BIG BIM4.0

Ecosystems for a Connected World

OMG Finith has done it again! His first book BIG BIM–little bim was a seminal book for the facilities industry. This time in a 400-page book with 25 case studies and hands-on exercises and tools he has combined the next book I would have written, along with documenting what is in the incredible mind of Kimon Onuma, along with about every other great mind in the industry. For those of you who may be thinking that we have milked all we can out of BIM this book is a must read and will set you straight in understanding that we have not even scratched the surface. For those of you still trying to figure out what BIM is and think it is a piece of software or just an expansion on CAD if you don't read this book you will have missed a huge opportunity. This book truly documents what the standard of care will become in the facilities industry over the next decade. Thank you Finith for all your efforts in the transformation of the facilities industry.

—Dana Kennish "Deke" Smith, FAIA, father of the U.S. National CAD Standard and, the first executive director of the buildingSMART alliance, where he worked to establish the US National BIM Standard to help improve international adoption of the powerful BIM toolset.

BIG BIM4.0

Ecosystems for a Connected World

By Finith Jernigan
With edits by Mike Bordenaro

4 Site Press

PO Box 222, Salisbury, MD 21803, USA
+1-410-548-9245
publisher@4sitesystems.com

ISBN 978-0-9855359-3-3
Library of Congress Cataloging-in-Publication Control Number: 2017901969
BIG-BIM 4.0, Ecosystems for a Connected World, February 20, 2017
Printed in the United States of America

We have made every effort to make this book as complete and accurate as possible. However, there may be mistakes, both typographical and in content. While the author has made every effort to provide accurate telephone numbers, Internet address, and other contact information at the time of publication, neither the publisher nor the author assumes any responsibility for errors or for changes that occur after publication. Further, we have no control over and do not assume any liability for third-party Web sites or their content.

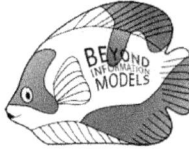

Contents

Application, Tools and Processes

PROLOGUE

Can you imagine using paper or CD catalogs of airfares, a travel agent, and the telephone to book your next trip? How long would it take to make your reservations? What happens when you need to explore other options? The travel industry has changed to allow you to do such things anywhere you have an internet connection.

You access vast amounts of pertinent data, in real-time. You decide the time, cost and quality of your trip—without knowing about the underlying complexity. You see only the information that you need to make your decisions—Nothing more and nothing less.

Similar things are happening in industries everywhere. When will the same happen to the building industry? Are you ready when it does?

BIG-BIM 4.0 lays out a systematic approach to establishing such an ecosystem and provides systematic examples of how to successfully use BIM to improve our entire built environment—buildings, bridges, roads, energy systems, water services, planes trains, automobiles, or anything we build. But there are many construction industry examples included because much of our energy and water use occurs in our buildings.

Included are case study examples of the issues, and workbook activities for you to practice. This book reveals the approaches used by many large companies, institutions, and government entities, and used by smaller, agile businesses. Develop confidence using a variety of tools inside that ecosystem—in a matter of days—Not years.

Dear Reader

When I wrote the first edition of BIG-BIM little-bim, BIG-BIM was presented as a conceptual approach to the use of Information Age tools and processes to achieve multiple goals. Only a few people were using Building Information Models in a systematic and beneficial manner at that time.

BIG-BIM no longer needs to be presented as conceptual. Those that are hanging on to the old perception of information in the building industry—as standalone systems exchanging information using file analogs—are missing the opportunity of the century.

Google and Uber are verbs. They blur the line between technology and the physical world and are leading the way into the Fourth Industrial Revolution. BIG-BIM is the built world's response to the fusion of the physical, digital, and biological spheres that are the hallmarks of today's most successful enterprises.

The impact of BIG-BIM goes far beyond buildings and those that plan for our assets. Now everyone is in the picture, even folks with no tie to the building industry. The way we do business is changing at a rapid rate.

You approach a building knowing that your phone will guide you directly to where you need to be for your appointment at 10:15 AM. At the proper times, the ecosystem signals the door to unlock as you approach (after it checks to be sure no one is lurking nearby), turns up the heat to make you comfortable when you arrive, and alerts the doctor to be ready to begin your exam at the agreed upon time. The sequence of actions triggers automatically because you and your Doctor added the appointment.

We can fundamentally improve how everyone gets what they need, when and where they need it. Luckily, the systems thinking that makes this possible has been around for a very long time. In graduate school, I was lucky enough to study with Buckminster Fuller and Alvin Toffler. Their theories and ideas continue to be among the best ways to understand how the cyber and physical worlds interact.

Long before my early experiences with Fuller and Toffler, they were envisioning systems much like those that are widely available to all of us today. Alvin Toffler was among the first to popularize the concepts of *mass customization* and *just-in-time production*. Buckminster Fuller's *Operating Manual for Spaceship Earth*, written in 1969, was a precursor and roadmap for what BIM is letting us do today—write the Operating Manual for the Built Environment.

Fuller's explorations of how humanity can survive on the planet Earth championed doing more with less and taking a holistic view of the world. His concept of *Comprehensive Anticipatory Design Science* is now practical and achievable using information models to visualize the vast amount of data freely available to us. Bucky predicted the overlapping of specialties that has focused attention on connected business processes by leading professional organizations. He taught that you could use technology to help us anticipate and solve problems with fewer resources.

Today, we can do what was talk and theory last century. We can use technology, guided by our innate talent and expertise, to look at our world in a more comprehensive way. As we break down the built environment and social issues that impact our world into bite-sized pieces, the theories of Toffler and Fuller are becoming reality. We are connecting technology to *do more (and better) with less.* Think of *BIG-BIM 4.0* as a user's manual to do just that.

This book has elements that provide an overview of where we are at today. It shows how to avoid common pitfalls. There are examples of what has worked well and instructions for practice exercises. This edition will help you establish an ecosystem that is shaped by your goals and allows you to practice the little steps that will help you achieve these aims.

Wishing you success, Finith E. Jernigan, FAIA

BIG-BIM Ecosystems

A mash-up uses information from multiple sources to create new things that may not have been considered when generating the original data. For example, one might mash-up facility conditions (from Workplace Management), space usage (from Scheduling), construction status (from Construction), operating costs (from Accounting), and a floor plan (from little-bim), into a web based GIS satellite view (from Google Earth) to present background information that supports decision-making in geospatial context.

Expanding on virtual building model technology first available in the early 1980s, the acronym BIM (for Building Information Modeling) was popularized beginning in 2002. BIM describes the virtual planning, design, construction, and management of the built world, using software on compatible hardware systems.

The terms BIG-BIM and little-bim were created for my first book to help readers wade through the ambiguity that underscores most discussions of BIM. Little-bim describes individual software programs and related processes, which too often do not connect well to other software or, if they do, rely on file exchanges in some form.

BIG-BIM is an ecosystem of applications and related processes that allow information to be shared via data exchanges and used by both experts and non-expert stakeholders for the entire life cycle of a building or anything that we can build.

BIG-BIM focuses on the future of information in the built world, moving beyond business-as-usual to embrace the changes happening in this age of the Internet of Things. BIG-BIM exploits the business process changes that are overtaking the built environment.

Data and information are paramount. Dynamic data is fed from distributed, shareable, and interoperable repositories, interconnected to encompass everything about assets.

BIG-BIM connects data, processes, competencies, and technologies from everywhere to increase understanding of what one is doing, in a significant global context. Business requirements, building industry data, geographical information, and real-time operations and maintenance information intersect to support connected decision-making using tools tailored to individual users and needs. Such are the stuff of the emerging Connected Age; the 4th Industrial Revolution.

The first and second Industrial Revolutions harnessed steam and water, brought the assembly line and taught us how to use electricity to mass produce things. The Information Age, or third Industrial Revolution, brought the internet, ubiquitous communication, and automation. The emerging Connected Age is blurring the line between the real-world and the technological world of the Information Age. Planning, design, construction, and operations all interconnect.

Given enough time and energy, the virtual representation of any asset can have as many attributes as the real thing. We share information and create *mash-ups* to understand the world in-context. The collection, updating and use of data are automated. Tools and processes end repetition. They maximize the efficiency of facilities and operations.

INDUSTRIAL REVOLUTIONS

1	2	3	4
The Age of Steam	The Machine Age	The Information Age	The Connected Age
c. 1784	c. 1870	c. 1945	c. 2008
Water & Steam Power Mechanize Production	Electric Power Creates Mass Production	Electronics & IT Automate Production	Technologies Fuse, Blurring Lines Between Physical & Digital

Without having to write code or design electronic circuitry, this book will show you how to work with others who are transitioning from 1st, 2nd, and 3rd Industrial Age tools to a world of connections between the cyber and physical realms.

No longer is this an aspiration for some future nirvana. BIG Data, artificial intelligence, the Internet of Things, autonomous vehicles, 3D printing, predictive analytics, nanotechnology, robotics, biotechnology, materials science, energy, and quantum computing are but a few of the areas with daily breakthroughs. With today's technology, you create a more sustainable, interconnected environment, and profit in the process.

Within BIG-BIM is a set of little-bim tools and processes crucial to design and construction. While little-bim does allow immediate and dramatic building industry business improvements by replacing 'flat-CAD' with BIM authoring and analysis on networked computers, there are many more benefits gained with BIG-BIM.

Little-bim has always been the hands-on use of different software tools and business processes to share information. It is important to have an excellent command of the little-bim software and processes, but the software is not the end goal. It is a small part of an active ecosystem.

Where BIG-BIM focuses on data exchanges, little-bim focuses on advanced graphics and file-based transactions using monolithic software product lines.

The work products and efficiency increase, but improvements are internal to projects; often little more than computer-aided-drafting on steroids. Advanced graphics, conflict checking, cost modeling and process simulation occur but are project-by-project oriented exercises.

It is an oft-repeated misconception that standardizing on one unified little-bim toolset simplifies the move into a BIG-BIM world. Nothing could be less true. Relying on a single product, application set, vendor product line or internally developed system, almost guarantees that you will be locked into a little-bim paradigm now and into the future. Do not be taken in by these software vendor or IT department-oriented sales pitch.

Organizations designed to deliver BIG-BIM work collaboratively to create or manipulate data using a myriad of standards-based tools in sustainable processes. Conversely, organizations that focus on little-bim cooperate, but use a limited set of file-oriented software products, a single hardware platform or, one brand of software often ignoring or misunderstanding the lifecycle benefits that come from a BIG-BIM ecosystem.

In either case, the goals of BIM focus on the people, environmental, and organizational changes needed to improve the sustainability and resilience of the world in which we live. Visualizing data about things—anything—provides a clarity and certainty that allows groups of people to make consensus decisions about complex issues.

Activities & Guidance

When electric saws came around, they significantly increased productivity AND increased the opportunity to cut your fingers off if you weren't careful. Use the Workflows, and Case Studies scattered through this book as a place to start to use BIG-BIM at little (or no) risk

BIG-BIM 4.0 is peppered with activities and guidance designed to educate and expose you to proven tools and processes that are new to you. They point you to next-practices, guide your discovery process and allow you to experience and learn from mistakes that don't impact real projects. Understanding the tools and processes will help you calculate your potential benefits from the use of BIG Building Information Models.

You can use the results of your completed exercises to demonstrate the benefits that come from BIG-BIM. Use what you learn to prove to your customers and stakeholders that they can see their projects earlier, they can make better decisions, and they can be more confident about the outcomes. With the proven results, you can establish based on exercises in this book, they will buy into the concepts.

Critical Capabilities

To help you make the leap to BIG-BIM, a SPECIAL SUPPLEMENT is included in the back of this book. This Supplement includes directions for exercises designed to overcome people's natural skepticism. By completing the exercises, you will connect to live BIG-BIM ecosystems and directly to topics throughout the book. Reading about a new topic begins the learning process. Doing it for yourself is the second step to building competence in any new area. Visit the SPECIAL SUPPLEMENT when you are ready to move beyond reading to tactile, hands-on, guided exercises.

For many, BIG-BIM requires a leap of logic. One crosses the chasm by becoming educating in the principles of connected systems. With education, you find answers to questions, such as: How can something so complex and all-encompassing be easier to use than the familiar tools? How is BIG-BIM even possible? Especially when some technology experts tell me it's a pipe dream? Or, something that will happen at some undefined future date? BIG-BIM 4.0 gives you the information you need to answer such questions, and to decide for yourself.

The BIG-BIM ecosystem needs a central hub to manage the data coming and going to, and from tools of many types—a BIG-BIM Server. The hub for BIG-BIM ecosystems must address two critical issues:

1. BIG-BIM should not impose hardware or software restrictions on users. Nor should BIG-BIM be limited to those with advanced training. Work takes place and is moderated using Internet-accessible, non-dedicated virtual servers, or cloud computing. Users access the system using any device capable of accessing the Internet. Desktops, laptops, tablets, and smartphones using any operating system are options.

2. BIG-BIM should foster rules-based planning, connecting authoritative data of all kinds in new and unexpected ways. Smart costing systems, finding connections among disparate datasets, analysis of Big Data, and simulations to find optimal solutions take place quickly. The system must transparently provide access to the core data in an open way, to allow spatial data to be visualized, manipulated, and maintained by all.

These issues are addressed at length later in the book. Without such critical capabilities, BIM will not deliver the things that people need in a BIG-BIM ecosystem. Today, the Onuma System uniquely demonstrates that it meets these criteria. The Onuma System fills a need that no other system on the market supports. The goal is not to push the Onuma System on you. With BIG-BIM the goal is to use the best tool for the job at hand, not to use only one tool.

Some find it easy to disregard the Onuma System as just another software tool among the hundreds that now exist in the Building Information Modeling space. Many of the detractors don't understand the difference between BIG-BIM and little-bim. Others scoff that the system is little more than an integrated dashboard or an object-oriented Javascript platform with no innovative technology. Even if true, they miss the point.

There are many reasons why enterprise clients such as the California Community Colleges opt to use the Onuma System after detailed technical comparison with the major little-bim systems. Use the knowledge in this book, and the exercises in the SPECIAL SUPPLEMENT to try BIG-BIM and make up your own mind.

Caveats

BIG-BIM 4.0 focuses on the things to consider as you move forward to become an active part of the connected world. The issues are complex and include so many topics that one cannot include them all in any single book. Because of this fact, this book focuses on educating people to understand issues critical to developing and using BIG-BIM ecosystems.

In a BIG-BIM ecosystem, anything is possible. People, tools, and processes of all types work together to achieve the goal of connected ecosystems. A properly functioning ecosystem enables connections, and this book includes some, but not all possibilities. There are other software tools, delivery methods, metrics, standards, and other things that will be part of the ecosystem as the Connected Age matures.

Web Feature Services (WFS), Key Performance Indicators (KPI), Omniclass, Job Order Contracting (JOC), Information Delivery Manuals (IDM), data dictionaries, taxonomies, the semantic web, and ontologies are but a few that spring to mind.

It's not that they aren't important—for they are—it's just that other things are more critical to the understanding of the BIG-BIM ecosystem and our part in the process. Adding to that is the fact that BIG-BIM is in a growth mode where breakthroughs happen every day.

All tools, methods and standards are welcomed and accommodated in the BIG-BIM ecosystem. However, each must be able to connect and share dynamic data with others. Merely claiming the ability to connect is not enough. Each must prove the capacity to connect. Demand that vendors show how to move data in and out of their applications. It is important to stick to this, no matter how flashy the marketing material.

This book refrains from making recommendations about which little-bim tools are best for you, for several reasons. First, there are too many to list. Second, little-bim tools are highly personal decisions, with many excellent options, and much guidance elsewhere to help you with such software decisions. Focusing on software detracts from the whole point of this book.

Just Do It!

In a BIG-BIM ecosystem, many interoperability problems vanish and the little-bim tools you use matter less than ever before. Select the tools that you find to be the most effective at getting the work done.

When you try to explain what BIG-BIM is, people's eyes glaze over because it isn't important to them yet. The concept may be simple, but it looks too complicated. Why waste energy explaining what BIG-BIM is? Just do it!

To efficiently use the powerful BIM tools and processes, industry professionals face many dilemmas. They strive for perfection. They work to stay ahead of the curve for fear that everyone else will pass them if they don't grow. Then they run risks by openly sharing their concepts and innovations. They react to these risks by holding their cards close. Then they can become afraid to take risks at all.

Fortunately, BIG-BIM offers a solution to solve such complex, multifaceted problems. Unfortunately, the complexity of the problems still requires careful consideration to avoid falling into old habits that can short-circuit the longevity of BIG-BIM.

The complexity of the issues addressed by information modeling makes it easy for some people to misrepresent BIM, making it hard for people to understand what is happening. It's even challenging to determine the best approach to the creation of Building Information Models. This complexity results in people continuing to work in the traditional way even though it isn't as successful as it could be. Selling technology isn't a winning strategy. Sell the benefits of what you can do. Don't sell the tools and processes. Your win rate will go up.

BIM is Not...

Although BIM may be far from the reality of many people, you need to understand what BIM is about. One way to understand BIM is to understand what BIM is not.

BIM is not a single building model or a single database. Vendors may tell you that everything must be in a single model to be BIM, this isn't true. They would be more accurate describing BIM as a series of interconnected models and databases. These models can take many forms while maintaining relationships and allowing information to be extracted and shared. The single model or single database description is one of the major confusions about BIM.

BIM is not Revit, Tekla, Navisworks, Vectorworks, SketchUp, ArchiCAD, Bentley, or any other product. Nor is it CAD on steroids. Those who don't understand the technology think that BIM and Revit mean the same thing. They are the same people who tell you that they use *CAD*, when they mean *AutoCAD*. They make *Xerox* copies even when using a Minolta photocopier. Software companies do a fantastic marketing job. These software tools are all excellent little–bim solutions, not THE BIM solution. You can use any of them and not be doing BIM at all.

BIM is not just 3D. 3D software lets you model geometry and is ideal for creating visualizations. 3D modeling has significantly improved our ability to communicate ideas. The output from 3D models are images and at heart little more than lengths, widths, heights, and surface material images. Images are not BIM. 3D is at best a view of the BIM database. With a 3D visualization, you still must interpret what things mean, how they connect to other things and where they reside in space. Building information models know all these. BIG–BIM knows how it relates to others in shared and standards driven ways.

BIM is not perfect. People input data manually and the more times they input the data, the more mistakes are made. Minimizing data entry allows you to capture knowledge quickly and reduces repetitive input errors. Data fed from authoritative sources minimizes manual entry errors. With BIG-BIM, you enter information once, leaving less chance for error and errors that do creep in are easier to find before they cause harm.

BIM does not have to be 3D. A spreadsheet can be used to help generate BIM. One example is a simple space needs spreadsheet. It includes space names, floor levels, space dimensions, and heights, department names, and other details. The data is in a standardized format. It is a useful tool, but not yet BIM. When you import this data into BIG-BIM, each line of the spreadsheet is analyzed and placed on a site as blocks of space with data, ready for further refinement. It becomes low-level of detail BIG-BIM. Go to the SPECIAL SUPPLEMENT to try this for yourself.

BIM will not remove people from the process. In many situations, the data supporting BIM will accumulate as a by-product of life. Our unique problem-solving skills will always be needed to assess this information. We will always be necessary. To find patterns, to design solutions and to make the informed decisions that drive our world. This will take less effort, and produce more. By reducing mundane data entry and other tedious tasks, BIM lets us work smarter, with fewer errors and faster than ever before.

BIM is not complete. Nor is it necessary for it to be complete. Some push to force completeness and consistency. Others argue that all standards and tools must be in place before BIM can become a lifecycle solution... if we do step one and make it perfect, we can then do step two, and so on. Others assume that BIM isn't possible unless everyone in the process is involved and can use the technology. Such positions defy logic.

BIM is not about any single standard. No single standard or approach does it all. Any approach that works today will change tomorrow. Standards and defined processes that are agile enough to work in the real-world are necessary for BIM. But all rules must adapt as the world around us changes. The fact is that we live in a world that is in a state of constant change, where a multitude of standards makes it possible to do what needs doing.

BIM is not about what we did yesterday. What we learned and did yesterday may inform what we do today, or they may be irrelevant. You need an agile mind and an agile approach to sort out which is the case in each action you take. At a rapid pace, we are moving to an era where technology is becoming connected to the physical world.

BIG-BIM is a framework for understanding the built environment ecosystem that we are creating. We coordinate by dynamically linking our expertise to the requirements of others to foster innovation and productivity that promotes growth. Moving to a more inclusive and connected ecosystem requires a shift in perspective and attitude that allows us to manage the ambiguity that is a natural part of our world. People need to understand the context and impact of their decisions, in enough depth to allow connections with the larger ecosystem. All within a framework that makes the information one needs available, when and where it is needed.

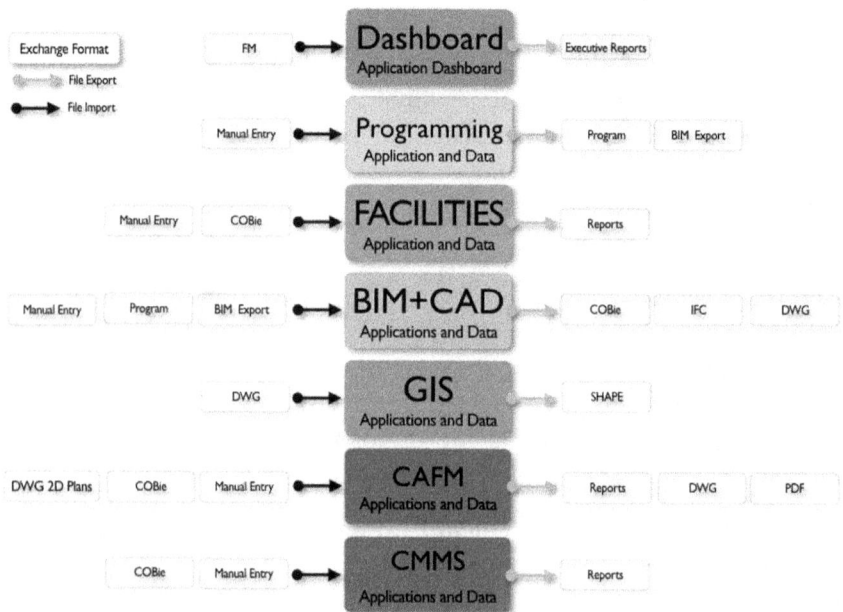

File exchanges (such as those shown above) whether via IFC or by other means are short-term solutions and do not rise to the level of BIG-BIM. Once a model is printed or archived such that the connection to its live data becomes broken (whether to a file, paper, removable media or a local or cloud server), it is no longer a dependable source of information upon which a BIG-BIM ecosystem can rely. Dynamic data must continue to be live, and linked, and the workflows for projects can not be built on a plan to manually import and export data to maintain the model.

User Manual

No matter who you are, use this book as a roadmap to future success related to any aspect of the built environment. Whether building something new or improving something already built, appropriate application of the principles assembled here will allow you to achieve surprising results sooner rather than later.

BIG-BIM enables large, diverse, and widely distributed communities of stakeholders to work with connected data to manage the built environment while working collaboratively in either real-time or asynchronously. If you want your small business or organization to enter the BIM world as a team, this book can be used as a source for establishing a team playbook. Similarly, small teams in medium and large businesses can use principles detailed in this book to launch connected business processes and web-based tools in pilot projects that grow the benefits for the entire organization.

This book provides the guidance you need to connect Building Information Models into your way of working. It shows how to do this without beginning anew. Bringing your current experience to the process is the starting requirement for the successful creation of a BIG-BIM ecosystem. You will learn how to create a plan visually and capture your insight and expertise into a Building Information Model that helps your project succeed.

What a model looks like is of less value than the information captured in the model. While realistic, 3D visualization is critical to the work of designers and constructors, for most others visualizing the data in models can be much more important. Your greatest value comes from getting your original information into software that helps operate and manage what you helped plan, design or build.

The greatest challenges to the full use of BIG-BIM are cultural, not technical. Creating Building Information Models, so that you can easily share the information you put in it with many others, using web-based software and mobile hardware, is the key.

The technical challenge is that you must use tool sets of all types in projects. It is necessary—and desirable—to work with a variety of tools and processes to achieve the best results possible today. There is great value in being fluent with many tools.

Leading the cultural challenges is the human resistance to change. Fortunately, BIM is well suited to simply augmenting existing practices, allowing a group to keep what works while enhancing or replacing the pieces that do not. The goal is to help individuals and groups of any size to explore, and demonstrate the things we have learned from using BIG–BIM for many years.

BIG–BIM 4.0 is organized around eight issues to focus on as you move forward in your exploration. In each of the eight key areas, we will discuss the theories and practices that ground the BIG–BIM ecosystem. Each focal point includes descriptions of common misconceptions, suggested solutions, checklists, case studies of successful actions used by others and workshop exercises related to the principles to provide guidance and practice for applying lessons learned to your work.

Issue 1.   Start with the End in Mind.

Change direction as fast as needs require.

Issue 2.   Enhance Strategic Thinking.

Explore and embrace new tools and business processes.

Issue 3.   Simple as Can Be.

Systems that are too complex, too finished, and too difficult to master.

Issue 4.   People, Not Technology.

Solve the problems that have long plagued the built environment.

Issue 5.   Assets, Not Projects.

Improved decisions from broadening our perspective.

Issue 6.   Share and Collaborate.

Size no longer determines what we can accomplish.

Issue 7.   Process Over Product.

People confuse process with product.

Issue 8. First Day Mistakes.

Dependable fact-based information; anecdotes and past precedents are no longer reliable.

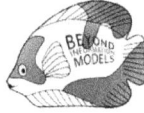

ONE

START WITH THE END IN MIND

As information modeling took hold at the turn of the century, there was a focus on getting good at one BIM software program or another. This emphasis on using only one BIM program was understandable for many reasons. People were new to modeling, there were limitations to hardware processing power, user interface graphic strategies were just beginning, and many other factors influenced how we interacted with the new tools. Vendors readily answered the, *what's in it for me?* question by showcasing the traditional process benefits provided with their software.

Many aesthetically significant projects were completed using a single BIM authoring tool. But the real, big-picture success of these projects and the success of their owners has proven to be limited by how well (or how poorly) the Building Information Models shared information with other software programs. If the information from the planning, design, and construction of a project could not easily move to the operation and management of the project, much of the information gained during the project was lost, much like projects completed with paper documentation and CAD files.

Shared Vision

The economic value and efficiency that come from BIG-BIM make us more competitive. We can access and use unstructured information to make informed decisions, in-context. BIM is increasing efficiency and leveraging the ability to support better those you serve. BIG-BIM is about connections of all types. Understand what BIM is and what it is not and practice the workflows in the SPECIAL SUPPLEMENT at the end of this book to demonstrate the value of BIG-BIM to others.

Successful enterprises are throwing away the hierarchical, single use systems and processes that defined their predecessors, and represent a revolutionary rethinking of how technology can spark innovation to serve their customers better. This new way of thinking comes as companies recognize that they have much to of value to share, without affecting their intellectual capital, or proprietary information.

Before building information modeling, and connected processes arrived on the scene, few groups even attempted to handle larger, systemic problems in the building industry. Efforts to solve the problems tended to focus on one group, or one project and rarely did the solutions filter through the industry. Few professionals attempted to share solutions they found outside their local area.

Every community, state and country looked at their problems as unique. It was a time before the high-speed, global communities and ubiquitous communications that we see today. The problems were complicated, but there was time to plan, study and find local solutions. Everyone took care of the problems that affected them personally and left others to do the same.

At many levels, little has changed. People remain convinced of the uniqueness of their plight. Local changes continue to be easier to implement than global corrections. Patchwork solutions are inefficient.

The built environment lacks resilience, is wasteful, inefficient, and too expensive to maintain properly. The building industry has no shared, strategic vision of how to proceed. Around the world, people are actively working to find solutions, yet a clear, shared vision of how to correct the issues has yet to emerge. Finding solutions to the industry's problems is proving to be difficult.

Global issues of many types affect us all and are so widespread that none are exempt. Business, as usual, is no longer enough. Systemic changes are needed in several areas. We face problems of poor execution, poor cost controls, and the recognition that traditional processes are deteriorating.

At the same time, project complexity has increased the pace and volume of change. As the industry embraces more technological innovations, the technology needs to be adaptable and easy to deploy, because, the business resources to respond to these changes are limited. The number and complexity of current and emerging systems have reached a level that requires input from multiple experts to select workable solutions. New tools and approaches are needed to maintain awareness and develop expertise with these new materials and systems.

The building industry needs to change how it does business to respond to these systemic issues. We face a *Complex and Wicked Problem,* where every step toward a solution exposes new problems, with no end in sight. Continuing, as usual, isn't a solution. There needs to be a better and more efficient way to work.

Is History Relevant?

Much of what happened in the last 30 years in software development and file-based systems from the Information Age are not where things are heading today. A tectonic shift has occurred, and holding firmly to the twentieth century approach; the building industry has yet to gain the dramatic benefits now available.

History may not provide the best framework to help us adapt to the changes we are now experiencing. From the historical perspective, we should be questioning many things. How does the explosive growth of the internet impact the construction industry? Is the success of Google, Facebook, Expedia, Amazon, and other web services germane to the future of the built environment? Why are construction industry organizations scrambling to redefine themselves while madly trying to retain the value in their old approach to processes, software, and data?

Answering such questions is grounded in recognizing key facts that continue to change today's built environment:

Access to timely and accurate facility data has become imperative.

Verifiable sustainability and resilience are no longer options.

Actionable information about physical assets is critical to the function of organizations.

Eliminating waste and inefficiency can no longer wait.

Business decisions made without facts lead to catastrophic outcomes for groups.

Large and small facility owners need to demonstrate leadership and competency to efficiently plan, manage and operate their assets.

The Internet of Things, mobile devices, building information modeling (BIM), facilities management and mapping tools are converging.

The building industry can manage each of these facts with currently available tools, within a BIG-BIM ecosystem. This book asks you to look at how we can best respond to them.

Cross the Chasm

Common wisdom tells people to hold their information close, for proprietary knowledge has value. For many people giving away information gives away value. Because of this viewpoint, many built environment software programs are designed to retain information, not to share it with other programs. Yet, paradoxically, sharing information with no limitations is the precursor to dramatic success.

Leaders in other industries are already working toward a more connected approach, with all the attendant benefits and problems. Those that embraced the change became more competitive. They endured disruptions to businesses resistant to change, but they also increased customer value, improved services, created higher quality and lowered costs. We can expect that similar levels of disruption and rebirth will happen in the building industry.

We face a fundamental opportunity—how to, in the face of such disruptive change, maintain the valuable information we have, to maintain (or improve) our positions in the building industry?

Many attempts at carrying existing information forward to minimize the need to re-create documents and other data have been made. The building industry has a long history of leading owners from innovation to innovation, each guaranteed to deliver significant improvements once all the information was in the new format.

Most of these innovations provided incremental improvement, but until now these attempts at future-proofing the building industry information have lacked the ability to maintain live data in ways that enable lifecycle use.

Project information will always be valuable. Owners need to insist that their project information is what holds the real value to their assets—not the software in which the data resides. The software will always be evolving and changing. Locking data into proprietary software no longer serves anyone's interests.

Your financial and time investment in software is at risk. At any time, your software can become outdated by an App that allows everyone to conduct the same business process more quickly and more efficiently. That is what software companies have a hard time telling you. But that is the reality that we face.

Industry in Transition

If getting the job done, on-time and under-budget means that you also must use pencil-and-paper or 'flat-CAD'—in addition to using Building Information Models—that is all right. This book is intended to help you to sort out the options in a way that works for you, one-step-at-a-time.

Making your information accessible on the web for the entire life of what you help build shifts the focus away from design and construction. Operations and maintenance become more critical—and rightly so. That is where most of the money goes, and where the greatest need for sustainability and resilience lie. Your transition to using Building Information Models in a BIG-BIM ecosystem is going to happen in conjunction with established procedures that are required by contract or, through legislation or, for many other reasons. Learn new strategies for the best ways to insert Building Information Models into your workflows. Because projects must be completed on time and on-budget using the resources available.

Reconcile yourself to the fact that much of the building industry remains firmly locked in the past for a variety of reasons. Resistance to change, antiquated legal requirements, lack of understanding about what is possible, and other reasons are keeping many locked into doing things only one way and not leveraging the power of today's connected tools and processes.

Resist the temptation to embrace only one software program in a little-bim approach and then thinking that you have addressed all your BIM needs. The one-can-do-it-all approach leads to a process little changed from the days of drawing blueprints. You may see some benefit, but this method does not allow you to use BIM to its fullest potential and does not support a full lifecycle approach to BIM.

Embracing a BIG-BIM approach frees information from proprietary limitations and makes it available in a web-based, services oriented architecture approach. This method leverages mobile devices as tools to use the information you create and manage.

Focus on Outcomes

The exploration of BIG-BIM requires thought. Start by looking at emotional and social issues related to using new tools and processes. The social and emotional issues will likely be the most difficult to resolve. The organization of this information will begin to form patterns that reflect your individual needs. Use the patterns to draft a framework for moving forward.

Before you go too deep into your exploration of BIG-BIM, it is important to understand what you hope to achieve with the expert use of Connected Age tools and processes. Use tools, such as mind mapping software, to capture your answers to the questions below. Study resources such as: *Business Model Generation* and *Value Proposition Design,* written by Alexander Osterwalder, et.al. at www.strategyzer.com to guide your process.

The requirements may seem obvious, but often the real needs can only be found by delving deeply. Look at your business with fresh eyes, and you will learn some interesting things. Listen to your customers, and they will tell of their concerns. Search and find the things that your customers most need from you. Rarely are the profound and penetrating questions asked. Answers to such question are even rarer.

To get you started, here is a list of questions to consider. Check them off as you find the answers for yourself:

- *Why would I want to do this? What's this got to do with my role in the building lifecycle?*

- *Why would a customer want me to do this? Do they even care?*

- *How do we sell this? To stakeholders? To staff? To our supply chain?*

- *Do I have to throw everything else out and start over? Can we still use AutoCAD, or Microstation, or….? My CAD people tell me that we can already do this with our current technology, why are my customers saying something else? We can do 3D drawings, and they look good, so... what's the problem?*

- *What's in it for me? What's in it for my customers?*

- *In what new areas can we see the benefit to stakeholders from applying these skills?*

- *What are customers missing that would improve their assets?*

- *What unrealized gains can we bring to new markets?*

- *Is this worth the effort and angst? To me? To my people? To customers?*

- *Where are the pain points for those in the new market? How do we justify the move? To new customers?*

- *How is this new process different, in a day-to-day office environment? Who is affected? What unresolved pain can we relieve?*

- *What should we do? Should we specialize? Or, become generalists?*

- *What are our skill sets? What does the new market value? What products and services can we offer?*

- *What are the first five things that we can do to improve how our work?*

- *How must you change your approach to projects? Can you look at the world with a fresh set of eyes? Can you transcend the artificial limitations that your legacy systems create?*

- *How do we assess our value in the new market? What staff resources do I need to do this? How can we most effectively do this? What savings come by implementing this process? For me? For my customers?*

- *How does our current business model need to change?*

- *What changes when we expand into new markets? How do we do new things that customers will care enough to buy? Can we differentiate ourselves from the competition? In ways that the stakeholders will understand?*

☐ *How does one modify a major facility management system to eliminate the need for training and support?*

☐ *How does one move from a files-based, welded together software approach into the app economy? How does a traditional business become agile? Without giving up market share and impacting profits?*

Mastery

In tomorrow's connected world, the gaps that come from relying on what one was taught years ago lead directly to failed implementations and BIM Washing. Proven mastery is the coin of leadership in this environment. See the details of BIM Washing in Part IV—People, Not Technology.

Establishing a BIG-BIM ecosystem requires active and ongoing involvement from an organization's most qualified people. To get the benefits of developing a BIG-BIM ecosystem requires leaders to have at least a base level of competency and commitment to the principals of BIG-BIM.

One does not have to be an expert in all parts of any system. However, to orchestrate a team of BIG-BIM experts, leaders need to become an expert in the underlying principles. When properly established, a BIG-BIM ecosystem will allow access to just the data needed by each stakeholder. The CEO can use dashboards to do his or her work. At the same time, with the same datasets, a middle manager can manage work orders; an engineer can do analysis; an assistant can enter additional data via a spreadsheet and the builder can check for conflicts.

To lead, one must learn to delegate some tasks and not others. There are tasks that a senior leader might assign after they understand the underlying logic or have tried and learned how to do it themselves. How this happens may vary widely from one person to another.

Understanding of BIM of any type does not come from merely listening to lectures or applying collateral knowledge. Take responsibility for your learning, to eliminate the gaps in your knowledge. Don't settle for understanding only 95% of the concepts or at some point; you will find yourself hitting a wall to the detriment of your business, your employees, or your projects. Do not skip this step, no matter how high and lofty your job title.

There are prominent examples of leaders who have others create models or other materials for them. For businesses where the leaders rely on making inferences based on old knowledge, this approach dilutes the value and benefits to the company and their customers. Others will argue differently. However, you should learn how to do some form of BIG-BIM with your very own hands, mind, and computer.

The Workflows in this book will help with this. Take the time and gain proficiency so that you can conceptualize the world in a BIG-BIM ecosystem—before pushing the effort off onto others or acting like you understand and know of what you speak.

Actionable and Dynamic Information

Accommodate, coach, and support new colleagues as you find your way to BIG-BIM. Capture your contributions as meaningful data and use them throughout the life of whatever you help build. There are repeatable workflows in this book that you can use with colleagues to explore compatibility.

It is not easy for most of us to accept that the information about our work is the rapidly becoming the most valuable part of what we do. But, this is the case in the Connected Age. Most people are in the habit of gaining the most value from their work on a project, not during the entire life of the information they put into the project. In this change of focus lie the building industry's greatest opportunities. Finding ways to get value from the future use of your information remains one of the holy grails of BIG-BIM.

Your journey to full utilization and advantage from Connected Age tools and processes will be easier if you find other people interested in exploring projects that show long-term benefits. Learn if current colleagues also want to work on projects that demonstrate the value of live data for lifecycle use. Or meet others interested in exploring web-based business processes with you.

As much changes in the process, you will want to build up a team that can quickly adjust to new tools and processes as they become available. Find team members that commit to adopting new capabilities as systems, methods and tools evolve. You have many resources at your disposal to grow your team of like-minded experts.

Understand that everyone on the team will have different levels of experience. Few will be fluent with all the possible options. Everyone will be learning and finding their way forward.

As the industry continues to transition, some of what you explore will seem counterintuitive at first. That is the nature of transitioning from the Industrial Revolution to the Information Age and now into the Connected Age. Some of the mindsets, tools, and processes valuable in the earlier Industrial Ages can be a liability in this 4th Industrial Age.

Fortunately, professional expertise and the ability to make critical decisions will never be a liability as you focus on information as your most valuable deliverable.

The process allowed control of critical components. The details provided by the building model gave us the resources to manage a complex financing package and to convince the City Council to proceed with securing additional funding to meet the project's needs. Being able to look at detailed information very quickly, early in the process allowed effective management of costs. Everyone understood what was needed to complete the project. And, roadblocks were then managed so early that they never seemed to become a problem. — William Gordy, Deputy Fire Chief.

A New Focus

It may seem natural to focus on becoming a software expert more than being an information expert. Yet, truly transformative benefits can only come when information is available and used in real-time for the entire lifecycle of each asset. Much as now happens for Internet-based transactions.

Many continue to work only in the little-bim world that involves traditional design and construction using file-centric workflows to produce documentation for the traditional process. And this is not likely to vanish overnight.

The built environment is complex, and the interactions are daunting. We need ways to support the complexity while at the same time providing for simple ways for people to jump in and use the available data. It is possible to create a system that weaves servers, data, and the many available tools together into a unified, yet loosely connected whole that supports better decisions and improves planning across the entire lifecycle.

To fully engage the power of BIM, the industry needs to embrace business processes that work more like the Internet, and less like the one-size-for-all, stand-alone and welded together software approach of the last century. When we all can create, share and reuse information about our area of concern in the built environment, better decisions are made, and dramatic improvements are possible.

One approach that helps little-bim experts share information about the built environment is named Industry Foundation Classes (IFC). However, it is currently a complicated development environment and many experts find that the difficulties far outweigh the benefits; demurring when asked to create new IFC compliant applications. And, this is especially true when applied to reconfiguring existing applications to be IFC compliant.

IFC is an international standard for interoperable sharing of data used in Building Information Models. The Industry Foundation Classes schema, or data organization system, makes it possible for information about rooms, spaces, chairs, tables, and anything related to the built environment, to be exchanged between any compliant software program. IFC allows sharing of geometry, topology, structural elements, spaces, terrain, structure, systems, furniture, time, constraints, analysis, people, work plans, costs, external data, relationships between these things, and more.

Industry Foundation Classes may become the centerpiece format for sharing and managing built environment data over the long-term. However, as currently structured, IFC remains focused on file (and single use output) based processes and is unlikely to be the central standard, except in little-bim exchanges that cannot reuse live data.

The concepts that ground IFCs have the potential to enable sharing across all built environment domains. However, after more than twenty years of development, the full expression of the concept remains elusive.

Only recently has IFC moved to wider international use. IFC remains a file-centric approach for only a limited subset of the industry. File exchanges with IFC are complex and require significant coordination and training to master. It is a standard for the Information Age, not the Connected Age.

It is not that IFC is bad—it sets a standard, and forms a basis for a lot of the web services, BIMxml, and other things. The problem is when people insist on IFC or nothing. This insistence on IFC has in some areas become so extreme that owners *demand* that teams deliver everything in IFC. The teams then *jam* all the data into Revit manually; sometimes even pulling out data from excellent databases.

They inject the data into the model and then try and get it back out again as COBie IFC; which is usually a disaster. Then the reaction is—*Oh, COBie does not work.* It is a crazy approach.

Let's look at this from the perspective that someone may ONLY want information on one piece of equipment or, the QR Code of the item or, any other type of information. Web services and other approaches allow them to access any of this data and use the information, in many ways, without needing to know IFC.

The all-or-nothing approach is hurting the industry, causing confusion, and dramatically slowing the benefits from BIM. With the IFC-only approach, it is much as if one said, *the only way to look at a BIM floor plan is to read the computer code instead of looking at a graphical view.*

The requirement that people understand the complexity before they can start connecting to built environment data makes IFC look a lot like a proprietary format that accentuates the complexity of the entire built environment.

Even with recent advances in some of the traditional software platforms, it remains a mystery to most people in the industry. Because of IFC's complexity, it remains a standard that is far from answering the overall needs of a complex and diverse industry. Today, it is best to do what you can with the small subset of software that uses Industry Foundation Classes (IFC) to share data about the parts of the industry that are defined. IFC is not the only open-standard at play and is unlikely to be the only standard required to satisfy the industry's needs. Many of the standards that underpin web technologies, geographic information systems, and database systems are also applicable to the needs of BIG-BIM.

To reach the full potential of BIG-BIM, users need to be able to use data without being required to become an expert in the underlying complexity. Agile, plug-and-play approaches that free the data for use by all software programs using service-oriented-architecture or other loosely coupled, flexible and scaleable frameworks are the key.

Using standards much like those that underpin the Internet, web services, and mobile devices can distribute information to those that have a need, whenever and wherever the need occurs. One such approach that could benefit IFC is to separate the underlying data from software and other components.

Dramatic benefits have been shown to come from separating the data and other components of software to move away from the welded together software, file focused approach that has long been the standard in the building industry. Such a move maximizes the benefit from Industry Foundation Classes and other open-standards while accelerating our ability to share and reuse the massive amounts of data generated across all parts of the building industry.

We need to encourage simple solutions while continuously developing standards that can guide a fast-changing environment where processes are neither simple nor easily defined.

Today, systems exist that offer much of this functionality. By connecting current, functional subsets of IFC with other standards and connecting loosely coupled data, such software works to support early stage planning, business decision-making, and management of lifecycle information. Data can connect from anywhere and everywhere in a mostly cloud-based environment while accommodating legacy file-centric operations that are essential to current productivity.

In this approach, end users follow the same rules that they have come to expect with other Internet-based systems. Such systems allow those with little or no technology training to experience the enhanced decision-making possibilities that BIG-BIM offers.

The buildingSMART alliance and their Thought Leadership subcommittee work to widely distribute this concept through a variety of initiatives.

Even with our day-to-day experiences on our mobile devices, most of us need to experience BIG-BIM for themselves. Without experiencing the power that comes from open-standards and cloud-based systems, few understand the potential and opportunities that such systems create.

Groups such as OpenBIM and tools such as program2BIM help the industry realize that by facilitating transparent, open workflows we can enable all to participate in BIG-BIM. Contact the buildingSMART alliance for access to their hosted GitHub, open-source prototype BIMplan Viewer concept. Also do a search for the xBIMTeam's GitHub hosted repositories of the open-source Xbim Toolkit project.

Benefits and Savings

You will likely find that financial benefits related to little-bim fall into the category of Cost Avoidance rather than Cost Reduction. Expect the bulk of cost avoidance benefits to be during design and construction. Both cost avoidance and cost reduction benefits are to be found later in the building lifecycle.

When people first consider using BIM, they naturally seek ways to quantify the benefits and savings they will gain from using the tools and business processes that are new to them. Over the last twenty years at Design Atlantic, we have found that our customers avoid spending 8-15% on their first projects that actively use BIM in any way. On repeat engagements, cost avoidance can reduce spending as much as 35%.

Some of the reductions are real savings—lower fees, lower costs, and greater efficiency. Some reductions are in the form of extra things that get done to make the project better—improved lifecycle analysis, enhanced project management, and a better understanding of outcomes. The remainder is in the form of unspent contingency funds, fewer errors, improved compliance, and lack of unplanned changes.

It is next to impossible to arrive at a scientifically validated Key Performance Indicator (or KPI) that accurately says, *I did this... it saved that.* There is much anecdotal evidence of the value of little-bim: early identification of system clashes that almost eliminate change orders; reduced material waste from dimensional precision; and, time savings from drawings that uniformly update because they connect to a visual relational database, are but a few areas where many have seen the benefit.

The problem with making a universal statement of benefits arise when one tries to tie them all together to create a one-size-fits-all savings formula. The industry and businesses involved are too diverse to make this practical.

Meaningful success metrics are needed to implement and sustain an effective BIG-BIM ecosystem. Do a web search to find and identify Key Performance Indicators (KPI) that allow you to measure progress, success, or failure, as you progress toward achieving your BIG-BIM strategic goals, little-bim activities, LEAN Construction, Integrated Project Delivery, and many other topics. Focus on the indicators that relate to how, and where, you work in the BIG-BIM ecosystem.

As you embark on your journey toward BIG-BIM, find or create metrics that resonate with you and how you work. Create your personal set of Key Performance Indicators. Did the work get done faster, with fewer problems? Were your costs more controllable? Were your customers happier with the process? The answers to these types of questions will be the real measures of your success.

In most cases, increased analysis, better control, fewer changes and adding new services seem to fill in any price reduction. Since the goal is better outcomes, areas that once received minimal attention can now be included in your project services. Some benefits are hard to categorize. Unspent contingencies are one such. Is it cost savings or cost avoidance, when you don't spend the contingency for unplanned changes?

In whatever form reductions take, savings accrue to everyone in the project. These savings are the result of reusing information, having more and better decision-making information earlier, better first phase analysis and more accurate information during operations and maintenance.

Companies have internal metrics that track results that are important to them. Take time to decide what you want to measure. Identify the type of cost data each of your customers or stakeholders like for making better, earlier decisions. Then use this book to help create your repeatable method for creating Building Information Models that respond to their needs.

Real-World BIG-BIM

One cannot send a fax to Expedia to book an airline seat, nor is it possible to use pencil and paper to send an e-mail. Likewise, the limited tools of little-bim cannot substitute for the connection that is possible with a BIG-BIM ecosystem. The same tools that allow one to collaborate on the Internet, allow one to plan, create and manage data in real-time across the built environment lifecycle.

Theory and conjecture are immutable parts of any discussion of BIM. The possibilities are endless. It is hard to separate the real from the fiction, especially when BIG-BIM enters the picture. BIG-BIM seems elusive and aspirational. It is only natural to ask, Does BIG-BIM even exist?

Some vendors and self-proclaimed gurus make it sound like BIG-BIM will happen at some undefined future date. They would have one believe that today, only little-bim is possible. Other vendors and gurus proclaim that they have the one-and-only way to BIG-BIM. The same crowd too often equates BIG-BIM with big projects. Usually, these misconceptions occur because someone's entire income stream comes from selling you some form of little-bim.

Until one delves into the details and looks closely, it's hard to dispute such claims. Study the issue and come to your decision about this topic. The only way to understand what BIG-BIM is about is to put your hands-on BIG-BIM to explore BIG-BIM as it exists today. This book contains workflows designed to help you in your exploration.

The workflows and examples focus on using the *I of BIM* to manage the data generated from many different sources. By exploring the workflows, one can experience BIG-BIM for oneself. Use the workflows to understand how one might create dependable, decision-making information, when and where needed.

The workflows address topics such as:

Creating BIG-BIM from spreadsheets.

Generating COBie spreadsheets from a BIG-BIM model… in one step.

Moving information and graphics from models created from spreadsheets to Revit for further development.

Moving information and graphics from models created from Google Earth to ArchiCad or Revit for further development.

Building data-rich lifecycle models on the web, with furniture, fixtures, and equipment, ready to use in the desktop tool of your choice.

To use the BIG-BIM workflows one needs access to a BIG-BIM Ecosystem. Go to the RECIPE FOR REAL-WORLD BIG-BIM in the SPECIAL SUPPLEMENT at the end of the book for the detailed recipe to get started.

Red Dots

Today, there are few commercially available GeoDesign and BIG-BIM systems. Explore the tools that are currently available to enable web-based information exchanges among different software programs to create similar workflows to those scattered through this book.

The convergence of information from Geospatial Information Systems (GIS) and Building Information Models (BIM) has enormous implications for the future of the built environment. In the domain of geography, this convergence has been called GeoDesign or GeoBIM. In the domain of building information, it is the foundation of BIG-BIM.

The successful BIG-BIM ecosystems involve a web-based bridge (or BIG-BIM Server) to allow data sharing among software from many different disciplines. The key is focusing on software that uses an approach to data sharing that connects not just applications, but people and processes. *Red Dots* placed on computer maps can now connect you to the complete code for everything about the building, activities inside it and an almost infinite amount of information for use on mobile devices in real-time.

The Red Dot can lead you to a massing model that begins to represent the shape and size of a building or fleet or stack of assets related to a building—or anything. Click again and zoom in and the massing model can begin to represent a more realistic version of an existing or new building on a more realistic geographic representation of that place on earth.

With the proper bridges, Building Information Models landed on geospatial models become the publicly recognizable graphic interface for sharing critical information about our built environment. These interfaces exchange information and connect that information in-context.

The technology is available to create virtual images of anything, at any level of detail that you want to see in the real-world. Go to the Exploration with a Global Perspective in the Special Supplement to experience Red Dot models for yourself.

Work process beginning with placemarks or Red Dots (upper left) that link to data from many trusted sources that can be mashed-up to support enterprise planning, emergency preparedness, infrastructure assessment and many other tasks. This ability to share and use data across all information domains is a model for successfully connected processes that can start with placing a connected Red Dot on a web-based map.

Information In-context

The concepts that drive BIG-BIM become simple when you focus on the data.

The use of loosely coupled, flexible, and scaleable approaches to web-based information sharing is not yet in widespread use in built environment technology. This method can be used to codify and connect knowledge about any subject. As an example, Expedia asks you to tell them where and when you want to travel, plus a few other preferences. Behind the scenes, they connect to the airline reservation system, the seat booking system, the hotel and car rental booking systems and more, and seconds later they feed you just the information you need to decide.

By flexibly defining how software programs can access the required data, we can enable the automation of many of the fact-based assessments that drive planning, design, construction, and operations in the built environment. Professionals are becoming more attuned to the power of this type of business process.

Thinking about such systems from the traditional perspective of the building industry, this may not seem possible or practical. From the viewpoint of the Internet, such systems are a natural extension of how the construction sector has worked for a long time.

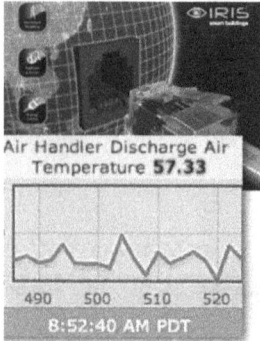

Live Sensors

Air Handler Discharge Air Temperature **57.33**

490   500   510   520

8:52:40 AM PDT

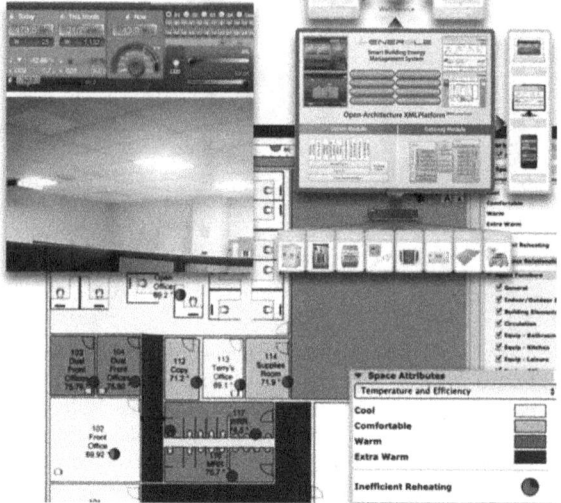

Embrace open-standards driven sensors and control systems that readily interface with information models

The Red Dot Model enables data from many sources to be used to leverage how you understand the world, in-context. Legacy data, data created in little-bim, sensor data, financial data, and much more can be visualized using Red Dots.

Such systems form an infrastructure that enables the reuse of services, knowledge capture, universal access, and transparent best practices. This contrasts with the brittle and expensive to maintain, tightly coupled networks that have been the technology centerpieces of much of the industry's history.

A model may be little more than a red dot on a map that someone uses to locate a restaurant. The red dot leads you to information: a menu; an automatic reservation system; a link to Facebook; a phone number; a general email address for those who prefer email, or any of hundreds of other things. Simplified interfaces are tied to multiple authoritative data sources to create value for users. Though a simplified example, BIG-BIM works much the same way.

How much energy does this building use? What spaces are available for my meeting at 1:30 PM? Where is this building and where do I park when I arrive? How much must we budget to correct deferred maintenance? I just got a pop-up informing me that my lab is at 87°F, who do I call for help?

These are the sorts of information, and much, much more that Red Dot Models make possible. The model leads to higher levels of information to quickly visualize a campus, building, space, component, or anything else.

Red Dot Models and similar concepts help us get our minds around how the building industry can take advantage of the world of information to manage information for the benefit of our stakeholders. They become an interface to allow you to connect information in-context to multiple massing models, and then to sketching software, before moving into more detailed design and analysis, to build greater value and benefit at each step.

By creating simplified access to data from everywhere, even realistic renderings that WOW! customers take on a new value. Images from little-bim that were little more than beautiful pictures now begin to support planning, design, manufacturing, construction, commissioning, operation, and management, in ways that anyone can use.

Basic Concepts

In the past, owners have been forced to delay decisions pending better information. Or they made decisions with little or not dependable data, resulting in catastrophic, real-world failures. A BIG-BIM approach makes it possible to use information to create a virtual ecosystem where early, virtual failures show how to avoid later, real-world failures.

A focus on shared information that supports the owner's mission through the entire lifecycle of a project requires a new way of looking at your business. Step back and look at the *first-principles* that drive your business.

How does your skill set and experience fit with your perception of BIM? Where can your experience have the greatest impact? Which of your internal processes and procedures map well to a BIG-BIM workflow?

How is your business affected by real-time information available on web-based mobile devices? Look at what is happening in successful management systems in parallel industries. Where have others experienced success?

Beginning in early 1997, my firm, Design Atlantic, conducted such an exploration. The outcomes led us to coin the term *BIG-BIM* to describe the ecosystem of processes we identified. We formalized the process with the goal of overcoming the shortfalls that came from doing our work the old-fashioned way. We decided to see the world for what it is, and what it can be, rather than defending what we were taught to believe. In broad terms, we conceived a system that revolves around eight basic concepts:

1.   Embrace Early Decisions: Take a decision-making focus. Jump in at the very beginning with the goal of eliminating train-wrecks later in the process. Embrace reliable decision-making information. Use technology to get a high level of quality information at the right time in the process.

2.   Take the Long View: Use a systems approach. Understand that transitioning how you work is a process. One can define and manage any process, so take heart, this is possible.

3.   Manage by Constraints: Constraints are anything that influences your work. Understand that you can manage complex processes by managing the constraints on your business to improve your work products. Manage the big constraints first. Cost is the key constraint to address if one wishes to manage work in the built environment.

4.   Be Collaborative: Embrace free and open communications. Know that people work better and make better decisions when they are informed about what is happening. Embrace processes that bring forward all points of view and all skill sets to the table early in significant ways.

5.   Adapt and Respond: No two owners (or project, lecture, process, study, replacement, etc.) is alike. Be agile and adapt each need. The system you develop (or any system) will always be in a constant state of evolution. If you are not growing, find another way to move forward.

6.   Optimize Processes: No one tool can do everything needed. There is always more than one way of completing tasks. Bring the most appropriate tools and methods to bear on each task. Understand the underlying concepts behind the tools and processes and to ensure that you have the greatest opportunities to solve problems.

7.   Manage Risk: Liability management is critical. Understand that by resolving issues early and proactively managing the process, you minimize your risks. Openly discuss and equitably allocate risks throughout the team. Use pain-share / gain-share concepts whenever possible.

8.   Share Information: The default position is to share. Intellectual property is important, but not the priority. Share information to achieve tasks, but also share information for the good of others. Know and understand that free-flowing information is a fundamental requirement of a successful BIG-BIM ecosystem. Without shared information, BIM and connected processes will never reach their true potential.

Embrace these basic concepts and adjust them to fit your needs. With a holistic understanding and dependable information available at the right time, our customers find it easier to make correct decisions—no matter how complicated or complex.

Fresh Set of Eyes

Most people want simple and easy to use tools and processes that get the job at hand done. Smooth, precise, and straightforward-to-use technology removes people's fears and enables change.

With a fresh set of eyes, you can see ways to help owners achieve their missions, with dramatically improved results. To do so, we must move beyond the traditional approach that we find most comfortable. The potential benefits are too great to continue as usual.

The more people struggle to maintain the status-quo, the more problems they cause. The usual ways may defer the pain, but it will not stop the inevitable transformations that are driving change today. No simple, painless fix will solve today's economic, social, political or business problems.

Mistakes are being made by well-intentioned people trying to sustain legacy tools and processes. This is particularly the case in the world of government projects. Too many resources are used in attempts to force existing systems to do things for which they are ill-suited. Often for systems with inherent flaws that will not work in the future, no matter how much time and money is spent trying to patch the holes. Patchwork solutions designed to upgrade old and faulty systems rarely work. They cost too much and give too little.

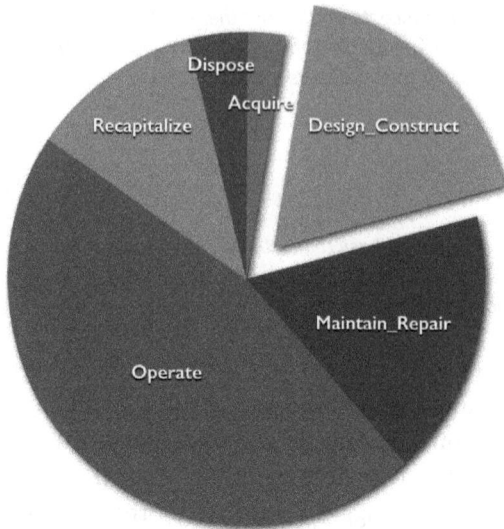

Studies suggest that of the estimated $7.2 Trillion annual worldwide construction industry expenditures, design, and construction account for only 18.2%. It is time for us to consider refocusing our attention on optimizing the remaining 81.8% which includes the parts of the industry that come before design and after construction. The $5.89 Trillion spent on disposal, acquisition, maintenance, repair, operations, and recapitalization of built environment assets is where the largest opportunities for savings exist.

The processes used for last generation's tools are too complicated and take too long to implement. The tools they produce are not always the best way to solve today's problems. People don't have the time, the interest, or the resources to understand the complexity such tools embody. Creating ever-more-complex and feature-rich tools doesn't solve the problem for most people. There are better and more efficient ways to succeed and become more competitive.

There are practical reasons sites such as Google+, Facebook, and Expedia became famous. They are easy to understand, simple to use and mask the underlying complexity. They overcome people's resistance to change, and no interaction with experts is required.

One can communicate one-to-one, one-to-many, and many-to-many to make things happen, no matter your skill or knowledge. The speed and extent of change have accelerated to the point that traditional approaches no longer suffice.

We no longer have the luxury to respond in traditional ways. Things change too fast. It is imperative to reconsider each part of what we do, in today's agile, fast-paced world. The industry's focus on design and construction is an example to consider:

Detailed design and construction make up a small percentage of the built environment, yet they receive the lion's share of the attention. They are the favorite subjects discussed in the media and by politicians. But, most people are not directly involved in design and construction.

We must broaden our focus. Design and construction are just part of a processes that impact the wider industry. Real estate, planning, operations and maintenance, and other functions are where most people interact with the built environment. These are the places where people need easy to use access to information to create solutions to complex problems that impact the greater part of our world.

A New Dynamic

It is worth the time to find out why your software programs are not sharing information in ways that are useful and productive.

The next tier of dramatic improvements will take place in operations and maintenance. Recognizing the opportunities, owners are striving to become better stewards of their assets. Efficiency, performance, and resiliency are but a few of the areas where they are working to track and respond in new and better ways.

Built environments and the missions they support are in constant flux. Buildings are re-purposed, new tenants arrive, new mandates are imposed. Work is outsourced. Work is done in-house. Occupants and functions change.

New business models change which metrics take precedence. National and international policies require new and unpredictable things to be measured. Most of the changes are incremental and slow, and they sneak up on owners. Others happen in crisis mode.

Whatever the case, the process of sharing information on the web is dynamic and diverse, which is ideally suited to this circumstance; but the subject is complex, with many subtleties. The subject is complex, with many subtleties. Owners are quick to understand the potential of the benefits, but they are wary of the hype. Owners ask: Is this just another fad? What's the problem? Vendors have sold stuff like this more times than I can count and they never work out.

With the mixed-messages they receive, and technology failures they have experienced, owners are rightfully a bit jaded. All too often legacy systems are failing, and vendors are concealing the fact that their systems fall short of fulfilling the need to share information in real-time. Begin by eliminating false expectations, establishing better compliance with existing information requirements, and learning how software programs exchange data.

Case Study
BIM–GIS–FM Fusion

The Foundation's study and testing confirmed their fears. Little-bim programs using file-based paradigms could not scale fast enough to meet their needs. They settled on the ONUMA System as the only option that offered the solution they needed.

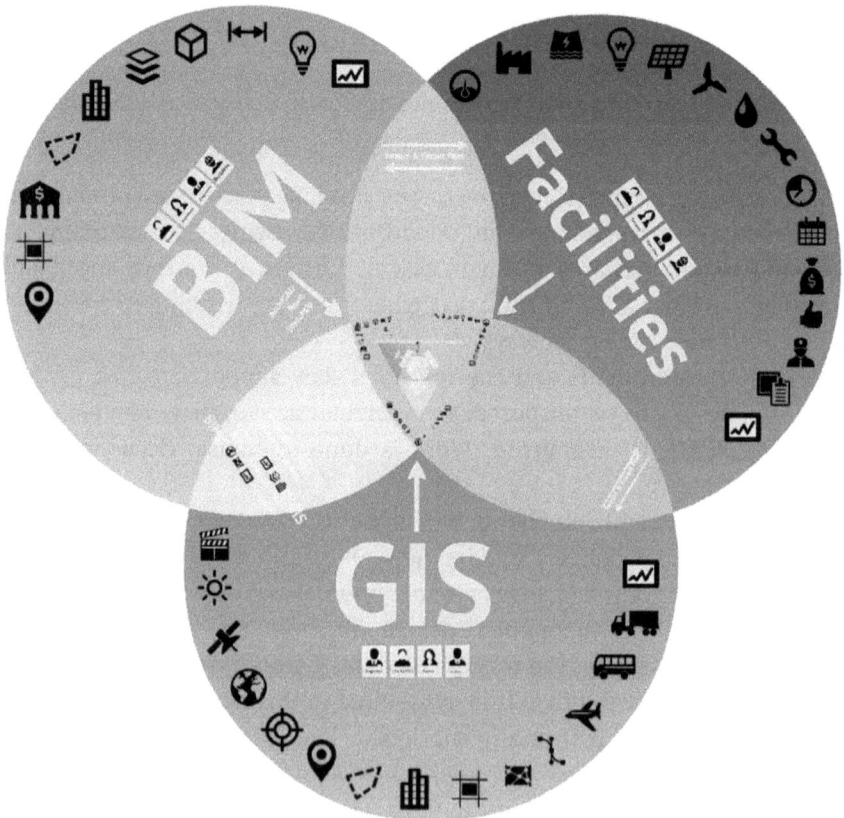

What are the interesting aspects of this case study?

Scalable, open, agile system to rapidly bimify 5,200 buildings and support a student population of 2.4 million students in 112 campuses—the largest higher education system in the world.

All Community College facilities and GIS data now connects to Building Information Models.

Innovations created a foundation for other solutions to follow, worldwide.

Demonstrates the value of going big, keeping it simple, implementing in a short time, while iterating as the system grows.

Location—California, USA.

It is rare to find an owner who has created consistent data across their entire portfolio, large or small. Few have attained this goal. The Foundation for California Community Colleges (CCC) web-enabled their data to allow for real-time viewing, editing, and updating beginning in 2002, for all districts in the system. Making it an easy task to *mash-up* GIS with BIM.

The Foundation has long advocated and used an open-standard approach to technology. When they found all the pieces to make a BIG-BIM ecosystem possible, it was time to capitalize on the fact that the Foundation's data was maintained to enable connections. They started by formally assessing and testing the major BIM tools available.

An initial pilot of one district started in late 2010 and became the proof-of-concept to show that it is possible to link FUSION, GIS, and BIM together. Originally the next step was planned to test the system in several more districts. Due the success of the initial trials, a decision was made to go straight into the linking the college's districts at a low-level of detail. And, it worked!

There is a tremendous waste in the AECOO industry. Proprietary and expensive competing solutions create silos of disconnected information. The status-quo is software applications that do not connect.

AECOO is the biggest industry in the world, consuming more energy and resources than transportation. Even with the explosion of new technologies, the tools, and processes to support this industry remain locked into traditional paradigms. Technological, cultural, legal, and other barriers hamper innovation. Without rapid change to the industry, the world's resources continue to be depleted at a much higher rate than necessary.

The interface for the College's system presents each of the 72 Community Colleges as a placemark in Google Maps. By hovering over or clicking on a placemark the user is given links to more detailed data. The user can then 'drill down' from this level all the way to views of furniture and equipment.

The BIG-BIM ecosystem that CCC created enables them to manage and interconnect data for design, engineering, construction, owners, and operators (AECOO) of facilities. Using a real-time mash-up of tools that enable users at many levels to interact and make decisions.

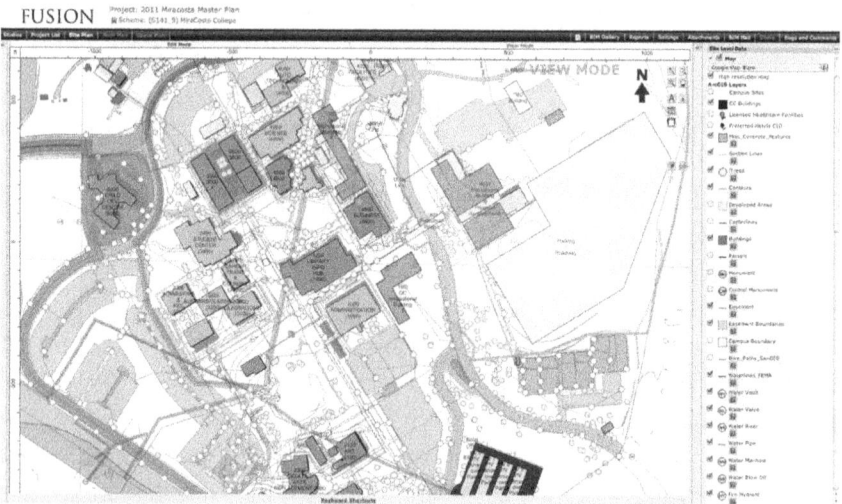

Owner spatial information mashed-up live into BIM. The system demonstrates why no one software can solve everything in the AECOO industry. Cloud computing, the Internet, and open-standards underpin the solution. CCC's answer to AECOO issues links Building Information Modeling (BIM), Geographic Information Systems (GIS) and Facilities Management information, making the innovation relevant beyond their organization. The opportunity for architects and architecture is enormous, but it will require a tectonic shift in how the AECOO industry operates. The revolution is happening now, and starting in California.

Summary

The California Community College's System is the largest postsecondary system of education in the world. The framework they created enables information at any stage of the lifecycle of projects to link to the other parts of the process. Interoperability, open-standards, and scalability are the oxygen that drive the College's ecosystem.

FUSION + CCC GIS + ONUMA

The Entire State of
California Community College System
in a Cloud Computing Environment
Linking FUSION with GIS and BIM

71 million square feet
2.75 million students
112 California locations

Implementation of this highly flexible system happened very quickly. Within nine months the connection of all districts as standards-compliant BIG-BIM, at a low level of detail, was complete. Of the 72 districts, fifteen had already added projects at higher levels of detail to represent the full planning to operations lifecycle. The remaining 57 districts are adding models and data of increasing detail, as the adoption cycle continues

There is no official completion date or occupancy date for the overall system. It is a process that feeds into itself. The system manages existing facilities, plans new services and, supports funding. Planning defines new projects, construction happens, and delivers projects. The data is fed back into the system to support operations as the cycle repeats.

One can think of the system as a user interface to built environment related information to enable better decision-making and visualization in any aspect of the built world.

Too often, the user interfaces that are available default to mathematical/statistical equations, spreadsheets, and graphs/charts. For those that are highly trained in the field under discussion, these interfaces can work quite well. However, for the others that might benefit are often left 'scratching their heads' and wondering of what the experts talk. They have little or no context on the interface and, therefore, find themselves talked down to or left with misconceptions and holes in their understanding. This approach results in too many incorrect decisions, misallocated resources, and conflict between parties.

The need for clear, easy to use interfaces is one of the issues that the system seeks to resolve. By enabling information to be connected to the environment, the system makes it easier to understand what is happening, what the big constraints might be, what works, and what doesn't work. The value that comes from connecting information is one of the 'aha!' issues that many have gotten during the BIM workshops. When one sees the world in a simplified graphic context; one that pops-up pertinent data custom to the level one is viewing; the decision points become clearer.

Planning can now happen connected into the full lifecycle. Data from existing facilities can be used to generate scenarios in real-time. The resulting decisions are then passed to project teams as BIM and GIS for implementation. The results are then pushed back into the College's system to start the cycle all over again.

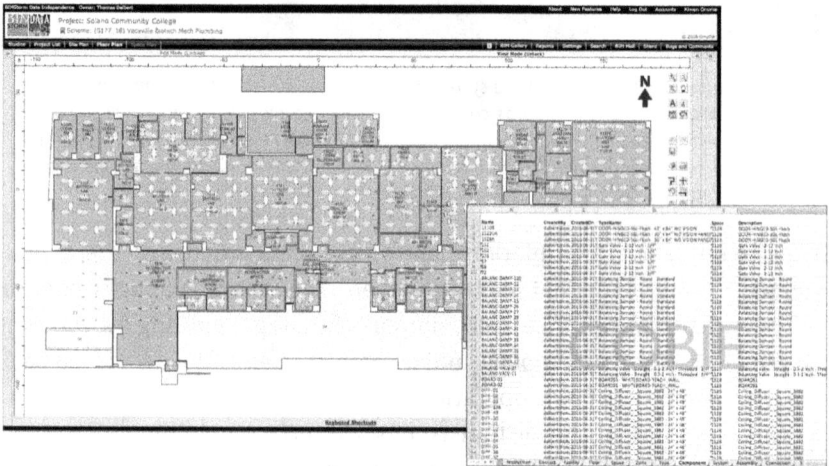

Data captured in the process is COBie-compliant and can be used to support procurement and management of building products.

Along with actual projects and ongoing operations, there is a need to innovate continually, test, implement, research and develop. The College's platform was opened to the entire industry where 129 participants from around the world worked with real project data to mash-up full lifecycle scenarios in a rapid two-day BIMStorm event.

BIMStorms have become ongoing industry events to allow for collaboration without the constraints of contracts, thus allowing for rapid innovation, exploration, and testing. The connection is an example of how BIG-BIM approaches can provide significant benefits that enable you to leapfrog over the limitations of a little-bim focus on a single software tool.

The Foundation's leaders determined that BIM was the logical way to go to overcome FUSION's limits. However, they could not see how a little-bim file-based system could scale to the level required. Nor could they solve the problem of how to get all 5,400 existing buildings into a single little-bim software program in an economical way.

History

The Foundation for California Community Colleges has provided facilities and building data services to the 113-campus system. Although the Foundation for California Community Colleges manages the data for all 74 Million Square feet of facility data statewide, each district is autonomous in their decision on how to use the information and tools. Services to the Community Colleges include the Geographic Information Systems (GIS) Collaborative and a facility management system named FUSION.

Before the FUSION System came online in 2003, the problem was that there was no way to consistently aggregate information at a statewide level. Each district operated as they saw fit using systems ranging from spreadsheets to proprietary databases, to DOS based systems. With FUSION, the colleges manage data in real-time in a consistent way across the entire portfolio.

FUSION is a facilities database that tracks condition assessments and develops cost modeling for capital construction projects. The system enabled member colleges to plan budgets and facilitate bond measures. While benefits came from FUSION, many factors limited implementation and sub-optimized the system's value. For instance, it was not possible with just FUSION to link to a graphical format to visualize errors in the data.

Add to this the fact that the districts needed tools to operate appropriately in a highly-constrained environment. They had no time to wait for the entire portfolio of buildings to be created incrementally inserted into a single little-bim software program. Budget constraints, demographic shifts, energy issues, and the dynamic nature of such factors were becoming a huge risk and liability to the systems operations. New strategies and solutions were needed.

Through the application of open-standards, the CCC BIG-BIM ecosystem natively supports buildingSMART alliance standards and makes the California Community Colleges' data available as IFC, COBie, KML, BIMxml, and RESTful web services at varying levels of detail. The end results are substantial savings of time, an inherent accuracy of information and a growing value in support of the CCC districts.

The connection enables data to be used by a broad spectrum of people, in many formats, at many levels of detail. One presents the information in the format that best supports decision-making whether that be tabular, charts, graphical, live or three-dimensional. Here, the data is consolidated in Navisworks to support construction.

In 2010, the college's system began to add significant functionality to the services once offered. Information that was previously available only in a tabular data format became two or three-dimensional building models. The system allows for fast pattern recognition, better decision-making, and improved accounting for facilities and assets.

In what seemed an instant, the colleges moved from broken systems to BIG-BIM. Ease of access and the power to capitalize on enterprise data were but two of the benefits. The College's system expands the capabilities of the colleges to manage and plan their physical space more efficiently. The system combines Facilities Utilization, Space Inventory Options Net (FUSION)—an entire inventory of facilities and areas, with the College's GIS Collaborative data about campus buildings and geography, interconnected with open-standard, web-enabled data sharing capabilities to create a highly viable BIG-BIM ecosystem.

The online platform makes real-time data available to all without users having to install or update software in the centralized system. BIM data exports in most standard formats for contractors and builders. Cross-platform compatibility allows for easy updates once construction is complete. Users produce project proposals and preliminary design plans locally and more cost effectively than before. One can view FUSION, GIS, and BIM data at several levels of detail. Maps become more than static representations, at a statewide, campus-wide, building, or room level. Reports enable users to aggregate data at any of these levels. The system lets users view and edit furniture, equipment, plus much more.

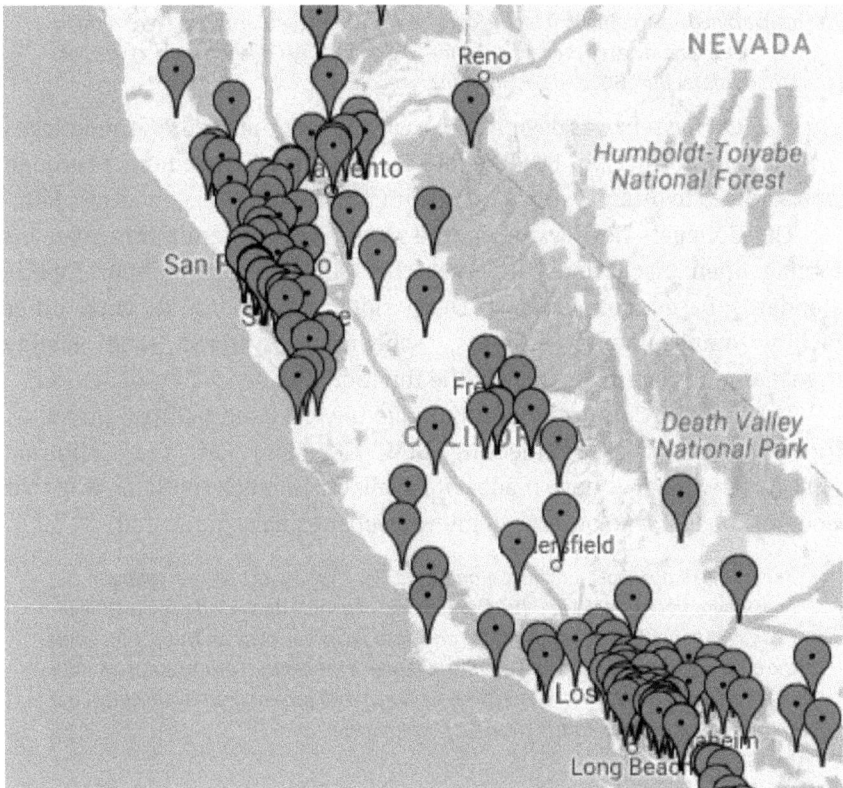

Little-Red-Dot-Model from the CCC system. Each placemark allows the user to drill down into greater detail about the asset. There is more discussion and detail of California Community College's system in the MORE CASE STUDIES section near the end of this book

Features and Opportunities

Technology isn't the largest roadblock to the implementation of BIG-BIM. Getting over the culture shock associated with change is the opportunity. Keeping things simple, implementing fast, and talking the language of the audience is critical, and exactly what is happening in the College's system.

Complex solutions need to be broken down into bite-sized pieces that don't evoke the cultural hurdle. The solution is an infinitely scalable strategy that allows connection across multiple disconnected processes. In a discussion of classroom scheduling, why mention GIS, BIM, or standards? Even if those tools are the engines that are driving our ability to visualize class schedule on a plan?

The state of California is a resource-constrained environment. In a resource-constrained environment, it is critical to be efficient in the use of one's information. This need for efficiency drove the California Community College's interest in open-standards for BIM, GIS, and Facility Management.

The FUSION System was designed to scale to meet the needs of the colleges for facility information. FUSION laid the groundwork to connect through web services to other systems, to maximize the value of Foundation data.

The College's new system is the result. The system's framework is forcing open discussions on how other solutions can support open-standards-based connections. Discussions are underway with other facility managements systems, scheduling systems, and energy management systems to include the functionality needed by all districts.

The state of California offers unique physical and political problems for any system. By connecting BIM, GIS, and FM, the California Community Colleges have made data available in much the same way that Google, Expedia, and other well known websites have pioneered.

BIG-BIM is about tools, processes, and attitudes that impact on everything in the built environment. Achieving the optimum mix of people and technology is difficult. Most, recent implementations of BIM and data focus narrowly on the project and the data about the project. This emphasis is one of the clearest examples of a failure to optimize both sides of the BIG-BIM equation. While project data is relevant in the short term, enterprise data is critical for the long run.

Real-Time Assets

The plug-and-play modular approach to connecting is the scalable way to enable future functions that one can plan today. The elimination of duplicated data and efforts and the easy access to complex information in a simple format creates a lower cost set of solutions.

It is now possible to build your travel plans to book a plane ticket, hotel room and rental car based on a specified schedule. Contracts and payments are negotiated and completed online. You receive automated updates as changes occur to allow rapid responses. Your records are accessible from any location on many different devices. After your trip is over, you can access trip cost information for personal or business records. You see custom subsets of the data to find, select and decide; without directly interacting with the underlying complexity.

Only when built environment projects result in information becoming continuously available, much like information about travel plans are accessible on the web, can true BIG Data/BIG-BIM ecosystems be possible.

When information about the built environment is available in real-time for planning, design, manufacturing, construction, commissioning, operations, and maintenance, the project is no longer the primary focus. Maximizing the value of assets becomes the focus.

Being concerned about the entire lifecycle of an asset, any built asset, allows more direct attention on the essence of the problem. At the US Coast Guard, pioneers of BIG-BIM thinking, it was said that, *if you can't explain how your work directly relates to saving people who may be in the water drowning today, you are not supporting the end goal.*

When BIM software programs make their information available in real-time they unleash their power to all stakeholders. Real-time access to information allows everyone involved to contribute throughout the entire lifecycle of anything we build

Much of the information management we do today is more analogous to paper files stored in a file cabinet than to live data that is always available. Everyone understands what happens when you lose track of a major paper document in a file cabinet. Similarly, information in an electronic file that can't be easily accessed by all stakeholders suffers from the same ills, although often much more acutely. As the World Wide Web evolved, massive benefits were discovered in safely sharing and reusing information.

As we will explore more in a later chapter, the focus is on ASSETS, NOT PROJECTS.

COBie Check

COBie keeps BIM honest. You can have a perfect looking little-bim and fail any one of the tests described below, making your COBie output worthless. If this is the case, your model is suspect, represents little more than graphical information and, will not cleanly transition to future use over the project's lifecycle.

The Construction Operations Building Information Exchange (COBie) was created to standardize and record the data about equipment established in the design phase and installed during construction for transfer and use during a building's operations. Developed by the US Army Corps of Engineers and NASA, today the COBie standard is actively supported by the buildingSMART alliance in the United States and the BIM Task Group in the United Kingdom. Many large US government projects use the standard. A modified version of COBie is also a core part of the mandate for BIM Level 2 in UK government funded projects.

COBie began as a spreadsheet-oriented structure formatted to support the import of information into computer-aided facility management and operation software.

Organized properly, one can export design and construction data into a COBie spreadsheet and transfer the data to facilities management tools, such as Maximo or ArchiBus. Some BIM authoring tools also allow the return of data after making changes on the facilities management side of the equation. This ability to move information, in both directions, between design, construction and facilities management is a key to connected processes in the built environment, yet is not possible in most little-bim today.

Originally COBie was a workaround to enable a subset of the data applicable to facilities management to move between design and construction little-bim into non-BIM computer-aided facilities management (CAFM) systems. Until bidirectional information flow between little-bim and CAFM became mainstream. While COBie is a positive first step, it isn't the end-game in the transition between construction and operations. In most cases, using COBie requires human intervention and active management, both susceptible to human error, for managing the data in Building Information Models.

To use COBie in a BIM environment you start by validating your model and asking two fundamental questions:

1. Does each room or space have a number?

2. Are room numbers duplicated? MOST CObie exports from little-bim fail these questions—even very sophisticated, cool looking 3D BIMs with tons of data. There is no reason to check anything else for CObie compliance, if they don't pass both questions. If they pass the first two questions, you next ask:

3. Are all components or equipment associated with a unique room number? Many little-bim also fail this test. For those that pass the first three, hard tests, you should ask:

4. Do all components have unique IDs?

5. Are there types associated with all components?

6. Are the correct classifications used?

7. Have the spaces been modeled correctly?

8. Are associated documents or attributes properly referenced?

None of the information described above is unusual. The same information should be maintained and managed in any well-documented construction document set—whether created by hand or in an electronic format.

In a BIG-BIM environment, CObie is created transparently as an output from your data and requires minimal human intervention. Once your model's underlying data structure is correct, magical things can happen in BIG and little-bim. One can move data to other systems and maintain live data for the lifecycle and more. Better supporting the owner's mission over the long haul.

Manage and Operate

A system is a network of interdependent components that work together to try to accomplish the aim of the system. A system must have an objective. Without an aim, there is no system. The purpose of the system must be clear to everyone in the system.
— Dr. Edwards Deming

When design, construction and facility management are entirely separate tasks in the lifecycle, projects take a linear approach: plan—design—document—build—operate. Tradition and preconceived notions govern. Each step features a different cast of actors. Rarely do they overlap. At each step, the actors work to deliver discreet products in ways much like their ancestors did, generations (millennia) ago.

Some of the steps are efficient—debugged over generations. Many others are outdated and wasteful. Each actor does their own thing. There is little regard for what comes next. Each actor and each component concentrates on its own niche. Each act as though they were independent of the others. Few do the things that might build an interdependent network.

In the RECIPE FOR BIG-BIM FROM THIN AIR in the SPECIAL SUPPLEMENT, you will create a very simple Building Information Model that has multiple spaces or rooms that comply with COBie. After you do the workflow, use the system to export a COBIE2 (Excel/XML) file. Then return and use what you learn in the to assess your model.

Their actions exhibit little agreement about the overall mission. Each focus on their own mission, with little concern for the mission of others and the resulting system. A BIG-BIM ecosystem relies on a continuous flow of information through each step of the process. To achieve this, a couple of things must happen.

First, the owners need to establish the end goal or aim of the system. Then, project leaders must connect (or integrate) each of the components and make them interdependent by sharing information across the entire system. Both functions require owners to take time and neither is ever complete.

Connecting the building industry's parts starts with a well-researched and planned process. A process that explicitly includes long-term sustainability and resilience. Structured and coordinated information models interface with data in web-accessible databases. The models pull data to enable decision-making, visualization, and analysis. Changes to the project are pushed back to continually refine and expand the database. Over time the data becomes more accurate and valuable. The effort begins early and must carry through into facility operations.

Such processes are critical to long-term sustainability. Ideally the data flows bidirectionally, is available in real-time and, is created with little or no added effort. As the project is designed and built, the data flows to the next steps transparently—while being organized to support future decision-making. This is the world of web services and the seamless connection of applications, data, and devices. Infrastructures for information exchange, such as Service-Oriented-Architecture allows applications to be *plugged* into the ecosystem.

Later we will explore the details and Core Concepts that make such a network the long-term solution for sharing information through all phases of the lifecycle. This approach has already transformed other industries and is beginning to impact the built environment.

Materials to help with COBie, and operations connected to design and construction, can be found at the National Institute of Building Sciences (NIBS) web site. Review the Means and Methods page, Using COBie Data section and download the COBie Responsibility Matrix. Look at the listing of Free Software in the online NIBS Whole Building Design Guide's (WBDG) Resources Page. Read through the information provided and watch a video or two. Near the bottom is a group entitled TEMPLATES AND ADDITIONAL RESOURCES.

Go to the Examples link and download one of the files. Open the spreadsheet and browse through the tabs to get an idea of how COBie is structured. Download the COBie2 Validator from the Onuma website. Note that web search will lead you to other products that also validate and organize COBie data. While on the WBDG or Onuma COBie page, also download sample COBie files. Use the Validator and sample file to practice and understand what COBie does and how you might use it to your advantage.

Connected Information

Uber makes more daily trips than traditional taxis. Wikipedia replaces encyclopedias which are outdated before publication. Travel sites let us book and pay for trips quicker and for less money, wherever and whenever it suits us. We order medical devices such as eyeglasses without the intervention of opticians. These are but the tip of the Internet iceberg.

Remain nimble and use the disruptions to your benefit. You needn't limit yourself to only a small part of the built environment.

Much of the industry involved with the built environment does not avail itself of the transformative benefits of providing real-time data that is platform neutral.

The concept of reusable, real-time, live data is contrary to how many BIM tool vendors have chosen to design their software. Vendors continue to keep information safely embedded within the bowels of their programs, making file exchanges necessary to share the data generated by their users.

The reality is that—NOW—most BIM software only stores information in proprietary ways, internal to each software vendor's program. It is possible to create applications that free the data for real-time use, with all the attendant benefits that we experience each day as we use the Internet.

The use of live information available in real-time creates disruption in whatever industry it occurs. The upheavals occur because Connected Age tools and processes can communicate essential information to decision makers so quickly that much of the uncertainty and time lag vanish. No longer must an expert intercede to help us do the right thing. Expert help now often comes from creatively using the available data resources, not from a live person.

Disruption may take many forms in the building industry. Soon, with a click of a button, people may be able to contract securely to get things done in the built environment.

The systemic elimination of wasteful practices will accelerate design and construction in ways never possible. Global teams have already started to prototype new ways of working that may replace traditional design and construction teams.

The outcomes from these trials lead one to speculate about what might happen to the timeline of a typical project. Consider a hypothetical example:

At project initiation: The Owner's project coordinator passes a BIG-BIM tender request to a preset, distributed delivery team. The coordinator concurrently authorizes the engagement of the team members flagged by the BIG-BIM ecosystem for the project, and;

A generalist design Architect in Rio then spends six hours to generate a little-bim concept in full compliance with the project's requirements embedding in the BIG-BIM tender;

At eight hours: views from the little-bim are captured, as they develop, in the ecosystem so that the Owner, Financier, and Bonding Agency can review and approve the engagement in the portfolio and global context. Input from end users, the operations and maintenance organization and others feeds into the ecosystem to assure that stakeholder needs are met.

Approvals and other decisions are made, captured, and responded to; all within the ecosystem. Funds are allocated and sureties are issued based on data in the BIG-BIM ecosystem tied to the international financial portal. Concurrently, the project is reviewed and permits are issued by the Building Authority, while;

The concept model goes to a specialist Architect in Chicago and a Constructor in New York for coordination and additional refinement. At the same time, access to the model is passed to Engineers in Helsinki and Dusseldorf who in twenty-two hours submit drawings to a Cost Manager in Dublin, while;

A production house in Budapest packages the teams' little-bim models and other data from the BIG-BIM ecosystem, adding detail for prefabrication and so that the Cost Manager and remainder of the team can tap in as needed to perform just-in-time quality assurance tasks. Responding to and correcting any issues they find, and;

At forty-eight hours: the resulting tender posts to a service that uses the data in the BIG-BIM ecosystem to manage the team's pain-share/gain-share agreement, puts fabrication resources into production and procures construction proposals to fill in the balance of the team at the project's location, and;

At sixty hours: ground breaking ceremonies take place; prefabricated components begin to arrive on site and construction begins...

Such a scenario is aspirational, yet well within the realm of BIG-BIM ecosystems of the near future. Every critical step has been prototyped and shown to be possible, within the timeframes shown. Engaged teams that take full advantage of the power of BIG-BIM will see such dramatic improvements in business processes.

Among the first disruptions will be a shift away from the narrow focus on the phases of a project to sharing information through all stages of our assets' lives. As all stakeholders gain access to lifecycle information, they will begin to have a more direct and positive impact on long-term project outcomes.

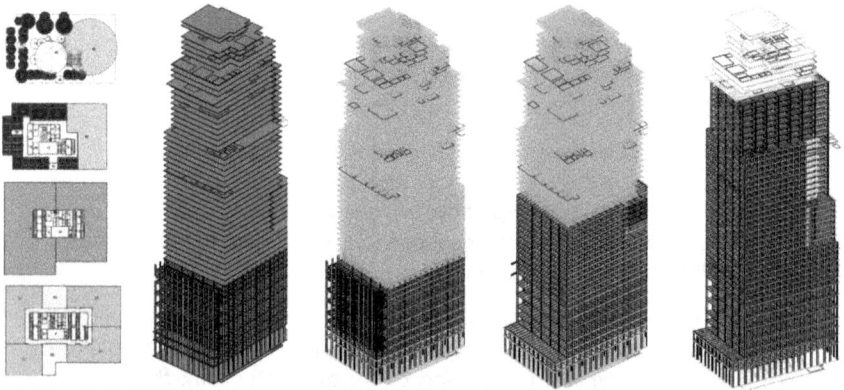

BIMStorms have been used to prototype the rapid development of projects using teams of widely distributed experts. In 24 hours, the high-rise structure above was created beginning with the diagrams in the upper left and progressing to detailed architectural, structural, and mechanical systems at the right.

This disruption will have both positive and negative impacts on current businesses. On the negative side, some established medium and large businesses will not be able to adapt, for a variety of reasons. On the positive side, the asset-focused view will work to minimize the cycles of feast and famine that have long characterized the building industry, while increasing opportunities for new and yet unidentified business ventures that expand upon current occupations.

Few practitioners today have considered the full extent of the possibilities. Use the disruptions to take advantage of the full breadth of your training and skills in the broader context. With the aim in the forefront of your mind, it is possible to connect your facility, equipment, vehicles, infrastructure, finances, etc., into BIG-BIM ecosystems in ways that allow people to say, I see what you are talking about.

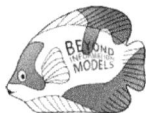

TWO
STRATEGIC THINKING

Most people working in the built environment do business the same way they have been for decades—while those that pay the bills demand improvement. No longer can we rely on the old ways and ignore the changes that surround us.

Fortunately, today's best tools are designed with ease of use in mind. The tools' complexity takes place hidden from view and doesn't require us to have expert knowledge to use them for our benefit. It is possible to establish your strategy for thinking big while starting with small steps.

Understand what has taken place in the travel, music, publishing, big-box retail, cable television, telecommunications, financial services, manufacturing and other industries. Similar disruptions will be impacting the built environment—SOON. Enhance your strategic thinking to tap into what has gone before in other industries. Focus on parallel situations that you can use to anticipate and align with a new, information-centric building industry.

Embrace systems that capture knowledge and then connect that knowledge to optimize benefit. Move your focus away from the different phases of projects toward managing lifecycle information and assets that support those you serve.

Silos

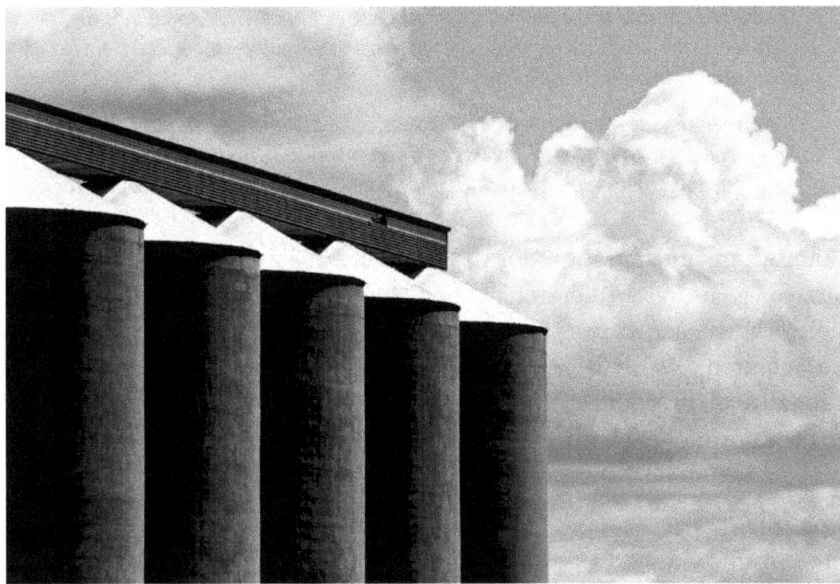

> *We have the power and tools to make the necessary corrections, breaking down the silos to overcome constraints between owners, tenants, lenders, architects, contractors, owners, accountants, lawyers, insurance professionals, and everyone else. Much of what we need is in place; the first adopters have blazed the way.*

There has been a rich history of quality management and improvement in other industries that the building industry has yet to embrace. Using the lessons learned from the successes and failures in other areas, we can break down the silos and disconnected processes that are currently constraining the building sector at every turn.

At the industry level:

Trade and legacy methods impose rigid systematic processes where each subgroup must recreate information at each step.

At the organizational level:

Departments impose disconnected systems with little sharing between functional groups; imposing disconnects that decrease performance and negatively impact the enterprise.

At the project level:

The surveyor does her work and outputs a site survey for the design team, who recreate the information to use geographic information in the building context;

The designer creates a concept, prepares bidding materials, and hands the documents off for pricing to constructors, who recreate the information in their systems for quantity takeoffs and implementation;

The builder constructs the project, prepares close-out paperwork and hands them off to the owner, who then recreates the information for multiple internal systems to operate and maintain the building;

The owner's finance department pays invoices; the maintenance department keeps the equipment running; the operations staff orders fuel and coordinates vendors; yet each maintains their own set of records and data, with little or no reuse between the departments.

Countering information silos traditionally required a combination of shared goals, flat hierarchies and increased internal and external networking—across the supply chain. In the building industry, more will be required. We will need to distribute systems that transparently capitalize on individual self-interests to impose new ways of working that make information sharing beneficial to all concerned.

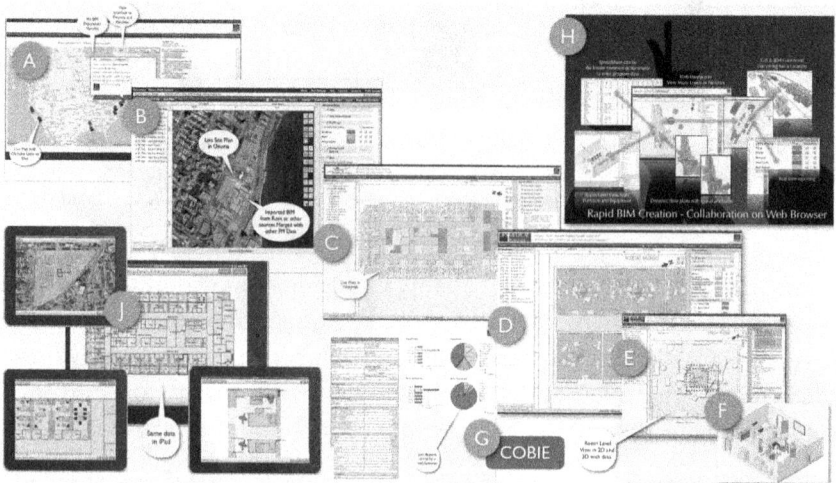

If you can make a Red Dot model (A above) and have completed the RECIPE FOR REAL-WORLD BIG-BIM, you have taken the first steps toward surviving the disruption coming to the building industry. You may thrive in it. The Red Dot models leverage BIMxml to disrupt the file-based approach of Industry Foundation Classes (IFC).

Current Conditions

To date, the little-bim software has not helped free information for easy use, although it has created compelling visualizations that have provided some level of benefit through coordinated documents, clash detection and in other ways. More benefits are possible.

Traditional project delivery processes are fraught with lack of cooperation and poor information sharing. Each step wastes resources and creates opportunities for error. Early Industrial Age standards and transactional agreements control the process. Results are undependable. We store information in file-based software systems that are hard to access by non-expert stakeholders. Other industries are realizing benefits from making data available as a service to any software that can navigate the Internet to send and receive information.

You do not have to learn anything about the software hosting airline schedules, rental car availability, or hotel occupancy to design your vacation. You go to Expedia or Travelocity, and use web services to access freely available information. At its heart, a system like Expedia is a real-time bidding and procurement system. Input your specification (name, destination, and date of travel) and the system returns a series of offers that meet your request. Select an option, make payment, and your purchase is recorded and validated. Much like eBay, Amazon, iTunes, Amazon Prime, Google Express, and many other systems, Expedia is a proof-of-concept for tools that serve similar functions in the built environment.

While some in the built environment have been pushing for this type of functionality for many years, others are just coming around to applying this kind of functionality to BIM software. Approaches using proven, standards-based tools like those we all use on the Internet can be leveraged to address the wicked problems facing the built environment. We can overcome many obstacles when we move beyond the little-bim graphic and files-centric focus toward the capture and reuse of live information.

For most of us, it is out of the question to return to the days of travel agents, print newspapers, paper billing, and the other technologies that were common before the Internet.

When we design, and create a new house or interact with a city's building department, we act like the Internet doesn't even exist. Indeed, we use computers for drawing lines and exchanging files, but most of the benefits stop right there in the built world. Why do built environment processes lag? It is a Complex and Wicked Problem.

Contemporary Problems

Gardening is not very complicated. You turn the soil, put the seeds in the ground and hope. You need lots of hope, because growing things is complex. You must deal with many uncertainties: the sun, the rain, and weeds. And, those are just the things you know about, the known-unknowns. You can plan for many things. The farmer can choose the right time to plant and can use the land properly, but weather, pests, and the other uncontrollable things make the difference between success and failure.

Today's strategic thinking must take into consideration four types of problems facing built environment professionals—Tame Problems, Complicated Problems, Complex Problems, and Wicked Problems. *Tame Problems are well defined with a straightforward problem statement.* The ability to solve Tame Problems is a step toward professional expertise and proficiency. You solved Tame Problems when you tested to receive a professional license.

Complicated Problems are difficult, but have a solution using your knowledge and processes. Building a building is not simple, but it's not complex; it's complicated. Complicated things are often hard to produce and might take a long time to build, but they are capable of being described in detail—down to the last brick, connector, or door. Design and construction can be accurately articulated and built, even by those that don't understand what they are building—If the builders comply with the letter of the processes and designs created by those that do know what they are doing. Failure is either due to poor compliance with the instructions, or the instructions being inadequate themselves.

We solve Complicated Problems with our expertise and knowledge to work out the steps, create the plan, and use them to implement the solution. The difference between complicated and complex is in the degree of uncertainty and the number of interacting, but independent components over which we have no control.

Complex Problems don't have a solution and may not have a solution, at all. Many of the problems that surround us are complex.

Feeding the hungry, population growth, fixing the building industry, and climate change are among the Complex Problems that affect us all. However, Complex Problems need not be universal issues.

Take the game of Lacrosse. The lacrosse coach cannot lay out every action in advance. Today a weak member of the opposing team could have her best game and score a hat trick.

How can you plan for that? You cannot know where things are heading until other things happen. Things are likely to happen about which you have no knowledge or control over. The unknowns and uncertainties that characterize complex tasks make them difficult to solve with traditional tools. By changing leadership behaviors, managing for outcomes, appropriate contracting models, system thinking techniques and experiential learning you can prepare for what some have called the *known unknowns*, but not the *unknowns*. To manage what we don't know that we don't know, one must plan for surprises.

The unknowns and uncertainties that characterize Complex Problems make them difficult to handle with traditional tools. Agile systems, crowdsourcing, and tools that manage how things interact lead us to the best possible solutions to Complex Problems.

Wicked Problems have no single discrete solution and each apparent solution leads to new wicked problems. Climate change forecasting is a classic wicked problem. Incomplete, contradictory and changing requirements make wicked problems hard to categorize or even recognize.

We address Tame Problems and Complicated Problems with First Order tools and techniques that help professionals follow the rules and focus on doing things *the right way.*

First Order tools and technology are the foundations for expertise and process compliance. Most of today's familiar paper-based tools (such as checklists), as well as desktop and file-based design software and related business processes, are First Order tools or techniques. Even a printed specification is a First Order tool, as are project scheduling systems such as Primavera or MS-Project. Licensing exams are passed based on memorizing a first order rule set.

First Order tools have helped create an amazing built environment but are not adequate to address the increasingly challenging set of problems the world is facing.

Complex Problems and Wicked Problems require Second-Order tools and techniques that focus on systems thinking, appropriate leadership and flexibility to respond appropriately to changing situations.

Second-Order tools and technology take advantage of real-time shared data to enable rapid and flexible assessment and responses. Second-Order tools and non-linear uses of big data lead to people-centered solutions that maximize resources and minimize error. Allowing one to rapidly model options and predict outcomes.

Software such as *Sim-City* was an early example of a Second-Order tool—model the virtual community with Sims, businesses, and other things and see what happens over time.

Today's biggest issues are often frustrating, and solutions seem to be far away. Many professionals continue to think that if they apply the First Order tools and techniques they have mastered to current problems, a solution will result. The news media announces failures, and reports sub-optimized outcomes that result from these failed projects every day. Too often such situations come about because someone has tried to force a discrete solution onto a Complex, Wicked Problem, based on application of First Order tools.

Viewed from this perspective, project failures may not be due to incompetence and mismanagement. More likely, they are due to rigid organizational adherence to using linear thinking on unrecognized wicked problems. Wicked problems don't have a stopping point. There is no test to show that one has solved a wicked problem. Rather than *right or wrong*, a wicked problem can usually only be described by *better or worse.* Every wicked problem is fundamentally unique and therefore does not have a repeatable solution.

Waste in the building industry, community planning, law enforcement in urban communities, the environment, energy, sustainability, connected processes, and most of the other issues that affect our future can be said to be wicked problems. Approaches to them using first order management tools alone will not produce the outcomes we hope for, even when used by trained professionals who have worked all their lives to gain expertise. If a problem is wicked, the traditional approach doesn't work. Prescribed linear methods will not solve wicked problems.

The approach to wicked problems requires more interaction than any linear sequence of steps provides. You don't solve a wicked problem as much as broker shared understanding and shared meaning about the problem and the possible solutions. Collaboration and communication are more critical than creativity to successfully addressing wicked problems.

A Second-Order approach to problems refocuses people toward communication, systems thinking, and collaboration. Creativity, insight, and innovation emerge spontaneously as the consequence of shared knowledge and shared responsibility.

Look at the work you do and study your projects and customers. How many of the problems you face are tame or complicated? How many are wicked or complex? Examples, case studies, and workflows are scattered through this book to give insight into the ways others manage problems of all types. Explore the available tools and techniques to build your system as you tackle the problems you confront. Refer to Wikipedia and other sources to build a more in-depth understanding of each of these problem categories. Many have been wrestling with these concepts for many years and extensive additional information is available to support your research on the topic.

Owners Demand Improvement

The little-bim workflows enable high-speed production while masking errors that make quality control difficult. Owners find themselves in a position where, even with the promise of little-bim, they can no longer rely on the traditional checks and balances to assure outcomes. Studies suggest that owners experience project schedule and cost overruns on 85% of all projects. The situation is better for some little-bim projects, but most are not. Today, the problems persist.

Owners working to handle the increasingly Complex and Wicked Problems facing us, demand improvement—and rightfully so. Getting to the root of the problem hasn't been easy. The complexity and fragmentation of the building industry made (and continues to make) interoperability a major issue. However, using little-bim on a project-by-project and team-by-team basis, has resulted in notable successes in the last ten years.

The path to more widespread success depends on BIG-BIM and the adoption of new, higher order tools. Second-Order tools and processes need to be further developed and adopted to provide improved approaches to the Complex and Wicked Problems owners face today. Solving the industry wide problems requires the right tools and processes, applied one professional and one company at a time.

Owners continue to demand paper or files-based plans and specifications from their consultants for bidding. The contractor then recreates the work to support construction. When construction is complete, the facility manager once again recreates the work to support operations and maintenance. And this happens even on little-bim projects using COBie and other tools.

The traditional project delivery process is fraught with lack of cooperation and poor information sharing. Each step wastes energy and creates opportunities for error. Tradition, age-old standards, and transactional agreements control the process. The industry is inefficient and undependable.

Core Knowledge

The errors caused by the lack of senior staff worsen as design and construction companies have yet to find effective ways to capture knowledge and make it available to support their teams. The new generation finds themselves starting anew even with well-established organizations. Often, little dynamic corporate knowledge is available, when and where it is needed.

Part of the problem raised by owners comes from losses in core knowledge and wisdom. The building industry is losing seasoned staff at a rapid pace. These losses have resulted in fewer people with the sound judgment required to manage the complex and dynamic environment that exists today. Throughout the industry, knowledge resources were lost in the Great Recession and are being lost as experienced people retire.

Some surveys predict that 50% of all senior managers will retire in the next decade. Companies are already experiencing the impact of these losses. Every year it becomes harder to hire experienced, senior staff. This loss of knowledgeable workers, inefficiency and lack of coordinated workflows will continue to plague the entire building industry.

Finding ways to educate those new to the industry is a major opportunity. The paradigm of long apprenticeships is no longer viable. People with little knowledge of the context and little or no discipline-oriented experience are doing many of the tasks traditionally reserved for those with significant core knowledge. We ask people to step into situations that are both new to the industry and new to the employee. Often without adequate support and planning. Learning as one goes has become the standard in many situations.

Knowledge-based systems are a partial answer. We need to find ways to capture industry experience and use it to build (or supplement) the wisdom required by the next generation.

Second-Order tools and techniques that capture the knowledge of those leaving the industry are part of the solution. Only by embracing such an approach—capturing the knowledge in the old-guards' heads and then connecting that experience to the needs of new people—can we head off drastic changes to the professions.

Machine learning to capture high volume and rote tasks are a place to start. Such systems used algorithms to train on known facts plus unstructured data that we generate during our life processes. With machine learning, computers can infer all sorts of things about us from our digital breadcrumbs.

Supplementing machine learning systems with Rule-Based Systems that emerge from Second-Order tools and techniques can help you to capture core knowledge for ongoing use through the entire lifecycle of our built environment. Such new systems do not eliminate the need for human experience.

Computers do poorly with novel tasks, requiring large volumes of past data to support machine learning. Humans are better at connecting the threads between things never seen to solve problems. There are (and will continued to be) critical tasks in most professions that need discipline-specific knowledge and expertise to solve problems that we have never seen. These are the places to focus your efforts.

Studies at Oxford University predict that one in two of today's jobs is at risk of being replaced by machines, it is critical that we understand the limits of machine learning. For the line between things needing human expertise and things that can be done by machines is becoming ever sharper.

Rule-Based Systems

Systems using machine learning can predict future outcomes. Use this predictive power with care, for this is a black-box approach with no easy way to confirm that the machine's inferences are correct. Critical things can be eliminated, and unplanned biases added, without any way to know. Recognize that machine learning systems need to be audited to ensure that the algorithms do not select for the wrong issues. Do not outsource responsibility to the computer. Rather, hold tight to your values and ethics and use machine learning algorithms to augment human decision-making.

Rule-based Systems use data to interpret and make connections between information to mimic some of the typical decision-making processes that humans can do.

A Rule-Based Systems might capture a formula that can act on a set of data. For example, the system creates a box with an area of twenty-five square feet (sq ft) and a volume of four hundred square feet for each first-grade student work space—resulting in a low-level of detail model of five-hundred square feet, eight feet tall to accommodate twenty students.

Rules-based systems using web services and service-oriented-architecture enable us to create requirements for how things relate. This enables rapid automation of repetitive, low-level decisions. Such systems can approximate the outputs that one might get from rules-of-thumb assumptions, or come close to the results from human manipulation of the same data. Everything depends on the complexity and sophistication of the algorithms used.

At all levels for all types of projects, there are immediate benefits as we connect data in distributed systems. By flowing reusable data from dependable and authoritative sources, through reliable Rules-Based Systems, we become faster and more efficient. Systems can then process significant amounts of information and represent the results in ways that get to the facts of Complex and Wicked Problems. Suddenly we can assess potential problems rapidly on an enterprise or portfolio scale, rather than one building at a time.

To date, many Rules-Based Systems have been standalone, it is possible to create systems that become middleware, moderating data from many sources and making outputs available in many formats.

Although a connected inventory of facilities (rather than a rule-based system) the California Community Colleges System was a step toward defining new program requirements to anchor their 74 million square feet of buildings and spaces, making it the largest cloud computing Building Information Modeling (BIM) + Geographic Information System (GiS) + Facilities Management (FM) platform in the world.

By generating Rules-Based outcomes your work is leveraged. Captured wisdom is made visible to those without deep knowledge. Much of the rote work that was once the domain of long-term employees now becomes available to everyone that must make the right decisions.

Most of the data in little-bim reside in files and single use outputs, such as PDFs, text files, and images, which can be out-of-date from the moment they are saved. Cataloging and managing thousands of such files for immediate access isn't realistic, especially for large or long established organizations.

In this form, using the data in these files is problematic. Live data enables the reuse of information to support opportunities such as rules-based systems, file-based data does not. The continued use of file-based systems results in valuable owner asset data becoming inaccessible for future use.

As new ways to connect live data emerge, owners like the California Community Colleges System are beginning to understand that inaccessible, unstructured, and out-of-date data, locked in hard to access files, are of little long-term value. The industry is starting to see rapid improvements in the availability of data, as the recognition of the value of shareable knowledge grows and systems to use the data mature. You have been exposed to the *think big, start small* approach to model building that begins to transform the way we can do business around the built environment.

The use of open-standards, like those that drive the Internet, enable Building Information Model data to be efficiently organized to allow developers to create tools which share data between a multitude of applications. One such standard, BIMxml, applies to BIM the same concepts as the ubiquitous XML standard that elegantly compresses data to enable online information exchange. BIMxml has proven in real projects to enable robust, highly capable models that help address Complex and Wicked Problems, such as those faced by California Community Colleges.

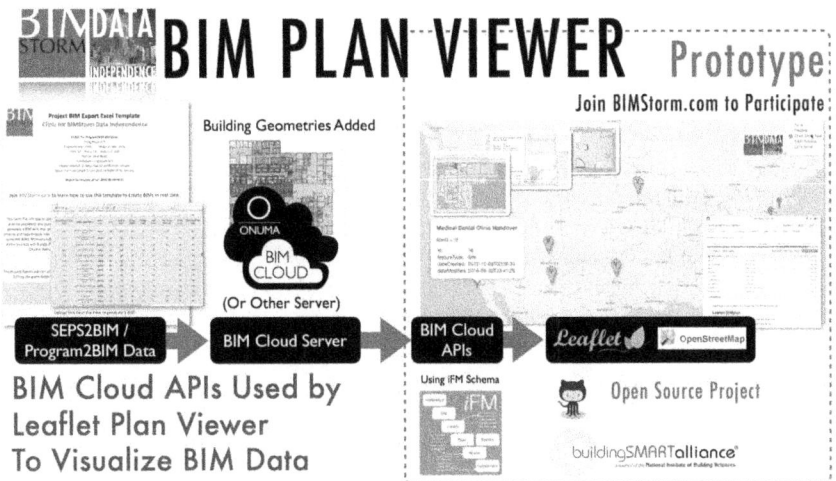

BIM PLAN VIEWER Prototype

Join BIMStorm.com to Participate

Building Geometries Added

BIM Cloud APIs Used by Leaflet Plan Viewer To Visualize BIM Data

Open Source Project

buildingSMARTalliance®

At the time that this book was wrapping up, the buildingSMART alliance Thought Leaders just announced the open-source BIM Cloud. Based on BIMxml and FEDiFM, the prototype enables access and update of BIM data from, and to, COBie the USACE (US Corps of Engineers) Facility Data Workbook, and other datasets, in real-time. The prototype BIM Cloud Server was released under an MIT License to allow others to work with and adapt the code freely. Go to https://goo.gl/LSrc66 to explore the buildingSMART alliance GitHub repositories.

Such models can change the way small or large entities do business. If you can dramatically reduce expenditures to become more resilient, you may be part of the future.

As discussed at the beginning of the book, Industry Foundation Classes (IFC) establish the classification for some types of data related to the built environment. For most users, the standard focuses on file-based exchanges focused on design and construction. Once IFC evolves to leverage loosely coupled, scalable and flexible approaches to web-based data sharing, it will be able to participate in a full lifecycle BIG-BIM ecosystem. Until IFC openly embraces live, web-based data exchanges—moving away from the brittle, tightly coupled, complex and expensive to implement approach—it will be stuck in little-bim; engaging the benefits of BIG-BIM through workarounds and file exchanges.

The EXPLORATION WITH A GLOBAL PERSPECTIVE in the SPECIAL SUPPLEMENT makes BIG-BIM data accessible to users. Within the Red Dots are links to models that use BIMxml in real projects that serve owners from the inception of plans through the entire lifecycle. This style of workflow was employed by the California Community Colleges Case Study earlier in the previous Part of this book.

Our Path to Better Serve Owners

BIG-BIM now makes it possible for anyone to connect much of what was only possible for the largest corporations at the time that Heery, CRS, and CM Associates created their processes. The procedures and philosophies that these visionaries created are a stable starting point for the use of BIM to meet customer needs better. If one does nothing more than using the tools to connect processes like those of early ACMs, customers of BIM-centered organizations will have more certainty of outcomes and smoother, more efficient projects. Connected processes enabled by virtual design tools offers ways to take their ideas to a much higher level.

In a world that is constantly changing, one needs to embrace change to keep up—and, not just changing technology. Our explorations touched every part of our business. We quickly learned that the people side of the equation is more important and needs more attention than the technology side.

Experienced consumers of design and construction services told us that Design-Builders and Agency Construction Managers (ACMs) consistently solved their problems with minimal hassles. They perceived that Design-Builders and Construction Managers focused on their interests, while Architects and General Contractors often did not. They told us that they were looking for better ways to understand and manage their projects. They were tired of surprises and cost overruns. Their input started us thinking:

What systems do Design-Builders and ACMs use to position themselves to better control projects?

Why do experienced consumers trust Design-Builders and ACMs to work in their best interests?

What makes Design-Builders and ACMs so successful in the eyes of these consumers?

Why would someone go directly to Design-Builders and ACMs? Often before talking to an Architect? What do they offer that makes sophisticated customers call them first?

We deconstructed how Design-Builders and Agency Construction Managers work. We looked at the tools that they use to sell and package projects for their customers. We researched the seeds of their approach to design and construction.

We found that the groundwork laid by a small group of individuals and organizations including George Heery, the firm of Caudill Rowlett Scott (CRS), and their affiliate CM Associates, took on new significance when viewed in the context of this exploration. Around the middle of the twentieth century, they created the profession of construction management, as they sought to correct the same issues that we are experiencing in the design and development process.

To those we interviewed, meeting needs in the highest quality way, optimizing the customer's time and money resources was more critical. The need was to manage risk and to control project outcomes—from all perspectives—time, money, liability, aesthetics, quality, serviceability, et.al.

These explorations identified a process that we call **defining the box.** Within the box are all the parts and pieces required for a competent designer and constructor to deliver a project that meets the customer's needs. The box contains a design concept with everything necessary for a successful design, an objective definition of project success, a primary strategy, and time and money control systems to make the solution possible. All with enough detail to allow the team to come to understand and implement as the work moves forward.

The process of defining the box was an early form of accelerated decision-making and lifecycle thinking to identify and remove potential problems well before the owner spent significant funds for design and construction. Every aspect of the project was open for discussion and scrutiny by the design, construction, and operations team.

By identifying problems early, in owner-centered ways, trailblazing ACMs and Design-Builders created an offering that could deliver on this process for their customers. By envisioning projects at the programming stage, and then managing the project, based on an agreed upon vision, they found that they could better control project risks, costs, and time. They achieved improved project outcomes for those who embraced the process.

Many of those we interviewed held the perception that architects and planners didn't handle the issues critical to early stage project decisions. Architects and planners placed too much emphasis on aesthetics and their personal view of projects.

Connect Values

When clearly stated, your values themselves become an asset. See ASSETS, NOT PROJECTS for more information on ways to apply your values to BIG-BIM.

Strategic thinking surrounding the use of a BIG-BIM ecosystem includes the connection of values into your business processes. Your system of values is the framework from which to make daily decisions. Successful business processes begin with such values. Without an agreed upon set of values, it becomes difficult to stay the course.

The tendency is to wander off-track or to revert to the comfortable way of doing things when there is no clearly annunciated set of values. To annunciate values in your strategic thinking, consider ten issues:

1. Plan for the lifecycle of the asset. Take the long view, knowing it can affect short-term gains. Be flexible and adapt to the inevitable shifts in business that are coming to built environment businesses.

2. Solve problems as early as possible in the process. Minimize waste at all levels—human, production, and resources.

3. Use technology to serve people and processes. Maximize efficiency to produce many different products quickly and efficiently.

4. Keep the customer involved. Get a good, objective definition of success. Make decisions based on proven results.

5. Empower people to be the best they can be. Educate leaders. Everyone is a lifelong learner.

6. Take responsibility and make things happen. Make quality THE priority.

7. Use consensus and rapid decision-making to understand the underlying need.

8. Team success is THE measure of success. Listen—communicate openly to understand expectations.

9. Define success at the beginning and set appropriate expectations. Early decisions have a significant impact on the final product (and they cost the least).

10. Share risks, costs, and information. Form partnerships with people you trust. Work together to create mutual self-interest for all parties.

Use the Connected Process Values list to begin the value list for your business. Develop your list with input from everyone. When it begins to take hold, post it for all to see and revisit your list often. Many little things, when done properly and consistently achieve great results.

The lesson to learn is that many small steps correctly focused will make a significant impact. Everyone shares in outcomes and anyone can stop the process to correct problems. Avoiding competition is neither possible nor in the owner's long-term interest. But competition that is destructive or undermines the objective cannot be tolerated. The obligation for ensuring this lies with owners and visionary leaders with a view to the long-game.

Use the best available technology, processes, and tools, to find solutions that work for you and your customers. It does not matter if you are a one-man shop or part of a large company—connected processes make it easier to solve the problems that happen on projects.

Case Study
BIMStorm

BIMStorms require people to share data to enable rapid and connected decision-making. The power comes from creating a common operating picture that all can use. Trust builds as those who experience the process work to solve problems and create solutions. For a detailed timeline of completed BIMStorms, see the BIMSTORM CHRONOLOGY in the MORE CASE STUDIES later in the book.

What are the interesting aspects of BIMStorms?

BIMStorms give people a first-hand experience of the power and possibilities that distributed processes make possible.

More than 35 BIMStorms with many different program focuses have taken place since 2008. Concepts that were innovative at the time are becoming mainstream approaches and used worldwide.

Each evolution of the BIMStorms offers glimpses of more things to come as the cloud and web services blossom.

BIMStorms celebrate expertise and experience. International and local experts communicate, examine, and propose solutions to a predetermined built environment issue focused on a geographic area.

Teams contribute expertise from around the world, creating a global perspective for the BIMStorm solution set.

Participants use rules-driven systems, business metrics, connected decision support, geographic information systems, and building information modeling in the cloud during BIMStorms. Participants use tools of their choice and access the web in ways that are familiar, contributing their information and expertise to group projects.

Location—Worldwide.

BIMStorms are online brainstorms using Building Information Models in proof-of-concept exercises that allow people to come together to experience the beauty and power of web-based information sharing. They are BIG-BIM and BIG Data in action.

BIMStorms concentrate on sharing the information in Building Information Models. Their power comes from linked live data from authoritative sources. It is an inclusive approach that allows anyone to participate. Frequently they occur over one to three days to show that, in a short period, extraordinary things can happen—when everyone works together in a connected information sharing environment.

At times, BIMStorms are held over a period of months to allow participants to experience real-world workflows of greater depth and complexity.

BIMStorms let people roll up their sleeves and experience real information modeling in ways that are straightforward and cost effective. No travel occurs to demonstrate your ability to work with people all over the world. BIMStorms are near zero carbon events; since everything happens in the cloud, and no one must travel to take part.

In 2008, BIMStorm Los Angeles was the first of public BIMStorm. This open demonstration showed what is possible using a service-oriented-architecture approach to information sharing in unison, by people all over the world. The event offered a first-hand experience of a BIG-BIM ecosystem.

In twenty-four hours, multiple teams with a total of 130 participants created more than four hundred Building Information Models. People from around the world collaborated in real-time with information models and many open-standards software applications. What may have been futuristic was proven possible.

BIMStorm Los Angeles was a watershed event that opened the eyes of the world to the possibilities of BIG-BIM. The event won an American Institute of Architects BIM Award for its innovative approach to using BIM on the web, something very new at the time.

Today, we look back and laugh at the simplicity of the technology when BIMStorms started. The cloud and web services were just beginning to blossom. BIG-BIM was an aspiration. The intersection of building information, geographic information and facilities management was conceptual to many; yet proven by the participants, who *landed* their models on Google Earth near the Los Angeles' Dodgers baseball stadium.

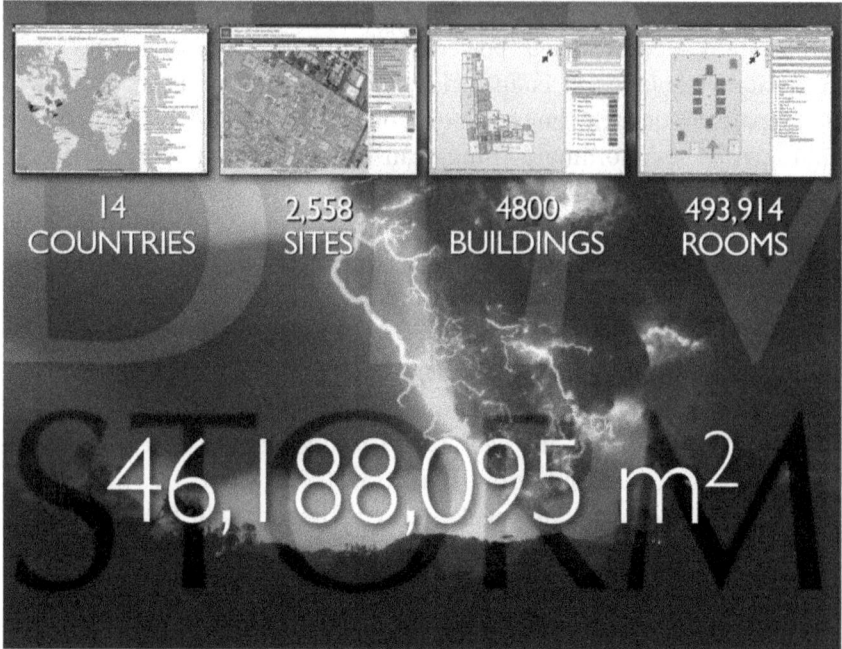

| 14 COUNTRIES | 2,558 SITES | 4800 BUILDINGS | 493,914 ROOMS |

46,188,095 m²

BIMStorms take many forms and have focused on sites around the world. They are live events offered at no cost to participants. One brings their enthusiasm, expertise and a willingness to collaborate on something new. The BIMStorm is the best way to get hands-on understanding and experience of how to use BIG-BIM. You invest your time; the remainder is free BIMStorm.com.

BIMStorms have changed over the years. First, BIMStorms enabled comprehensive design and industry participation. BIMStorms involved architects, engineers, and those in facility leadership positions. Quickly they transitioned to encompass wider design and industry participation.

Early BIMStorms were designed to give people a clear understanding of where the technology was heading, making it easier for people to plan their personal transformation to a more connected and collaborative world than in the past.

Commercial BIMStorms that support customer needs have been in demand since 2010. The commercially focused version of the BIMStorm has been used to design for organizational change—EcoDistricts, major facilities, statewide school systems, and health-care facilities. Thousands of people from all levels of society and all specialties have now experienced a BIMStorm in a variety of forms.

Since BIMStorms work with open-standard and interoperable data, experts can quickly extract the information they need, using both traditional or innovative tools, at any stage of the process. Expert participants can then post their professional take on the matter to enrich the data of the ecosystem. Concurrently, other users provide reviews, post input and monitor progress.

People are starting to understand why we must move toward a BIG-BIM ecosystem approach and away from our reliance on files and siloed processes. BIMStorms show how each of us can be part of the BIG-BIM solution. BIMStorms react to individual, environmental, and public needs in ways that offer informed decision-making. Rather than the politically charged processes that have become the norm in society.

Design Fiction
BIMStorm Chesapeake Bay

Design fiction, isn't fiction but a technique for thinking ahead, predicting future technologies, potentially influencing policy, but most importantly creating debate by asking what-if? In this way, fiction can be used as a tool to help design future societies and technologies, giving the public a say on it too. — Imagination Lancaster

Growth in the development of BIG-BIM Ecosystems has been slow and steady, led by visionary organizations such as the US Coast Guard, the California Community Colleges, and the US Veterans Administration. Connected systems in the cloud are gradually emerging as critical for managing systems in the built environment. There may lie the means for handling societies' most pressing issues.

BIMStorms have been but one of the tools used for prototyping and debugging systems to make possible the power of BIG-BIM Ecosystems to respond to wicked problems in our society. BIMStorms offer the ability for people to use their energy and skill for the greater good. The vision of BIMStorm Chesapeake Bay that follows is an opportunity for the 13 million people that live, work, and play in the Chesapeake Bay region.

This proposal is intended to simulate thought and offer one vision for how BIMStorms can be used to achieve results in an environment where there are no single, declarative solution... only better or worse options.

BIMStorm Chesapeake Bay offers hints into how BIMStorms might improve our ability to manage wicked social and environmental problems. It is designed to illustrate how interlocking BIMStorms might bring people together to find solutions to some of the most vexing wicked problems we face.

The Chesapeake Bay region is beset by significant wicked problems: Problems that involve changing the behavior and mindset of millions of people, thousands of organizations, and too many individual opinions to consider. These problems are moving targets, with no right or wrong solution. These situations require that information be readily available, in ways that enable people to make informed decisions.

In recent years, isolated programs that did not respond to stakeholders with different outlooks and needs have usually failed. In this environment, federal and state mandates show marginal results at best. BIMStorms connect and engage people.

By empowering people to make decisions and trusting in the wisdom of crowds, BIMStorms provide the tools to work with wicked problems. The BIMStorm Chesapeake Bay program begins with three connected BIMStorms that focus on the fishing, crabbing, and shellfish industries that have long been a staple of the region.

BIMStorm Chesapeake Environment focuses on sustainability and environmental policy, giving those concerned with energy, greenhouse gases, and other conservation issues a forum.

BIMStorm Chesapeake Air & Water builds on the previous BIMStorm while focusing on drinking and industrial water resources, wastewater, and storm water. Biological nitrogen removal, storm water remediation, and aquifer protection are but a few of the issues this BIMStorm handles.

BIMStorm Chesapeake Agriculture and *BIMStorm Chesapeake Fisheries & Aquaculture* focus on these the region's farming, and seafood industries, seeking ways to maintain and improve these resources.

The next three, connected BIMStorm focus on infrastructure. *BIMStorm Chesapeake Infrastructure* is followed closely by *BIMStorm Chesapeake Utilities* and *BIMStorm Chesapeake Transportation*. Participants in these BIMStorms primarily focus on roads, public transportation, significant regional utilities, and the other manufactured systems that support life in the region.

The seven connected BIMStorms are followed by four BIMStorms designed to address critical issues that impact the region. Each is a wicked problem that has longed plagued those working to resolve regional problems, and each BIMStorm builds on the unique issues identified in the first four BIMStorms.

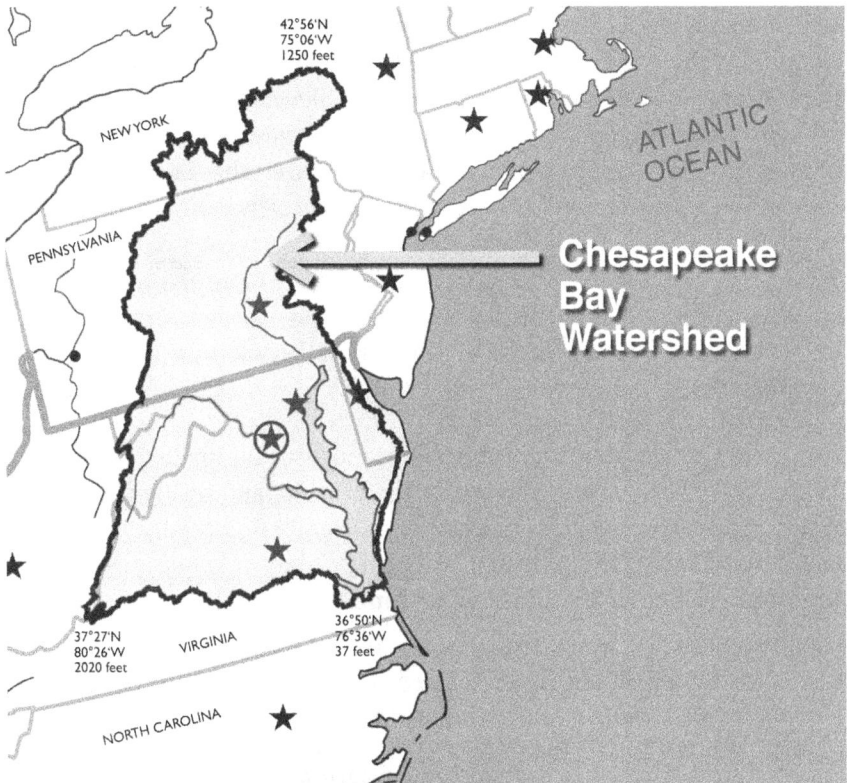

The processes used in all the BIMStorms are highly representative, relying on the wisdom of crowd's concept. Each participant has a voice in the decisions. Residents of all states in the Chesapeake Bay watershed (Maryland, Virginia, Pennsylvania, the District of Columbia, New York, West Virginia, and Delaware) participated.

BIMStorm Chesapeake Industry looks at regional growth patterns and zoning. Teams analyze current development patterns and find opportunities for improvements to support better the recovery efforts. Much of the area has been industrialized for many years. These industries have contributed significantly to the problems with the Chesapeake Bay.

Mining, hydraulic fracturing for natural gas, and abandoned industrial sites throughout the watershed are a key theme in BIMStorm Chesapeake Industry. Pollution sources, often far from the Chesapeake Bay itself, have long been a substantial contributor to the problem. Industrial pollution sources offer one of the largest potentials for correction, although they will require significant resources to clean up.

BIMStorm Chesapeake Housing tackles another major issue with the region's ability to recover the Chesapeake Bay. There are many initiatives in the area aimed at consolidating residential development and moving residential development from sensitive areas adjacent to the bay and its tributaries. Maryland's Smart Growth Initiative, the Chesapeake Bay Critical Areas Program, and others have made inroads in finding solutions.

Few of the past housing programs in the region have been highly successful, in part because they impose requirements on one state (or region such as the Delmarva Peninsula) alone, allowing others to continue business-as-usual. There are conflicting standards. A goal of BIMStorm Chesapeake Housing is to change this paradigm. Only by coordinating local requirements to achieve compliance throughout the watershed will real change happen.

BIMStorm Chesapeake Safety & Response focuses on making the people and assets of the region safer, more sustainable, and resilient to future events. Emergency services professionals usually find themselves in the role of planning for how to respond to local emergency services needs long after the designers and planners were done.

BIMStorm Chesapeake Safety & Response enables emergency services planning to switch from a reactive to a proactive model. Designers and planners create solutions together with local emergency personnel. Best of all, international experts help make the process happen quickly, in an extremely economical way. The process highlights real solutions for even small urban areas and allows emergency services professionals to experience the state-of-the-art in connected planning.

The Chesapeake Bay recovery will take many years. Much growth will occur in the process. It was essential that emergency services planners find the most economical and efficient solution to handle each step of the way. The BIMStorm Chesapeake Safety & Response process offers significant advantages to emergency services personnel who participate. They can determine emergency services delivery needs from in progress design and planning. They visually assess critical and high-risk areas as they will evolve.

Emergency planners can create phased-in and connected emergency services delivery plans tied to community planning goals. While this takes place, they extract equipment and personnel requirements for each phase of the process to optimize for capital and operational cost and capital needs. They create an engine that allows for future flexibility and changing planned futures.

As design and planning teams create solutions BIMStorm Chesapeake Safety & Response teams assess the ebb and flow of support needs. Teams evaluate critical needs (population densities, population types, criticality of functions/building types, changes to access patterns, etc.) at any point in time.

From this data and the emerging design concepts, the BIMStorm Chesapeake Safety & Response team relocates emergency services equipment, staffing, and facilities. Teams build timelines for facility design and construction and develops capital budgets. Provisional plans are created to respond to growth. At the same time, team recommendations flow back to the other BIMStorm teams to develop their concepts.

BIMStorm Chesapeake Communities deals with the issues unique to the cities and towns in the region. Teams began to resolve the full range of issues that affect the Chesapeake Bay. This BIMStorm requires the teams to move across many levels of detail as they explore possibilities throughout the region.

At one level of detail, teams assess greenways, transportation systems, and changes to zoning patterns. At another level, teams zoom in to evaluate and develop solutions for individual structures that anchor the larger opportunities. In some cases, groups propose solutions to localized problems.

Teams create options that best fit the millions of interrelated issues in the region. As directions emerge, the teams' work is reviewed, analyzed, and commented on by thousands of people monitoring progress. As viable options emerge, the teams model them to find the points of failure, make corrections, and present the results for comment. Options deemed to be acceptable to the largest group of participants move forward for further consideration.

The final two BIMStorms focus on wrapping the work from earlier BIMStorms into implementation programs; with defined budgets, strategies for next steps, and ongoing action programs. Without a defined plan of action for the future, the time, and energy put into the program might be of little long-term value.

BIMStorm Chesapeake Bay is the capstone BIMStorm, connecting each of the proceeding BIMStorms to create a master information model. In this BIMStorm, the work from all other BIMStorms was evaluated. Options were assessed. Priorities began to be assigned. The goal is to reach a consensus on next steps, priorities, and the way to recovery.

Now that the issues are on the table, participants in the region can debate the merits of each option and arrive at a direction.

BIMStorm Chesapeake Restore & Governance is the final, public BIMStorm focused on broad, regional-scale planning, design, and governance issues as the effort moves toward full implementation.

Finith Jernigan

The vision of BIMStorm Chesapeake Bay, combined with the workflows and process described in BIMStorm Cork Point (included in MORE CASE STUDIES), defines a framework for constructing BIMStorms with the potential for resolving some of societies' most vexing problems... in a transparent, collaborative environment

THREE

SIMPLE AS CAN BE

Complexity can become a trap. The real value comes from modeling systems that are simple and easy to use. Most people do not have to become experts to get benefit from BIG–BIM.

Much of what is needed does not require highly specialized systems or highly trained experts. The complexity of BIM can remain hidden from most users. Most people need information to do the task at hand and should not interact with the complex nature of BIM. Much of what we need to become more sustainable and resilient in the built environment is possible with simple information models. In systems that benefit anyone, without regard to training or specialized knowledge.

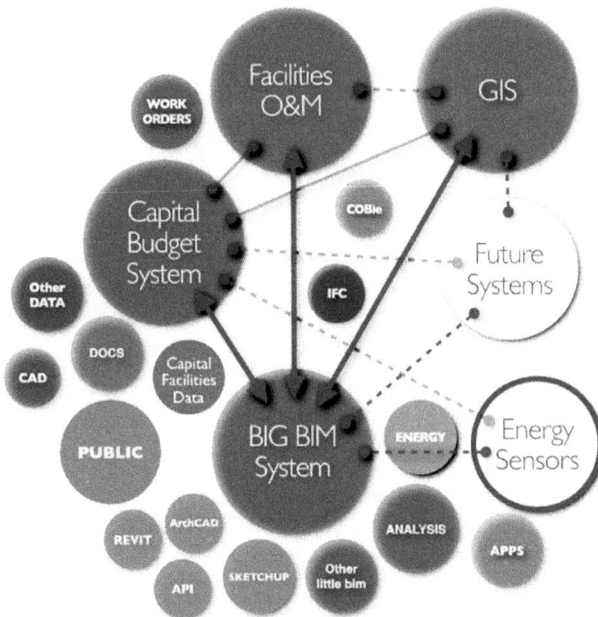

Start Now

Starting is important and does not have to be complex or daunting. Keep things simple, and start BIG–BIM this way:

Learn by doing. Do not spend too much time pondering, discussing, analyzing, and fretting or nothing will get done. Do not wait until you have taken classes, for technology changes so fast you must learn to keep learning about new tools and processes on a day-to-day basis.

Use the information that you have now. Do not wait for more or better data.

Get rid of non-performing tools. Use only the tools that work for you.

Think ahead and decide what you want to achieve.

Make what you do now mesh with what you plan. Don't waste a lot of time for no reason.

Use what you learn to change how you work.

Practice some of the Workflows in the SPECIAL SUPPLEMENT. Move through each of the Workflows and then, repeat the process.

Data Is All Around Us

Few key players in the industry understand how to accommodate the emerging Connected Age. They may be expert in planning, architecture, engineering, construction, or any of the hundreds of other specialties. But, when it comes to building information modeling and connected processes, they miss the boat. Recognize that many of the experts use little-bim exclusively, with a lot of trial and error. They continue to focus on design and construction using Information Age tools that are not up to the task at hand. They blithely repeat the same mistakes, thinking that their expertise in other areas tracks to BIG-BIM. Usually, it doesn't.

Every day, we use the products of others already moving down the path to connection. Your grocery store is connected. Your local car care shop is connected. Your bank's systems are connected. Connected processes affect everything you do aside from the building industry. Connected systems and processes occur more places than you may realize. The travel industry is an example of a connected system.

Airline ticketing is tightly connected. Did you buy your last airplane ticket on the Internet? If so, you went to a site and typed in a few parameters, when, where, and how long, and hit enter. The system searched all available flights to your selected location and gave you the chance to fine-tune your trip. The system quoted the cost, took your money, and booked your flight—Quickly and efficiently.

Behind the scenes, many systems are tied together (connected) to make this happen. The complexities of the systems to track the thousands of planes was invisible. The systems to maintain the engines to keep the aircraft safe were transparent. You will benefit from the personnel tracking system when it gets the right pilot to the right plane in the right airport at the right time. Such items critical to the safety and security of your trip took place, without your knowledge. Many systems connect to let you book your ticket from the comfort of your home.

Such systems are widespread in other industries. Even with such precedents all around us, many professionals in the building industry act as if we can continue with the same thousand-year-old approach. What stops building industry professionals from embracing these new processes? What prevents the industry from doing a better job of managing time and costs for projects using these time-tested tools and methods? Could we survive in an environment that does not reward waste and inefficiency?

Many people in all segments of the building industry focus on the complexities, without understanding the underlying concepts. Some of them have long focused on standards and the future. They have focused on high cost *test cases.* They spend a lot of time in committees preparing rules that contain jargon that few can understand. They debate the minutia of data exchanges. When people argue about whether BIM is the best name for what we do, RUN.

Their concern for the minutiae; standards and interoperability, is necessary for the future, but it does not help you to do real work today. Nor does it move the industry to a less wasteful and productive future. As an industry, we are missing the forest for the trees.

Without clear, affordable, and dependable ways to manage and exchange the information that you are developing with models, you may not see the potential long-term returns on your investment in time or money.

For a group of small business users, little-bim is a more efficient delivery system day-to-day. But, little-bim does little more that improve traditional processes. With a BIG-BIM ecosystem, the data in your models becomes valuable long after you design and construct the project. You tap into an ecosystem that is as big as our world. Best of all, those that are thriving on the Internet have already found (and use) the standards that make it possible today. You can too. Consider this in your long-term plans.

Over time, your decision will enable you to benefit from evolving technology or not. Data in your models allow cost, environmental analysis and more. Links to Google Earth allow evaluations in a real-world context. Connections to authoritative data inform decision-making. You decide how many, or how few, of the benefits, flow to you and those you serve.

Go to the RECIPE FOR BIG-BIM FROM THIN AIR in the SPECIAL SUPPLEMENT to create your model from thin air.

Elephants and Gorillas

Much of the volunteer work on BIM reminds one of the Indian parable about the BLIND MEN AND THE ELEPHANT. Each group focuses intensely on different parts of the need as they journey through their exploration of BIM. In turn, each group creates solutions from their limited experience and perspectives. Each committee's individual perspective becomes the only answer. Rather than recognizing the opportunity and seeking the ability to explore more of the elephant, the blind men focus only on the part that they choose to perceive.

The building industry isn't monolithic. It is diverse and touches upon everything in our lives. The built world is so widespread and includes so many different players that no central organization can hope to create or manage this change in this environment.

Leaders of government agencies and large enterprises (the thousand-pound gorillas of our world) focus on broad initiatives, politics, corporate profitability, and other factors, far removed from the details that drive the problems. While some leaders understand that there are problems and talk about subsets of the solutions, comprehensive, public engagement and investment are lacking. Without consistent leadership from the top, little changes.

The leaders may talk about the possibilities and say positive things, but there is little real action, and more money is spent printing annual reports than is spent to correct industry problems.

From a mission focus, this shows a lack of strategy and vision on the part of the leaders—not a lack of altruistic intent in the pursuit of a worldwide movement. To such leaders, the changes required to enable a change to BIG-BIM is a luxury that their funders (legislators or shareholders) do not allow them to pursue. Whatever else happens, at the enterprise level people understand that their business models may not do well if things change dramatically.

Only by clarifying the value to each participant will large corporations and government agencies embrace the change to BIG-BIM ecosystems. This lack of a clear set of strategic values that can be easily understood by non-experts has resulted in a worldwide movement that relies on the volunteer efforts of groups of dedicated individuals and corporations worldwide.

Development of BIM has relied on individuals and small businesses to invest significant percentages of their resources in the effort. International groups have been working for more than thirty years to define standards and create systems that will deliver on the promise of BIM. Their efforts have regularly run into funding issues and a lack of focus. Most of the work continues to be done by volunteers. With all the inherent problems.

Some of the groups tacitly deliver the message that to play in their sandbox one had to use their version of the elephant (e.g. standards-compliant tools). Even with the best of intentions, they limit progress, advancing their inner vision of the elephant that is BIM. Most volunteer groups have merely added complexity in a very complex and hard to understand part of our world.

Worst of all, decades of volunteer and underfunded work have resulted in tools and standards that usually require specialist knowledge and training. They need too much effort and limit access to a small subset of experts rather than to the much larger group that would see a direct benefit from the tools. For many, the strategic value is hard to see.

Many were initially slow to embrace the tools that came from the volunteer and vendor focused efforts. The personnel and money investment costs were too high. Few of the systems could handle the extensive data required for high level needs. None of the products could manage all the necessary information. No single server product could handle the necessary tools.

Only in recent years has the movement toward the BIG-BIM ecosystem started to make substantial progress toward solutions for these problems. Leaders of corporations and government agencies are beginning to see the strategic value. Look at the elephant from the perspective of everyone.

Business, as usual, is not the answer. The solution will not happen in an environment where a small number of proprietary solutions are the only option. Solutions driven by a limited number of the thousand-pound gorillas that drive traditional software markets in the industry isn't beneficial to the industry's long-term needs.

The solutions will only come with simple systems that can grow and naturally adjust as processes evolve and mature. Systems that may be quite complex internally, yet are simple for everyone to use and understand with little or no training.

A complex system that works is invariably found to have evolved from a simple system that works. — John Gaule

Core Concepts

Alvin Toffler, the author of the 1970 classic, Future Shock wrote, *the capture of connected knowledge in an organized way should drive planning.*

The concepts that drive planning in the BIG-BIM ecosystem include:

Core Concept 1. Data is a Strategic Asset

Core Concept 2. No More Welded Data

Core Concept 3. Embrace Open-Standards

Core Concept 4. Mobility and Access

Core Concept 5. Service-Oriented-Architecture

Core Concept 6. A Strategy for Security

Core Concept 7. Encourage an App Economy

Core Concept 8. Align the IT Department

Core Concept 9. Ecosystems for Facilities

Many of the case studies in this book are demonstrations of how to capture connected knowledge for planning, and much more. All relied on these core concepts to drive their success; or wish they had.

Core Concept 1. Data Is a Strategic Asset

To make your data more valuable: (1) do not allow any application to prevent linking your data to other applications, and; (2) make sure your data can outlive any software application that processes it. Never allow applications to hold your data so tightly that it becomes difficult to move to a new software tool.

Software developers create applications that are often feature-rich. Intentional or not; underlying the features are a profit-driven goal of keeping you and your data captive in the system. Many software applications make it easy to import data into their system but then make it difficult or impossible to get data out.

The first task for any new project is to verify your ability to reuse the existing information. To do that one does not need to understand the enterprise's underlying business. What is required is data from the vendor or IT department about their web services capabilities and their ability to make the information accessible. When that is determined, one can use the information in a BIG-BIM ecosystem that uses web services.

It is imperative to ask questions. *How much will it cost in time, effort, and money to get data out of system X when we decide to migrate in the future to other systems?* Ask for a live demonstration to test first-hand how this will work.

Follow up with more questions. *Does the application have an open Application Programming Interface (API) that allows access to the data? Does that API allow for one-way or two-way access to read and write my data? If the application is web-based, is it possible to access data through web services?* Once you know the limitations, it is then possible to make informed decisions.

Prove for yourself that what you are told is possible, and not merely air-ware and dreams. Try to understand how to make the connections by asking questions such as:

☐ *Web services: YES or NO? If YES, in what format?*

☐ *REST or SOAP? What API is used to GET? To POST?*

☐ *What kind of data can you export out as tables and graphics?*

☐ *And, does the tabular data have IDs that relate to the graphics?*

☐ *Can you provide: 1) sample database output of GIS or CAD, and 2) sample tables of the database(s)?*

If you hear complex and unclear answers, begin to worry. Often this is the first sign of a problem. If you cannot easily (and quickly) get outputs and samples for review, the data in the system under review is locked down, or will be difficult to reuse for other applications.

It can take significant work and become overly expensive to engage in lengthy discussions with vendors or IT staff to dig out the information from existing systems. Documenting the database structure, creating translation tables, and most other approaches take too long and are rarely successful.

Discussions in this area usually go around in circles for a long time. It is much more productive to ask that they provide data to prove that the data is accessible and available. Then move forward in other areas, if they cannot quickly produce what you request.

BIG-BIM revolves around connecting to the data that others have created and maintain—which need not be difficult or complex—if data is not locked into proprietary systems. Even custom spreadsheets for processes can be used to import/export data for connection into BIG-BIM. Changes to the data can then be directly reflected in BIG-BIM, to enable live interactions.

Mandate that your data be maintained in a way that is easy to access, and verify that it is happening; for too often it doesn't. Your data is an asset made more valuable as more authorized users can securely access it.

Core Concept 2. No More Welded Data

Most people don't care how the details of BIM work; they just want to do things now.

Efficient management of assets is one goal of BIM. To achieve this aim, we must move beyond applications and systems that don't (or can't) talk to each other. Data must move seamlessly.

Most of the software products we use daily weld together the data and the application needed to use the data. We have come to accept this approach to software solutions, even though they trap facility and business data. We didn't know that we had other options.

In these products, the data and the applications are so firmly welded together that it's hard for owners to access and use their data. For those using BIG-BIM, it is often easier to create new information than it is to use the data held in these welded together applications. Especially for tasks never imagined at the beginning.

Data welded into most of these software programs make sharing information cumbersome, at best. It is hard to access and use the data embedded in applications, even internally. To connect such software applications, one must find a way to export data from one application and import it into another application.

In the past, solutions emphasized the tight coupling of data to the software. Tightly coupling data, the user interface, and security were a feature intended to make it easier for us to manage the data. When we only needed one software application, this may have been a benefit. Now there are thousands of software applications to handle the many tasks that are critical to the built environment. The tightly couple approach now makes it difficult, if not impossible to use the same data in other software.

Developers spent untold hours in the creation of systems and standards to enable the exchange of data via files. With marginal results when viewed in a lifecycle context.

Experts joined the standards development groups to further the cause with like-minded individuals. They prepared to change in 20 years or so when they had agreed upon how these complex systems would connect. They spent their energy on the expectation that the details must be agreed upon to be functional in BIM.

Both groups seem wedded to decisions made far in the past; when tightly coupled, or welded together software seemed the only option. Even though the context and technology have changed to make the earlier decisions suspect, or worse. Their approach has not achieved the promise of BIM over the last 20 years. Now we need to share data, not exchange files. We need to move ahead in a world of unstructured information.

To make matters worse, today there seems to be a bunch of developers and pundits with arc welders making sure the data and applications stay welded together. Is it in their personal best interests to do so?

It is a curious fact that most systems that firmly weld the data to the application don't even go as far as file exchanges. They rely on single use outputs such (pdf, chart, graphics, or other media that is not directly machine-readable), to compare data from different systems manually. Or they re-type data from one system into another.

The development practices that the old-line leaders have been using to protect their eroding turf are slowing the penetration of BIM into the marketplace. In a world of agile development and web services, the traditional software development approach costs too much and takes up too much oxygen from the discussion of the future of the built environment.

Export and import of files-based data is a one-off operation, one that requires significant manual effort. Even if one is successful in sharing the data held in welded together systems, one creates the new problem of keeping the data synchronized. As data changes in one system, one must go through a process of keeping the data the same in another system. To maintain synchronized data, careful attention to the version becomes critical.

The proponents of welded together applications espouse seamless and synchronized exchange of data as a hallmark of the BIM concept. However, the continued reliance on welded together tools and the import and export of file-based data are counter to this stated end goal. Welding together data, the application and other parts of the software gives you fewer choices over time. Tight coupling makes one dependent on one piece of software to manage the data. When the time comes that a change is required, for any reason, your data is not readily reusable.

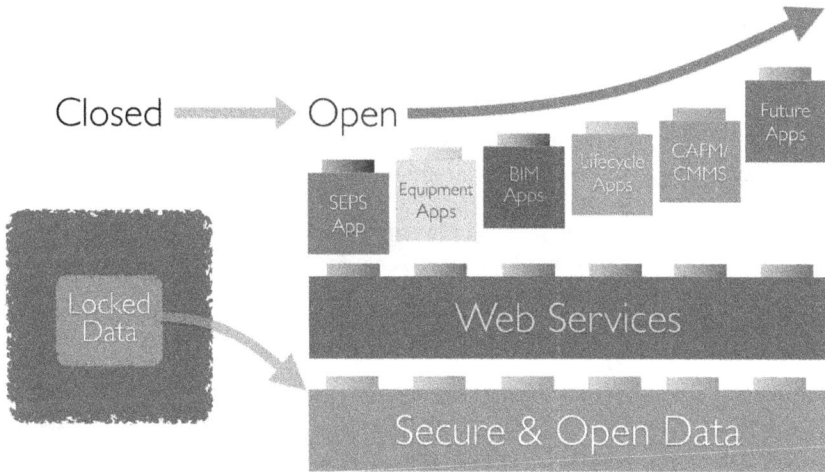

Separating data from the applications that use the data creates a more efficient process—With fewer errors. Data that can be accessed when and where needed is more valuable over the lifecycle of an asset.

The technology and systems available to us have moved to a different paradigm. Imagine having to export an airline's schedule to order an airline ticket. Download the book containing the carrier's offerings. Make your selections, and then import them into the carrier's system. The carrier then synchronizes your selection. If schedules, costs, seats, or anything else changed while you downloaded, selected, or imported, you start over. From the beginning. How many people would do this for themselves?

Today's on-the-go access to real-time airline schedules and ticketing require no manual synchronization. It just happens in the background for you. The same should be true for BIM.

Loose connections allow you to plug-and-play at will. If one module does not work, unplug it and plug in the next one. If something better comes along, plug it in. Much as one can interchange kitchen appliances. Even things not yet invented will plug into the system.

The most important takeaway relating to data accessible through web services is that the only reasonable way to connect all levels and stages of a project is by overlapping building, geographic and facilities data. That is what web services enables that the monolithic software approach does not.

It is impossible to contain all built environment data in one file or even a single vendor's software system. Making built environment data we- accessible is the only viable way to connect efficiently to the systems that we are creating in the BIM, GIS and built environment ecosystem we call BIG-BIM.

Core Concept 3. Embrace Open-Standards

No single application can support everything required by facility owners. Standards act as the glue to allow the sharing of critical pieces of information across systems over the lifecycle. Standards enable the ability to solve problems that otherwise seem insoluble. For example, a BIM holds data needed for design and construction as well as data for FM. The standardized name and ID for a space or piece of equipment that resides in BIM can be the glue to locate that piece of equipment in FM. Standards codify such things.

The Internet is a way for computers around the world to talk to each other. The Web is a system of web pages and sites using the Internet to make the sites accessible. The decision to make them open systems that comply with open-standards are major reasons behind why they are now universal.

Accessing data isn't enough. Without standards to define and moderate such things as connections and use, data is of limited value. Open-standards are central to connecting the data across traditionally siloed solutions. The buildingSMART alliance, the Construction Specifications Institute, and others create rules that support this type of need.

It is important to know and understand the standards that apply to your data. Do you plan to use data from Building Information Models (BIM) in your Facility Management (FM) applications? What standards do the applications accept to connect BIM to FM?

The welded together BIM systems that most are familiar with continue to have a purpose although primarily in the design and construction realms. In a BIG-BIM ecosystem, you move data into these systems to seed them for on-going development and out of these systems to capture the information that they create.

BIG-BIM seeds the welded together systems with all the pertinent information that exists at the outset of projects: space requirements, budgets, LEED requirements, financial constraints, owner decisions, GIS/topography/survey data, space needs, equipment, functions and much more. The ecosystem also becomes the repository for information coming from construction phase systems and processes.

As the project moves toward completion, the BIG-BIM ecosystem seeds commissioning, captures as-built conditions and can at any time fully push the data to COBie for O&M use. After construction, the system automates the aggregation of all project information and operations needs, with or without a Computer-Aided Facilities Management (CAFM) system or an Integrated Workplace Management System (IWMS).

At every stage of projects, the latest and most accurate existing and new information is available for refinement and pushed back to the ecosystem. This pushing and pulling of data allow the ecosystem to grow over time and enables up-to-date data to be available for ongoing decision-making to evaluate design performance, assess the impact on future financial needs, etc.

Without BIG-BIM it is possible to move data from Step A manually to Step B… to Step X, but, this can be a long and arduous process. Why would anyone continue such wasteful actions? In a world that tolerates zero errors, fraught with scarce resources and ever-increasing time pressures, it is best to use open-standards to make data sharing as easy as seamless as possible.

Within a BIG-BIM ecosystem, executives, managers, and staff continue to do what they have always done—if that is all they choose to do. BIG-BIM imposes very few additional requirements on them. Should they wish to expand their horizons into property management, early stage validation, O&M, and other areas, they now have the data to make that, and more, possible. BIG-BIM ties things together to enable the opportunities. When data flows smoothly in an ecosystem of shareable and reusable information, BIG-BIM is agile.

Core Concept 4. Mobility and Access

Agile... solutions evolve through collaboration between self-organizing, cross-functional teams. It promotes adaptive planning, evolutionary development, early delivery, continuous improvement, and encourages rapid and flexible response to change. — Wikipedia

Expectations of end users on mobile devices change everything. People expect to be able to pull up an App to get to any data about the task at hand. And, that app better not have a long learning curve. If it does, users just move on to the next app. Access to the data needed for on-the-go operations is now the norm. The May 2013 McKinsey Report entitled, *Disruptive technologies: Advances that will transform life, business, and the global economy,* by James Manyika and Richard Dobbs identified disruptive technologies that are transforming everything around us. The authors cite the Mobile Internet as the disruptive technology with the greatest potential economic impact in 2025.

Mobility and the disruptions it is causing affect the built world in direct and subtle ways. Buildings are, by their nature distributed assets, and a perfect use of mobile technologies. Connecting built environment data to mobile devices will transform how we interact with our surroundings. Even now, the Internet of Things (IoT) is changing how we do things; even in our homes. Mobile data will create a climate where buildings become an interface to knowledge for those that inhabit them.

Formatting data properly for web sharing makes it easy to use on mobile devices. It helps the end user quickly find the relevant information in a sea of data. Look at sites such as Yelp, Zillow, and Google Maps to understand how powerfully connected data is now and can become in the future. Let your mobile device locate you on an interactive map with information about your surroundings in-context, customized to match your preferences and needs.

In the past, we waded through a stack of paper documents. Or, more recently dug through a virtual stack of digital files. To get to the one nugget of information needed to decide. The BIG-BIM ecosystem acts as a clearinghouse or 'neutral' repository for the data to support mobility and accessibility.

Your mobile dashboards show you options, locations, facility data, menus, prices, reviews, directions and so much more. It is all done without knowing anything about the underlying complexity, by regular people like you and me. This level of connection to facilities is no small accomplishment. One might think that such systems are BIG-BIM. Without the intervention of any traditional design or construction professionals!

Disruptive Technology helps create a new market and value network, and eventually disrupts an existing market and value network..., displacing an earlier technology. — Wikipedia

Core Concept 5. Service-Oriented-Architecture

For simplicity, we might describe Service-Oriented-Architecture (SOA) as an approach to software development that creates modules of functionality that work together under a web-based ecosystem.

Desktop computing and 20th-century programming paradigms have taken the built environment down an unsustainable path. At the heart of a solution to this problem are decisions about how to manage data and applications. Until recently the focus has been on ever more powerful desktop systems running tightly coupled tools and file-based exchanges of information. The Internet and mobile computing are emblematic of the simplified interfaces that are replacing files and desktops across the world. Loosely coupled tools that rely on defined and interoperable interfaces are evolving to become the de-facto approach.

SOA is much more conducive to the addition or editing of a module without having to rework the entire source code of the application. It allows for enterprise agility, by enabling rapid development and modification of the software that supports the business processes. Its other main advantage is it allows for the data to become much more accessible to other applications and consumers of data.

In traditional software design, all needed data exchanges must be defined, and each type of transaction must be programmed into the application. If new types of data exchanges become necessary in the future, each must be individually programmed into the application.

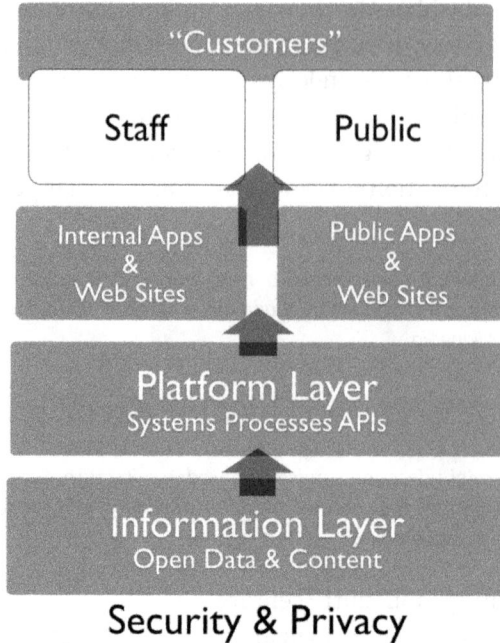

"Customers"

Staff   Public

Internal Apps & Web Sites   Public Apps & Web Sites

Platform Layer
Systems Processes APIs

Information Layer
Open Data & Content

Security & Privacy

SOA provides a much more flexible, scalable method of addressing data exchanges. Once a set of data is made accessible, that programming effort can be reused for any other requirement that may emerge over time.

Much like a consultant provides a service, data becomes a service—A service to the larger ecosystem. Service-oriented-architecture practices are a seed of BIG-BIM. Think of ways that services might support a simple architectural model:

You query the model; how many rooms do you contain and how big are they? The Room Service comes back with—fourteen and 4,234 square feet, or a list of each room and the room's area, or a plan showing the rooms with their net and gross areas, or a massing model in GiS to show the three-dimensional rooms in-context;

Which air conditioning systems are in the area bounded by this box? The engineering services come back with a list of the systems that cross into the box and itemizes the components that reside in the box;

Where is the sewer clean-out closest to Sink S-32? The operational service sends the GiS coordinates and a live map to your cell phone to help you find the clean-out covered by ceramic tile in a closet;

Air-Handler R-1535-C4 is sending error messages, who do I call to fix the problem? The facility management service sends you the details of the unit, warranty information, and auto-calls the company to schedule a technician based on your time constraints.

A newly hired maintenance supervisor queries the model. Where is the lunch room and do they take credit cards? The knowledge-base service sends a map to her cell phone and a copy of today's menu which includes a list of all payment methods.

Data conceived and used in similar ways is what people mean when they talk about service-oriented-architecture in the construction industry. Knowledge of design and engineering become but one of many shared services. By shifting our data into machine-readable formats, we make the data accessible, for known, and yet-to-be know uses. The end user does not need to worry about the technicalities of SOA. All they need to know is how to use their apps to get to the data.

Dramatic cost reductions are a benefit that comes from facility data handled this way. Service-oriented-architecture eliminates the redundancy that comes from having to build and manage the same data in many applications. SOA is the framework for allowing any application to use the data needed today, as well as in the future. This approach is the main ingredient for future-proofing one's data.

Where organizations have created datasets, it is best if they become the authoritative source of information on the topic. The company creates and maintains the integrity of their data. Their subject-matter experts then sustain the data, reducing the redundancies caused when multiple people try to create or maintain, the same (or similar) datasets. Others push and pull the data for use where needed.

It is best to keep standards data the same way. The organization creates and maintains the open-standards. Others use the rules to do things not imagined by those that created the initial structure. The open-standards body maintains the repository and arbitrates the proper application of their criteria.

The ability to use data in new and unexpected ways is one of the primary values of a services oriented architecture approach. Since business value trumps technical strategy, users assess the available information to find solutions to new problems, quickly and flexibly. Systems evolve to meet strategic goals at all levels. Rather than merely pursuing initial perfection to achieve project-specific benefits that may change over time.

You work from the assumption that maintenance of old and new data must take place in such as way that it can be read, processed, and exchanged using widely recognized data standards. One way to do this is to assume that the web browser is the end user's primary interface. Making sure the data and tools all run on browsers frees everyone from having to load extra software. Working within the web browser also helps to maintain security, while keeping data ready for many uses, when and where needed.

As an industry, the service-oriented-architecture approach helps us to realize the value of our data over time. Most facility owners already have a great deal of useful data awaiting optimization and use. Using this existing data allows the creation of new tools, quickly. Then you can add new capabilities as understand, and needs evolve.

Building tools to use existing data, over time, has the added benefit of making the training of new users more manageable. Training programs can grow slowly, in parallel with your new tools. To enable a gradual approach to BIG-BIM that connects stakeholder data sources.

Service-Oriented-Architecture . . . software design in which application components provide services to other elements via a communications protocol . . . Independent of any vendor, product, or technology. — Wikipedia & Microsoft. Service-oriented-architecture can also be thought of as the oxygen that drives the efficient use of facility data.

Core Concept 6. A Strategy for Security

By necessity, monolithic systems classify everything at the same level of security. Administrators set the level for the entire application to the security level needed for their most sensitive data, putting everything in the same category. What results is that access to even the lowest level, the information requiring the least security, becomes difficult to use. Rather than protecting critical information, everyone is faced with obstacles to even the most mundane tasks. At that point, human nature takes over.

Service-oriented-architecture principles are intended to minimize, or open, boundaries between applications and differing technologies. This opening of applications requires that one move beyond the model of security that is hard-coded within applications. Layers of security need to permeate throughout everything. Security welded into applications is no longer good enough.

Legacy systems and monolithic applications do not provide the granular level of security needed in today's environment. With threat levels growing, these systems have become difficult to use, even within the confines of individual organizations. The tightly coupled data built into such regimes, make for an all-or-nothing approach to security.

Users who need to get to the data may not be able to access the information they need to get their work done. Too often, this results in the creation of workarounds that make the system less secure and vulnerable to attack. Workarounds intended to overcome the restrictions imposed by one-size-fits-all security emerge so that the work can get done. Even in highly restricted environments.

A goal of BIG-BIM is to make data available; but, that does not mean that access should be a chaotic situation. Organizations must provide levels of security appropriate to the data they expose and share.

Your data becomes more secure when managed with a strategy that considers the organization's functional needs, from top to bottom. All enterprises and facilities have sensitive information that must be secured. New approaches, new standards, and new technologies are rapidly evolving to handle this need.

With a services-oriented architecture approach, it is possible to put into place more granular levels of data security, increasing the safety of your data. The organization can then build a strategy around protecting data at the level needed for each item and interaction.

Core Concept 7. Encourage an App Economy

Apps are powerful tools that do many things, better than any tool set that has gone before.

The App economy has exploded with easy to use software applications that impact everywhere and every day. Bite-sized applications loaded on phones, and other mobile technologies are profoundly changing the way we do business. These Apps are changing how we interact to get just the information we need, when and where we need it; to make decisions of all kinds. Apps bring new interfaces for managing complex data within the reach of most organizations.

The App economy is causing a proliferation of new solutions that deploy small, nimble solutions at a fast pace. Off-the-shelf Apps using external data interact to replace customized, welded together applications. Common traits that make Apps compelling:

Apps are always online. Working 24x7, Apps keep people informed and engaged. Apps access data in the cloud and share resources with other applications.

Cloud Apps allows multiple, simultaneous users to work in ways where none must compromise.

Apps feel personal, intended to fit our individual needs, and behave as we wish. If they don't, there is always another option.

Apps are secure at many levels, allowing us to store data securely at a lower cost. With the added benefit of being able to scale into more space as needed.

The best Apps are convenient and easy to use. Simple, easy to use and adaptable to work in a range of environmental situations.

Apps in the built environment sector are just beginning to have an impact. Hosted in the cloud, BIG-BIM Apps can enhance any organization's data, and how the enterprise uses the data. Within BIG-BIM ecosystems Apps can display an organization's data as 3D boxes representing projects, buildings, and spaces. Any of these boxes can (and does) carry detailed data at a very high level of accuracy and enables in-context visualization of data, plus much more.

Apps connect us to geography, are location aware and give us the ability to mash-up data in-context to make better decisions. Cloud Apps enable trouble free, fail-safe operations that work with complex data.

For those that have only embraced little-bim, the graphic representation of models in BIG-BIM ecosystems may seem a bit primitive. One must dive into the data to understand the complexity that these systems enable one to manage. The data these ecosystems connect are much more complete and accurate than the little-bim that enamors so many of today's design and construction professionals.

Immediately after importing a spreadsheet that lists Room Name, Room Size, and Floor Level, a BIG-BIM ecosystem can generate a building information model with an entirely functional work-order-management capability. A model that can be publicly accessed on any web-enabled device. If you add Room Number to the import, you can also immediately create standards-compliant COBie files and do many other high-order tasks.

BIG-BIM systems quickly create value and benefit with each increment of added data. While much of the effort around little-bim focuses on graphics and management of the processes via Levels of Detail or Levels of Development, such complexity is irrelevant as BIG-BIM functions at any LOD, at every stage in development.

In the past, the norm was large, monolithic applications that were expensive, complicated to create and deploy and, required extensive training to use. In today's fast-paced and ever-changing environment, that approach is no longer affordable or sustainable.

The new norm is agile and flexible Apps that are much easier and faster to create, easy to deploy and usable by everyone with minimal orientation. Link to Program2BIM to test this yourself for free.

Core Concept 8. Align the IT Department

The best IT professionals are shepherding their businesses through the disruptions that are now turning entire industries upside down.

The role of Information Technology (IT) is shifting—emerging from the confines of server rooms and into the role of high level business strategists and digital provocateurs. Since the advent of computerization, much data has accumulated. Often the information is just not available without significant (and sometimes extreme) effort. Overcoming such issues is one of the major technology quandaries in existing organizations.

Business profitability, risk mitigation and policies generated from outside IT are too often the core source of the problems. At heart, IT staffs are the innovators that embrace change in the technical side of businesses. IT folks may worry about the limitation of SOA, but normally they wholeheartedly marvel at the potential. Rather than being the origin of the problem.

With the constraints that impact traditional IT, they have been unable to quickly respond to ever-changing business demands. This has resulted in too many IT departments morphing from creators and maintainers of the technology infrastructure, into policing organizations, driving the data use policy of organizations.

In this mode, IT leaders cite data security and keeping the systems running as the reasons for such unplanned shifts from technology as logistics support to, technology as a driver (or a barrier) of organizational progress. Adding to the confusion are tightly coupled systems, that have evolved to include features that made them overly complicated, difficult to maintain and brittle to changes.

Much too often Information Technology (IT) departments, with the best of intentions (or with mandates from non-technical corporate lawyers), lock down user access to data and systems to the point where technology becomes a handicap. As systems become more complex and fragile, the more risk the organization assumes. IT control and monolithic systems come together to create enterprises where too little gets done. Worst of all, even small changes can disable such systems.

Most established enterprises have much data, in many formats. Most of the data is in welded together software systems. The datasets are in the form of spreadsheets, Microsoft Access databases, SQL databases, document management systems, accounting systems, geographic information systems and more. Held in files or other single use outputs the data is subject to data rot and often of little long-term value. Long-term use is often dependent on reentry or manual conversion of existing data.

Access is limited and challenging, even within the organization. Often only a small number of individuals can access and use the data for their purposes. Sometimes due to the level of training required. Other times due to access restrictions or lack of resources. The reasons are myriad.

When it becomes hard to get to the data that people need to do their work, they create personalized files to get their jobs done. Central resources that feed the organization's greater need become little more than dreams. The database and system are there; they just cannot be used effectively. The real jobs get done by diligent people using spreadsheets and other files. Otherwise, they would be doing little or nothing.

As organizations wrestle with this issue, there is a growing recognition that IT must learn to support new ways of managing the data, rather than being a bottleneck to productivity. IT Departments are finding themselves on the front lines of a computing generation gap.

On one side of the gap are experienced IT staffs with little understanding of today's consumer-friendly technology. They impose restrictions that once made sense but which today work counter to corporate needs. It seems like they don't understand that in the new economy, success depends on connecting the unconnected applications, data, and devices.

On the other side are a new generation of technology consultants and connectors working to use embedded data to get things done as efficiently as possible by eliminating self-imposed roadblocks. Reconciling this conflict is critical to an organization taking advantage of the ever-increasing amount of information they own.

An organization's technology systems need to allow for structure, flexibility, accessibility, and adaptiveness, within a secure environment. Systems must support both internal and external needs. Today, data is becoming more connected into all aspects of business. Organizations are finding that their data can be the backbone of resilient and sustainable decision-making when connected to a BIG-BIM ecosystem.

Historically, much of an organization's data was controlled by others, for there was no other way. Many large datasets regarding the built environment were traditionally in the hands of Architects, Engineers, Contractors, Owners, Operators, and other professionals. Today, this information can be linked and used to improve business processes. Organizations are beginning to recognize this fact.

To benefit from the connection of such external information, IT must revert to the task of maintaining the technology, to support the corporate need. Decoupled data, a services oriented approach and an App economy are the tools that make this possible.

Issues with Information Technology are not confined to the building industry (http://dilbert.com/strips/comic/2007-11-16/).

Ecosystems for the Built Environment

Wikipedia defines an ecosystem as—a community of living organisms in conjunction with the nonliving components of their environment, interacting as a system.

The world we inhabit is an ecosystem that changes and grows. The ecosystem never stops changing. It is chaotic, expanding and contracting over time. We have learned to impact the types and directions of some of the changes. Sometimes for the good. Too often not.

We have long had the tools to assess and manage changes in the ecosystem. However, they have not been available to most of us. At the highest level, with enough time, money, and experts we could analyze and act on any issue. We analyzed in a linear fashion, informed by experience and anecdote.

We had limited access and few resources to interrelate and correlate complex interconnected components. That is a big part of the reason that design and construction have worked the way they have for thousands of years.

At first, little-bim appeared to be the solution to change this paradigm in the construction industry. Unfortunately, little-bim is little more than a step toward the goal. BIG-BIM manifests the larger change in the built environment, building on the infrastructure created by the Internet and the World Wide Web. The systems that they have spawned have exposed the universal solution to managing our assets. Looking closely at the promise of BIM in a search for the things that enable the solution, we found:

We need the ability to connect data of all types.

We have the capacity to mash-up information of all kinds.

Our tools must let us visualize the problems before they occur. We need to test virtually—minimizing cost and optimizing outcomes. Zooming in on the results that are most likely to be successful over the entire lifecycle of entire built environment.

We need straightforward and easy to use tools that enable informed decision-making connecting the information we need at the proper time and place. Nothing more and nothing less.

We have the tools to build connections and interactions between people, places, and things in-context.

The data in the ecosystem must be protected even as applications change.

Only recently have our tools brought the capacity to predict outcomes in the context of the day-to-day activities of ordinary people. The goal is to create an ecosystem that allows and encourages flexibility while maintaining a structure of standards. Systems of many types become an ecosystem for today and tomorrow within a framework that supports the changes that are inevitable. The ecosystem guides both internal and external development and allows us to grow and adjust to an uncertain future, knowing that we have the tools to adapt to uncertainty. The ecosystem is sustainable and resilient.

Optimize How We Work

Over the last twenty years, much of the energy associated with BIM has gone toward developing industry standards for the distant future. These efforts focused on creating standards that, at their core, rely on file exchanges and the welded together, monolithic application environment of the last century. If you want people to follow your standards, they must be flexible and easy to use in the real-world.

The Core Concepts work best when there is adherence to immediately actionable standards. Clear standards that are transparent to the workflows that they impact. Standards in the building industry have become highly detailed and much too involved, as they attempt to deal with every potential issue that might develop as BIM moves toward a theoretical end state that no one can predict.

Cataloging and accommodating the known-unknowns has become a herculean task. One that is only partially successful. The dichotomy is that without building industry standards for naming things, defining connections and coordinating between diverse needs, many of the applications currently available may forever remain disconnected from the world of BIG-BIM. With such standards, some of them will, at some undefined future point, become interoperable in a BIG-BIM ecosystem.

Some significant (and well known) owners mandate that, *if you want to work on these premises, you must use the specific file exchanges we demand.* They are so focused on today's issues that they aren't considering what they are doing to themselves in a connected future?

Unfortunately, the standards development process has gotten so complicated and lost in the details that some ask—Do we need such elaborate standards, and who is going to follow them in any case?

Personal, corporate and government agendas drive outcomes, while publicly standards development groups espouse agendas based on consensus. Thousand-pound blind gorillas seem to have created elephants—and, decided to call them BIM standards.

Many of today's BIM standards are intended to guide software developers in the creation of systems that simplify user business processes. However, they are not doing a good job in fulfilling that goal. Too many developers move to other things as they realize the lack of clarity that characterizes BIM standards. The complexity and format of the criteria, coupled with arcane development processes result in flawed implementations and confusion. In many situations, they become more of an impediment than an enabler of productive and focused work.

There are other standards at play. Standards that directly apply to the building industry are not the only ones that are critical to the future of BIM. Look at the example of the Internet and the world-web-web. Both are standards-based environments that have become successful by setting flexible controls and getting out of the way. They let innovative people do what they need to do, mostly as they choose to do it.

Such approaches to standards are more elegant than those that have long been the focus in the building industry. These standards are rigorous and the process the community goes through to develop and maintain them is laborious and painful, but the outcomes are flexible, simple and effective. At their core, they are incremental and iterative.

Those developing solutions outside the building industry recognize that software need not be a massive monolith, but can be an amazingly organic entity with complex moving parts that interact with each other. Thus, they give more importance to adaptability and constant compatibility testing, than to prescriptive mandates.

Why should something as complex and elegant as the building industry and BIM be any different? To achieve a global scale BIG-BIM ecosystem in a reasonable timeframe, we need to move away from the current standards development processes for building industry technology. Toward universal standards that are agile, open and aimed at innovation and benefit today.

Historically, building industry standards focused on public safety and welfare. Zoning, plumbing, electrical and structural codes are examples. Within the design segment, standards focused on a uniform understanding of drafting conventions.

As the industry moved from manual drafting to computer-aided-drafting, standards were created to control the flat-CAD production environment and often focused entirely on a specific CAD application. Offices also created internal CAD standards to manage the application they chose to adopt.

Such rules seemed to be necessary for the unrefined technology that was CAD. These standards leaned toward hundreds of layers, pen tables, and prescriptive requirements. They made navigation and understanding difficult and imposed systems that worked for one instance, not for all cases. They required that users be highly trained and proficient in the use of a standards-based application. They were, and are, inflexible.

They were by their nature impediments to change and are one factor in the building industry's decline in productivity since the advent of personal computers. Using such standards, in most cases, adds little to a BIM workflow. Adding complex, hard to apply rules to a mature BIM system is unnecessary and does not optimize the work effort.

A connected process using little-bim must be flexible and allow for easy transitions between projects, tasks, and people. It needs everyone to understand, without a data table or rule book. Doing this requires things like common and understandable names.

For BIM to become universally successfully, industry standards must become more elegant and foster innovation.

Case Study
BIM Guidelines

With the move to a little-bim solution, one can usually abandon such things as layers and pen tables without penalizing your work product. To be effective, little-bim initially needs only a few attributes, and to be compatible with BIG-BIM these attributes need to be standards-compliant.

What are the interesting aspects of this project?

Owners have learned that BIM permits them to make informed decisions with greater certainty of outcomes.

Owners have proven to themselves that BIM reduces costs, achieves higher productivity, increases building performance, and reduces errors.

Most importantly, owners have come to understand that they can phase implementation of guidelines, models, and delivery processes, to connect with existing legislation and available financial resources.

Knowledgeable owners know that the BIM implementation process must be positioned correctly to match the needs of their individual market.

Location—Wisconsin, USA.

No new legislation was required. The owner tailored the guidelines and standards to fit within current procurement and delivery mandates. The State did not mandate workflows. Consultants were allowed a variety of software products to achieve project goals. The focus was on deliverables with the best chance of reuse over the lifecycle of State facilities.

Critical tools had to be compliant with international standards. The guidelines accommodated current practices while building toward a future state that relies on authoritative data and real-time data exchange.

Some multi-facility owners understand both the potential of BIM and the issues created by reliance on file-based data exchanges. Using owner driven *proof-of-concept* projects they have proven and documented how BIM delivers benefits. With their success, momentum has built within the ranks of large property owners.

However, for owners with large asset portfolios or public mandates, the optimal path to successful implementation remains unclear. Often there is legacy legislation that imposes requirements on procurement. Most need to maintain relationships with vendors of long standing. These owners rely on the support of the professionals that provide services for their facilities.

Overlaying all of this, many of the professionals that work for these owners remain uncertain about the impact on their businesses. As the owners see the benefits of using BIM to enable asset lifecycle management, the professionals see confusion and the potential for interruptions to profitability. Uncertainty breeds fear of change. The state of Wisconsin, when faced with these issues, tackled the problem in a measured and planned way.

First, State officials informed and educated those that work on the State's projects. An extended fact-finding and input process began that included seminars, surveys, and presentations. By 2008, pilot projects were in progress. These steps resulted in Wisconsin publishing, *Building Information Modeling, a Report on the Current State of BIM Technologies, and Recommendations for Implementation.* The report documents the State's multiyear review of BIM.

Using the lessons learned, they next focused on creating guidelines to meet Wisconsin's requirements. Using a local team supported by national experts, Wisconsin then drafted a set of standards that closely aligned with the State's unique political and commercial needs. In doing this, they set the pace for property owners everywhere, becoming the first to require BIM use on State projects. *BIM Guidelines and Standards for Architects/Engineers,* went into force on July 1, 2009.

The guidelines mandated BIM during design for projects over $5 million and set the foundation for BIM during construction and operations. The guidelines and standards were designed to reduce costs, to be sustainable and to maximize informed decision-making.

The goal was to get work done properly without limiting competition. The idea was to get the tasks done in the best way, recognizing that no one tool or suite of tools can do everything needed. The guidelines are flexible, conservative, software-neutral and don't require bleeding-edge technology. Tools not proven in real-world tests and 'vaporware' are not acceptable.

Design teams are required to update models during construction. At project closeout, the owner receives deliverables that represent the completed facility. In multiple file formats, to accommodate future changes. Wisconsin's guidelines are a first step toward achieving the long-term benefits that come from asset lifecycle management.

Rather than attempting to change everything at once, the State elected to change incrementally. Work began in 2010 on additions to phase into the connection of facilities management and GIS. Work on alternative design and construction delivery methods started in 2011. Each step took place in measured ways that accommodate Wisconsin's vendors, the political environment, and the evolving state of the technology.

Too many other owners have spent significant time and money to mandate BIM standards that are software driven and impose unnecessary market constraints. Wisconsin managed to avoid such problems.

Strange as it may seem, many owners have not understood the conservative and build-on-what-we-have approach. Rather, many have mandated the use of the one-software-platform-approach and created complex requirements that restrict competition. They have codified legacy processes in ways that hamper their chances of achieving many of the near-term benefits of little-bim, and minimize the long-term potential of a BIG-BIM ecosystem.

Case Study
Program to BIM

More than $113 million is spent annually by one US government department on the administration of work orders alone. Trimming a conservative 10 percent from their process would shrink their annual costs by $11 million. The savings, nation and world-wide could be staggering.

What are the interesting aspects of this system?

An approach leading to the development of a vision that becomes an ecosystem of tools to support the varied needs and skill sets of many people.

Capitalizes on the use of web-based capabilities while leveraging mobile technologies that have exploded in public and private industries within the last few years.

The move to a service-oriented-architecture approach enables a future-proof, flexible foundation for new developments and features while supporting quick development cycles.

The systems are about creating a community of ALL professionals with an interest in driving interoperable standards, improved processes, and digital workflows. It also is about moving data from early planning through design, construction and into operations and facility sustainment, using live information exchanges.

iFM established a vision of the technology hub—a software and App ecosystem—for the rapid and agile deployment of tools and practices to dramatically improve efficiency and effectiveness.

Location—Worldwide.

The ability to capture and use lifecycle data is no longer just aspirations. Some are doing it today. Owners of facilities of all sizes, including those owned by the federal government, use BIG-BIM. The Department of Defense (DoD) Military Health System (MHS) and the Department of Veterans Affairs (DVA) are pursuing an aggressive connected strategy for facility planning, design, construction, operation, and retirement/ modernization to reduce the total lifecycle cost and create world-class facilities.

A fundamental building block of such a strategy is planning for facility space and equipment requirements and the related expenses. MHS and DVA recently completed a series of projects through the National Institute of Building Sciences centered on strategic planning, roadmaps, and proofs-of-concept projects that use BIM, geographic information systems (GIS) and facility management (FM) to support lifecycle value.

The team sought to enhance legacy products such as DVA's Space and Equipment Planning System (SEPS) and MHS's Defense Medical Logistics Standard Support Facility Management (DMLSS-FM) system to enable them to become live tools in a BIG-BIM ecosystem supporting DVA and MHS missions. The team's work products resulted in the development of an ecosystem called FED ifM.

SEPS Data - Services Oriented Architecture

Space and Equipment Planning System (SEPS)

The purpose of the Space and Equipment Planning System (SEPS) is to create Programs for Design (PFD) and Project Room Contents (PRC); defining space and equipment needs for facilities. The SEPS user community consists of 655 government employees and 200 consultants.

MHS and DVA identified strategies and recommendations to enhance and sustain SEPS in support of medical facilities planning by the Portfolio Planning and Management Division (PPMD), the Air Force, Army, Navy, and Department of Veterans Affairs as they conduct Facility Life Cycle Management (FLCM) planning and programming around the world. These offices gather input by interviewing medical facility personnel. This data is then used to compute project scope and to estimate the costs of initially outfitting (equipment and furnishings) facilities, using the SEPS application.

SEPS forecasts space and equipment need through a complex series of business rules related to mission, workload, and staffing or other inputs. Outputs, in the form of projected space, equipment, and their costs, are calculated using the SEPS application.

In October 2012, a Strategic Plan for the enhancement and sustainment of SEPS began. The team first reviewed current capabilities and workflows critical to end user communities. They also worked closely with the software developers to understand the technical makeup of the underlying system and data structures, with the goal of creating immediately actionable results rather than creating general strategies.

The Strategic Plan also created the opportunity to make small, modular steps toward the goal rather than making massive commitments to time and resources upfront. This approach allowed for feedback and appropriate course corrections as development proceeded into new territory.

Process

Unlike prior versions of SEPS (which were monolithic and file-based), SEPS 3.0 is built entirely as a web-based application. This immediately enabled much-needed capabilities such as multi-user collaborations on projects and sharing of criteria and project data in real-time. It also eliminates the time-consuming tasks of administering and managing the installation of SEPS for each user on each computer. With proper credentials, users log into the application and have access to the latest version of the tool, standards, and criteria as well as the most recent project data.

SEPS users process a series of input data questions about Mission, Workload, and Staffing. From those sets of data, a project program generates in the form of required spaces and equipment.

This list of Spaces and Equipment defines the preliminary basis for a project. The data in SEPS may then be used in systems such as the Parametric Cost Engineering System (PACES) to study cost implications at a high level. With this preliminary program and budget in place, the project can be contracted out for design and construction.

This shift towards a web-based platform introduced an entirely new set of possibilities for future versions. The team can now move SEPS to implement service-oriented-architecture, a significant improvement in the core system's configuration and architecture. Before version 3.0 SEPS was rooted in tools and processes from the previous century. Access to building data was tightly coupled, closed and highly inflexible. With version 3.0, this changed dramatically.

Legacy accomplishments in the ecosystem:

SEPS 3.0 corrected Single User Limitations that forced users to fall back to a manual process, consuming too much time and creating too many errors.

SEPS 3.0 corrected major problems in project workflows, saving much lost time and accuracy.

SEPS 3.0 enabled online, offline and versioning controls as well as transparent synchronization of online and offline data as it goes in and out of the system.

SEPS 3.0 enabled connections to other tools to improve shared information across multiple devices in a facility lifecycle timeline in flexible and scalable ways.

SEPS 3.0 enabled the importing and exporting of as-built data to support modernization projects. The ability to compare completed designs to the original program and the completed project or as-built data was a crucial part of this effort.

The SEPS 3.0 platform allowed for the creation of new interfaces within SEPS or direct connection with other applications using the SEPS data, as the work progresses.

SEPS 3.0 enabled data consistency between SEPS and published documents. SEPS 3.0 is beginning to manage the process of matching documents posted in static PDFs and Excel files within the system with the data the system needs to generate output on-the-fly, rather than serving as a repository for static files.

SEPS 3.0 enabled a much larger user base than in previous versions and has the potential to scale. More users of SEPS 3.0 will drive the quality, use and value of the product.

SEPS 3.0 improved the accuracy of automated Program-for-Design and better review and coordination of manual edits to the data. Making SEPS more user-friendly decreases the learning curve and is a critical goal of future development.

The SEPS 3.0 is no longer a monolithic architecture and now has an API (Application Program Interface) which removes many of the limits to enable better support of other business processes as more stakeholders and systems provide data or use data from SEPS 3.0.

SEPS 3.0 enabled security and access controls on even public information that maintain the necessary security between each part of the system.

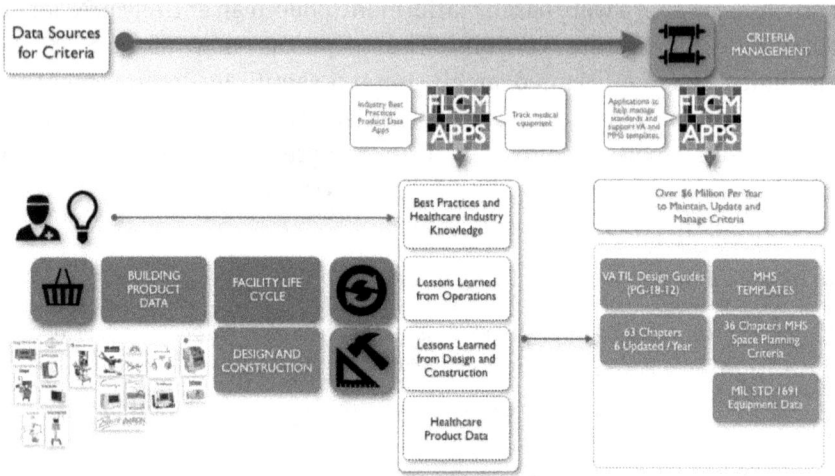

SEPS 3.0 relied on file-based, published standards. A goal is to connect to live versions of external standards and to manage architectural and engineering criteria updates into the system as machine-readable data that can be used in managed ways, by the full range of potential users.

Due to the breadth of needs throughout the lifecycle of facilities, no single system or monolithic system can solve issues in an organization. From an industry outreach perspective, this is a real opportunity for vendors and consultants who are willing and ready to jump into this ecosystem and marketplace of apps and data.

Open–standards are a starting point; they create a common language. Also needed is access to data—to latch onto the explosion of mobility, agility, and small modules of functionality that plug–and–play with each other and that can scale over time. To solve big problems with small actions repeated often.

Collaboration & Standards

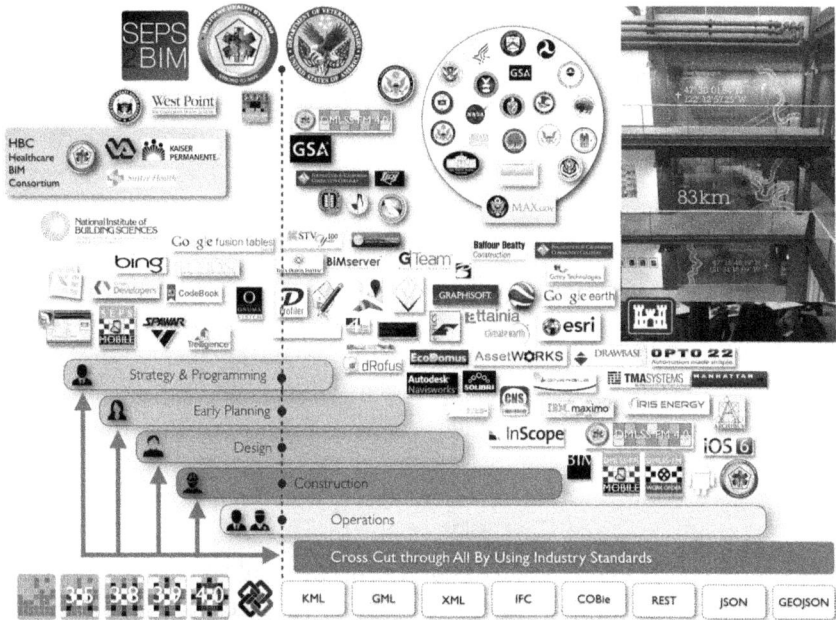

Computerized Maintenance Management System (CMMS)—specifically, preventive maintenance (PM), work orders, asset management/real property, project management and reports; and Computerized Asset Facility Management (CAFM)—specifically, drawings (drawing repository), space management, keying control, Real Property Inventory Requirements (RPIR) and reports were the critical components to this facilities management system.

Many consider Work Orders to be the low-hanging fruit, an easily identifiable and current problem area that is a primarily single-use and paper intensive workflow with a strong potential for significantly improved seamless digital data flow. However, work orders are just one of the many facility management functions that need of significant improvement. The potential savings that could result from optimized facility management services will be enormous.

Much like Global Positioning Systems, iFM offers the building industry an open platform for facilities.

FED iFM

Facility management—encompasses multiple disciplines to ensure the functionality of the built environment by connecting people, place, process, and technology—International Facility Management Association (IFMA). To meet even higher expectations in today's fast-paced, data-driven world, that original concept has morphed into a broader, more encompassing principle—Integrated Facility Management (iFM).

The US Government portfolio of facilities is a massive 3.35 billion square feet with an annual operating cost more than 30 billion dollars. Plagued with antiquated IT systems, arcane procurement processes, and inefficient operations, iFM (Integrated Facility Management) was created as a shared information service to lift the building industry and create an opportunity for change. FED iFM is an initiative to create shared and standard practices for integrated facility management in federal agencies and the private sector.

FED IFM is flexible and scalable. The system engages private sector owners, architects, and professional organizations to build a bridge of collaboration and shared interests; and enlist technology service providers to build platforms, applications, and App marketplaces to access DVA and MHS data repositories. The goal was to foster a technology hub vision—a software and App ecosystem—for rapid and agile deployment of tools and innovative practices that dramatically improves efficiency and effectiveness. To better use data from early planning through design and construction, into operations and facility sustainment.

Open-source, as well as proprietary technologies, were evaluated within a connected platform of cloud and server-based environments. In October 2012, the MHS Tricare Management Activity (TMA) initiated a project to develop a five-year roadmap for DMLSS-FM.

The roadmap was intended to guide the production of a corporate CAFM/CMMS system using best practices and current and future technology to resolve problems from facilities data which is fragmented, causing extensive manual work to analyze information across the entire enterprise.

Using lessons learned and strategies developed in the concurrent SEPS Strategic Plan, the team improved data access dramatically, maximizing value and enabling a wide variety of hardware and software options.

Two of the many flowcharts that describe criteria as activities flow, from construction into operations of facilities. The vision is for ifM to be a technology hub of software and applications used for rapid and agile development of tools or innovative practices for moving data from early planning through design, construction and into operations and facility sustainment.

The team was also able to align the system with another government initiative, *Digital Government: Building a 21st Century Platform to Better Serve the American People.* This alignment contributed to DVA and MHS adopting a strategy to decouple their data from specific applications to create a flexible system capable of using the underlying data from an ever-growing number of hardware devices and software apps available for end users.

The strategy and subsequent recommendations developed by the team resulted in the connection of facility management with other parts of the BIG-BIM ecosystem. Decoupling data from applications enabled new opportunities and required new strategies. A key strategy was to develop an ecosystem of tools able to leverage things that are already available in the industry. This approach enabled such elements as the rapid incorporation of technologies such as RSS tagging, RFID scanning, and simple apps on mobile devices for everyday tasks.

The goal is to build bridges of collaboration and shared interests in achieving the FED iFM vision and to enlist technology service providers to build platforms, applications (apps) and app marketplaces to access agency data repositories and to foster and enable the realization and success of the FED iFM vision.

This project has implications for BIM, GIS, FM, and open-standards worldwide, as it engages the healthcare industry, both in the federal and private sector, on a plan of action for the future. The goal is to build bridges of collaboration and shared interests in achieving the FED iFM vision and to enlist technology service providers to build platforms, applications, and app marketplaces to access agency data repositories and to foster and enable the realization and success of the FED iFM vision.

Platform as a Service

The iFM is a Platform as a Service (PaaS) created on top of MAX.gov, a shared service among government agencies with over 100,000 users. MAX.gov enables FED iFM to benefit from many features already built in the MAX system (e.g., secure logins) while offering new facility management tools to all existing users.

The iFM sandbox is an ideal environment for developers and owners to create tools and solutions that can plug into the iFM PaaS while creating new opportunities and introducing the facility management community to the power of shared data. You should participate and become part of the iFM community.

Disruptive Technologies Conference

Conferences abound in the world of BIM. Often such get-togethers become little more than places for professionals to socialize with their peers, but not always. During Building Innovation 2014: The National Institute of Building Sciences Conference and Expo, the full-day *Healthcare Facilities Lifecycle Workshop* introduced the concepts of FED ifM and iFM to the world. Attendees included representatives from federal agencies, architect-engineers and consultants involved in healthcare; technology vendors; and industry organizations.

The workshop began by introducing the topic of *Disruptive Technologies—advances that will transform life, business, and the global economy,* as presented in the May 2013 McKinsey & Company report on 12 disruptive technologies, four of which are directly related to healthcare facilities and facilities management: The mobile Internet; the automation of knowledge work; the Internet of Things; and cloud technology.

The presenters emphasized that one of the trends driving iFM is that: technology is becoming transparent and straightforward to use. Information silos are rapidly disappearing as agile, and nimble development is deployed using Apps which quickly focus on delivering a minimum viable product.

No single software solves everything. Standards focused on smoothly moving information from one application to others can now be used to enable shared services for facilities. Such are the underpinnings of mobile technology and distributed computing.

The mantra of iFM is to start simple and iterate.

The iFM concept follows the *White House 21st Century Digital Strategy.* An important component of this strategy is that data is at the core; systems, processes, and services all rely on robust, interoperable data. The digital strategy requires *layers of digital services, to include security, information, platform, presentation, and customers/users.*

A second presentation emphasized security as an over-arching and enveloping construct. To support the disruptive technology of cloud computing, the National Institute of Standards and Technology (NIST) is guiding the Department of Defense in establishing an overall framework for security that supports layers of digital services.

Today, facility data is not well defined or well protected, which is a huge security threat. iFM fixes this. It sets out a security structure that enables more collaboration in a controlled yet open way (and yes, you can have both).

The originator of the FED ifM concept, and Chief of Operations & Lifecycle Integration for the Defense Health Agency also provided his perspective on facilities in the federal marketplace. The accomplishment was to create real integrated facility management.

The essential elements of the program include: CMMS which provides the means to manage the data relating to the Real Property Installed Equipment (RPIE) for the facility and its associated preventive maintenance, work orders, and project management; and, CAFM which provides the means to manage space utilization for facilities in a graphical manner linked to relevant CMMS data. The CAFM also provides a means for MHS to comply with Real Property Inventory Requirements.

The broader connected vision pulls together a variety of technologies from new systems, including BIM, GIS, and COBie; together with existing systems, such as SEPS and DMLSS-FM, resulting in FED ifM as the connection construct.

The working groups driving FED ifM created a sandbox environment on Amazon Web Services and invited developers into the sandbox. Because it is a common need, other government agencies, as well as the private sector, have shown an interest in ifM. Industry outreach continues with In-person Progress Review (IPR) meetings. Building on the success of the *Healthcare Facilities Lifecycle Workshop*, broader collaboration is planned moving forward.

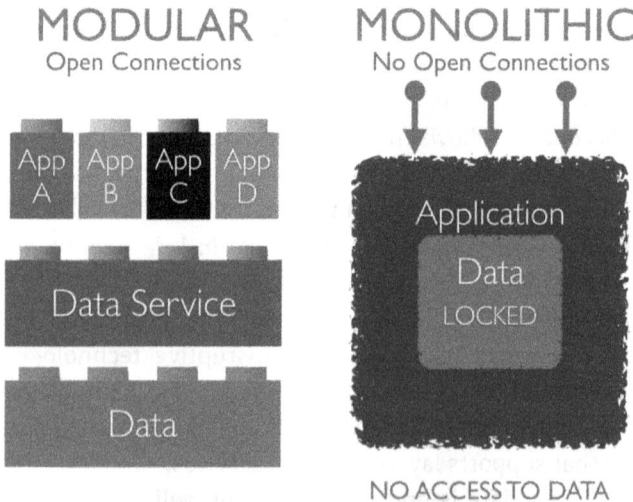

MODULAR
Open Connections

App A | App B | App C | App D

Data Service

Data

MONOLITHIC
No Open Connections

Application

Data
LOCKED

NO ACCESS TO DATA

Facility management is evolving to become a hybrid of proprietary tools that can communicate better with open-standards. A combination of established Commercial-Off-The-Shelf (COTS) and open-source tools, new agile, modular methods, and procedures for making connections are becoming the norm.

The goal is to reduce redundancy, enable an environment that is application neutral and decouple the data from the application. Data cannot be trapped. Future FM will combine easily understood and developed standards that foster the needs of all sectors of the industry to connect their solutions. A balance will emerge where standards will not be too rigid or too loose, with no dogma; as simple as possible, but no simpler.

Mobile devices overtaking desktop PCs was unimaginable four years ago, but that is what has happened. Managing buildings, spaces, equipment, and people is the same thing—different names, but the underlying iFM backbone is the same—built on open-standards of BIM, GIS, and FM. The building owner, occupant, facility, and tools/devices will be fully connected, with open, but secure data at the core of this framework.

Program to BIM gives the federal government the ability to capture and use lifecycle data in new ways that are economical and efficiently deliver on their missions. The ecosystem enables agencies to capture and maintain vast amounts of data and program requirements that can them be served up as needed to support planning, design, construction, and operations. The system leverages SOA and a variety of BIG and little-bim tools to get the work done the best way possible, with the greatest certainty of outcomes.

Experience Program to BIM for yourself. See the latest developments and experience the results of work in this Case Study by going to the FediFM or SEPS2BIM website. Also visit the MAXGov website for an overview of the ways that the US government is working to create a simple, user-friendly system with easy access to services and tools to support day-to-day work.

Finith Jernigan

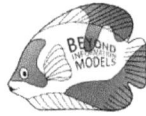

FOUR
PEOPLE, NOT TECHNOLOGY

The solution is people enabled by technology. Technology isn't the answer; it is toolsets that people can use to become an expert in our world. Technology gives us the facts; we take the facts and decide how to use them.

The BIG-BIM ecosystem is the place where people use technology to leverage what is possible. Within the ecosystem, value comes from synthesizing information and managing complex situations at a very high level, using tools and processes that mirror today's best and most efficient business processes. Use proven technology to enable in-context decision-making, to become an active force in the economy. Take charge and lead the way.

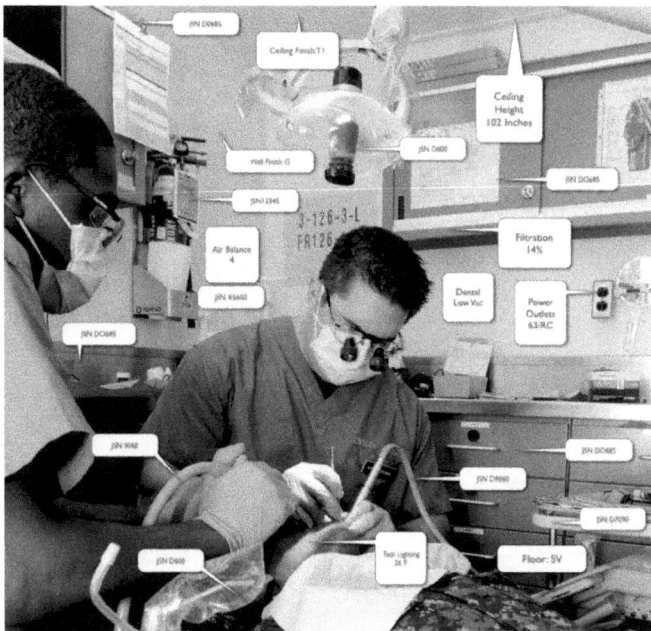

Opportunities

It isn't enough to have good ideas. Only when you act and implement can you make innovation happen day in and day out. Deep knowledge in a handful of areas and broad interests are the defining characteristics of tomorrow's leaders.

Today, those with deep expertise in one skill set, balanced by passion and the ability to interconnect with others across what may seem like unconnected disciplines, are thriving.

The volume of information that affects what you do every day can be a blessing or a curse. You can either embrace the information or let it inundate you. There are strategies for managing information to maximize its value in your life. Examine the new ways of working that underpin BIM, in the context of your beliefs. In the Workflows of this book, you will find opportunities and possibilities that can enable great things—even on your current work.

Make a checklist of the opportunities for establishing a BIG-BIM ecosystem. Here are a few of the possibilities to get you started:

- ☐ *Embrace design thinking and find ways to make design part of everything you do (whether you are a designer, or not);*

- ☐ *Think about entire systems, not only components, and manage your business processes by constraints;*

- ☐ *Manage teams so that design and implementation happen in parallel;*

- ☐ *Create early decision-making processes to improve the quality of project outcomes;*

- ☐ *Understand the value of tradition and legacy systems, but don't let them overshadow connected business decisions;*

- ☐ *Define mutually beneficial objectives with your teams to create more value. Share the pains and the gains;*

- ☐ *Enforce good communications and knowledge sharing to build strong project teams; and,*

- ☐ *Find ways to become part of connected supply networks with others of like mind.*

Automation is about People

What traits and skills are needed for someone to be great at BIG-BIM? Make a list for yourself. How well do you match your list? Plan to fill any gaps that you find.

Automating processes, need not destroy the things we value. Connected processes will always be about people. There will always be personal intervention in the process. Automation of the process can reduce the mundane tasks and let you focus on critical issues. Automation gives you more decision-making information in ways that are easy to digest. Often, automation changes how we work and what we do, enriching the things we create.

We can automate much, but not everything. Not everyone has the training and mindset to quickly embrace technology and the creativity to get the most from BIM. Add to that the complexity and confusion of the traditional building industry and it is easy to understand why BIG-BIM is so hard for some people to embrace.

Some people resist the thought of using technology to automate work practices. They fear overlaying this level of control on their process. Such fears are counterproductive to connected processes. By allowing such attitudes, you are positioning yourself for a sub-optimized process.

The process works best when you use the technology to improve understanding of alternatives, at the BEGINNING. By adding the detail, richness and speed that comes from the technology to the creative problem-solving of experienced professionals and motived stakeholders, we achieve more.

The best outcomes seem to happen when someone with a design thinking mindset uses the tools to evaluate options and hone in on the concept for projects. This level of enlightened automation of the process allows you to deliver just-in-time decision-making—even for the smallest project. By better supporting your customers, you become more valuable. You use your training and natural skills to synthesize information. You expand your ability to conceive and manage complex processes.

People Matter

BIG-BIM relies on transparency. People of all levels get the data they need to do the tasks at hand. When and where the data is required.

The illiterate of the 21st century will not be those who cannot read and write, but those who cannot learn, unlearn, and relearn. — Alvin Toffler

Most discussions about technology in the built environment focus on tools, followed by processes, with a smattering of organizational change. These are the hard face of information modeling and connection. It's hard to identify a BIM training program, seminar, or forum that focuses on people. The focus on the hard side of the equation, to the exclusion of the soft side—the people side—might not be surprising to you, but does it make sense?

My answer is NO.

By investing our energy in people, we build more robust, vigorous solutions. For the first time, BIG-BIM and the Internet allow individuals to leverage their abilities and resources to be direct competitors with the largest organizations. The world has changed and those with the foresight and skills are using the strength of BIG-BIM to leverage their abilities.

Little-bim thrives on technical complexity in a world of narrowly focused experts. Sold by large organizations, little-bim has slowed adoption of BIG-BIM benefits that are a threat to the status-quo. The focus on little-bim and the complexity it creates is simply because visualizing little-bim is easy; simpler to understand, easier to quantify, and easier to sell. It is because of legacy thinking and inaction. Whatever the reason, the focus on software, processes, and organizational change isn't enough.

For many years, specialists have worked in isolation. Their areas of expertise are now beginning to intersect in the larger conceptual framework of the built environment. Now is the time to go all in on BIG-BIM. Professionals are finding that geographic information, facility information, utility information, operations information, business information, political information, sustainability information, and every other form of information are intertwining.

The domains that professionals in each of these areas control are becoming blended. New professions are rising to respond to this convergence. The barriers between disciplines are slipping away. Society is pushing toward integrating and connecting all parts of our world—To the dismay of traditionalists.

If the built environment included only design and construction of projects, the traditional approach could be refined to improve quality and value. But the project-focused use of information modeling is only a small slice of the whole; the built environment is significantly larger, and needs much more than design and construction focused BIM can provide.

The building industry is in a state of transformation. Much of the discussion about resilience in the face of catastrophe, sustainability, zero-energy, and conservation is moot if the issues don't connect in meaningful ways. Technology and societal issues now intersect to create new things every day. The changes are in an always-on mode, and you can't hide and hope that things will go back to the way they were.

People see, and use connected processes every day. They buy things, they make reservations, interact with their friends and colleagues, and do a myriad of other things. Built environment issues can be handled much the same.

The building industry is beginning to feel the pressure to involve everyone in the process. Otherwise, the problems the industry faces are too big and too widespread to handle effectively. The key to leading this change is the ability to bring people of all types together to achieve significant results.

The Deloitte Center for the Edge's 2009 *Shift Index,* found that only of every five workers in the United States is genuinely passionate about his or her work. A recent Gallup Poll indicated that one of five employees are so disengaged that he or she actively seeks to undermine colleagues at work. Of course, most of us are in the middle of these two extremes. In a BIG-BIM context, studies such as this are frightening.

Put people first to improve and energize the changes that BIG-BIM brings to the way you do business. Inspire people by connecting to individuals with a broad sense of purpose. Go all in to create change that drives growth. Invest to develop leadership and talent in a culture of continuous learning. Practice inclusive leadership that enables people with the skills needed. Reinforce positive behaviors, listen, take input, and give credit where it is due.

Change is hard, especially when we don't trust those that lead. People resist change, especially when it is imposed on them. Too often leaders wait too long to act. They focus only on the short-term with no hope for the future or, subscribe to the one-off thinking that they can go back when the crisis is over. Such approaches play to people's fears and do little to ease anyone into the change.

In the transformation to BIG-BIM, education is the critical issue. Education helps people build confident relationships with the unknown and keeps us moving forward. Education to change the way that people interact with the built environment must become part of the BIG-BIM equation.

Too often, we confuse training with education. Training is simply about learning how to use a tool or process. Important, but far behind the need to educate. We need everyone to become educated in the concepts that drive BIG-BIM.

We can do better using the same problem-solving skills and education systems that drive other successful programs in our world. We have the luxury of deciding how we want to continue, but we don't have much time. For the building industry is currently in failure mode, and the system is primed to implode. As an industry and as individuals, we can work to make changes that support our interests. To move beyond legacy issues that make the system unsustainable and brittle.

Building industry professionals need to become directly involved in education. We need people that are passionate, curious learners. Become a life-long learner to build a society that values transparency, and inclusiveness; a society that is accountability-based and thrives by being sure about outcomes. Industry pundits estimate that millions of professionals need the education to connect technology issues and processes into their work. These professionals are finding it increasingly difficult to get appropriate direction because of sales hype and disinformation.

Close behind those now in the workforce millions of young people are seeking innovative and compelling ways to combine technology into their lives to build a better tomorrow. To that we need to add homeowners, tenants, shopkeepers, doctors, lawyers, and everyone else in our world. For in a world overlaid with the Internet of Things, everyone is rapidly becoming engaged in the process.

Can a collaborative and connected work environment that connects systems, tools and, processes in BIG-BIM ecosystems improve life? It did for us. While the first step may seem daunting, use the power of the Internet and the ecosystems it spawns to help you over the trust gap. Take the risk to embrace the Connected Age, and do things that you have never done.

Find ways in your local community to close the gap between innovation and education delivery. Find ways to move the innovations taking place in industry, into the classroom. This needs to occur at what may seem like the speed of light. There are significant examples and prototypes for how to get this done throughout this book and across the blogosphere.

Educate for Tomorrow

Those of us born before 1970 may not understand how those born after 1990 use technology. To Baby-Boomers technology was an acquired skill. To later generations technology is ubiquitous and a way of life. See one example of the way that this new way of looking at life is being expressed at the Khan Academy.

Today's young learners are open and fluid in their use of technology. They use technology much differently than those who found technology later in life. One small example is that few of today's students wear wristwatches, and if they do it as a fashion statement—not as a timepiece. They are so wedded to their mobile devices that a wristwatch is no longer a necessity.

We live in a time where knowledge work far overshadows the line workers of yesteryear. Previously, students could absorb the information that came from their professors, then regurgitate what they learned for the test and, get the degree. We trained for job compliance in a small world.

We must find new forms of education that more closely align with the work we will be doing tomorrow. We must refocus curriculum and reconnect education with a new future vision. In the Connected Age peer-to-peer engagement will replace top-down controls that were designed to normalize factory workers. The emphasis will be on supporting those eager to learn; with a passion to participate, rather than on testing. Rather than controlling students in static classrooms, education is already beginning to focus on experiential learning, in real and virtual environments.

Lectures, accreditation, and testing are the underpinnings of the traditional school system. This system seems focused on creating one topic experts or requires learners to be lucky or exceptionally focused on surviving the process with their creativity and curiosity intact. We teach to the lowest common denominator, honor and support the top 5 percent, and do harm to the majority in the middle—without malice, with the best of intentions, but we do it.

This educational model does not work well for BIG-BIM. Should we be concerned that a person can't get a PhD in a broad subject area? While BIG-BIM is at heart the broadest of subjects, touching on everything in the built world? We are no longer educating for industrial age workers. The system needs to turn away from teaching tools, and single focus experts, and toward connections as a way of thinking. When it does, we will see a generation of BIM experts.

The single focus, one topic expert has his or her place, but BIG-BIM relies on those that understand interconnected communities, overlapping systems and complexity.

If little changes and our education systems continue as usual, improvements in the built environment will be limited. Our systems will continue to strive for sustainability and resilience with little chance of truly solving the problems. We need the will and knowledge to understand that each of us has the ability and resources to become relevant to the future. We are no longer a station on an assembly line. We are in the age of the technology-empowered individual.

Slow adoption and linear, tradition-bound educational delivery systems must become systems that reward those that more closely connect teaching with what is happening in the real-world. Making this change is a real opportunity for educators.

Tomorrow's training will be about truly changing people and helping them blossom in peer-to-peer learning environments. Coaches will engage with students, urging them forward and holding them accountable to themselves.

Education today values cooperation above collaboration, and few teachers seem to understand the difference. Cooperation says: *Don't get in each other's way.* The cooperation model was created to train workers for Henry Ford's assembly line. It isn't valid with today's students.

Collaboration is an active involvement of people working together. Collaboration amplifies the value of many individuals and articulates ways to create opportunities. Collaboration is a high-fidelity notion that bridges the disconnect between education and the rest of the world. We need to develop academic standards that value collaboration as a core competency. Collaborative processes and connected tools are the mechanisms that make BIG-BIM possible.

The education system that evolved following World War II is under attack from many directions, and rightly so. People are tired of continually escalating costs, wasted effort, and ineffective teaching.

Educators take too long to learn about technology. Then they take too long to incorporate innovations into the classroom. Teachers need to learn ways to reduce the gap between the entry of a new technology and its practical use in the classroom.

Most lack the will or incentives to change, especially about current and pending conditions in the real-world. As an example, some community colleges still teach computer-aided drafting. They continue to train people for jobs that are in decline or extinct. They take too long to see changes outside academia, too much time to prepare once they know, and too long to apply the appropriate learning processes. Many students on leaving school find that the real-world functions nothing like the lessons they have learned.

Educators need to create their personal narratives about the future. They need to figure out what technology and systems will help them to train the next generation how to achieve these futures. Educators must begin to look at new ways of teaching to ground their students better in the theoretical knowledge that will drive the future. Teachers must learn new methods to reflect the ways of working that are emerging.

Rather than teach best practices of today they need to show next-practices that drive into the future. Educators need to stop teaching to an industrial era paradigm. The focus should move toward system thinking and problem-solving. Teaching someone how to operate a mouse or to draw a line in CAD is no longer appropriate.

Instead, educators should be asking their students to answer the question: What technology would you use to solve this problem? In fairness, we must recognize that the pressures on our education system are more severe than ever before. In this time of change, education requires systems that are flexible and responsive. Schools face the same issues as the built environment. Both ecosystems must change, or the pressures will force the change.

In a perfect world, school systems would quickly embrace the new reality. Course content and delivery mechanisms would change. Interdisciplinary, collaborative skills focused on society's narrative of the future should be the norm. The reality is that overcoming the inertia of earlier Industrial Revolutions is a major roadblock to forward motion.

Technology has created a chasm between generations unlike anything before. The scale of the issues creates problems and tremendous opportunities. Within the education system, we can find the seeds that, properly nurtured, will become the drivers of future success. Bridging this gap requires the education system to:

Teach people to be curious and life-long learners. At its best, our education system instills a passion for learning and the context needed to succeed. Individuals with broad interests and expert level knowledge are likely to be the best practitioners of BIG-BIM.

Focus on next-practices, not best practices. Technologies such as service-oriented-architecture, information models, model servers, web services, asset management and connected systems drive the solution. The education system can support these technologies.

Increase the importance of critical thinking and problem-solving. Teaching people to use their cognitive abilities is well entrenched in the system. Analytic thinking, conceptual thinking, pattern finding, and information seeking are learned in many educational programs.

Make people skills connected to technology a priority. Education for the human side of the equation is far behind education for applying technology itself.

Become the champion of systems that make the individual powerful and productive. Crowdsourcing, high-performing teams, collaboration, and connected decision-making need much more attention.

Focus on emotional competencies at all levels. Without the motivation, influence, self-confidence, teamwork, awareness, empathy, and flexibility that defines emotional awareness, information models and systems will always be sub-optimized.

Research organizations and academia must become more connected with the rest of the world. Theoretical research is needed to clarify how both professionals and the public will use and interact with new tools and processes. Applied research that models how groups and large-scale collaborations will use the tools, processes, and systems is essential. We also need case studies, test cases, and real-world trials to convince the skeptics.

It can be said that; one prototype is worth a thousand meetings. This book is an attempt to help in such matters.

Knowledge Economy

As you assess strategies for the future of your business, ask questions such as:
* *How dependent are we on knowledge workers?*
* *How many of our workflows, tools, and skills remain grounded in industrial age thinking?*
* *How complicated and expensive are our company's tools.*
* *How much time is required to deliver our organization's best and most valuable work product?*

Planners favor systems that worked well during the Kennedy administration, but no longer serve the public. Facility managers find themselves in continuous crisis management with limited ability to act proactively, because they don't have the tools and processes to be proactive. Architects draft by hand or use a file-based process. Contractors continue to return to technology that the expert builder of the cathedral in the thirteenth century would recognize.

Do you know people or companies that still work these ways? The world has shifted, yet too many of us continue working the usual way, with all the attendant problems. Like it or not, we live in a knowledge economy where the line between information producers and information users is vanishing. We, as individuals are becoming sources of knowledge and self-educated experts rather than just consumers.

Anyone can open any web-connected device and access a virtual firehose of data. One may need help to organize the data feeds, but no longer does one need to be an information technology expert to take advantage of the opportunities. Technology has leveled the playing field; we can work directly with information. We live in the age of the autodidact with the accumulated knowledge of the ages at her fingertips. Individuals can make an unprecedented impact.

The shift is forcing organizations to reconsider how to expand their boundaries, and even reevaluate their core competencies. Enterprises are building ecosystems that enable them to redefine their core competencies and respond to the digital transformation to connect systems, data, and devices.

Organizations of all types are finding themselves faced with a new reality. The explosion of information can be overwhelming, especially when considered from the perspective of established companies.

Many factors influence how an established enterprise will react to the power of the individual. As you explore the areas that need attention, before you react, there are many questions to ask. A checklist of some possibilities might include:

☐ *Do many of our processes take place in silos of activity? Are there areas that are difficult to connect with others?*

☐ *Is our data complicated and disorganized? Did this happen without anyone knowing?*

☐ *Have our staff members created spreadsheets and light databases, transaction-by-transaction, to get their work done? If so, what motivated them to take this approach?*

☐ *Does work done with a worksheet in the past now require extensive databases and connected decision-making tools? Does management believe that the correction is too hard or costs too much money or takes too much time?*

☐ *Are our response times slow, and getting slower?*

☐ *Are competent long-term employees leaving? Taking with them the organization's accumulated knowledge?*

☐ *Is most of our work done with a system containing thousands of files and single user outputs that are unmanageable in real-time?*

☐ *Do we have a data normalization problem of immense proportions?*

People in companies that need to adjust to the shifts in society often feel overwhelmed and revert to the usual way of working—even during formal change programs—because the solutions seem too hard. They want to compete but inertia, fear of lost revenues and lack of the right people resources are barriers to them changing.

Some of their problems are simple to resolve, once a strategy and framework for the future is in place. Businesses can hire people to create databases and build domain knowledge; both require easily taught and learned skills. Other problems require much greater will and a rethinking of the company's entire business approach.

Create a plan for how you will attract value creators. What talents and skills are important to you and your business strategy? Can you find people with expertise to match your needs and, the skills to function in an app economy? Where will you find them? Must you create them yourself? If so, you should consider a strategy for making this happen.

Competency

A competency is a pattern of behavior that sticks. A competency comes from a combination of knowledge, skills, abilities, and motivations. It isn't only about technical expertise, experience, or age.

We are amid a systemic and comprehensive change to how things work. Only by finding individuals with the necessary competencies can companies make these adjustments needed to be successful in the digital transformation. People with such skill sets are hard to find. Without them, companies find it hard to embrace BIG-BIM.

The change requires new skills—competencies that may not fit the traditional checklist or database. Skills that can be developed by practicing the Workflows in this book. Some of the competencies and traits that those who will thrive in a connected future exhibit include:

Creative competencies—People with creative competencies know and understand a range of problem-solving techniques. They have an ability to use logic to identify different approaches and the judgment to analyze their strength and weakness. They also have the capacity to synthesize and reorganize information to find better ways of doing things. They bring fresh ideas to solve problems and lead groups. Look for people that like to sketch or seek solutions to problems, the idea people.

Mashable competencies—People with mashable competencies can quickly identify the nature and cause of issues and the dynamics that define them. They have a constant desire to improve and ability to identify, collect, and use only the information that is necessary. They think creatively, even when it isn't popular. Those with Mashable competencies understand the underlying principles that are the foundation of technology and use them to improve outcomes. Look for people that can pick up a new software product and start using it with little or no formal training.

Emotional competencies—People with emotional competencies listen to others and to try new ideas. They are curious and an open mind to the ideas and solutions of others. They are observant and understand others' behavior. They voraciously study to find innovations and trends in various fields. Emotionally competent people are well-rounded personalities that seek information from all areas of life. They can relate unconnected ideas to find novel approaches to situations. Look for the person that you can depend on to diffuse situations... the informal human relations director.

Futurist competencies—People with futurist competencies are good at predicting the outcomes that will result from changes. They are often the first to understand changes that have occurred. Those with futurist competencies are good at creating a narrative of an ideal working condition and planning strategically. Look for those that continually think up new ways of doing new things or using existing things in novel ways to get new things done.

Change competencies—People with change competencies understand the phases of change and the barriers to change. They can evaluate and identify those things that promote and inhibit change. They have a willingness to act against traditional ways of working when they slow development. They have a willingness and ability to take calculated risks, yet know when to stop and figure out the right way before doing something. These people have an ability to encourage and reward others for initiative and creative work. They facilitate change initiatives. Look for those that quickly adapt to changing conditions who can find the opportunities in any new situation.

Enterprises have a hard time hiring people with process knowledge and expertise. They need people who are intuitive about managing processes and can envision success in a global context. They need people with the capacity to persuade others to their point of view. They need people capable of finding patterns in the complexity. These skills are highly valuable and hard to learn. They are challenging to evaluate and impossible to include in a database.

Companies need people with the capacity to create value. They need people to connect the dots between their products and services and their customers. These needs exist in all industries, business types, and places.

Case Study
Lost Momentum

People are more important than organizational structures. Structures we can design if we have any administrative creativity. — Bill Caudill, founder of CRS Architects, winner of the AIA Architecture Firm Award, and named Firm of the Century by Texas A&M University College of Architecture.

I left graduate school at the height of a recession. Jobs were scarce. After nine months of looking, I got my first job in a real office. At that time, they were a progressive growing business. A company sharply focused on productivity and profitability; that taught how to carefully budget and manage projects. They were constantly looking for better and more profitable ways to do things. They accepted the innovations of that era; overlay drafting, paste-up, and any other hand methods that got projects out the door faster.

The company was a very detail-oriented company, quietly controlled (informally behind the scenes) by one of the first Certified Construction Specifiers (CCS). He taught me to pay attention to the details.

The company's senior designer would produce a sketch. The rest of us worked out the details. We eliminated the problems. If someone made the effort and spent the time to resolve conflicts, we picked up most of the problems in the process. As a fallback, the company had people full-time on construction administration to catch anything that others missed.

They did Design-Build and Design-Build-Leaseback, but most of the projects were Design-Bid-Build. My first project with an agency construction manager started in 1980. In the mid-1980s, things began to change for the company.

The specifications writer retired. I left as work fell away and they hired new and less-experienced people. People sued them—several times, usually for something that they missed. The construction administration department could no longer talk their way out of the errors and conflicts with the documents.

The senior designer started to accept only waterfront projects for close friends. He didn't have the time to handle the details and no one with enough experience was available to do it for him. They went from a high-profitability, growing, and dynamic business to a static one. They lost their momentum.

The principals were perceptive enough to know that they needed to change something. They hired a management consultant, who met with limited success. They tried mergers, without success. They made functional changes. In 1984, I returned in a leadership role.

My new partners expected things to work just as they did before 1980. However, it was not possible to roll back the clock. Now there were more and hungrier competitors. Economic conditions had changed. Staff expected higher salaries and customers were demanding more in less time. Computers were becoming an issue. The company's inertia was gone.

Construction Management and Design-Build had taught that it is much more cost effective to have all of the issues examined as early in the process as possible. I knew that projects that were properly budgeted and designed within the budget had a much higher chance of success. We hired a senior construction manager to work with the senior designer to correct the problems, without changing workflows. Rather than solving the problem, hiring the construction manager signaled the end.

The partners resisted making additional changes and refused to fund solutions. As a group, they had tried too many things, without success. They began to practice willful ignorance. They took the—*we will try one, and if it works, we will talk about another,* approach. Little ever worked to their satisfaction. Computerization was becoming a problem. Partners' attitudes were—*You can try it if you want, but I will never touch a computer.*

A longtime drafter could try Cadvance, but only if it was profitable immediately. The company's engineers were trying AutoCAD, and they hired a drafter who knew how to use Microstation on UNIX, so they tried that too. None of it worked out.

With much pain and after years of trials and months of meetings, the firm's leadership authorized a group to find the best solution for their fourth or fifth CAD system. We looked at everything on the market—worldwide. We choose to concentrate on products that would work within an Agency-Construction-Management approach. We developed a rough business case for the process. In 1990, long before it was called BIM, we found the technology that looked like it might solve the problem. We began to look at how we could tweak our process to make it happen.

We ended up buying ArchiCad. It worked with our rough business case. We started with one seat. We trained two people in the week after we got the software. Within nine months, the entire staff was using ArchiCad, and we had five seats, with no additional outside training. A senior designer was using ArchiCad to prepare all documents. Drafters were using ArchiCad for construction documents. New interns were producing virtual reality fly-throughs after only two days on staff. The software worked. Mainly because of the working team moving ahead with zero company support.

The company's first software success didn't mean that things were getting better. It became apparent that we could not correct endemic organizational problems by buying new technology. The projects done per the rough business case went well. The projects done in a regular way did not. Broader changes to the firm operation were required, but not forthcoming.

The partners continued their willful—no technology bias and the business splintered into disconnected studios. We could not reach a consensus on how to move forward. Organizational change was not possible due to the legacy issues.

By November 1996, the problems had reached an impasse and Design Atlantic Ltd was born. As often happens in such situations, Design Atlantic Ltd resolved never to repeat the same mistakes. We decided to use technology as a tool to create better projects. We conceived a test platform for new ways of doing business. We did what was needed to be successful.

Don't let your business go the way of the company described above. Embrace change and do what is necessary to adapt to a connected way of working. The need to place people first, and to change rapidly are more acute now than before...

People Who Get It

You will find yourself in the process of constant reorganization of the highly creative individuals who deliver the process. You will find it difficult to create organization charts in this environment—because they change so fast. An organizational chart done today will be very different tomorrow. In practice, if you can create an accurate organizational chart of your team, you may not be doing BIG-BIM at all.

The BIG-BIM ecosystem needs to balance three essential elements—people, processes, and technology—to compete in a global economy and provide the information that decision makers need. Connected organizations are highly fluid. They bring the best team to get each assignment done, keying every staff member, at all levels, into the process.

With connected processes, people are much more important than structure. Since BIM and connected processes are rapidly evolving, they require different skill sets and different ways of looking at staff. With a connected process, the staffing structure is best when it is flat—with even senior staff participating at all levels.

Hire people that *get it.* People with vision are your priority. If you are an established business, these people will become your agents for change. If you are starting new, these people set the pace and define your processes. Everyone should connect into the process, from bottom to top. Don't fall into the trap of letting senior staff or firm leaders push this off onto young professionals that are (or seem to be) technologically adept. Allowing experienced staff to opt-out is the first step toward a failed implementation.

Experience has shown that several types of individuals become important as you move forward. You are looking for the ability to synthesize data and problem solve within the framework that you establish. For simplicity, we call this individual or group the Change Agent. The Change Agent must be able to communicate the vision and overcome the complacency that comes from long held beliefs and inertia. The Change Agent must have, or must build, power sufficient to overcome any roadblocks to the process. Over time, the Change Agent will ingrain the process into every aspect of your business. The Change Agent may wear all the hats or, a company leader might be the Change Agent with support from many others.

The Change Agent should start by bringing people together to create a series of small wins. Many small, incremental successes have been found to be much more successful in sustaining change than waiting for the big win. As more staff members buy-in, the process will reach a point where everyone is doing it, all the time. The Change Agent, leading by example, is the single strongest approach to embedding connected processes into your business.

With constant attention from the Change Agent and others in the company, you can achieve the full benefit from connected workflows. In time, you will find that your staff will reach a comfort level with the process. Over time, you make the changes required to support your BIM process. These changes should mirror the interests and talents of you and your staff.

The Change Agent must continually reinforce the process, even after your business fully internalizes the processes. As this happens, you will find that you need to create new positions that better mirror the way your staff is working.

To deliver the BIG-BIM process, we created a new type of project manager that we call 4Site Manager. The duties of the 4Site Manager include responsibility for connecting processes and a strong understanding of the impact of cost constraints on project outcomes. The job adds the responsibility for actively finding places where we can eliminate repetition. It requires a hands-on ability to work with modeling tools and data structures to manage information. Our 4Site Manager's priority is the owner's advocate—looking out for the owner's interests, both short and long-term. Flexibility, open-mindedness, and a broad understanding of the BIG-BIM process are all hallmarks of a person who can be successful in this position.

Cautionary Words for Owners

Several years ago, I attended a presentation by a corporation that is a BIM Leader with 300 employees. A principal and the company's CIO gave the performance. Between them, they made at least five glaring theoretical errors regarding BIM. Software vendors had planted the theories to further their position and the company's technology leaders believed the hype. The company used the software but did not understand how to use BIM to solve owner information needs for the long-term.

We are in a time of change, and some would say upheaval—a time of great confusion. A time where uncertainty allows unscrupulous actors to prosper. Too often those that profess expertise are the ones that create the biggest risks to any BIM implementation.

Confusion creeps into discussions of BIM for a variety of reasons. The complexity of the subject, coupled with market driven self-interest has led to many misunderstandings. The confusion created is usually unintentional, but sometimes not. The best approach is to be wary and to question everything, no matter how plausible or enticing the message.

BIM Washing is the name given to the subtle (and sometimes not so subtle) misrepresentations of BIM. It is pitching an incomplete idea using buzz words and hyperbole. BIM washing is to be avoided and should be called out for what it is.

Promoting a single software solution for meeting all BIM needs is bim washing—PERIOD.

Making BIM presentations, sales calls and reviewing the work of others when one does not have a hands-on understanding of the tools and techniques is hypocritical and bim washing.

Generating misleading reports and making images that appear to be generated in a BIM tool, but are presented with the intention of masking one's ability to manage data or graphic representation in BIM is bim washing.

Saying you can provide BIM services without first demonstrating capabilities in a practice session, demonstration or some other hands-on manner is bim washing.

Owners are the most frequent victim of bim washing, and sometimes the damage is self-inflicted. Because BIM has become widely popularized but remains poorly understood, BIM is expected by many customers without them knowing how to state the need.

Give me a BIM, any BIM, because I don't know enough to ask the right questions. This lack of clarity by owners makes bim washing, and unsupported marketing claims a concern, particularly for those that take the time and make the effort to learn how to deliver BIM professionally. Whether an owner or conscientious practitioner, the first and best, way to prevent bim washing is to understand that successful BIM is about sharing information among many programs and not an issue of picking a single, *right* BIM software program.

Letters to the editor, blog posts and seminar topics are increasingly application-centric. There is an unhealthy reinforcement of the concept that BIM is a just technological commodity, and all that you need to do is buy the right software to be successful. This false position supports the sales of vendors and consultants but does not accurately represent the fact that successful BIM revolves around connected processes supported by technology—not the other way around.

Self-styled experts selling a misguided vision of BIM may represent sophisticated approaches that require significant training and expertise. They make the path forward unclear. At best, they sub-optimize the adoption of BIM's potential. At worst, their smoke-and-mirrors advance personal agendas while harming others' ability to move forward. They leave those new to the subject wondering whether BIM is possible for ordinary people or worth the effort. Be on your guard and use the following checklist to help you determine if you are being bim washed:

☐ *If you think that by doing large projects using one of the big-name authoring tools, you are doing BIG-BIM—you have been bim washed;*

☐ *If you have standardized on the product lines of one software developer—in the cloud or not—you have been bim washed;*

☐ *If you output to files, whether DVDs, hard drives, or cloud servers as anything more than a workaround to allow little-bim—you have been bim washed. Beware, for in this case you are also promoting Data Rot;*

☐ *If you focus on LOD (whether Level of Detail, Level of Development, or Level of Definition), use manual methods to compare data and outputs of different systems or re-enter data from one system into the other—you have been bim washed;*

☐ *If you think that BIG-BIM will only happen in some future nirvana after all standards are in place—you have been bim washed;*

☐ *If you believe that BIG-BIM is an option only for those with large staffs, extensive training, and significant budgets—you have been bim washed;*

☐ *If you are laser focused on n-D (3D, 4D, 5D, etc.) rather than focusing on getting the right data to the right people in the right manner so they can make better decisions—you have been bim washed. It is not about the limiting of data to precise dimensions.*

In each of the cases above, one's heart may be in the right place, but it is still bim washing. Misconceptions about BIG-BIM have been the basis for presentations, educational programs, and chats around the water-cooler. Often well-meaning people lead others down the wrong path assuming an understanding of what they are advocating.

Using Building Information Models in a BIG-BIM ecosystem is worth the effort, but the issues can be daunting. Especially if you are establishing processes to share information among many software programs to visualize solutions while maintaining live data. By going through this book, completing the Workflow sections and understanding some simple concepts, you will inoculate yourself from bim washing or from becoming at risk of spreading bim wash.

A New Process

Unless your CAD/BIM Manager is also the CEO, he or she isn't the one to lead the process. If leadership for your BIM process becomes centered on your CAD or BIM Manager or other IT staff, you are positioned to remain in little-bim for a long time. Focused this way, you will end up with less than optimum results.

When talk around the water-cooler turns to BIM, the topic is often yesterday's CAD Manager and today's BIM Manager. Do you still have a person that does little more than manage the technology? If you do, you need to rethink how they will work in the BIG-BIM ecosystem.

Successful BIM implementations happen from the top-down. Far too many executives have seen the change to BIM as beneath them, insisting on pushing implementation in a manner much like their last major software update. To their chagrin, they find out that the process isn't living up to the promises. Some of those who approached BIM this way find themselves starting over after years of testing and training... At significant cost and lost inertia.

Technology-oriented staff members are critical to BIG-BIM. As your most technologically skilled employee, the person that is now your CAD/BIM Manager may (or may not) add value to the process and your company. But to do this in a BIG-BIM environment, they also need to have the proper people skills. The process isn't about technology.

Facilitating action is the key... not technology. It is about bringing people together in connected workflows to create better projects and more satisfied owners. The need to innovate and the pace of change impose a need for more high level strategic involvement than ever before. Using technology to solve problems and find the problems before they happen in life is the goal.

Properly connected a CAD or BIM Manager providing technical support, but focused on outcomes and discrete projects, has a place in this environment. Across the board, Information Technology (IT) staff should be enablers to support the goals of a BIG-BIM ecosystem. Earlier in the book, as part of the Core Concepts, we detailed the issues with misaligned IT departments that many are experiencing. Today, they may at best be redundant or at worst, harmful to a BIM process.

Until recently, CAD Managers (and BIM Managers) were critical to maintaining the complexity. This notion is on its way out. The focus of industry technology is on a trajectory to move away from the highly complex standards and layering conventions that are the hallmark of yesterday's systems. Such complicated approaches to standards are on their way to becoming transparent to users and connected into the tools.

BIG-BIM relies on tools that are standards-compliant, yet easy to use. In this environment, many people work with tools requiring limited technical know-how. Your teams need to interact with authoritative information sources, normalize data and manage web services connections. Teams will need people that can create and maintain databases, websites and, ideally, web applications. Someone must maintain and monitor security while making sure that everyone stays connected.

People fluent and fluid in many applications and many disciplines— not focused on only one, are the new standard to thrive in this environment. Users interact with the information critical to decision-making without needing to experience the complexity that underlays the current need. An expert intermediary is usually not required. Understanding the context is essential, directly controlling the complexity, not so much. Keep this in mind as you organize your team to work in this environment.

However, you handle the CAD / BIM Manager issue, realize that you cannot abdicate leadership for connected processes. Connected processes using BIM is a core business function requiring executive-level leadership. It needs people who are powerful in your organization. Experience has shown that if you leave this to middle management or treat it as CAD management, you will experience mixed results.

Do you need a BIM Manager in your organization? Or, do you need to define a new role of Information Manager or Process Manager? Decide for yourself. Do you need to dedicate a professional staff member to this task? Or do you need a computer technician? Is your staff better utilized to focus on your work? Rather than on your tools? Assess current and future systems. Will your systems need dedicated support or not? Will the complexity that underlays the current approach to little-bim subside? How will you organize your team to work in a BIG-BIM environment? Write the tasks and responsibilities that must be handled.

It's a Team Sport

Creating a cadre of non-traditional experts ready as the need arises, gives your teams added depth and strength. With a prescreened group of specialists, you may be able to increase your presence, better support your customers and create unique service offerings.

Think of yourself as the coach. In today's world bringing experts from many realms together and getting them to act as a team is an accomplishment. Too often seems as if you are herding the proverbial cats or coaching a power forward that won't share the ball, even if she loses the game.

BIG-BIM gives you a framework and tools to use in focusing experts of all types on delivering services across the life cycle of the built environment, to provide value in a context that is much larger than traditional design and construction defines. The conception that any one discipline can understand and support all areas of the built environment is flawed. The scale and scope of the issues are enormous.

Leaders in all disciplines are finding that their teams are much different than in the recent past. The level of expertise required is outstripping the generalist's ability to adapt. To respond to these demands today's projects often include an array of experts. Every project includes one or more specialists rarely involved in the recent past. Coders, psychologists, economists, security professionals, accountants, facade consultants, and many other specialists are required to support today's projects.

Adding new experts to projects imposes new issues. Tapping into expert talent has long been a tool for opening new markets and developing new expertise. When done, in a planned and organized fashion. Often experts come from disciplines with little connection to the established norms of the building industry.

In some cases, their work practices are difficult to incorporate. They don't understand what you expect of them, the format for deliverables or the context in which you work. Some have little or no consulting background. These experts require support and education to help them to integrate with your new connected process. Without such support, they may with the best of intentions, undermine project goals.

Other experts already use processes that connect planning, design, production, and operations. They may be further down the path to a connected process than your organization. In this situation, learn what you can from them and adapt your processes as required. Use these experts as an opportunity to learn from the experiences of others. Let them help you to build on your connected process expertise.

All you need is a willingness to change business and design processes, a commitment to embrace new technologies, a high level of responsibility and real leadership. You must be a great coach!

Outline your processes to connect nontraditional team members. Take the lead to incorporate them into the BIM process.

Communications

We have more than one stakeholder that quietly, behind the scenes follows every project communication, wherever they are in the world, 24x7. They only jump in when they perceive that something is going sideways. When they jump into a discussion thread, we take their input seriously. You quickly learn that if you don't hear from them; proceed with all due haste.

We still use email daily, but for how much longer? Texting, tweeting, and social networking have become essential. You get your news from the web. When you buy something, ofter you use a credit or debit card. When you travel, you make your plans with Expedia or one of the other travel sites. Your tools are mobile and app oriented.

The Cloud and social networks connect your work and personal networks of people and devices. For much of what you do, hard-copies and their digital counterparts are last generation's technologies. What a change from a few short years ago. In this highly-connected environment, unify the best available resources to allow everyone involved to stay easily informed.

The goal is to build trust, simplify communications, minimize errors, and keep everyone in the loop. The speed and frequency of communications make it critical to plan for your communications systems.

Too often, a business puts phone lines in place, sets up email, buys access to an online presentation system and considers the job complete. It is not even close. Multiple modes of interaction are the new normal.

There is no standard way of communicating that works for everyone. Some will engage in one-on-one communications that happen many times an hour. Others will monitor progress passively, only to participate when they see something of interest or concern. Your communications systems must accommodate both extremes.

Some prefer to communicate via written formats; others prefer verbal communications. Some communications are best when handled informally. Others require strict control. Mobile communications tools, video conferencing, screen sharing, webinars, and other technologies come into play. Each has their place. Include them in ways that further transparency and trust. A few things to consider as you move forward:

Email should only be used for noncritical communications. Email does not support the level of communications and collaboration that BIG-BIM requires. Email permits too much uncertainty. Too many opportunities exist to act counter to the needs of true collaboration. Too many things are missed. Communications are too critical. Consider taking a different approach.

One must have a way to collect every piece of data that the team creates and to put the information into a context that is usable and repeatable. You need something more than standard email. The tool you need is something like the BIM Mail that connects to the BIG-BIM data.

There are many overlapping communication needs in building industry businesses. Tools that enable financial management, project controls, marketing, correspondence, reference libraries, enterprise storage, electronic agreements and other tasks are critical. Blogs, websites, social networks, and cloud-based storage add to the mix. BIG-BIM adds models and object libraries, model servers and interfaces to your supply chain at new levels. Tools to administer or manage construction, manage facilities after construction, or manage facility portfolios are also critical.

No single solution handles all needs. The world has moved away from big software that did a few things well and many things half way, toward the world with apps that may only one thing, but do it perfectly.

Building industry businesses need to make every bit of their data accessible to this larger world of information. Behind the scenes, apps connect to shared data. Think of invoices that directly link to project tasks and submittals that directly attach to the room and air-handler where they apply, throughout the lifecycle of assets. Soon we may come to rely on these connections to maintain a real-time understanding of our global assets.

The Internet has been the proving ground for most BIG-BIM communications. It has evolved from a place for geeks to talk to other geeks, into a place where all of us get value. Widely distributed and web-enabled database applications that push and pull information give clues toward the capabilities on the horizon for the building industry.

Systems such as Yelp, Expedia, eBay, Amazon, iTunes, Amazon Prime, Google Express, the UK's NBS Product Library, BIMObject, Autodesk Seek, and thousands of others actively connect data from many sources to interact with users in ways that were thought to be impossible a few years ago. Such systems combine geographic information, product information, social networks, commerce, and other data to enable people to make near real-time decisions with just the information needed to decide.

BIM Mail is a fundamental step toward a full BIG-BIM ecosystem. Think of BIM Mail as a BIM social network. With BIM Mail, you access your organization's users and set up groups of people for your team. BIM Mail messages flow from and to your live models.

BIM Mail connects project communications directly to the BIG-BIM at the geographically referenced location that is appropriate to the message. Messages sent with BIM Mail give recipients a link back to the live model or file location so that they can see discussions in-context—no more rooting through files to find the drawing referenced in an email.

Using BIM Mail, you maintain a record of project communications. Decisions retained within the model support future understanding—reducing uninformed decisions later in projects—now you know why something was selected or what made a detail necessary, even years later.

Sketches with comments, external links, file attachments and many other forms of information are embedded. The idea is to enable team members to participate actively in the discussion about the project within the geospatial context of the model. BIM Mail is the glue that ties together connected teams and the enabler to allow hundreds of people in many locations to successfully work on projects concurrently.

Today you may not need to connect your data, tomorrow that will change. BIM Mail maintains connections to the place in the model in which you are working and need to track.

Discussions and attachments made within the Site Level attach to the Site, those to the Floor Plan attach to the Floor Plan, etc. Users review and comment in near real-time and context. At the same time, communications are time-coded, tracking changes to maintain a record of all actions. In practical terms, this means that communication about a site, building, room, or component becomes part of the building information model. Allowing the logic behind decisions to be followed from ideation to implementation and used, in-context.

> *Look at your current communications tools, with an eye toward eliminating (or at least reducing) the reliance on email. Document the tools you now use. Analyze how the data they create is archived. Evaluate your alternatives considering how you work and who you work with.*

When BIM Mail isn't available, opt for the best of breed web-based collaboration tools. There are always issues that fall outside any system. You will need to adapt and fill the gaps, working with more than one package to cover all the bases. We use many of Google's tools and Basecamp's suite of Web-based collaboration tools to supplement BIM Mail.

These days most people know and use Google's tools, at some level. Basecamp's products are a study in simplicity. Either can get the job done, if an immediate connection to models is not required. We use these tools knowing that our data is readily available in a form that can be connected to our models if needed. Onuma, Google, and Basecamp embrace the fact that most collaboration failures come from unclear communications and their products show it.

Basecamp's products make project communications and sharing as clear and as simple as possible. However, that is sometimes not the real problem. The communications problems that occur with BIM Mail, Google and Basecamp's products often revolve around a team member's refusal to allow others access to group communications tools. When this happens, decisions are made, out-of-context, and the traditional communications problems that have plagued projects over the years are the result.

No one communication tool will cover all business needs. There are a wide variety of business-related tools that exist to fill building industry communication needs. After testing many products, running cost analyses, working with customized solutions, and falling victim to a lot of hype and false promises; BIM Mail and Basecamp's tools have stood the test of time for us. They have been the best combination for our business, so they are what we use. We look for, and demand several things when we evaluate communications tools. Here is our basic checklist for the things we review:

☐ *Define the need and assess the functionality of the available options.*

☐ *Pricing structure. We typically eliminate any product that has per-project or per-user costs. The concepts of per-project and per-user costing work against the goal of every project and everyone using BIG-BIM (or little-bim for that matter). When we buy a new tool, we make sure that there are few roadblocks to full implementation as possible. We are looking for value for our investment, within the context in which we work.*

☐ *Easy to use? Look hard and critically at ease of use. We can usually tell within minutes if a potential new tool is going to work out.*

☐ *Does the system restrict our data? We absolutely, positively NEVER allow vendors to hold our data hostage. Use systems that give you access to your data, even if at some point, you move to another vendor. Make sure that you own your data and that the system allows interconnected and shareable data. Look for terms such as Open-Source, Open-Standard, and Web Services API to be sure that your data isn't locked away where you cannot get to it in the future. Try the vendor's backup system and see what you get, as early as possible.*

☐ *Does the system try to do too much? We are wary of the all-in-one communication systems. In a world of apps, the path to excellence is to use the absolute best and most affordable tool for each job, rather than relying on an all-in-one package. Traditionally the all-things-for-all-users packages have been very expensive and at best offer mediocre performance. On the surface, managing multiple database systems to handle business needs is more complicated and costly than using an all-in-one solution. When using multiple systems, this technology has gotten so inexpensive and so mature that there is no excuse to delay or charge for this level of support.*

*Transparency leads to self-correcting behavior—*Admiral Thad Allen, US Coast Guard.

Do Something Different

Take every opportunity to reinforce the concepts in your network of staff, consultants, and customers. Do something that you have never done. Take a risk. Learn a new skill. Build deep knowledge and broad interests to become an expert. Success comes from planning, doing and, producing results.

From the beginning, we worked to create and use information in every part of our projects. With the side benefit of better documents and nicer images. Our underlying goal was to level out the cyclical nature of our business. We were tired of the ups and down. We believed that the tools we now equate with BIM, and new processes would generate opportunities for residual income streams.

In the early days, we realized that we could not sell the tools and process directly. Stakeholders didn't care how we solved their problems. No one was willing to pay extra. The benefits were not apparent or easily measured. The concepts were too complicated. The whole idea was foreign to everyone, in and outside the industry.

When we talked about the technology, people's eyes glazed over. We were geeks before geeks became fashionable. Only by using the technology and processes to do a better job, was there any justification for embracing this new way of working. We stopped talking about how we worked and the tools we used. Internally, we used the tools and adapted our processes to do better work for our customers. This strategy worked. It was not long until we had schools, environmental centers, healthcare facilities and many other project types completed, in BIG-BIM—Without much fanfare.

The term BIM alone did not describe what we were doing. It certainly didn't explain how we were working. The models were only a part of the equation. What got the results were all the things that revolve around the models. By delivering better results in an environment where owners had better decision-making information, we could create better projects and become more valuable. Customers were willing to pay to get their projects done better.

The term BIG-BIM was intended to describe better what was happening in our practice. BIG-BIM became synonymous with using technology to improve processes to relieve customers' stress. To help them get certainty about their projects. You can explain this to customers. It is easy for them to understand that they benefit if you use technology to get them more and better decision-making information, earlier in the process. Customers see value in certainty. They understand it and are willing to pay for it.

Case Study
Count Custodians

When one experiences a BIG-BIM deployment one learns that it is impossible to preplan for everything that will change as the ecosystem matures. New things happen, often in unexpected ways and often with significant unplanned benefits. Such benefits are hard to quantify, but can result in much of the return-on-investment from making the change.

What are the interesting aspects of this system?

When a BIG-BIM ecosystem in place, new things happen, and new opportunities come to the front.

Illustrates the rapid turnaround that is possible when new uses are found for the data in BIG-BIM ecosystems.

Illustrates the time and resource savings that BIG-BIM ecosystems can offer over current approaches to the counting problems that plague many of current funding and management systems.

Shows the phased-in use of facility data to get immediate benefit from implementing BIG-BIM ecosystems via file exchanges as an interim step to live information exchanges as resources allow.

You may have read the title of this Case Study and thought, this couldn't apply to me. You might want to reconsider.

The email thread that follows comes from communications between the Manager charged with controlling State-wide funding allocations and the person that maintains a school customer's ecosystem. The conversation details the types of unexpected benefits that happen every day with BIG-BIM.

Those that fund public schools work hard to distribute scarce funds equitably to support education. Federal, state and local governments allocate their resources in a variety of ways. In some cases, it is as simple as, *the school needs $X, here you are...* In most cases, the decision revolves around some computation that may (or may not) relate to actual need. Often the calculations to determine allocations require the use of a metric, such as—dollars per student, support staff per type of classroom, or square feet per projected student population. These parameters often require complex calculations that require data inputs from many sources. Facility data, census data, enrollment data, standards for costs and time, and much more come into play.

Location: Delaware, USA.

Some school systems use custodial count as a funding metric. Custodial counts impact directly on personnel funding and require a complex assessment that relates funding, area, space type and use.

Committees meet to agree on the procedures; legislatures enact laws to enforce implementation, and capital facility administrators work to apply the metrics equitably. How much money each school (or school system) receives is directly tied to these metrics and how they are applied. The process is laborious, complicated, and fraught with the potential for errors of all types.

The email thread that follows illustrates how BIG-BIM can help one to standardize the capital funding process while improving efficiency and fairness. It is also an example of the significant, unplanned benefits that come from implementing a BIG-BIM ecosystem:

To BIG-BIM Manager—Friday afternoon.

Hi—It was yet again another very informative meeting this morning. Thank you for taking the time. Attached is the spreadsheet the State uses to calculate the custodial units.

Equivalents of classrooms as mentioned may be any space that isn't called a classroom, yet is an instructional place, such as a library. A library can be equivalent to one or many classrooms depending on its size. We take the average classroom size and divide that into the library square footage to determine the number of equivalent classrooms.

Many times, a stage in an auditorium is used as a music classroom and can count as an equivalent classroom. For offices, the State takes the average size of an office, per our standard formula. Then we either count a whole bunch of smaller spaces as one office or count the number of offices that fit into large front office areas where on the floor plan may show just a big open area, vs. the actual partition walls.

Attached is the construction formula/parameters of the size of buildings the State will fund. The State's formula is where we find the average sizes of classrooms and offices. — Capital Project Manager

To Capital Project Manager (with cc: Director of Facilities & Operations for the school with a BIG-BIM ecosystem) — Friday evening.

We added a metric to the high school model to manage custodial counts, as you suggested. The short version:

We created a new metric called Custodial and exported all spaces in the school to Excel. We then categorized each space based on your Excel spreadsheet and pushed the spreadsheet back into the model.

At that point, we had every space in the model classified, per the State's standard for computing custodial needs, so that we could have the system do the counts. In the case of the cafeteria and other spaces dependent on seating, we added a prediction for seats. We don't have data on actual seating counts.

We then re-exported the data to Excel, deleted unused columns for clarity and connected the appropriate categories to your spreadsheet, so that it now computes from the model data. The spaces tab within your spreadsheet came directly from the high school model in the BIG-BIM ecosystem and were only cleaned up for clarity.

We did no calculations outside your original spreadsheet. As part of this exercise, we combined categories from your spreadsheet to simplify the counts (i.e., locker rooms and gang toilets both have a 0.5 multiplier, so they became a single type).

This entire exercise started at 5 PM today and took 1:45 hours. At this point, even using the spreadsheet approach, a new school with spaces categorized in the system should take about 20-minutes total. Should this same effort happen via web services, it would be complete in near real-time. Creating the web services links will take a couple of days to prepare, should you wish this report to be functional state-wide. Hopefully, this will give you some valuable ammunition for your discussions. How long does it take to complete the same effort manually?

btw. The categorization is visible in the model by turning on the Custodial attribute for any building on campus. We can pull images from the model to show this if they are needed. We don't know what the high school's current custodial count is, so please don't use this for any State to District negotiation. — BIG-BIM Manager

To BIG-BIM Manager — Tuesday morning.

Wow, this is great!

If I were to take high school plans today and started a custodial evaluation it would take me at least 3 hrs, between evaluating the floor plan, double checking, entering the data, and starting the official notification. If there are no ambiguities in the plans, where I would have to contact the district for clarifications. Uncertainties in school's plans frequently make it take much longer.

As per my records, I have this high school at (21) custodians, and your calculations show (27). I must go back and see where the discrepancies lie.

As earlier mentioned, it took me more than three months to finish another school district's total Custodial Count evaluation on 32 buildings. As we often find, they had many ambiguities in their plans. — Capital Project Manager

To Capital Project Manager (with bcc: Director of Facilities & Operations) — Tuesday morning.

Thanks—If the Districts have their plans in the system, the process of 'permanently' removing the ambiguities would occur naturally. The only variable might be in situations where they are planning new work (the proposed high school addition is at the bottom of the Spaces tab, as a for instance).

Were the other School District's plans added to the system, and you opted for the spreadsheet export approach, you 'might' need an hour to do this. Were you to choose the web services approach; you are looking at the time to open the system and go to reports. In the three months that you took previously for the other district, you could have done this assessment for most of the Districts in the state, including the input of the core models for the schools.

Classroom counts are as accurate as the information that we extracted from the State's current facility database.

Suggestion: You might want to consider revising the formulae to compute 'equivalent classrooms' from the total teaching areas calculation, now that you can get to actual square footage per use type. That way, any space used for instruction would be treated the same, rather than a 1200 square foot classroom getting one custodian and a 4000 square foot media center (@750 square foot per custodian) getting 5.33 custodians for a total of 6.33 custodians. As an 'equivalent classrooms' formula: 5200 square foot of instructional space divided by 900 square feet per custodian = 5.78 custodians. It could even get more precise by assigning one value to traditional teaching stations and a different value to non-traditional instructional spaces — BIG-BIM Manager

To BIG-BIM Manager — Tuesday afternoon.

At a past Metrics Committee meeting, we had talked about how the custodial formula is way overdue for an overhaul. Many schools now, to take the most advantage of their space, put rows of computers in their halls (as a common space area), where students take tests or perform other computer work (therefore deeming it an instructional space).

We can take the square footage of the hallways and divide by classroom area for equivalent classrooms. Another sore area is the heating plant. Systems and methods have changed for heating whereas, in the past, more hours were needed to run the old boilers, etc. The last time the custodial formula was officially updated was more than a decade ago. — Capital Project Manager

To Director of Facilities & Operations, — Tuesday afternoon.

Having your school in the can allowed us to respond to one of the State's concerns with a couple of hours of work, in a way that the State's Capital Project Manager may not have seen before. Perhaps it will kick things over the top. — BIG-BIM Manager

It should come as no surprise that people use metrics to further their own ends and to maximize funding. BIG-BIM makes the tools available to connect data from many sources to make such funding decisions with facts, in near real-time. Leveling the field for all schools.

FIVE

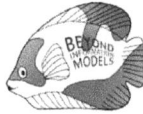

ASSETS, NOT PROJECTS

Professionals working with the built environment tend to focus on projects as the end goal. A key to the future is to focus on ASSETS as opposed to discrete projects.

With a project focus, improvements from a little-bim approach correct only a tiny subset of the problems we face. Global solutions require a broader context. Fixing projects may ease the symptoms but does not cure the disease. The industry must embrace the larger world of built environment assets.

A New Focus

There is a growing awareness across the building industry of how critical it is to move toward managing assets, rather than merely managing projects. When we think of something as an asset, it tends to get our attention for a long time. When we think of a project, we think of something that is going to be over at some point. Usually in short order.

Our built environment, in all its forms, is something that we want to think about for a long time. When we think of our assets as projects that are complete; bridges start crumbling, buildings lose energy efficiency, and manufacturing facilities lose productivity. Without on-going attention, our projects eventually become worthless assets.

It is easy to see the effects of project-think. When the National Parks Service recently celebrated their 100th Anniversary, a Washington Post lead story was about the $11 Billion in delayed maintenance last year. We all suffer from the potholes, poorly maintained bridges and other deterioration that comes from deferred maintenance of our highways. Every hospital, school or public building has an ever-growing list of unfunded, deferred maintenance items for their facilities. Untold billions of dollars are needed to overcome the systemic problems created by our focus on projects.

Thinking about our built environment as an asset promotes the holistic, lifecycle thinking needed in our increasingly complex world. But what is it that is meant by ASSET?

Paraphrasing the definition of asset from the International Organization for Standardization (ISO)—an asset is an item, thing or entity that has potential or actual value. Assets include people, property, real estate, information technology, fleets, infrastructure, intellectual capital, resources, financial holdings and more.

Based on this definition, everything in the built environment can (and should) be considered an asset. The ISO 55000 Asset Management, and ISO 15686 Service Life Planning standards codified the fact that the information about our assets needs to be managed using defined processes. The standards call for the establishment of a BIG-BIM ecosystem for managing asset information and total costs of ownership— for without full control of the information related to your assets, you don't know what you have and can't support the objectives or purpose (the mission) you are working to achieve.

The Coast Guard frequently operates in emergency conditions and it is not surprising it became a leader in connecting mission thinking to asset management using Building Information Models. Without asset management, the Coast Guard wouldn't have real-time information about their ships—knowing their location, how much fuel and supplies they have, and a myriad of other things. They couldn't have the right amount of fuel and supplies in the correct locations for their Cutters to rapidly refuel, resupply and head out again. In emergency situations, such information becomes more than valuable. It becomes the difference between life and death.

Showing how your assets relate to each other using Building Information Models is beneficial to the success of any entity. Funding discussions become easier to manage with accurate information that visually represents conditions. Relating finances to the built environment using models allows informed decision-making by any stakeholder—not just subject-matter experts—before errors cost significant money, time, or pain. Because BIG-BIM enables the storage and enhancement of information, the common goal of including all interested parties and assuring the necessary quality at the lowest reasonable cost, becomes possible.

Information is an Asset

It may seem counterintuitive, but by focusing on assets, many of the highly complex tasks that now require training and expertise become easier for all stakeholders. New processes and new ways of using data become possible.

Information about the built environment is an asset. When you treat information as an asset, you begin to make a mental shift that allows you to adopt useful web-tools and business processes. BIM becomes the standard information source to find the value in your assets as professionals move toward connected decisions.

Establishing a BIG-BIM ecosystem that defines how to share information in an open and secure manner is the starting point. Enterprises with structured information quickly find productivity and economic benefits as they move to BIG-BIM. Organizations with poorly structured databases, freeform spreadsheets, and disconnected snippets of information find that they have much more work to do to make the BIG-BIM transformation.

Those with much experience in the vagaries of planning, design, and construction have learned that the smallest errors in decisions at the outset of projects can have significant consequences. Things that seem like minor issues, that can be easily corrected later, often escalate to become major problems as things progress. The BIG-BIM ecosystem helps find and correct these minor issues early, to minimize their impact later in the process.

When data is connected, and shared among many software programs, the information begins to inform decisions in unplanned ways that reveal project opportunities and expose potential threats. You minimize first day mistakes. The goal should be to connect everything possible in automated ways. Yet, in many cases today, we continue to make file exchanges... knowing that we will change as soon as possible.

Moving toward a focus on assets moves us toward connected (systems) thinking. Asset-focused professionals are concerned about the assets through their entire lifecycle. With such a focus, those working in different phases begin to understand the downstream (lifecycle) impacts of what they do.

Most tasks in the facility lifecycle require only simple graphics or no graphics at all. The BIG-BIM ecosystem uses high complexity graphics requiring powerful, dedicated computing devices when needed but does not burden the process with that load at other times.

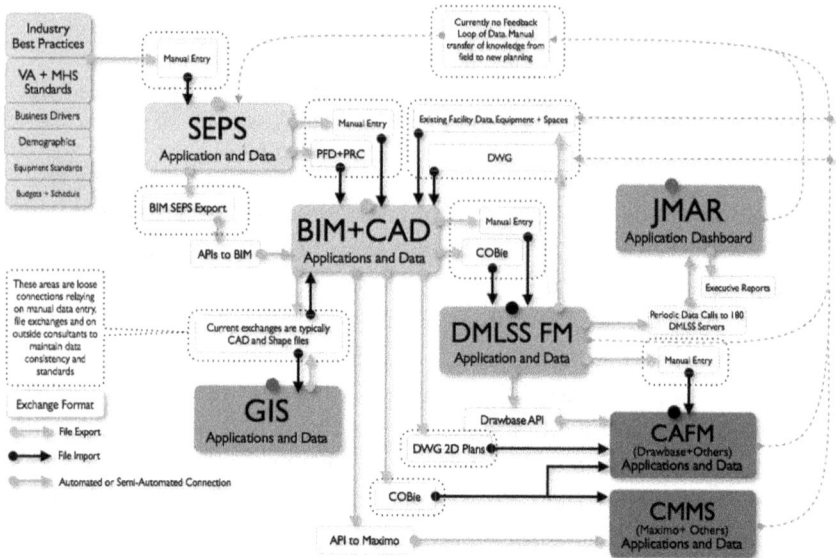

Web-enabled models give you the means to visualize the information about your assets in powerful and precise ways. Data comes from internal, and external sources and is analyzed and refined using a myriad of tools. The process makes the data about assets richer and more complete. All with the goal of increasing the owner's certainty of outcomes.

For example, Facility Managers get along quite nicely without visual models of column baseplates and other structural systems. They get great benefit from motor sizes, filter numbers, pump ratings and other mechanical data points that may need little or no graphics. BIG-BIM tools efficiently enable sharing asset information in a way that best supports individual needs.

The Structural Engineer, knowing what the Facility Engineer might need from the structural systems, makes them available to support facilities management. Conversely, the Facility Engineer, understanding what the Structural Engineer will need when the next renovation occurs, does likewise. You begin to build a self-sufficient cycle of people working to seed lifecycle needs, rather than merely fulfilling project needs.

Suddenly, the industry leapfrogs current approaches. If asset information is available through open-standards, new tools and processes can be more readily adopted to provide the most up-to-date benefits possible, while using existing data and infrastructure, rather than starting anew.

Organizations are successfully deploying BIG-BIM ecosystems to help them manage their assets. Case Studies in this book trumpet their successes. People in these organizations benefit from tools that give them just the information they need to make the decisions at hand. They experience little of the complexity, even when working with highly complex systems. The complexities are transparent to their users.

When you used Expedia to book an airline ticket or Yelp! to research, find and rate a restaurant, you used a system that functions like BIG-BIM. You only interacted with a tiny, focused part of a much larger system. Behind the scenes, is a highly complex ecosystem, but you only interacted with the parts you needed, to do what you needed to do. Today, much of the work done by companies is like the manual creation of the PDF files that you downloaded for your trip to Frankfurt.

Using today's little-bim or most other standalone software programs might be thought of as the equivalent of logging onto Expedia and requesting a PDF download of all the flights from Dublin to Frankfurt so that you could select a flight at some future date. By the time you completed the download, read through and understood the many pages of schedules and went back to book your trip, things would have changed, and you would have to start over. You would have been better off calling a travel agent.

The only difference is that the firms send someone to each of the airline's offices, copy down their schedules on a notepad, return to the office, type the flight schedules in a word processor, print them as PDFs and upload them to a server for your downloading pleasure. Not only is it slow, but filled with redundancies and inefficiencies.

Worst of all, this is how little-bim software programs work today. Most Internet sites would be of little use and totally dysfunctional if they worked this way. For school systems, healthcare systems, government agencies, and most multi-facility owners the little-bim processes provided by most of today's design and construction professionals are frustrating. Their processes don't respond to the needs of asset owners and operators.

It is now common practice for internet sites to do the things much like the functions needed in the building industry. Asset owners need to make connections between many different data sources to do what they must do to achieve lifecycle benefit.

Some owners and a few design and construction professionals are doing the same type of things with BIG-BIM. People use their models as graphic interfaces to get the information they need and don't have to be concerned about other issues. They make asset information readily available, using systems that can push and pull information from anywhere using a service-oriented-architecture type of approach. They have learned that asset data isn't worth much if it is not accessible and accurate.

You have the power to change the game. Use BIG-BIM to start with better information. Increase the likelihood that decisions will result in better and more sustainable outcomes. Achieve the vision of BIG-BIM by tying together the traditional one-off project approach with asset management. Look at the building industry in a new light to become more resilient. Information is a critical asset—establishing a BIG-BIM ecosystem that allows your asset information to flow to many people over many platforms is the way to go.

Asset Information: Levels of Detail

Packing LOD into discrete steps may be beneficial, if the goal is to create a contract production requirement. But only if the aim is to control the work of a room full of technicians. It does little to help an owner coordinate and manage the complex data that connects to the BIG-BIM ecosystem over time. Be wary of those that push to require systems that focus on delivering a specific LOD. They are reflecting traditional ways of working that sub-optimize the BIG-BIM ecosystem.

Big Data is a term understood to describe the vast amounts of information available to us all. It is important to realize there are different types of information available about every asset. Different people want to know different things at various times about an asset. The requests for information occur in different sequences depending on the data, the project, the team, and the owner.

Descriptions and explanations don't do justice to the ability of an information model to handle the complexity of built environment activities. For this reason, this book includes Workflows and Case Studies that allow you to get more hands-on. Over the last twenty years, much effort has gone into trying to quantify the information contained in a model over time.

The concept called Levels of Detail (LOD) attempts to order the information required at different phases in the design and construction processes. Conceptually, you need less detail at the beginning of a project. You add more details during the development and construction processes, followed by even more data when operating the project. While different LOD approaches divide project phases into five, six, seven, or more steps, there are in fact too many levels of detail to count.

Level of Detail Origin Story

A manifestation of BIG-BIM might have the highest possible LOD from the standpoint of data and the lowest possible LOD from the viewpoint of graphic representation. In fact, a Red Dot model, or tabular database can carry every imaginable data point.

On the morning of January 15, 2004, on an airplane headed to Cleveland, Ohio, Kimon Onuma sketched out what was to become known as the concept of Levels of Detail (LOD). In the sketch, he referred to the idea as *Data Repository Model, Level Definition*.

The idea was to describe a sequential model development process implementable in a fiscally constrained environment. It involved first connecting existing information and making it computable. Gradually, over time, information was added in ways that required little new funding. As facilities changed, the process was captured to make the information in the model more complete. Until the model grew to become a virtual representation of the real-world condition.

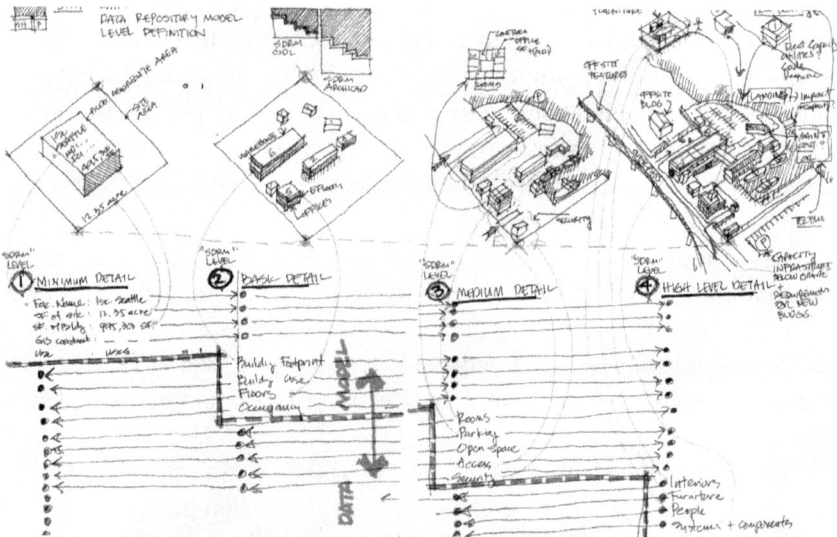

Over time, the LOD conception has evolved to be a foundation of BIG-BIM and the basis of our ability to integrate data in ways that enable connected decision-making.

Since the release of *BIG-BIM little-bim* in 2006, many have written about Levels of Detail, Levels of Development, and similar structures for making Building Information Models. When you read their material, you understand the positions that different organizations and systems have taken. For example:

> *Most focus on LOD as a prescriptive requirement. LOD is used to define what must be included in the model to conform to a contract or team working requirement. Others focus on LOD as a measure of capability. In this view, LOD divides users and companies to assess their competence, much as one might use a qualifications exam. Another segment uses LOD to describe the stage in the development of the model. This approach most closely aligns with the early vision.*

> *There are also hybrid approaches that try better to define LOD and the inherent complexity of information models. These approaches either break out information from the virtual model or create new acronyms that, in their view, better describe the process of developing models.*

None of the approaches accurately represents what is happening as the model develops. Each is a rough approximation of what is taking place with little-bim. In a BIG-BIM ecosystem, LOD has almost no value. There are near infinite levels of detail for many metrics and data in BIG-BIM.

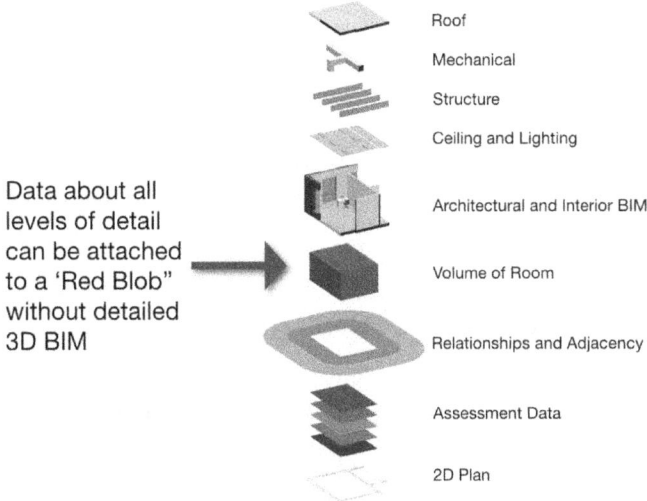

Roof

Mechanical

Structure

Ceiling and Lighting

Data about all
levels of detail
can be attached
to a 'Red Blob"
without detailed
3D BIM

Architectural and Interior BIM

Volume of Room

Relationships and Adjacency

Assessment Data

2D Plan

For most currently accepted LOD definitions, the Red Dot model would at best be the lowest level. Most LOD scales ignore the data, even though the data is the most valuable part of the model, by far. The data could represent everything about the Red Dot model, up to and including the data for drawing a highly detailed graphic representation of the object the Dot represents.

Use LOD as you must. In some situations, you will have no choice if you wish to participate. Keep in mind that LOD is little more than a mechanism for assessing, controlling, and paying for work modeled in desktop authoring tools. The real value and most of the power falls in other places.

You can create information models in steps, with little or no data loss in the transitions. By setting up a concept that defines a long-range plan for data, information models can be implemented much like one might implement a contacts database—over time. In a BIG-BIM environment, this is the preferred means of moving from zero to a resilient and fully realized enterprise model system.

BIG-BIM becomes beneficial very quickly, especially when created in an agile development environment that isn't sequential, and it can be added to continuously as asset conditions change and new information becomes available.

You start with a container or little-red-blob on the site. You then collect and connect existing data. Then you add massing, then some spaces. You tag areas for costs, metrics, and type. This, and that are added because they are available, or it seems like the data might be beneficial. You throw everything you have into the little-red-blob that is quickly becoming a data-rich information model.

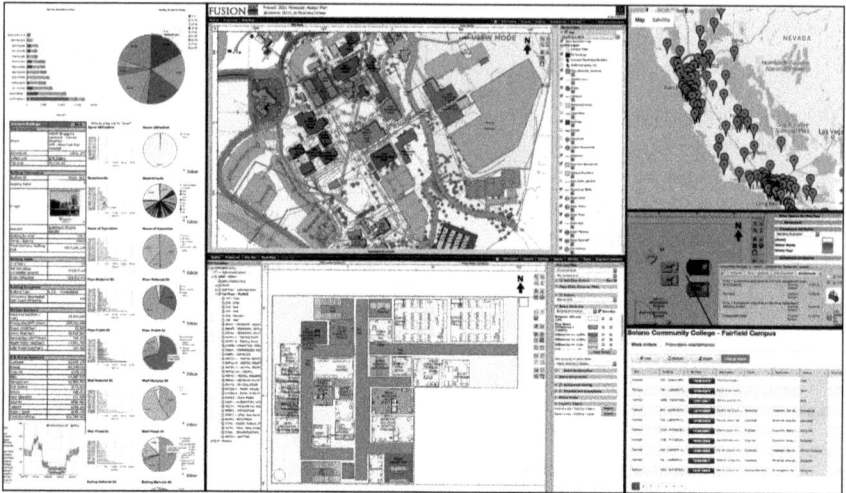

From step one, the model is computable. It can compute areas, show relationships, generate pie charts, and plans showing metrics. You can visualize blocking and stacking. Project costs are overlaid with a timeline to enable ta better understanding of the overall concept. Will the facility fit on the site? Can we afford to move forward in this direction? Can we use this approach to satisfy mandate X?

BIG information models progress through an infinite number of Levels of Detail. The graphic representation is one of the less important items on this scale. Models at any LOD can be (and are being) used to manage assets and portfolios in some of the largest enterprises. In a BIG-BIM environment, even the lowest LOD model can give an owner the ability to do capital asset planning, work-order-management, scenario planning and much more.

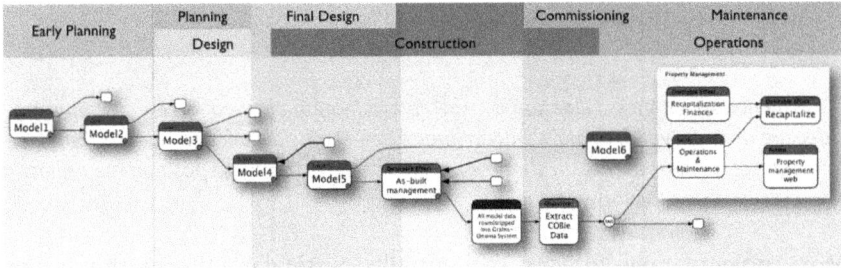

The sequential processes at the heart of most uses of LOD harken back to the siloed workflows that most BIM experts seek to eliminate. Is a systematic process that mirrors workflows where each trade builds their model the best way? Is this the best way to manage the life cycle of facilities?

LOD has little value beyond helping to describe processes that use little-bim authoring, analysis, and collaboration tools. Only when confined to control of design and construction operations is LOD necessary. In this arena, LOD helps to control the sequence of events, the scope of work product and contract compliance. Outside this area, LOD quickly falls by the wayside. LOD assumes a sequential process in the development of information models, as occurs in design and construction, some of the time. The reality is that things are complex and messy. Most of the effort does not happen sequentially.

Look at each task and stage of the BIM process. Understand that, contrary to many publications, Levels of Detail is little more than a coarse-grained approximation of what is taking place. There are too many LOD to count. This is where BIG-BIM comes to the rescue. Embrace the fact that models at all stages can simultaneously be maintained as live assets. BIG-BIM enables the data and models to be used when and where they are needed to get the job done. Across the lifecycle of built environment assets.

Validation: Planning Process

The dictionary defines validation as: the determination of the degree of validity; to declare or make valid; to mark with an indication of official sanction; to establish the soundness of; corroborate. In short, you use the tools at hand, to position the project for success, from as many viewpoints as possible.

Most projects move forward sequentially, particularly during the design and construction phases. The effort to deliver design and construction projects in a BIG-BIM ecosystem focused on assets, fall broadly on little-bim tools and the processes they enable. However, there are changes in approach that you should consider, some subtle and some not so much. The sections that follow detail what happens in the design and construction phases of lifecycle BIG-BIM.

In a BIG-BIM ecosystem, projects ideally start with processes designed to validate owner needs and objectives about their use of assets. There are many approaches to consider. In the UK, validation might rely on Employer's Information Requirements (EIR), Asset Information Requirements (AIR) and other highly formalized tools. In other venues, validation might look much like a highly-detailed feasibility study. Whatever the format, validation processes form the foundation for all further efforts. The underlying goal is to explore and eliminate the potential train-wrecks before one designs, builds, or expends significant resources.

Eliminating the obvious, and sometimes not so obvious, errors at the earliest stage of a project minimizes the unintended consequences of decisions made with too little information. One is of course still making predictions, but now they are predictions supported by validated data. You can describe the validation process as *filling a box with all the information, parts and pieces required to create a successful project.*

The process starts with gathering all the available information, structuring the information for open sharing. You quickly use available tools to create reports for expert and stakeholder review of project details, to best define and understand current conditions and desired outcomes. You see project information in many ways, allowing insight into critical early decisions that will impact the entire lifecycle of the project.

Validation helps determine the types of models required, the procurement approach, construction methods and other elements of a project. Data about finances, user needs, energy and much more connect in-context, using BIG-BIM tools—resulting in improvements in productivity and profitability throughout the lifecycle.

Validation of project needs and objectives focuses everyone's attention on the first decisions that make-or-break projects and confirms owner requirements. It gives the owner a high level of certainty about the validity of their intended outcomes. To help others achieve this goal, you will need to consider five core issues:

1. Use technology to give immediate access. Clear and open communication is the priority. Without this, nothing else is possible.

2. Optimize your working practices, methods, and behaviors to get maximum value for the beginning steps. Create a culture where the team can work together to envision projects—before anyone designs anything.

3. Build structures that capture everything, then share the information. Eliminate repetition so that you do your work once and use the information for many purposes. Obviously, you can't share everything with everybody. Security will always remain an issue. However, we can share most of what we do... and we should.

4. Capture everything in dependable and reusable archives. Use real-world rules about how things relate to each other to eliminate the mundane and speed critical decisions. Pay attention to the details.

5. Use everything at your disposal to make things clear. Reuse data whenever and wherever possible.

Prototypes created during the process enable decisions about costs early in the process, significantly improving the accuracy of capital budgets. By handling these core issues, your process becomes more efficient, and you reduce downstream errors. Project results show significant improvements.

We have seen our ability to better predict bid results improve by using the process. Our public bid results rarely exceed the stated budget. Our projects progress more smoothly and finish on time.

Our customers seldom spend much, if any, of the budgeted contingency funds. We have fewer change orders and fewer requests for information than our colleagues that are not using a preliminary validation process. One might dismiss these results as flukes. Nevertheless, we have consistently seen such outcomes for more than ten years.

The comprehensive set of data created for the models becomes the base for further development and remains relevant even after completion. The models give the owner immediate value well beyond the costs of preparing the Validation Study. The models generate seed data that gives the design team the ability to begin their work at an advanced stage. The prototypes immediately enable work order systems and can populate structured data systems, such as COBie and other standards-based approaches to jump start operations controls. The data from the Validation Process has many uses in many realms.

Knowing where and how to apply the data for immediate benefit becomes your expertise. Validation isn't a linear or automated process. It requires human intervention and is the place where experience and knowledge have the greatest impact on project outcomes.

Start your first Validation Process by identifying the strategies for successfully designing, constructing, and managing the facility, project, or process. Then create a clear, objective definition of quality. When you define success at the beginning, you begin to set appropriate expectations, develop solid project controls, and have a better way to measure your performance over time.

Standardize the way that you do Validation Studies. Keeping in mind that each study will have different issues and needs that require attention from various types of professionals. Focus on your customer's needs with laser-like intensity. Exploit the successes that come from this focused approach. Then repeat the process. Over time, you will begin to see quantum gains in your results.

The size and technical expertise of your business will drive your approach to Validation. Adding Validation to your toolbox makes you the steward of the owner's assets. The process creates an archive of information in interoperable databases—allowing others to benefit from it for many years to come. Validating owner needs and objectives to result in information that is itself an asset is smart.

The internet and BIG-BIM don't solve all problems without human involvement. Nor do they always provide the right answers. Sometimes the answers they provide seem correct but are in fact wildly inaccurate. The wrong search terms, degraded data and other factors affect the answers. People with the expertise and knowledge to identify and manage such issues remain the linchpins of fact-based decision-making in this environment.

Blogger and columnist, Kevin Drum put it best when he wrote, ...the Internet is now a major driver of the growth of cognitive inequality. Or in simpler terms, the Internet makes dumb people dumber and smart people smarter.

Data Integration

Often, finding the information you need to do the right thing is a major task, fraught with smoke and mirrors. Refer to the Core Concepts—Data Is a Strategic Asset *for the right questions to ask if you find yourself in this situation.*

Repeatable, substantiated, and documented project information—who, what, where, why, when and always how—is integral to the successful Validation process. The more one knows about the details that may directly or indirectly impact the project, the better chance you can envision potential outcomes accurately.

Start by focusing on site and location related constraints. Do you have access to high resolution and real-time Geographic Information System data? Or is Google Earth your best resource? Do you have access to a boundary or topographic survey? Are they tied to a coordinate system that will allow them to be used to supplement and inform GIS? Do you have GIS layers for hydrology, census, and other applicable data? The list of data, while long and exhaustive, is vital to understanding the project.

Next, focus on time and resources constraints. Who will be involved? What are their restrictions? When must the project be ready to occupy? Is the owner connected into a BIG-BIM ecosystem? Is a connected delivery team in place? What can they do? What drives costs in this location?

Consider all of the other issues that impact the project. What are the points requiring critical decisions? When must the decisions occur? Is documentation available for existing conditions? On paper, or CADD? What little-bim resources are available? Does the owner have a capital asset management program connected with their business process and other asset information?

These questions represent only the beginning. Depending on the answers to such questions, you may find that your data integration effort revolves around connecting data, data extraction and verification to support your project. In most situations, today, owners have not created nor implemented BIM of any type. Nor have they connected their archives and business processes. In these cases, your efforts become much like any traditional fact-finding and site survey task, with the added requirement of processing the results to connect with a BIM software program.

Whether you are connecting existing data or creating new digital assets from scratch, manage the project information within a standardized data structure. The goal is to capture normalized data that easily connects with rules-based planning systems. Ideally the data should be added to an open-standards-based BIG-BIM server.

If access to such a tool isn't available, manage the data so that your organizing structure will easily map to others. Make sure that each bit of data appears only one time, so that updates will need to happen only once. Use some form of an open-standard shared database structure that allows normalized information connections to other tools. If you must go this route, a low-level example might be a normalized spreadsheet with correctly named predefined rows and columns for use in seeding BIG-BIM systems.

Amass a group of tools and resources that enable you to rapidly fill-in-the-blanks about any project issue.

Program Analysis

Your goal is to uncover, and objectively study the issues that must be addressed to create successful project outcomes.

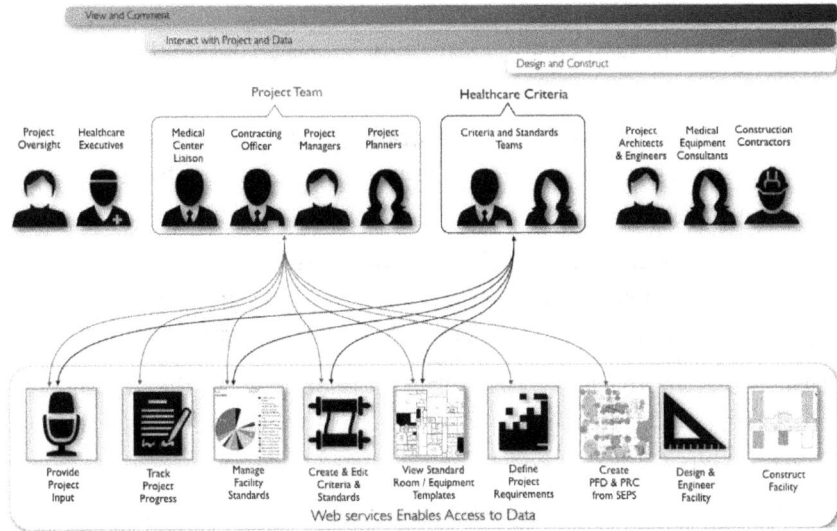

Everyone does not need the same information, the same support, or the same access to data. The main purpose of Program Analysis is to understand the asset, the unique needs of each group, and to develop initial concepts for realizing highest value. Become fluent with the opportunities, customer issues, concerns and constraints.

Delve into the organizational issues, environment, and programming constraints of the project. This step generates much the same type of information as the traditional Feasibility Study. Start by looking at user needs, physical requirements, schedule, function, and strategy. How will these issues be managed? How should the project proceed?

Many options exist for how this step takes place. Explore the requirements using tools that allow you to visualize information in meaningful ways for all stakeholders to understand. Mind mapping is one highly effective tool for analyzing and presenting such information. Mind mapping tools allow one to assess relationships and communicate them through the entire team. The mature mind mapping tools connect budgeting, resources management, and scheduling. Most link via file exchanges to schedule programs such as MS-Project. Some mind mapping tools also enable direct external links to the web.

Today, mind mapping tools lack a way to directly link to BIM. Either manual connections or workarounds are needed to move the data from mind maps to normalized spreadsheets and then to BIG-BIM tools.

Hopefully such workarounds will vanish as new apps are developed to better integrate the types of information that mind maps and spreadsheets currently enable. Until then, here is an option that may work for you:

Block out the project workflow and strategy in a mind map and then use the resulting structure to lay out the project's components in BIG-BIM, before moving to little-bim to refine concepts.

Use the same mind map, to add durations, resources and start dates to generate time schedules. Then export the map to MS-Project, clean up the hierarchy and import into ArchiCad to do time-based modeling.

Use a similar approach to define program relationships, then output to a spreadsheet and import into BIG-BIM for visualization and further development.

Consider other tools that will allow you to do similar types of functions. Tools to consider are Trelligence Affinity, Beck Technologies DESTINI tools, and the Onuma System. At the time of this writing, all three products are commercially available. These products feed directly to robust little-bim authoring and production documentation tools. Explore emerging tools such as BuildingCatalyst which are cropping up in the area, as well.

Do a web search for mind mapping tools. Download the one that seems most interesting. Read the getting starting documentation. Create a mind map with five branches:

☐ *Why do I need to use BIM?*

☐ *Why do I NOT need to use BIM?*

☐ *What do I know now?*

☐ *What do I need to know?*

☐ *Ways to fill in the gaps in my knowledge.*

Prototype

Understanding the process of sifting your information to make it increasingly precise is essential to the creation of sustainable and resilient outcomes that closely align with the full range of project needs.

Informed decisions at the beginning are critical to reducing first day errors in projects. Traditionally, early decisions are made with few facts, a lot of anecdotes and unsupported conjecture. Often the key decisions are delayed until much later in the process to accommodate traditional workflows. For many projects, early decision-making is limited to an owner's *oohing-and-aahing* at beautiful renderings supported with few hard facts. The decisions are emotion-based approvals for an inadequately supported concept.

From that point, the first day mistakes begin to build. Finding a better way around this dilemma is the main reason to conduct validation studies. If seat-of-the-pants decisions can lead projects astray, do decisions based on repeatable facts increase the chances of success? The answer is a resounding—yes, they do!

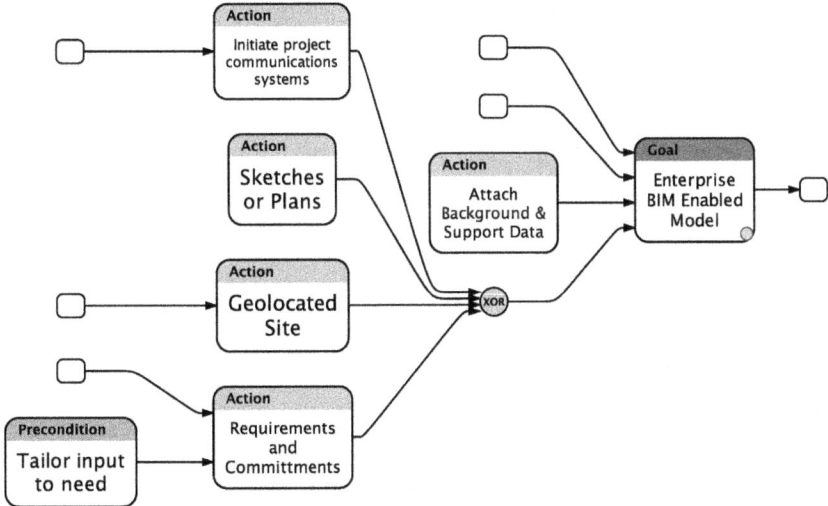

The Validation Prototype adds information models to the virtual box that contains everything about your project. You give owners the facts and the graphical views they need if they are to make informed decisions.

The decisions one makes also become part of the prototype's facts. They enable one to revisit earlier decisions to inform future decisions. We work in an iterative world where decisions build upon each other. Avoid mistakes later in the process by capturing the timing and reasoning behind early decisions.

You rapidly create a conceptual solution to the issues posed by the project. With a solid understanding of the project's business, management, and design needs, you can begin the process of creating one or more solutions. The prototype you build need not be THE solution, but it must resolve all major project needs.

The information from the prototype becomes the baseline for all future development. The solution becomes the platform for studying and testing assumptions. It becomes the Objective-Measure-of-Success for the project.

You can look at creation of the virtual prototype as a sifting process. At the start, there is too much information to work effectively. As the process progresses, one sifts through the data, keeping only the information needed. At some point in the process, one arrives at a prototype that contains only those things critical to the solution.

We often produce several types of prototypes in our validation processes. We use models with low level graphics and deep data to study relationships, site layouts, timing issues and to seed construction, energy and operations cost analyses. We use models that allow complex geometry to study systems, aesthetics, engineering issues and to produce imagery for discussion. Planning anything of value requires much more than detailed 3D models. It needs cold, hard facts.

Facts can be sparse at the beginning of projects. However, early in projects, facts are often more important than graphics. Traditionally is has been hard to find all required information at the beginning of projects. Especially for projects that are one-off or unique situations. This lack of readily available information is one of the reasons why the traditional process evolved the way it did.

Things have changed with the advent of BIG-BIM and databases. When reliable data exists, it connects to and informs your validation models. Some of the facts come from data embedded in parametric objects. This is quickly becoming a source of truth about items from forward-looking manufacturers of building products.

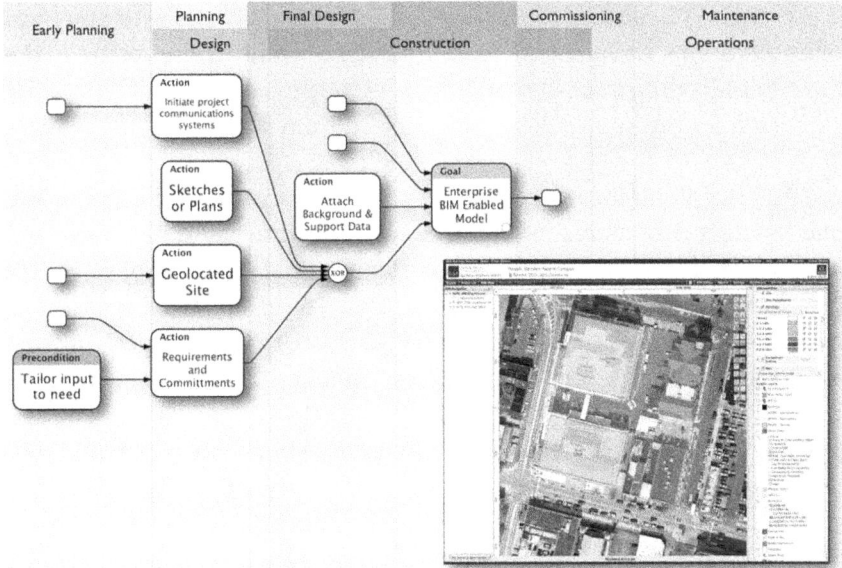

30 Minutes to Conceptual Site

Depending on the capabilities of the modeling solutions in your tool sets, models at this stage may range from a study of geometry with rules-based parameters attached—to virtual building structures created from intelligent planning objects—to a complete virtual model with floors, walls, ceiling, roofs, and much more...

When facts are not available, we now have access to computable projections, knowledge bases, standards, accepted practices, and experience to create near approximations that get us close to the actual answers; until they can be replaced by better, more reliable information later.

Part Two, STRATEGIC THINKING reviewed the power of Rule-Based Systems. As an example: if you are designing a kindergarten classroom for twenty children you can—with a high degree of certainty—project the number of desks, light fixtures, toilets and much more. You can compute the square footage required, as well as ceilings, walls, and floors. You can project most of the things that make up the classroom. At an accuracy that is far superior to the guesswork and experience based approach we relied upon at this stage in the recent past.

A mature BIM solution allows you to embed these parameters in the virtual prototype. These parameters can be in the form of textual data such as product descriptions that enable quantity take-offs and space allocations.

The data can also be represented as intelligent objects with graphical representations to validate a task. Is a dental chair in the room? Is the room in the right part of the building? Will the projected cost of the quality standards in the model keep the project from achieving the owner's budget?

As you fill-in-the-blanks in the prototype's parameters, you create placeholders that represent the best available answers to items that are known from experience to be required. Understand the range of values for placeholder assumptions or you may create a flawed analysis. For example, if you are adding a placeholder for Snow Removal, to seed an operating cost estimate, you need to understand the range of costs for those tasks near the project.

Validation Prototypes can include enormous amounts of information—often with little or no user intervention. The facts and parametric data are never complete, for they are much like a living thing, growing over time. These prototypes can connect external data, generate new data as they develop and enable you to add data over time. This ability to connect everywhere is what makes the BIG-BIM process so compelling.

How will you create clear, objective measurements of success for your projects? Pull out your notebook. Outline your ideas about the types of information that is needed. Jot down all the ways that you and others measure the success (or failure) of your projects. Begin to define a system with objective measures of success to use for your projects. Profitability can be one, but more is required. Look at things from the perspective of all team members.

Define the Scope

It is amazing that some professionals are just now beginning to understand that over 50% of the data required for operations and maintenance are created during the design process.

Embedded and connected data allow any level of model to function up or down the built environment lifecycle (i.e., you can use the earliest BIG-BIM for work-order-management or procurement of Design-Build services.) BIG-BIM at all levels can connect with the Internet of Things (IoT) and many types of business data. The ecosystem enables visualization and management of data from any source and use of the data from any network connected device.

Usually, we create the validation prototype for a project as we study constraints, opportunities, and threats during the earliest phase of development and planning. At this level, the prototype serves to define the scope of the project. It establishes a framework that contains all the parameters for a successful project. It immediately supports connected decision-making.

BIG-BIM during the design phase defines the solution that you are planning. Often little-bim takes on the lion's share of the effort at this stage. The BIG-BIM system typically acts as middleware for the data for procurement, permitting and documentation, and is tailored to meet the needs of the delivery methodology selected. (i.e. a Design-Build oriented BIG-BIM might focus on defining critical owner needs and have little to do with support of a more traditional Construction Document bidding set for a Design-Bid-Build project.)

During the project execution phases, BIG-BIM begins to focus on capturing the data generated during construction. Data for things like trades coordination, project controls for schedules, supply chain connection, and cost management collect for downstream uses. As the process unfold, the constructors add in place and as-constructed detail information to support the next step, Operations, and Maintenance (O&M).

The greatest benefits from the BIG-BIM ecosystem come during O&M. Linked together, existing facility data, work-order-management, links to equipment and other information geared to the efficient use of facilities begin to offer owners new ways of working. Since a well-planned process eliminates repetitive work, you smooth out your internal process and work more economically. No matter which stage you enter the ecosystem.

Create a validation prototype during O&M to guide a systemic renovation. Or to model and manage campuses across the continent. Create a validation prototype to capture all the information spun off by the construction process, ready for use later to handle Integrated Facilities Management needs. Or, do as we normally do and create a validation prototype as the box to organize and manage your project from beginning to end. You decide the entry point and the scope for your BIG-BIM ecosystem.

Framework

How many architects, engineers, and other people that create models plan for their BIMs to be usable well into the future? A few? Most of them seem to have missed such a long-term vision in the rush to get their work out the door.

Conversely, most people trying to use BIM downstream from design and construction think that the effort will have long-term benefits of some kind. And they are either being duped or fooling themselves. Such confusion does not need to happen. There are better ways.

Today's information models can serve as links to the built environment of tomorrow. The industry needs to move beyond the approach currently in vogue if we are to achieve this goal. Most of the Building Information Models created today are created in ways that guarantee that the models will never reach their potential. These models are destined for virtual file cabinets and data rot. Whether people understand or acknowledge this fact.

The building industry is in the early days of learning to create permanent digital assets in the growing BIG–BIM ecosystem. In this ecosystem, models don't have to become fixed archives; they continue to develop to fit future needs while improving what we do today. When the BIG–BIM ecosystem is widespread in the built environment, our models will reflect real-time and real-world conditions.

Today, we plant the seeds for a connected future where the threads from the things we create carry into the future. Since much of our building stock is already constructed, renovations are a good place to start.

Traditionally, every renovation project begins from nothing with a process designed to verify and document existing conditions. As a rule, every remodeling begins with confirmation of as-is conditions. Because the as-is situation is (or will soon be) already in place in a BIG–BIM ecosystem, the verification process is more efficient.

Using the data in your ecosystem, you may start with better, more current information about a facility; with the initial data entry process, all but eliminated. So are the mistakes that invariably accompany the manual confirmation process that now happens with every renovation or addition. The process can be much richer and significantly faster, bringing to bear information on all changes that occurred during construction and after completion.

There are two axioms at the heart of every renovation:

1. It is impossible to predict how a building will change over time, and;

2. Each renovation will start with the need to understand existing conditions.

Today, most models with few of the mundane and known issues preset. One has little choice. Few have yet to create live, archival models from which one might otherwise begin. Even fewer organizations have invested fully in the BIG-BIM ecosystem. This situation starts to change as one embraces models as prototypes.

Models connected into the ecosystem are not stagnant. Even when created with little-bim tools, they can contribute to making the ecosystem ever richer. At every stage of development, models are useful or valuable. Some lessons must be learned if you are to achieve the benefits.

Analog Process - Even with BIM

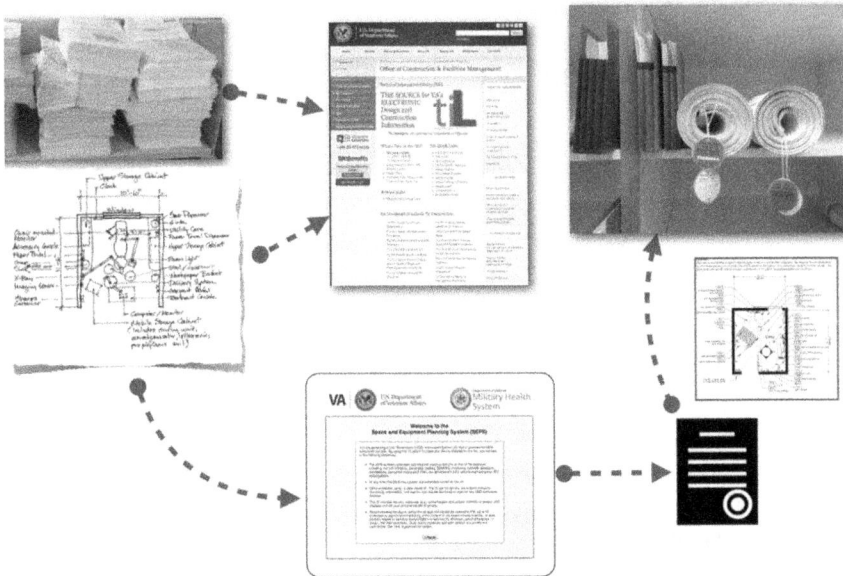

The reliance on paper, and paper equivalents, such as files, makes it difficult and costly to transition information from design and construction into operations and maintenance. Even little-bim relies on such analog approaches. In a world where we are surrounded by data, can we continue to sort through masses of files to find what we need?

Adding too much data to models too early isn't practical. In practice, one does not have the information, time, or budgets to recreate the real-world in the virtual world—not at the start of projects. Design your prototypes with just enough data to support the current need, nothing more. Building toward the future. Information that one embeds in prototypes should be as accurate as possible, given the information available. There are couple of ways to do this:

1. Document everything that goes into your prototypes as accurately as possible. The quality of representation trumps quantity. This approach requires that everything that goes into the prototype is verified and configured to match reality closely. Even better is to capture actual conditions via open-standards to match reality exactly. Ideally, you represent an air-handler as an actual digital object with every parameter possible. In fact, the air-handler begins as a box that represents the correct size, includes the right manufacturer's data, and has fundamental properties for inputs and outputs. The detail added matches up with reality and requires time to confirm. The assumption is that more detail will be added later by others, building upon what you do now.

2. Document what is needed for decision-making for each stage of development within an aligned frame of reference. This approach requires that the prototype contains accurate representations of quantities and other items that will be necessary to make fact-based decisions.

A little red dot accurately located in geographic space might represent floors, walls, and ceilings. It includes the actual size of the unit and connects to external databases of air-handler data, physical properties, and business facts. The data is then made available in a graphic or numeric form to support analysis and decision-making. The assumption is that the prototype is a living resource that will adjust as more and better data becomes available from any source.

Either approach connects into a BIG-BIM ecosystem. The first relies on human-centered quality control and often results in files-based outputs that are difficult (if not impossible) to maintain as living assets. This approach results in high early stage costs and a major time investment.

The second approach relies on external, authoritative data and focuses on decision-making and other areas that require human intervention. This approach can happen very quickly and can minimize early stage costs. Successful implementation of BIG-BIM requires the careful balancing and informed use of both approaches. Usually an enterprise's prototypes become more complete over time, as money and other resources allow.

It is not unusual to create a graphically compelling 3D object that looks real while having almost no further value in the process. Remember that you are building for the future and make sure that the underlying data doesn't get shortchanged.

Prototypes serve many purposes and take many forms. A design and construction prototype may be entirely unlike one designed to guide a major renovation in an occupied hospital. The model designed for an urban revitalization might be nothing like the one intended for an office space consolidation. Some will require graphics oriented little-bim and others will do well with data that can be visualized in GIS, or even with Red Dot models. You decide what is best, depending on the need.

We have found that models develop best in a systematic process that adds the correct data, at the proper time to support the decision-making process. To do this, someone must be knowledgeable and capable of understanding the subtleties, to ensure that inconsistencies are correctly managed. This requires trained and experienced people in the process. When the responsibility for prototypes is passed without control to untrained or inexperienced staff, bad things can happen.

As more modeling software enables web-based data sharing and becomes widely available in the building industry, it is likely that developers will create tools that automate more of the process. In other sectors, such software apps have seen rapid acceptance and a broad deployment, via the Internet. Until the same happens in the building industry, modeling depends on expertise—as it always has. Use your expertise to guide the process, tailoring your prototypes to each situation.

Clear your mind of preconceptions and any sales pitches you have heard. Forget (at least temporarily) everything you have heard about market share and what your competitors are using. Go to at least three major BIM authoring tool vendor websites and download their free or trial software. Read and complete the getting started documentation for each. Try a few of the trial examples for yourself. Which is best for you?

Cost Model

Using BIG-BIM's abilities to quickly define viable options and then connect the options to time and quality, the line between Definitive Estimating and Order-of-Magnitude Estimating blurs. The Cost Model becomes a constraint on the design solution and the baseline for cost control during construction and operations of the resulting assets.

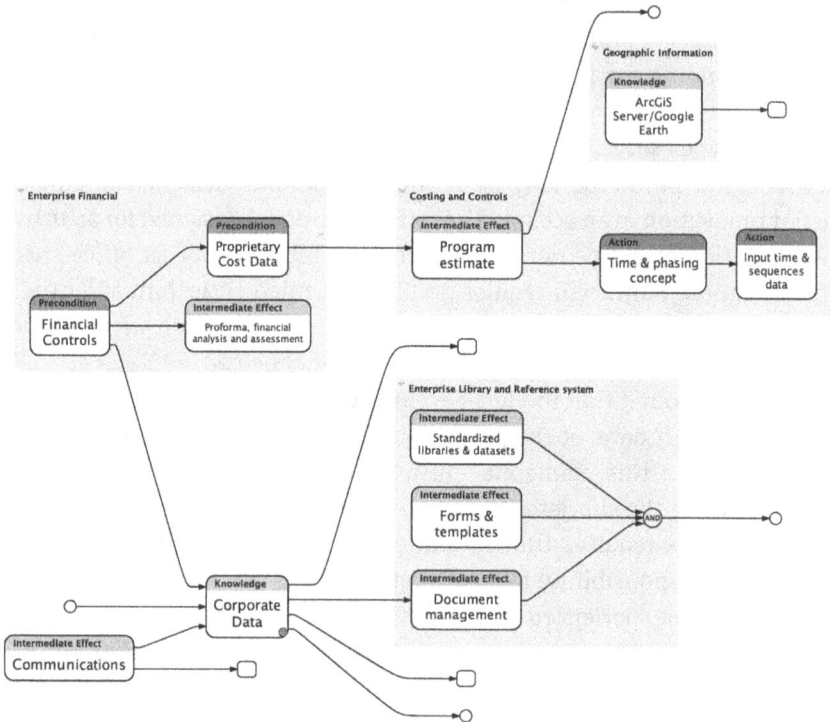

A well-planned Cost Model is the core of the validation process. The process outlined above works to help you to envision where the project might go and to identify problems early. Rather than starting with eye-candy, the model begins with informed projections that become the objective measures of success, as the project proceeds.

As your BIG–BIM ecosystem develops, use cost management as a constraint to both establish valid budgets for projected elements and to better align the design and construction process with budgetary requirements. The goal is to set boundaries and restrictions on time, costs, and quality to increase the certainty of outcomes. Cost modeling is like the *Programming Phase Estimating* used by agency construction managers and pioneered by George Heery, CM Associates, and others in the late 1960s.

When developed collaboratively with the owner, this approach has proven to be an extremely useful tool for controlling project outcomes, and is one of the best ways to embed cost constraints in your BIG-BIM development process. The goal is to create prototypes made of of models that contain all the things required for a successful project.

You have options as you transition into a process that focuses on cost-as-a-constraint. Create an association with a good estimator. Get additional cost management training. Hire someone with estimating skills. However, you do it, jump into cost controls as a baseline part of your process. We find it best to use a combination of off-the-shelf estimating tools and internal cost data to arrive at cost projections in our Cost Models.

As you create your system, start by finding a tool that allows you to compute costs at the granularity that your projects require quickly. Your system should enable rapid what-if planning, ideally making real-time changes to the cost estimates as you refine your prototype models. The *BuildingCatalyst* knowledge-based cost and facility modeling and the *Onuma System* both offer such capabilities.

There are any number of online and hard-copy tools and databases available to seed cost data needed by your system. Options worth considering include: the Whitestone Research facility cost benchmarking, modeling, and forecasting system; RS Means *Cost Data*; BNi *Building Costbooks*; Design Cost Data and their *D4Cost* Interactive database for preliminary cost estimating, cost modeling, 'what if' scenarios and cost research. There are several ways to connect data from these tools to your prototype model. Here are the basic steps to start your prototype Cost Modeling process:

☐ *Define the project's requirements and understand the programming issues. Start scheduling and strategy assumptions in tandem with a need analysis. See the DEFINE THE SCOPE chapter for more on this topic.*

☐ *Visualize and document a strategy for delivering the solution. How will the project be designed and built? How long will it take? What is the plan for procurement and implementation of construction? Create a clear timeline. Use one of the many new web-based scheduling apps with capabilities like Microsoft's Project or Oracle's Primavera. You may also want to consider mind mapping tools that connect timelines, scheduling relationships, and a more free-form representation of information.*

☐ *Factor in durations, your project strategy, and phasing. Without understanding phasing, estimates may miss critical costs. Without a clear vision of how the work will take place, risk management is more complicated. See the PROGRAM ANALYSIS chapter for more on this topic.*

☐ *Create a prototype model of a solution that responds to the issues you have identified. See the VALIDATION chapter for more on this topic.*

☐ *Add quality data and markers for costs to the prototype to enable the model to generate cost estimates, or develop quantities and unit costs for a more traditional, mostly manual process. Go conceptual with square footage costing or more detailed with component-based estimating. In either case, costs generated in the process rely on quantities extracted from the prototype model. Missing values can be computed using rules-based tools and knowledge-based projections. Fill in the gaps from your experience and common sense.*

Within the model, data comes together in a number ways. Some of the data can be highly detailed, even at this early stage. Other information is highly parametric. These variations create a need for estimating that can be both very detailed and very conceptual. It is best to balance the project needs, your expertise, and available resources with the type and granularity of the estimating approach. The following are common ways of costing projects in the Cost Model:

Costs based on quantities from the model and parametric rules-based cost data. Within the prototyping tool, costs and building area directly link together. Change the size of any space, and the cost changes by an equivalent amount. In this mode, unit costs are placeholders representing the middle of the market for each project type. One might think of this as volumetric estimating, with greater control and without the need to manually take-off the building areas.

Costs based on quantities extracted from the model and external cost data. Change the size of a space and the cost changes proportionally based on customized unit costs developed in another tool or through direct links to an external database. Combine multiple systems such as the *Onuma System* with RSMeans' *Cost Data,* BNi *Building Costbooks,* and DC&D Technologies' *D4Cost* system for these estimates. The precision of outcomes depends on the capabilities of the external tool and the knowledge of the user.

Cost Model based on preliminary project description and standardized classification system data. Quantities, units, and rates are entered based on standardized data classifications (such as Uniformat), using a combination of manual input and export/import from normalized spreadsheets.

Costs and building areas directly link or are computed independently. One might think of this as assembly or unit price estimating, depending on the the classifications that are input. This approach offers the ability to create a more nuanced and detailed view of project costs.

Costs based on quantities from the model connected via web services to external standardized classification system data. Quantities, units, and rates are imported or connected with web services directly to the model. Costs and building areas directly link or are computed independently. With web services, this approach offers the ability to interconnect external cost controls bidirectionally with the prototype. As changes occur in the external model, they reflect in the prototype and vice-versa: Systems such as iFM, and SEPS2BIM now enable linkages between product manufacturer/vendor product databases, owner requirements and BIG-BIM to create dynamic Cost Models for projects.

Dynamically linked external cost estimate or budget model. Space names, areas and Uniformat classified data are imported or linked into the prototype from tools such as BuildingCatalyst. Using this approach, non-graphic, planning *what-ifs* are completed in the exterior system and either linked into the prototype via web services or imported using a standardized workflow. The information from the external tool is utilized to generate 3D spaces that contain the attributes supplied, in effect auto-generating a model.

> *Cost management within the validation process has come a long way since the first release of BIG-BIM little-bim. Vendors now focus on making links between cost data, owner requirements and spaces. It is no longer a dream to be able to estimate dynamically, in-context. You can (and should) do it today, for every project.*

Cost Model: Assumptions and Alternates

> *Beware: Do not skip this step. Without the assumptions and alternates you may find it very hard to get buy-in and agreement on the Cost Model.*

Include an audit of the data and identification of the places that offer the possibility of changes both additive and deductive as part of the Cost Model. Use BIG-BIM tools to capture every step you took and every decision you made as the project developed. You can do this without BIG-BIM tools, if you must, but recognize that this critical step is tedious when done manually.

List the assumptions you have made along the way. What items did you include (or not include)? Why? What codes did you refer to in the process? What factors did you assume when you selected approach A over B? Make a list of everything you assumed. To help others understand how you arrived at your solutions.

Brainstorm how the model can be made better, using every criterion you can imagine. Can spaces be eliminated? Are the overall costs too high? Too much parking? Too little? Will other finishes deliver the lifecycle benefits required? Pose alternatives based upon your assumptions, such as: *the costs include marble floors in the lobbies. What is the impact of changing the floor finish to ceramic tile?* The prototype, coupled with the Cost Model and analysis tools gives the ability to assess such what-if alternatives in many ways. Lowest first cost vs. lifecycle operations costs? Durability vs. aesthetics? Installer-A vs. Installer-B? Such questions should be addressed, in detail. Everything is fair game as you assess options quickly with a properly constructed model.

- [ ] *List and estimate the costs of every addition or reduction that the owner might wish to consider as they decide about the budget.*

- [ ] *Evaluate user needs and study alternative strategies to offer solutions that might improve the project. Detail alternative strategies that might negatively impact the project.*

- [ ] *Offer compromises that might be possible without undermining basic project requirements.*

Identifying alternative approaches give the team a platform for discussing options. Frank and open discussions of alternative solutions work to assure that the validated concept meets the owner's needs at all levels. The owner makes the final decisions. She decides whether to accept or reject any alternative proposed. On the surface, the goal is to economize and refine. Beneath the surface, the goal is to challenge and validate conceptions—or misconceptions.

We have found that exploring options for alternate approaches, reductions, and additions create tension. The realism of Building Information Models landed on Google Earth allows people to imagine the finished project clearly and results in some people taking proposed changes personally. Conversely, the realism is often misinterpreted as a much more complete state than is the case. Both conditions become obvious in these discussions. To the benefit of reaching an agreed upon vision of the final project.

The expression of emotional investment in the alternate approaches serves as an additional validation of the direction that the project is taking. The realization the project is in the early stages, albeit with enormous amounts of data and many decisions made helps the team more clearly understand the process. While discussions can become heated, all gain understanding from the expression of different perspectives, and the Cost Model serves the team well.

Cost Model: Comparable Projects

When we don't offer appropriate comparisons ourselves, our Cost Models can be compared to others using out of context, general numbers that don't relate to the asset in question. One must be proactive to head this off. Include five or six comparison projects within each validation process.

The final component of the Cost Model is a group of comparable projects that can be used to compare where your project stands relative to others. Owners want to understand how their assets' performance compares with similar assets. It is human nature. Each of us wishes to understand our costs, in the project's context. Owners will compare the costs we provide to the costs that others paid, or to the design benchmarks for the asset you are prototyping.

The comparable analysis is how we address this issue. Compare similar projects to the project in question by actively seeking and presenting the details so that the owner can make more accurate evaluations.

We have found that DC&D Technologies' *D4Cost* system is our best source for project data for comparisons. The *D4Cost* tool allows one to select multiple projects from an extensive database of historical cost data. During the process, one can search for project type, building use, construction type, size, location and more. First, we seek recent projects of similar type and size to the project we are validating. The projects are then localized and date-adjusted using DC&D Technologies' algorithms. Each of the projects is then customized to become apples-to-apples comparisons with the Cost Model.

Cost Model: Contingencies

Changes such as revising the project scope, amending prior decisions, providing updated information, extended schedules, expanding services, or adding additional consultants become easier to handle when managed within a budgeted contingency. By streamlining the need to negotiate extra costs, you minimize the need for uncomfortable situations that can jeopardize the owner's relationships with the team.

Unpredictable things happen in the real-world. One can manage some. Others are outliers or *Black Swans* that are rare and extreme. The outliers upset any vision and plan. It is also hard to determine ahead of time the precise scope of every item, and the assumptions that will change as the project moves forward. Even with a reliable prototype, it's hard to plan for every conceivable service or item required. In simplest terms, the goal of any cost management process is to eliminate (or at least minimize) uncertainty. Completely removing uncertainty and the risks it imposes isn't possible.

To manage the unplanned, and unpredictable risks it is critical to include contingencies. Correctly structured, contingencies allow the owner to respond to the manageable unknowns. Contingencies are not the only tools that one uses to manage project costs as, scope adjustments, and alternate approaches to delivery come into play. Contingencies allow flexibility as the project moves to completion. Many factors drive the amount and types of contingencies:

Scheduling and phasing factor into the contingency. When there is timing uncertainty or an extended timetable, costs accelerate. Rather than inflating the expenses in the model to allow for unknowns and potential problems, you establish contingencies to manage scheduling uncertainty. You administer the project within the constraints imposed by the contingencies.

The ability to make reliable early decisions is dependent on understanding the needs and having a conceptual solution. A precise design and clear communication are the owner's best tool for controlling embedded 'fudge-factors' in bids.

Producing perfect procurement documents has yet to occur. No matter how skilled or how highly compensated, no human has yet achieved perfection.

The quality and accuracy of site information are critical. The convergence of BIM and GIS in prototypes offsets some of the issues with location data at the earliest stages of projects, but not all.

Financing should be locked in or include a separate allowance for added costs.

Contingencies are part of the Cost Model to allow you to manage these and many other factors. Managing added costs for legitimate changes must be as easy as possible. Confrontations cost money. The contingency eliminates the need to obtain repetitive formal approvals–a huge barrier for many public projects since you have already encumbered the funding. Including contingent funds in your project budget, is a far better way to manage costs than taking the adversarial approach. Finally, a reserve fund helps one to receive a better product and avoid needless headaches and legal wrangling.

Some people have unrealistic expectations about project costs. These expectations often result in conflict and confusion. Unrealistic expectations have proven to create additional costs and can lead to unexpected project problems. Unrealistic expectations include:

The belief that: "Once we sign the contract, you should provide all required services or products. Whether included in the project scope or not."

The belief that: "You're the experts, and I relied on your knowledge of required services when we negotiated your fees."

The belief that: "Sharing project data with other stakeholders will avoid conflict or controversy."

The belief that: "It is possible to refuse to part with more money, regardless of the cause."

Keep expectations realistic. Realize that even with the best of intentions and the highest quality process; changes will happen. Plan for them and projects go smoother. Use contingencies and a realistic budget to manage better. Define contingencies during the validation process. They are a project cost, just like everything else in the project.

As the project moves forward, step-to-step, your contingent funds adjust to enable flexibility and to allow you to react to changes quickly and efficiently. Contingencies included in the Cost Model fall into three categories:

1. Design Contingency. If you start with a validated concept, you have a clear idea of where your project is going. As your project moves from conception to design through production and procurement, the contingency serves to manage 'design creep' allowing you to add or remove cost items as you learn more detail about your project. Without this flexibility, either the project must exactly follow the validated concept or, at bid day, outcomes are likely to be very different from the original budget.

2. Construction Contingency. Change orders during construction are inevitable. No matter the delivery type. Most constructors expect additional money for every slight change, whether such changes result from errors, substitutions, unexpected site conditions or owner-initiated changes. During construction, the contingency fund sets aside a portion of the budget. Either a dollar amount or a percentage of the estimated construction costs. The construction contingency pays for the costs due to the imperfect nature of the process.

3. Project Contingency. Beyond the design and construction-related changes, budget for other unexpected costs. Typical project changes include schedule delays; changes in agency requirements; programmatic changes; owner-initiated design changes; unknown site conditions; unexpected construction cost escalation; added financing costs; and additional professional fees. Construction operations, market conditions or other factors may also drive these costs.

Within a BIM project, you manage project finances by managing the contingency. As the project progresses, the contingencies go up and down as you react to day-to-day needs and decisions.

Monitor progress against the contingencies to give your project the best chance of finishing on-budget and on-time. Use the status of contingencies at project completion as an objective measure of financial success.

Start your next project by creating a connected project strategy. Toss out the preconceptions and standard approach. Put yourself in the bidder's shoes and write the actions you will take to minimize the need for contingencies and safety factors. What can you change in the process to improve clarity and understanding? While maintaining the interests, and needs of the project? Diagram your approach and measure your successes and failures as the project moves forward.

Limits and Possibilities

The validation process enables owners to make initial planning decisions based on real-world facts. Even with facts, early decisions are but projections and speculation. Because of this, early decisions are not static. They grow and change as the project moves forward. These early decisions became the measure of project success.

The pace of change, design problems, and economic complexity increase the opportunities for catastrophic errors of judgment. Projects that are over budget, late, and not fit for the intended use are symptoms of the problem. Solutions that quickly and economically guide those who make critical project decisions are rare.

The goal of the Validation Process is to define the framework of activities and components required for project success. Successfully achieving this aim, results in a solution that has a high likelihood of matching the owner's requirements. The prototype, when infused with all known and projected data that will impact outcomes, optimizes decision-making.

In-context decision-making data makes the process of visioning the project more reliable. The known, and known-unknowns are cataloged, managed, and resolved. Designing ways to handle the things one does not know that one does not know remains the opportunity. Good early decisions, implemented correctly, lead to better outcomes and an improved ability to capitalize on opportunities. Even in a world of uncertainty.

The final product of a validation process is a precise definition of the limits and possibilities designed to guide the steps that follow. The results from the process serve several functions: they codify the space use program and measures of success for the project; they become the statement of owner requirements to guide further development; they make the cost constraint a priority; and, they become the basis of procurement documents.

BIM Linked to Geography

The traditional disconnects between site information and building information no longer need to exist. Building and geographical technologies are merging to become one. This convergence is taking place, despite push-back from entrenched professionals in both camps.

The worlds of geography and the building industry are converging. This convergence is one area with tremendous opportunity for improving how we live, work, and play in the built environment. Today, when you hike, bike or drive you are as often as not guided by geospatial information. This information is defined using latitude, longitude, and altitude to place you anywhere on the earth. You can see your path, select from the amenities that are close to you, and companies can advertise products from nearby stores right to your cell phone. We live in a world where much of our technology is geo-aware.

In the recent past, buildings and other structures were little more than boxes or photographs in this geospatial world. By adding detailed built information to geospatial information, one can interact with the complete code of everything about the built environment. Together this information forms a continuum with enormous benefit to the built environment.

This convergence of technologies has been growing since early in the twenty-first century. One could say it began with the Keyhole satellites that eventually gave us Google Earth. For the first time, with Keyhole data non-experts could visualize geographic data without the baggage that came with other, expert Geographic Information Systems (GIS). They could zoom into a site and get a real-world view, without knowing much of anything about GIS. The limitations revolved around the fact that one had to be part of the Federal government to get access.

Along came Google™. Google acquired Keyhole in 2004. Keyhole then became Google Earth™ and geography and the built environment were finally coming together to allow BIG-BIM. Buried deep in this fantastic development was a deep, dark secret that might have stopped progress in its tracks.

The secret revolved around a simple question—*Who owns the data?* Proprietary information could scuttle the whole system. There needed to be a way to make sure that the information would remain free and usable. There needed to be standards... not Google rules; but standards that were public and shared with everyone.

Without such standards, Google Earth would continue to be a truly refreshing tool. With such standards, it could become the basis for new ways to do business that allow us to achieve true sustainability. On April 14, 2008, Ron Lake, chairperson, and chief executive officer of Galdos Systems Inc. announced that the Open Geospatial Consortium (OGC) had adopted Keyhole Markup Language (KML) as an OGC standard. This announcement created the basis for moving forward with confidence.

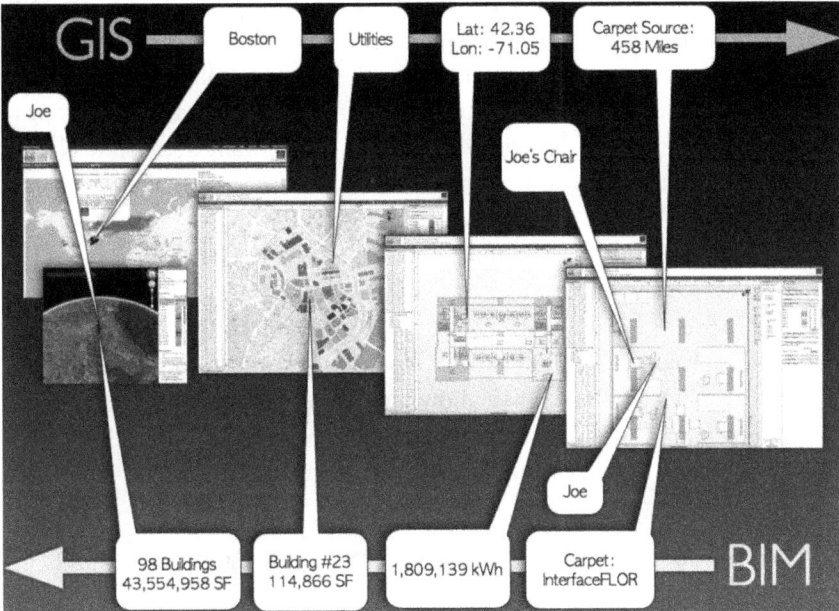

We can now set up and share geographic information directly linked to the design and construction process. We now know that we have a stable and repeatable way to communicate and assemble information. And, it is entirely due to an open-standard that makes an exceptional product even better. By connecting data, we can now get the information needed; across the life cycle of our facilities.

This is the world where geographic information technology enables much of the app economy. And the building industry is either too dense or too self-absorbed to realize that it has been left behind. The construction sector continues to default to the usual ways of doing business, as the rest of the world embraces the change.

Manually coordinating infrastructure with building needs results in too many errors and wasted effort. It is no longer economical to maintain site data in silos that don't support the full range of building industry needs. By connecting building information with geographic information, communities and professionals work more efficiently and more economically. With the added benefits of better coordination, improved environmental resilience and reduced downstream error.

The site information that you include in your prototypes can take many forms, depending on the stage of development. Your options range from detailed site survey to working with satellite imagery. Everything from traditional property and topographic surveys; to full Geographic Information System access via web services; to publicly accessible cloud-based site information comes into play. Geographic data connects into every modeling step in a BIG-BIM ecosystem.

Today, publicly available tools such as Bing and Google Earth are the most readily available and inexpensive source for early stage georeferenced site data. With careful consideration of the data sets used, these tools provide a surprising degree of accuracy and ground-truth. They explicitly include context. They allow one to maintain prototypes within a consistent and repeatable framework that others can work with as well. There are issues to keep in mind:

Not all Google Earth data is currently at high resolution. Aerial photography or other satellite mapping managed within a more robust GIS server framework may show finer detail.

In some contexts, Google Earth or other GIS data may not conform to manually prepared survey information. Whether this is an issue of accuracy or adjustments made in the field by surveyors, is sometimes difficult to determine.

Site data is best when it accurately represents ground-truth—where the imagery matches real-world conditions. Anything else is an approximation and will, in the long-term, require correction. Keep this in mind and evaluate each situation based on the data at hand and the long-term use of your prototypes. Sometimes tradition, metes-and-bounds surveys, and the official public records will differ from the GIS data for any number of reasons. Find a knowledgeable, and licensed land surveyor and get him or her to help you sort it out.

Google Earth usually meets the standard for granularity for early stage models. You will find that Google Earth provides the best and most consistent level of site data to support this level of development.

Sign up and get familiar with Google Earth Pro. It is free as of the beginning of 2015. Zoom to one of your project site's and add a polygon that approximates the site's property boundaries. Save the polygon and import it into the Onuma System/Revit/Archicad/Bentley/Vectorworks/SketchUp/et.al. to begin geolocated site studies.

Reusable Data

When users of the data create independent spreadsheets or simple databases, with no easy path back to the authoritative database, chaos reigns.

Underpinning BIG-BIM ecosystems are archives of asset information. These archives can take many forms. Ideally, the archives are open-standard compliant and shared, via web services. Conceptually the goal is for each kernel of data to be maintained in such an archive by those with the most to gain from keeping the information live and up-to-date.

The rest of us can then access and use the data as needed, knowing that we are working with the best and most accurate information. This authoritative source data forms the foundation for BIG-BIM and connected decision-making.

Consider what happens when a little-bim user manually enters or imports data via any of the files-based protocols:

Immediately the data becomes suspect and must be re-verified. Was a digit transposed during manual data entry? What changed between the time the data was exported from the source and then imported to the current use? What is missing?

When the same little-bim user completes her work, and wishes to send the updated data back to the source, how does that happen? How does anyone know that the new data is compatible with the data of origin? How is the replacement data validated to meet the needs at the source? Who makes the call?

These are a small fraction of the questions and issues that occur when data is transferred via manual and files-based exchanges. In many cases, questions like these defeat the attempt at maintaining shared and authoritative data—even for organizations with the best of intentions.

Those that maintain data understand that the information in their charge must be managed and controlled. The complexity and direct intervention required to properly keep the data can become an overwhelming task. Any system for organizing data must allow consistent and safe ways to store and find information. Data must be shareable, in coherent and repeatable ways.

Many in the building industry don't appear to understand these simple facts. This unwillingness to comply or lack of awareness may be the reason that the building industry lags so far behind other areas in today's app economy. One cannot eliminate disconnected processes and work that occurs in silos when there is no way to share information effectively—All Information.

In a paper-based system, management of information created libraries. These libraries started as isolated; oases spotted throughout society. As technology evolved, so did libraries. Today they are connected via networks and the Internet. Libraries share and collaborate to disperse the information housed within, and outside, their walls; whether the information is physical or digital. The building industry must do the same.

In the BIM world, web-enabled model server ecosystems are equivalent to the physical library. These servers function is to keep information alive and fresh. These servers are structured to host model data so that it can be added to and updated under strict quality controls. Within the ecosystem, everything is time tracked, interconnected, and enabled to interact with all available authoritative source data.

The systems that hold the greatest promise for long-term resilience use a service-oriented-architecture design pattern. The servers act as middleware, enabling components to provide services to other components using communications protocols over networks. These servers are independent of vendors, products, and technologies.

IFC Model Servers and proprietary model file servers such as Graphisoft's BIM Server and Autodesk's A360 project collaboration software remains focused on design and construction, using files-based data exchanges, albeit in the Cloud. As more building industry tools move toward the paradigms of the broader world, more options will develop.

You will need to develop a strategy for model storage and sharing that will let you move to new model server capabilities as they become available. Keep in mind that without the ability to manage and maintain live data, your projects will be subject to Data Rot. Anything copied to a hard drive, storage media, file or paper immediately begins to deteriorate, even if the files are virtual or in the Cloud. Only with live real-time data, which is what model servers MUST be all about, does your information remain viable for the lifecycle.

In the transition from an industry focused on little-bim as the endgame to one centered on the BIG-BIM Ecosystem, there will be compromises. In the short-term, not every bit of data will be able to move to web services or a to service-oriented-architecture approach to data sharing.

Campus and Portfolio

The reality is that low-cost models are now being created to meet the lifecycle needs of multi-building and multi-facility owners. Using combinations of both BIG and little-bim, GIS, business tools, and facilities management, large owners have implemented BIG-BIM ecosystems to manage the lifecycle needs of millions of square feet in thousands of locations.

At the time that *BIG-BIM little-bim* was released the response from enterprise owners, when confronted with the need to move their facilities information to BIM was: *we could never afford that and even if we could, we don't have the time to wait for someone to build us a bunch of models.* They were spot on in their assessment of the industry. Only a handful of hearty pioneers were willing to make the leap in those days.

Jump forward to today. For many enterprise owners, little has changed. They consider their existing facility assets based on what consultants tell them and abandon all hope of moving to lifecycle BIM. To these owners, BIM still demands a high cost for creating existing facility models. The excuses for not moving forward ring of 2006. Who can blame them? The industry continues to foster this belief with a combination of bim washing and a fierce adherence to little-bim.

Simple masses that represent campuses and buildings in Google Earth create a comprehensive understanding of entire portfolios of assets. Rather than focusing on the graphical information in the portfolio, these models focus on making the owner's data accessible for users with little or no connection to the building industry. Users click on the system and step-by-step, move from satellite level views; to the region; to the campus; to the building; to space; and down to the level of devices and equipment. Finding the information, to do what they need to do, when they need to do it.

The models include equipment inside the facilities. Furniture, fixtures, potential recycle value, structural soundness, surface conditions, and almost any other factor is accessible in a simple box model. The data can be used to make lifecycle decisions, such as: *Which facility should get renovated next? Where is my meeting, and what times are already reserved? Should we spend the last $15,000 in our budget to paint Room 2346 or to patch the roof on Building 86-3?*

One need not focus on one model at a time. An established BIG-BIM ecosystem allows the simultaneous creation of models in many forms which contain data for any level of detail. Each can generate information for further development or use in other models. They are the foundation for storage, maintenance, and access to data about the organization's assets.

Within the BIG-BIM environment, even Red Dot models and little-bim can vastly exceed the information and accuracy of any flat paper or CAD as-built. Fully mature BIG-BIM ecosystems are orders of magnitude more complete.

Traditional renovation projects start with field checks, measurement verification, and new base plans. Owner-provided electronic as-built documents are often uncoordinated, incomplete, or out-of-date, requiring designers to create new base plans using field measurements. Renovation work has long required special attention to sort through the mess.

Now, as a facility asset moves to become a renovation project, a more detailed model is either accessed from the BIG-BIM ecosystem or built using little-bim. In either case, little field verification takes place as all changes that occurred since the beginning are in the ecosystem.

As the renovation progresses, the model is updated, adding new design solutions, the results of field review, analyses and studies, field verified documentation and other items. The model aggregates any CADD or paper as-builts, houses asset information and is the starting point for further design. Such models, especially when seeded from the BIG-BIM ecosystem, are economical and result in superior procurement document quality within standard fee and time limitations.

Some of the lessons we have learned to work with enterprise owners to model existing facilities include:

Start little-bim installations one building at a time. A phased approach to as-built models is often the only solution when there is a requirement to deliver standalone little-bim, because funding to document existing conditions is often limited, even for the largest owners.

Start BIG-BIM installations so that all facilities within a campus or portfolio are modeled in a quick, low level of detail manner to act as the data buckets to hold owner information that will be attached to the ecosystem. The contextual and decision support benefits of BIG-BIM take much too long to emerge when you use a traditional process of fully developing one building at a time at a high level of graphical detail.

Get immediate benefit by creating Current Condition Models in BIG-BIM to hold legacy information (areas, coordinates, program data, and planning rules). These models can be upgraded to include geometry and detailed facility data over time, as budgets allow.

Models are ideal candidates for rules-based systems. Start by modeling the first project. Each additional project should take the same course. As the owner renovates or replaces facilities, the models become ever more precise. They build up the institution's storehouse of information. Connect these models to other asset data using BIG-BIM as middleware.

Portfolio owners within multiple facilities can have any building or use type. They can have new projects or renovations. They can involve infrastructure assets, or not. In this environment, the capital improvement plan is king. BIG-BIM of the entire portfolio is an ideal way to manage this complexity.

The management and elimination of deferred maintenance are a constant in extensive facilities and multi-building campuses. Budget restraints often force managers to focus on one capital improvement project at a time. Owners face a dilemma of where to apply limited funds. The ability to manage deferred maintenance is one of the major benefits of a BIG-BIM ecosystem.

For enterprise owners, the best solution is to develop a BIG–BIM ecosystem that includes models containing site information and massing models for facility assets. Projects within the model can take many forms, depending on the available information. Existing installations may start as little more than boxes to hold legacy data. As projects are developed the BIG–BIM ecosystem captures the results and becomes richer.

Information moves from conception to planning, design, and construction into operations and maintenance. At each step, the BIG–BIM ecosystem becomes more resilient, sustainable, and economical. Value builds as the owner learns how to connect to capital budgets and facility processes. Those able to plug into the process become valuable. In fact, they may be indispensable.

Build an existing condition model as the starting point for your next project. Use the BIM tools that you have available to create and document the basic information needed for your new project. Keep in mind future project needs and the long-term use of the model.

Construction Asset Value

Correctly configured, BIG-BIM tools can automate many construction information sharing processes, such as clash detection, validation assessment, and scheduling. But don't just use the model for construction support. Planning for the end goal is critical to the process. When you think of the long-term use of information, you are contributing to a successful BIG-BIM ecosystem.

The information in an appropriately created BIG–BIM ecosystem is not limited to use in any one phase of the lifecycle of assets. The information is highly valuable during construction. You can use the information with any construction delivery method, but the business processes for accessing and sharing the asset information requires planning and forethought. Tailor, your approach to what best serves the owner. Start by understanding the long–term use of the model:

☐ *Will the model be used for public bidding to General Contractors? For negotiated Design-Build? For publicly bid Design-Build? For Integrated Project Delivery? Each will require a different approach to the model.*

☐ *Will the constructor use the model for conflict checking, or for 4D or 5D analysis? If so, model to allow this to happen. Plan your production process accordingly.*

☐ *Are design and construction the only need? Or, must the model support the entire facility lifecycle? Is the model part of a BIG-BIM ecosystem, or a one-off, graphics-centric model? Each case requires a very different approach.*

☐ *Will the model become a long-term asset for the owner? To support facility management and operations? If so, the model will contain much data. How will this data be managed as more data generates? Build the connections to support this data.*

☐ *How will you connect other team members' data? Do all involved understand the specific needs of this project? Is everyone involved committed to the long-term goal?*

Practices for Better Outcomes

Enterprise BIM, Integrated Project Delivery, Construction Management, Design-Build, Design-Bid-Build and Turnkey-delivery represent only a handful of the wide range of delivery options available to you as you seek ways to connect design and construction into a BIG-BIM ecosystem. Whichever delivery methodology you choose, there are consistent practices that improve outcomes and lead to the creation and management of assets that are more resilient and sustainable.

Market forces have historically separated the designer and builder, with little regard for the fact that working together is key to project success. To overcome the dysfunction and inefficiencies of not working together closely, alternate approaches to design and construction emerged. These alternatives proved that early collaboration could improve project outcomes. BIG-BIM takes things up several levels. BIG-BIM works to reconnect the designer and builder using shared data sets that allow visual clarity and a better understanding of what is happening in the construction process.

By accelerating and supporting early collaboration on processes, we can use BIG-BIM to improve design and construction. Whether negotiating with Design–Builders from a conceptual model; helping understand a Design–Build model; bidding general contractors from a detailed construction phase model; working in a connected project framework with federated models, or using any of the hybrid approaches to modeling and development.

Focus on clear communications and answering all questions, quickly and comprehensively. Create an environment of trust and knowledge. No matter which delivery method you choose, these seven attitudes and actions will help you to achieve a more connected, collaborative process:

1. Represent the owner's interests and requirements in all you do. Transparently, document decisions and make them available for all. Provide more information than is expected. Fill-in-the-blanks. Respond quickly and collaborate easily.

2. Use the model to know that the design is on target. Define everything precisely, with graphics and data. Include a user-friendly project website to keep everyone informed.

3. Tailor the process to the project and owner's needs. Customize the model to match the chosen procurement method.

4. Strive to eliminate unknowns and uncertainties. There are no stupid questions, no matter how obvious or mundane they seem, especially during the procurement process. Every question that you avoid or miss will return as a problem, at the worst time.

5. Respond quickly and make dependable decisions. Learning to resolve issues before they become problems reduces placeholders and contingencies buried in bids, resulting in bidding that is more responsive.

6. Freely share your data—ideally, by sharing your model. Even share the data through file-based and flat formats, if that is what others require.

7. Understand that holding your cards close is the opposite of collaboration. Get the best for the customer. No matter how competitive the bid market.

Embrace these practices and you will get better results from your projects and improve outcomes for your customers. By applying the seven practices to projects using traditional delivery methods, you will see improvement.

Some find it difficult or unmanageable to embrace connected project delivery processes. To them, the change is too much, too fast. Fear of the unknown, a bias toward doing things in a traditional manner, and owner reticence contribute to a infinite range of variations between the base and enterprise levels. Because of these factors, one must be creative and adaptable.

Connected processes require adaptability and collaboration. At a basic level, these processes revolve around communications and understanding how to make traditional relationships work more efficiently. When close and collaborative commitments exist within teams, projects are more successful. Improved decision-making, better project controls, less duplication of effort, and an understanding of cost and scheduling issues are indicators of such projects.

There are many variations for how connected processes take place. Although there are common threads, every project is unique and requires a tailored approach. Because of this, little-bim projects require customization by informed and knowledgeable professionals. Anything less can lead to problems.

Look for new ways to adapt traditional processes to achieve connected process results. Know that none of the traditional options, even adjusted to include collaborative processes delivers the outcomes that people see from Integrated Project Delivery in an Enterprise BIM environment.

Be Nimble

Halfway measures added to traditional methods usually rely on the good intentions of the team and are often difficult to enforce and monitor.

Technology and education might be the keys to curing industry fragmentation, but those are long-range systemic needs. Most have a much shorter and much less holistic view of the industry. Foremost in many people's thinking are changes to traditional delivery processes that will cure the problems.

There are time-tested methods for delivering projects. Delivery methods, such as Design-Bid-Build, Design-Build, Construction-Management-at-Risk, and Agency-Construction-Management are a few of the traditional options. It isn't too hard to understand the fundamental differences between the available options. The subtleties and complexities of each option can be harder to assess.

The traditional options came about as ways to manage time, money, and the problems that people experienced as they built things. The sad truth is that none of the options fulfills the need for the high-performance process that will overcome the problems that plague the industry. Some come closer than others. Some may have worked once upon a time, and are no longer effective. Each has its place. These are the methodologies that have been used to get the industry to where it is today. They are not the ultimate solutions for tomorrow.

It is possible to include some level of collaborative processes in any traditional delivery method. However, these hybrids are at best half way measures and often result in sub-optimum outcomes. Some, such as Design-Bid-Build, are, at their core, not collaborative at all, and results reflect the confrontational nature of this method. Some, such as Design-Build, are easy to manipulate to overcome some of the problems.

As one considers the options and seeks the best approach to each situation, questions abound. Start with this checklist:

☐ *What is the best format for constructing the project?*

☐ *Will your conceptual information model already include all required Design Development documents—as soon as you compose your views on standard sheets?*

☐ *How much more effort will be needed to create bidding documents?*

☐ *Is your model geared toward creating biddable documents or beautiful pictures?*

☐ *Do you have a constructor that can work from information models? If so, are your models up to the task?*

☐ *Do you have a design prototype that will allow for connection with the constructor?*

☐ *Does your model include the basics to support 4D and 5D? Did you model all systems?*

☐ *Which delivery process will be best?*

☐ *Will your conceptual model and validation data provide enough information for bidding Design-Build?*

☐ *Will your models reduce bidder uncertainty to achieve better results and smoother projects? Or, add to the confusion?*

☐ *Must the process look a lot like a traditional Design-Bid-Build? To satisfy some bureaucratic need or mandate?*

☐ *Will you have to produce public bidding documents?*

☐ *Will you need to comply with a rigid review process that has defined submission requirements?*

☐ *Have you built your model to a level that complies with the submission requirements?*

Whatever your answers, be nimble and adjust traditional processes to be more collaborative. The informed addition of connected process features within traditional delivery methods has been shown to improve projects. The benefits are small, but can be significant.

The largest benefits come from delivery approaches that allow the most interaction between all team members—owners, contractors, subcontractors, suppliers, fabricators, and designers. For projects that must use traditional procurement processes, the greatest benefits come from well-planned hybrids using collaborative forms of Design-Build or Agency-Construction-Management. To understand how to tweak traditional delivery methods to achieve what is possible, look at each of the available options.

What follows are the broad categories of delivery methods, in order of relative ease in creating a connected, collaborative process that directly interfaces with BIG-BIM ecosystems. All approaches work in some cases and go astray in others. Each is subject to failure in situations of poor performance.

The strategies that fall into the traditional options have evolved to enable risk averse design professionals to off-load project risks onto others. Because of this risk aversion orientation, these choices are, as a group, less than ideal ways to achieve BIG-BIM delivery goals.

We begin with the two options that offer the greatest promise for the future: Enterprise BIM and Integrated Project Delivery. We then review the most traditional options: Agency-Construction-Management, Design-Build, Turnkey-delivery, Construction-Management-at-Risk, and Design-Bid-Build.

Download samples of standard agreements for each of the delivery approaches discussed from the American Institute of Architects Contract Documents website. Contract relationship diagrams are also available.

Enterprise BIM

Enterprise BIM allows for the engagement of any service or system that is open and accessible, to support organizational needs. All processes tie into the owner's live models to enable a connected team to work in real-world, near real-time context. There are few restrictions on tools, yet each party to the project can collaborate with the same data to achieve the owner's goals. All share in the risks and rewards of a process designed to eliminate the train-wrecks well before pouring concrete or expending significant costs.

Enterprise BIM revolves around the creation of an ecosystem that connects and maps infrastructure into business operations. The ecosystem has a lifecycle viewpoint—from management, into an early design, through construction and into the operations and maintenance of assets. For an entire enterprise, whether housed in a single building, a group of built assets or multiple campuses distributed widely.

Goals for such systems include reduced costs, increased sustainability, resilience, and improved organizational decision-making. Pre-established, long-term relationships, integrated supply chains, and BIG-BIM-enabled teams support this level of connected business processes. Delivery of Enterprise BIM engages many systems, tools, and people to create distributed networks in support of the activities of the enterprise.

Geographic information systems, document management systems, Building Information Models, business management systems and much more, feed to and receive real-time data which can then be mashed-up to support connected decision-making. Organizations are not limited to the features, updates or availability of any single application or approach to construction. By loosely coupling data, the enterprise takes advantage of many resources to better plan for today and tomorrow.

The enterprise becomes part of a sustainable ecosystem for today and tomorrow. Growing and adjusting to an uncertain future in times of uncertainty. In the ecosystem, hybrids of any project delivery approach can be used to support enterprise design and construction needs.

Multiple *brands* of sensor systems interface via mash-ups to enable management in a single web interface while accommodating the needs of those with no direct connection to the building industry. GIS, BIM, business systems, and facilities management data aggregate to create global views of the organization's status, at the level of detail appropriate to any user.

Multiple professional firms work on projects, using different processes and tools, and feed data to the organization's planning and facilities management systems, to enable a common operating picture for those that make decisions. Multiple contractors, under a variety of delivery methods, build facilities, using their choice of software solutions while pushing and pulling data, to and from the organization's BIG-BIM ecosystem.

The ability to interconnect people, places, and things, enables many tools and approaches to become connected into an ecosystem to achieve results.

Integrated Project Delivery

Integrated Project Delivery, or IPD, is defined in Wikipedia as: a collaborative alliance of people, systems, business structures and practices into a process that harnesses the talents and insights of all participants to optimize project results, increase value to the owner, reduce waste, and maximize efficiency through all phases of design, fabrication, and construction.

The development and construction team connect as planning starts. The group is contracted to work together under some form of Pain-Share/Gain-Share approach that rewards for doing the right things well. A team creates models and transitions from conflict checking, through scheduling and cost management, acting as the focus of all project documentation. At construction completion, the team and models transition smoothly to operations and maintenance.

IPD is an approach that offers the promise of better design, improved sustainability and increasing the certainty of outcomes. When used for projects in an Enterprise BIG-BIM ecosystem with established teams, IPD is an ideal way to maximize the long-term value to owners. When used for design and construction only, IPD is a big step toward correcting the issues that plague traditional projects.

The goal of IPD is to level the playing field for the owner, architect, consultants, contractors, and subcontractors. Collaboration, information sharing, openness, and transparency are essential to the process. The owner, principal designers, and builders remain involved from early design through project completion. Negotiating new, collaborative IPD agreements built on pain-share/gain-share principles requires early stage investment in time and money. The long-term benefits far outweigh the short-term expense and effort.

IPD harnesses the knowledge, talents, and insight of the team to increase project value, reduce waste and optimize efficiency through all phases of design, fabrication, and construction. In this environment, it is in the best interest of everyone to efficiently solve problems. In ways, that work to the benefit of all. Passing blame and scapegoating are reduced and replaced by an environment that encourages productivity and quality work. The success of projects depends on this approach.

IPD needs an owner that is willing to pay for the value received. Also needed are planning, design and construction professionals whose goal is to earn a profit by adding value to the project. Owners that don't pay for actual value-added and professionals that depend on error, waste, and inefficiency to make a profit, guarantee IPD failures.

Decision-making in an IPD process isn't hierarchical and bears in mind the expertise of multiple parties. Dynamic leadership changes often. Moving from those with expertise in a realm to optimize delivery in all areas of the project. The project benefits from the depth and breadth of knowledge that organizations and members bring to the team. One size does not fit all as the process accommodates each member of the team. Team building, Initiation, and Contracting.

Business interests align through shared risk and reward that depends on project outcomes. Underpinning IPD is the sharing of risks and rewards (with or without an incentive pool) in a collaborative environment. IPD can take many forms and happens at many different speeds. A checklist of the basic steps for a typical IPD project might include:

- ☐ *Programming and concept development.*

- ☐ *Validation or Extended Schematic Design. During the design process, involvement from consultants and specialty contractors works to achieve cost savings. Their input works to detect clashes and other issues early in the process. Well before construction starts. Eliminating costly design errors. The result is fewer requests for information and fewer change orders during construction.*

- ☐ *Detail Design, Analysis, and Implementation Documentation.*

- ☐ *Agency Review, Quality Assurance, and Buyout.*

☐ *Construction. You manage problems and optimize the project for efficiency before construction. Shared responsibility and BIM tools enable the team to control the process from beginning to end. Trade coordination, scheduling, cost management and all other aspects of the process benefit from front-end planning designed to eliminate construction waste. When members directly benefit from the efficiencies they create and the problems they avoid, construction improves.*

☐ *Close-out and Commissioning.*

☐ *Operations and Maintenance.*

The building industry's focus on projects rather than owner assets, tend to narrow or limit the potential of IPD. In the future, IPD may grow to become a support tool that brings pre-established teams of experts to bear on handling owner assets for the entire lifecycle. In today's IPD, the steps above look much like the steps in any traditional design and construction process.

Some large interdisciplinary teams embrace IPD as an opportunity to better address the need for a more holistic and sustainable approach to projects. Locally, smaller firms and smaller customers also see the promise of IPD. A lack of legal precedents, inflexible procurement regulations, lack of experience and inertia and a significant early stage investment in time and money to negotiate collaborative agreements continue to be the primary reasons that Integrated Project Delivery is a goal rarely attained.

Evidence from early implementers promises as much as 25% reductions in costs and length of time required to deliver projects. The evidence also shows a greater certainty of outcomes. Even with such benefits, the organizational complexities and unfamiliarity with collaborative work environments make IPD rare in today's contracting environment.

A small number of owners have taken the risk and applied IPD to their projects. The results are projects that utilize emerging technologies in ways that may lead to a more comprehensive use of IPD. However, today most focus on real returns in less comprehensive ways.

Much too often, teams continue to modify turnkey-delivery, design-build, construction-management-at-risk, and Agency-Construction-Management in the name of IPD, with mixed results. All achieve some of the benefits. None reach the full advantage.

Visit and subscribe to James Salmon's, Collaborative Construction Blog to get ideas about the issues and needs of Integrated Project Delivery, with a focus on connected agreements. Download a copy of the American Institute of Architects commentary on their Integrated Project Delivery documents from their online Contract Documents system. Download other Collaborative Agreements from the Association of General Contractor's ConsensusDocs web site.

Agency-Construction-Management

Agency-Construction-Management, or ACM is a method for managing a construction program. Agency Construction Managers work as an extension of an owner's staff. They are the owner's agent. In this role, the successful construction manager becomes the advocate for the owner's needs.

The underlying concepts in the Integrated Project Delivery process are like those used by many of today's most successful agency construction managers. When properly managed, this approach closely approximates Integrated Project Delivery and can achieve most collaborative project benefits discussed elsewhere.

The designer test-fits the owner's requirements, using the Building Information Model to minimize the unknowns. The goal is to provide the team with high level graphics and data to improve their understanding of the project, as early in the planning and design process as possible. The Agency Construction Manager then develops the Cost Model.

The Agency Construction Manager also takes on the responsibility for managing the cost constraints, by controlling the project's contingency. By automating management systems, the team also provides rapid, 'near real-time' processing of submittals, communications, and facilities management support.

Rather than the collaborative, multiple party agreement that underpins Integrated Project Delivery, the owner becomes the contracting entity between all parties, backed by the construction manager. The Agency Construction Manager holds no trade or design contracts. The owner is a direct party to many more agreements than in any of the other

The ACM manages the contracts and surety bonds in the owner's interest. Since the Agency Construction Manager isn't the contracted entity, risk management via bonds or other means come from the project's trade contractors, rather than from a single contracting entity.

The ACM also manages costs in the owner's interest to ensure that payments to contractors occur at a pace that minimizes the risk of default. Since the agency construction manager does not hold any contracts, the ability to create windfall (or hidden) profit opportunities is limited.

Short of Integrated Project Delivery, Agency-Construction-Management offers the most transparent and collaborative strategy for project implementation. The contractual underpinnings of this method lead to an open and free exchange between all parties. With a construction manager acting as a trusted advisor to the owner and a design team contractually obligated to share and collaborate, Agency-Construction-Management offers a significant step toward Integrated Project Delivery, in a format where the owner's additional management costs are minimal.

Download and read the American Institute of Architects reference material on Agency Construction Manager as Advisor.

Design-Build

The traditional Design-Build process offers owners a single point of design and construction responsibility, early price lock-in, and the potential for shorter delivery times. It also limits the owner's ability to manage quality, and verify the cost of changes. The focus is on low cost as opposed to high quality or owner needs. In a BIM-oriented Design-Build project, the owner has opportunities to manage the process better; to rebalance costs, quality, and owner needs.

Many owners opt for Design–Build because of the promise of a single point of responsibility for design and construction. Many believe that this option offers the easiest route to reducing the impact of cost overruns and conflict in projects. Managed correctly, this may be true.

Design–build started as a contractor led process with minimal support from the lowest cost design teams. General contractors, capitalizing on their ability to be first to the owner, used design–build to create new work while minimizing *interference* from designers. This approach often led to compromised solutions and shoddy workmanship—with the best of intentions, but not always. Too often Design–Builders offered prices that did not accurately reflect project costs, based on imperfect understanding and poor documentation.

For such design–build projects, change orders and extras required to meet the owner's real need are commonplace. With an owner that is uninformed; quality is driven down to save on costs—all with the owner's (sometimes) unwitting acceptance.

Such forms of design-build fall far short when managing built environment assets over their lifecycle. More is needed if the goal is to pay the lowest reasonable cost for the quality (and quantity) of project required to meet an owner's long-term need. Creative management of the design-build process is necessary to bridge the gap. One way to bridge the quality and needs gap is for owners to create a detailed standard to guide the Design-Builder's performance.

Owner concepts are quickly test-fitted and evaluated using early stage validation models to minimize uncertainty with the goal of eliminating many of the unknowns that drive the cost variation in Design-Build. The Design-Builder works from the owner's validation model to create detailed design and then to price and implement the work. The comprehensive vision represented in the owner validation model defines design-build performance requirements.

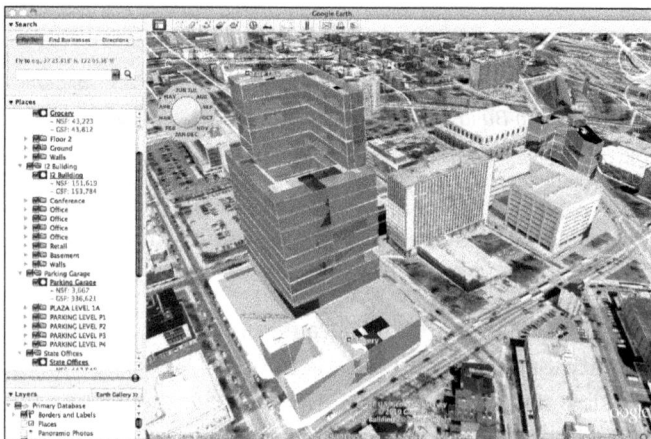

The project's vision expressed in BIG-BIM 'seeds' the Design-Builder's design process and acts as the 'bridge' between the owner's requirements and the Design-Builder's process, to achieve many of the long-term benefits that owners seek.

The owner receives the quantity and quality that is needed. The goal is to reduce or eliminate the uncertainties that force design-builders to embed contingencies. You give them what they need to best price and build your project. A high level of information about customer requirements coupled with clear communications can result in very successful Design-Build projects. Many benefits come from adding such connected processes to a Design-Build project.

There are issues to address:

Always require fully engineered and professionally sealed design solutions for design-build projects. Without this step, too many things can be done using little more than system components pulled from catalogs with little or no engineering input.

Today, few engineers have changed their methods to accommodate Integrated Project Delivery or this model of Design-Build. Because of this, design-builders often rely on performance criteria at the design stage that may or may not describe the ideal solution for a project, rather than connecting an engineered concept. This approach is a compromise that can be a project's weak point, resulting in cost escalation or underperforming systems. As more engineers develop a connected engineering process, their systems will be able to be test-fitted and analyzed within the validation model.

The direction included in performance criteria also needs to be modeled and analyzed. If the engineers assisting the owner are not yet working in a connected manner, their performance criteria documents are also a weak point in the process. Without engineered guidelines, the owner is pushing an open-ended responsibility for systems' design onto the design-builder team. Properly managed and contracted this scenario can allow the design-builder freedom within a defined framework. However, in many cases, this is counter to the goal of establishing the certainty of outcomes that is an underlying principle of connected business.

In many markets, the entire design-builder team is NOT functional in BIM. Owners, therefore, lose the long-term advantage that comes from a connected process, when you hand off the project to the design-builder. If the design-builder team isn't BIM proficient, the benefits effectively stop at the point of transferring the validation model. In this scenario, the owner receives superior bid outcomes that come from comprehensive pricing documents. But, receives few long-term benefits.

The short-term benefits still make the process valuable. However, much of the value to owners comes during operations. A partial solution to this dilemma is for the owner design-build consultant to maintain project models and project records in a parallel process. This parallel process lets the owner keep the long-term benefits, although at additional cost.

Even with design-build, the goal should be to contract with teams that can connect with the process. Standard agreements to support design-build, in an integrated-project-like workflow, are available. Many of the issues related to transparency and collaboration are evolving as new contracting and procurement tools emerge. Even with the best of intentions, the owner and design-builder remain as separate entities. There is always the potential for conflict between the parties in Design-Build.

Substantial opportunities still exist for participants to create benefits for themselves while harming others, without anyone knowing what occurred. Outcomes using design-build will continue to depend on good intentions and ethical behavior. Do what you can to maximize the good will and proper actions of all participants.

Download and read the American Institute of Architects reference material on Design-Build. Also, read the Association of General Contractor's guidebook on Design-Build from their ConsensusDocs web site.

Turnkey-Delivery

Turnkey-Delivery involves assigning full responsibility for the project to a developer entity. In this option, the owner monitors the developer's progress and may participate in any, or all, phases of the process—Or not. The developer hires the designer and constructor and provides a single point of delivery responsibility.

Connected processes can take place within the developer team if pain-share/gain-share internal relationships are in place. To achieve a close match between an owner's need and the final product requires carefully prepared agreements and a clear scope of requirements. The standard of the developer entity's performance, in the form of a model that validates the owner's need, is a good place to start.

This *validation model* can define a vision for the project, itemize program requirements and detail owner needs. This model can then serve as the measurable standard of success for the project. During the validation process, owners with BIG-BIM tools can test fit to eliminate solutions that will not meet their need. When completed in tandem with the developer entity (as a two-step process) this model can act to engage the team in ways that foster collaboration.

Relationships and outcomes in a Turnkey process can be adversely affected by concealed intentions and business self-interests that hamper collaboration. Since the developer assumes full construction and delivery liability, transparency of financial information can suffer, causing participates to disengage and focus on the individual rather than team or project needs. Collaboration between the owner and other participants usually depends on good intentions and ethical behavior. Substantial opportunities exist to create benefits for the developer entity while harming the owner or others, without anyone knowing what occurred.

Some owners require a turnkey-delivery package that includes the operation of the facility following construction completion. The owner retains the option of operating and managing the facility themselves or employing the developer and leasing the project. This extra layer of services can be used to the owner's advantage.

> *By mandating tight connection of data throughout the process, it is possible to implement connected workplace management and other tools as the work proceeds, if the developer entity has (or can obtain) the level of technical support and systems required to efficiently capture and manage data throughout the process.*

Construction-Management-at-Risk

Responsibilities for the entire project are like those of Turnkey-delivery when an owner opts to use a Construction-Management-at-Risk (CM-R) approach. The key difference is that usually, a large general contracting company acts as the developer, eliminating one layer of organization and associated costs. The Construction Manager supports the Owner while retaining responsibility for delivering design support and construction.

Many jurisdictions favor this option for large, high visibility projects. Because of their size and complexity, these projects offer opportunities to highlight individual model features, sometimes with little downstream value. These are often big projects that have come to rely on little-bim and where anecdotally, much bim washing occurs.

Visualization, clash detection, 4D, 5D, cloud-based project controls, bar-coding and laser scanning have all featured prominently in such projects. Even when the resources to implement lifecycle BIM exist, it remains an open question as to the long-term benefit that accrues to these projects.

While the box for BIM is usually checked off, few that use CM-R work with a lifecycle BIG-BIM ecosystem. Team members use BIM tools to improve their documentation—in their interests. The designer benefits from better and faster imagery. The contractor uses management tools to coordinate better the paperwork and people that build the project. Little changes except for the software.

There are many places where some level of collaborative delivery can relate to this option, making this a great approach for those that wish to try individual model features and select connected delivery features in ways that are easy to control and show to others. That said, CM-R retains many of the fundamental flaws associated with the design-bid-build option.

Few of the contractual relationships and work processes change to reflect the need for a collaborative pain-share/gain-share approach. The process is fraught with concealed intentions and business self-interests that hamper transparency. Once past the point of agreement on a Guaranteed Maximum Price, the Construction Manager assumes full construction liability. Information sharing, especially financial information sharing, often suffers. A Construction-Management-at-Risk project might proceed like this:

The design team is selected using a qualifications-based process. The CM-R does not hold contracts with the designers, who work directly for the Owner.

The Construction Manager is selected independently, using a price and qualifications-based selection process.

The design team creates a concept for pricing. They use the owner's programming, with input from the Construction Manager.

The Construction Manager prices the concept and delivers a guaranteed maximum price. With the contribution of the design team, owner, and subcontractors.

The Owner and CM-R sign an agreement at a Guaranteed Maximum Price after any adjustments and negotiation. The Owner contracts for construction with the single CM-R entity. The Construction Manager provides a single surety bond.

The design team creates a set of construction documents.

The Construction Manager re-prices based on the construction documents. The Owner and CM-R adjust the guaranteed maximum price for any changes.

After amendments to the Guaranteed Maximum Price, the CM-R is authorized to proceed with construction. Usually, the CM-R is required to bid trade contractors and then consult with the owner before awarding of contracts to other entities.

The CM-R builds the project per the construction documents and has project control, much as in the design-build method. Changes that take place during development become change orders. The CM-R and Owner share savings based on an agreed upon formula.

On the surface, the Construction Manager at Risk approach offers an improved model of single point responsibility. The reality can be quite different. As the project progresses and construction starts, the Construction Manager at Risk is no longer required to share financial details. Suddenly, detailed negotiations with trade contractors, the actual value to the owner of change orders, and the cost of project support staff become an issue.

Even with a Guaranteed Maximum Price, the Owner is often harmed, without realizing the impact. Savings that should accrue to the Owner too often accrue to the Construction Manager at Risk. The Construction Manager at Risk, in strict compliance with the contract, has many opportunities to enhance project outcomes to his or her company's benefit.

Download and read the American Institute of Architects reference material on Construction Management as Constructor. Also, read the Association of General Contractor's guidebook on CM-At-Risk.

Design-Bid-Build

Design-Bid-Build or DBB is the traditional design and construction process in the United States. A design team, working for the owner, creates a set of Design documents, and then assists the owner in obtaining a Bid from a General Contractor. The General Contractor, working for the owner, then Builds the project. No contractual relationship exists between the Design Team and the General Contractor.

Design-Bid-Build is the most difficult option to restructure for collaboration and connection. The decision to use this option has little to do with collaboration, connection, long-term needs, sustainability, or resilience. This option has long been a favorite of government procurement personnel and for public bidding.

When asked to describe the reasoning behind the choice of this option, many cite the belief that Design-Bid-Build works in the publics' best interest. Advocates would have us believe that this approach is the best way to assure everyone that we are getting the best value for their money. This was true, once upon a time in a land far, far away, but for many years, the truth has been much different.

Relationships between the owner, the architect, and the general contractor are intentionally adversarial in the Design-Bid-Build process. Case law and established standards of care related to Design-Bid-Build are clear. There have been thousands of court cases and much precedent. For many, this option is a promise of unplanned change orders and litigation. In fact, some large, well known owners budget their projects believing that litigation is a guarantee.

The effort required to overcome such issues is significant. Design–Bid–Build has produced more sub-par projects, more lawsuits, and lower productivity than any of the other categories of options. History has shown that it often results in increased conflict and people working at cross-purposes. Design–Bid–Build projects are often late, significantly over budget and the highest cost approach. Some find this counter-intuitive, believing that Design–Bid–Build offers the only way to be sure of the lowest price. This belief has repeatedly been shown to be false.

Faced with Design–Bid–Build as the only procurement option, all participants must focus on the principles of how and why people collaborate effectively. Connected delivery benefits become more a matter of all involved striving to do the right thing despite limitations of contracts. The owner must take a leadership role in this effort.

In this minimally connected environment, the focus may be on using a traditional process and maintaining building operations and maintenance data within the prototype model for downstream use. The designer creates a model which they then handoff to the construction team. The construction team then creates a construction model, often from scratch for use in conflict checking and other tasks. At the end of the construction process, the team hands the owner a file to seed operations and maintenance. Refer to the COBIE CHECK chapter earlier in the book; for this is the model from which COBie was drawn. Most of the traditional inefficiencies remain when using DBB, even with the addition of COBie.

Download and read the American Institute of Architects reference material on Conventional project delivery. Also, read the Association of General Contractor's materials on General Contracting.

Case Study
Community Center

The Director of Parks & Recreation commented: *We picked this company because of the way they focused on helping me to understand our project in the early stages, using BIM. As a department head of a rural county, I don't often get involved in design projects. Each time, I must ramp up my knowledge of design and construction.*

What are the interesting aspects of this project?

Modified public bid Design-Bid-Build for project delivery using little-bim that connects to a BIG-BIM ecosystem.

Downstream reuse of building information models to support phased delivery.

Stopping the building's decline and all other parts of this project occurred in a severely constrained fiscal environment. Few funds were available, and then only when tightly managed throughout the projects.

Front loaded project decision-making using connected processes and tools to improve outcomes.

Location—Denton, MD, USA.

Caroline County, Maryland received an unused Maryland National Guard Armory, built in 1938, with the agreement that the County use the facility as a community center. The Armory is an example of late–1940s military design with stepped parapets, cast stone trims, and projecting steel windows. The building was in poor condition throughout, due to deferred maintenance. Only after stabilizing the shell to stop rapid deterioration could the County's needs be met.

The armory came with many restrictions and required the county to maintain and restore the building, monitored by the Maryland Historical Trust. The detail and accuracy of little–bim allowed management of these requirements, while fulfilling the County's needs for the project.

Designers understand that one good job leads to another. In this case, a recently completed and successful renovation near the Armory resulted in an interview to adaptively reuse the building for a new Community Center. During the process, if became apparent that selection committee members understood the benefits of early decision-making support designed to make their project successful. They didn't call it BIM, or think of it as connection, but they knew that tight cost controls and certainty of outcomes were critical.

In the end, the owner cited the ability to connect BIG-BIM based processes into the traditional delivery process as the deciding factor in selecting the team. The selection committee knew nothing about BIM, but they knew that they needed more than what the traditional design process offers.

Opportunity: Support owner decision-making and review process.

One can use commercial-off-the-shelf (COTS) little-bim technology to leverage one's ability to deliver a scope that exceeds Owner expectations, even for the smallest renovation projects. In this case, we used such tools and our knowledge of the processes to help the Owner make early, informed decisions. The team proactively worked with the County to find strategies for completing the project, based on facts and opportunities.

Since you always start by understanding the Owner's needs and issues, for the Armory, we made field measurements, generated a facility conditions assessment and an as-is model as the first tasks. The team then modeled repairs and a design solution.

Mind maps were used to consolidate early data collection processes: Embedded data was used to project time requirements and analyze costs; mindmaps organized the text documents required for submissions. and; mindmaps were used to capture requirements and for space programming with Parks & Recreation staff.

Next, this information was placed into an existing conditions model, which became the basis for the design concept model used to validate Owner needs and requirements. From this model, we extracted existing and proposed quantity data to support the creation of a program estimate. The project's program estimate is a parametric Cost Model tied to project assumptions, a delivery strategy, and a schedule. From the program estimate, it became apparent that the available funding would severely limit the County's ability to pay for the project.

County staff knew that they didn't have enough money to do the entire project. The team responded by reworking the concept model and program estimate to identify the scope of work that fit within the available funds and by adding projections for future phases. The concept model, which included phasing, and aligned program estimate formed the basis for all further work on the project. With incremental additions, this model allowed extraction of construction documentation for each phase and subcomponent. Furthermore, the program estimate became the tool for managing costs and time through all phases. The project was completed successfully from these documents.

When completed, the Validation Study created from the mind maps, concept model and program estimate was presented to the County to assist them in understanding the short and long-range goals of the project. The same data was presented to the State of Maryland to lock in funding.

Opportunity: Coordinate phasing to match funding.

The program estimate, coupled with the early details from the model, became a tool for the county to allocate available funds. The decision came down to: abandon the project and return it to the State; immediately find much more money, or; construct the project in phases.

The decision was made to do the project in phases, as funding became available. Phase 1 included repair to leaks in the roof, wall systems, plus adding an elevator, accessible toilets, and a few interior improvements, deferring all remaining work to future phases.

The Director of Parks & Recreation commented of the process: *The design team provided detailed information, from the beginning. Their approach helped me to understand everything that was going into the project. This understanding led to questions that I may not have asked in a normal process. In other projects, I got floor plans and sketches and had to assume that they included everything. When the details finally came, we often found that we needed changes. The changes then took a lot of effort, took too long and cost a lot. With this process, the details, and a clear picture of what was involved were apparent. If I wanted something changed it happened quickly, and I could see how it affected the entire project before I spent too much money. It allowed us to educate ourselves.*

The team designed and documented the project in ArchiCad to produce construction documents for Phase 1. The project was then publicly bid to General Contractors. The County awarded the contract within the budget established by the program estimate.

Due to scheduling constraints defined in the program estimate, the elevator was pre-purchased. As the construction process unfolded, the County adjusted to expend budgeted contingency funds as defined by the program estimate. The little-bim models simplified understanding and management of the changes, reducing errors and construction problems. The County got the project they paid for, and more.

Construction of Phase 1 was completed on-time and with minimal problems. The project management database and the little-bim model captured as-builts, submittals, and changes for downstream use. Available funds were exhausted. There was little hope that funds for the remainder of the work would be available anytime soon. Before fully shutting down the project the county did a limited amount of clean up work.

> The County Engineer commented: *Being able to break out the elevator portion of the project to allow for early procurement saved a lot of time and enabled us to meet funding schedules. Being able to create a 3D model of the building was also a great asset in providing a clear vision of the project. Typically, the commissioners must look at 2D plans and elevations and no matter how often you see those; it is hard to envision what you are going to get. The 3D renderings made it clear.*

At multiple times during Phase 1, the Maryland Historical Trust requested a window analysis to support future work on the building's exterior. Using details extracted from Phase 1 as-built model and photography documenting existing conditions, this study was completed and submitted for review, at minimal cost. Design work terminated upon completion of a historical window survey.

Because of the funding constraints, the project then went dormant. The building remained mostly unusable. The County had a weathertight building that was only accessible once one managed to negotiate the half-flight of stairs into the building. Finishes were old and tired. Heating was sporadic and expensive to operate. Lead and asbestos remained problems.

On a Friday, two years later the team unexpectedly received a call from the County. The project was again a priority. Needs had changed. The Department of Parks & Recreation was directed to move from the County's central office building, as quickly as possible. Funds would be made available to make it happen. The Department wanted to move to the Armory. First, they wanted to ensure that the building could still become a community center, as well. The Department's requirements had changed dramatically, and they could no longer be sure that everything would fit into the building.

Opportunity: Manage evolving programmatic needs.

Asbestos removal, and lead remediation of the Armory's firing range, followed by to-the-shell demolition led off work on Phase 2. During the process, we managed to salvage the hardwood floor system in the original drill area for reuse in the renovation.

Once that was complete work began on the balance of the project. Work included restoration of the exterior and new windows and doors meeting historical guidelines. Work in the interior adapted the space for the new uses while retaining as many of the historical elements as possible.

> As the process unfolded, the County Engineer commented: *The community center project continues to progress very smoothly and efficiently. The team has worked great together. The communication throughout the entire process helps the work progress without many complications.*

The Phase 1 as-built little-bim allowed the team to reassess and redesign the project, and to reset the project in a two-week period. The first task was to re-establish communications system and to reassess project requirements. In the two years following completion of Phase 1, the tools for project analysis and online communication had improved dramatically. The little-bim authoring tool used for Phase 1 had undergone significant upgrades.

The team reactivated the as-built little-bim and completely reworked the earlier concepts, in short order. The County received the decision support information that they required to move forward, quickly, and inexpensively. All due to little-bim that included a dependable upgrade cycle that enabled the models to be transitioned into later versions quickly.

The restart required the team to reevaluate the Owner's program needs and redesign to accommodate the changes. Beginning with an inventory of Parks & Recreation's current and projected space requirements, the team reviewed and verified needs, again using mindmaps. Then the team updated project programming and the program estimate which was quickly approved by the County.

When complete, the new concept for the Armory housed the Parks & Recreation Department offices in the basement, created a recreation center on the first floor and housed support facilities on the second level.

In two weeks, the project went from abandoned-in-place to a phone call, to approval to proceed with the redesigned project. Faster and less expensively than in the traditional process. The process required minimal fieldwork, because of the as-built little-bim from Phase 1. This effort alone saved the County 50% in fees.

As the details for Phase 2 emerged, the updated little-bim was used to prototype problem areas. An acoustical dampening system was incorporated to manage sound transmission between the basketball courts and the office areas. One of the first Variable Refrigerant Flow (VRF) systems in the region enabled space-by-space control of temperatures in a highly sustainable way.

A Construction Project Manager said of the process: *From the start, the communication and information were clear and handled with quick turnaround. Questions were handled promptly and in an organized fashion. With a renovation, there are always hidden problems, but the architect had an excellent understanding of construction and the building and worked with us to resolve any issue quickly.*

The design progressed, and we extracted construction documentation for public bidding. On November 13, 2008, the fully restored Community Center was dedicated to retired Maryland National Guard Adjutant General James F. Fretterd and opened to the public.

The success of the Armory project is more about people than about technology. Little-bim enables faster and more accurate delivery of services, but people working collaboratively to achieve the Owner's goals is the real measure of success.

The Director of Parks & Recreation commented: *As a manager, I look for small manageable pieces that fit into place to organize and get things done. This little company works big. The principal designer is visionary and looks for the right tools to get things done in the most efficient way. The project manager has a strong construction background. The design team generates the ideas and creates the concepts, and their PM gives me the assurance that the details are being worked out in practical terms. The relationship provides us with a "yin/yang" approach. They turn with ease and adjust quickly. Larger companies are like dinosaurs or ocean liners; they take a long time and a lot of effort to turn or change.*

Enterprise Assets

Historically, facilities have not been considered mission-critical assets. Buildings have been necessary but not been as vital components to success or failure of the enterprise. People, money, location, transportation, and marketing have always been critical; buildings, not so much.

This traditional view of the built environment is changing, as resources become tight and new and unexpected events impact business sustainability. The ability to respond resiliently, to maintain and enable other business functions, has become of prime importance. Events with catastrophic losses of such functionality due to storms, earthquakes, and terrorism, have demonstrated the need to look at built environment assets differently. Long-term success now requires a connected approach to all enterprise assets, including built environment assets.

Business planners have long used data to understand and plan for functions considered critical to an organization's mission. Financial, marketing, and management planning are long established and mature systems. Geographic information systems and facilities management are in the mix. All continuously generate data.

While other areas embraced shareable and reusable data, the building industry remained focused on paper and files. Most of the components of the built environment have therefore remained in silos that do not connect or impact on enterprise asset planning. The opportunities that come from making this data shareable and accessible seem obvious.

Few organizations connect all the information they make. The enterprises that have tried have found the process to be costly. The complexities have overwhelmed businesses at all levels. Many have failed in the quest.

The enterprise BIG-BIM ecosystem changes the equation. For any multi-building and multi-campus organization, the benefits are significant. Geography becomes the unifying framework that connects the data from everywhere.

Complex data is available when and where needed, for use by anyone, much as on the Internet. The ecosystem is dependent on web services, cloud computing, open-standards, information sharing and interoperability between tools.

Case Study
Integrated Decisions

Because government agencies are big, often the issues they face are not handled efficiently. Add to this mix: disconnected functions; outdated procurement systems; institutional inertia, and; risk averse management systems. There is often no easy way to manage their wicked problems.

What are the interesting aspects to consider?

Those leading the move to BIG-BIM at the national level are working to make all data securely visible, available, and usable when and where needed for accelerate decision-making.

National initiatives are beginning to allow people to work more openly and collaboratively to make better decisions and improve governance.

Forward-looking agencies proactively work to create BIG-BIM ecosystems by educating themselves on the principles that drive the ever-evolving benefits of technology.

Location—Worldwide.

The US federal government faces a unique set of asset management issues. Agencies appear robust and monolithic until one digs deep and sees the high level of broken systems and inappropriate processes in place. They seem to have enormous resources until one realizes the vast numbers of missions they support.

Many attempts, at great cost to taxpayers, have been made to use technology to manage the challenges faced by government agencies. The results have been less than stellar. Agencies make plans and discuss improvements. They allow, and sometimes demand that software vendors create solutions that are not open and transparent. All while lauding their innovation programs and paying lip-service to technological innovation. The waste amounts to billions of dollars.

When it comes to BIM, many Federal Agencies do not understand the big-picture issues and are using a little-bim approach as a hand drafting and CADD replacement. These Agencies tend to adopt static, vendor-centric little-bim implementations that are unsustainable and lack resilience. They are focused on BIM as software and BIM using only one software program.

Such agencies' attempts at technological solutions have been too involved, too insular and, too hard to use. Failure, in the form of having to start anew after spending much time and money on a flawed approach, is highly predictable.

Fortunately, some in the federal government are moving in a different direction. They are bringing the Internet, web services, open-data, information exchanges, and the App Economy into the mix. Initiatives like MAX.gov, the General Services Administration's 18F office, and the GovLab.org have been created to enable access to information—With the goal of improving the process of governing the United States.

The massive ship of state is slowly turning toward Open-Data and Web-based information exchanges. Rather than relying on manual filing and single use approaches for data exchanges, they are exploring a service-oriented-architecture approach to web-based information sharing.

Such initiatives and openness did not happen overnight. Within a small number of government agencies, individuals experimented, tested and, prototyped ways to use data to govern better. To work faster and smarter. Their efforts have often been at odds with their more traditional and entrenched brethren. The agencies leading the move to BIG-BIM create systems that focus attention on shared knowledge resources in a net-centric environment. They shift to many-to-many exchange of data that enables many users and applications to access the same data to extend beyond yesterday's focus on standardized, predefined, point-to-point interfaces.

Government agencies that are leading the way are using technology to better their missions and transform how they do business. They actively pursue connected strategies for facility planning, design, construction, operation, and retirement/modernization to reduce the total lifecycle cost and create world-class facilities.

The people that are the champions of these changes face challenges to organizational and cultural collaboration, business processes, workflows, and technology. Problems manifest themselves in many ways, including:

Organizational and cultural issues hinder mission performance. Agencies find it difficult to collaborate efficiently with outside service providers such as architects, space and facility planners, and consultants that need to access information to deliver affordable services. Overcoming the inertia that comes from traditional systems can, at times, overwhelm the best of us.

Collaboration is often difficult or non-existent. Single user systems abound. Data is not consistent or normalized to any open-standard. User access is limited due to arcane and training driven requirements. Existing technology and management make a hard job much harder.

In-situ business processes and workflows rely on static documents or manual data entry with the inherent human error that results. To work around the mistakes work is done contrary to published and legislated standards. Too often even internal documentation and rules are at odds, due to manual and file-based systems.

Efficiency and service delivery conflict with both internal and external security needs. Workarounds to enable work to be done, create unmanaged security threats. Agencies are working toward improvements in the management of cyber security of facility related applications, data, and devices.

Although the leading groups are encountering multiple change management issues, they continue to strive to innovate and move toward BIG–BIM ecosystems. Over time, the efforts they are making will result in a more effective and efficient infrastructure for the benefit of all. The leading organizations work to improve how they visualize and use facility related data from the world view down to the device level. They work to connect the dots throughout the entire facility lifecycle. In some cases, such as with the US Coast Guard, these organizations provide leadership to the industry. The agencies leading the way toward BIG–BIM are:

- *Relating to more (and more types of) stakeholders, both internally and externally. Within and outside the government sphere.*

- *Working to leverage technologies such as Building Information Modeling (BIM), Geographical Information Systems (GIS), Facility Management (FM) and, mobile platforms to connect with the downstream use of data.*

- *Seeking ways to improve feedback between planning, design, construction, and operations, and their criteria and standards. Within the agencies leading the way, standards and masterplans are becoming living, breathing documents, rather than being updated manually and printed on paper or other single use approaches.*

- *Extending agency capabilities with cloud computing, the consolidation of data centers and virtualization. Leaders emphasize accessibility and reuse of computable data, rather than hosting and filing paper or its' digital equivalents.*

- *Using little-bim and a variety of other software tools and processes to create BIG-BIM ecosystems.*

In most cases, little-bim continues to gain acceptance throughout the architecture and construction sectors of the federal government. Involvement of little-bim in planning and engineering are close behind, trailed by acceptance in operations and maintenance. The strategies of the leading agencies include the use of BIM, geographic information systems, operations, and business data to support their missions in the most effective, efficient, and assured manner while remaining consistent with national security, operational requirements, and best value enterprise business practices.

Go to GOVERNMENT LEADERSHIP CASE STUDIES in the MORE CASE STUDIES section later in the book for details of the work done to move the US Federal Government into the Connected Age.

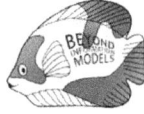

SIX
SHARE AND COLLABORATE

Technology makes it possible for the smallest organization to compete in markets once the sole domain of large corporations. The same tools make it possible for large companies to deliver in markets once only served by small entities. Both situations require changes to how building owners and businesses approach projects and assets. Both conditions require changes in structure, process, and attitude.

Hierarchical command-and-control organizations are falling by the wayside as few enterprises have the dynamic leadership needed to best respond to the complexities they face. Replacing them are groups based on distributed sharing and collaborative, process focused organizational structures. This collaborative environment requires that we form teams designed to bring the appropriate skills to bear on issues. Collaborative planning is critical to their success.

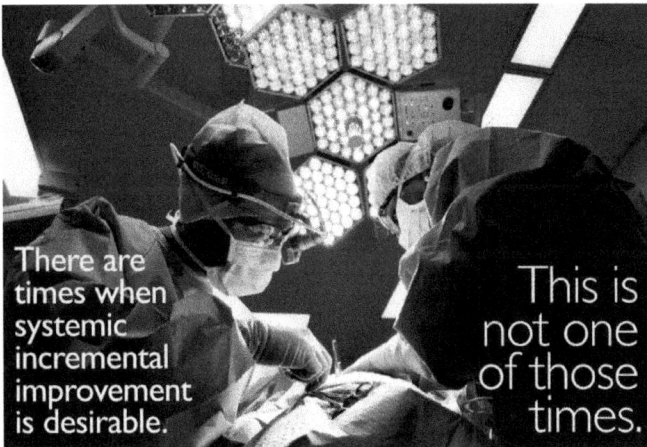

There are times when systemic incremental improvement is desirable. This is not one of those times.

Future Organizations

Create a fully connected structure that can use available tools to leverage assets and skills. With such an organization, you can work smarter and create more with less.

The world becomes flatter every day. The line between the large corporations and the small company grows very faint. This leveling of business is happening because technology has developed to a level that allows the small business to compete on a one-to-one basis with the big corporation. The small business can produce the same quality, the same public persona, and the same (or better) results. Strategic alliances and tools available on the desktop and the Web enable the small business to work big and compete with anyone. Several characteristics shape the organization of the future:

- ☐ *They can sustain innovation;*

- ☐ *They thrive on open and collaborative relationships;*

- ☐ *They embrace flat organization structures;*

- ☐ *They use adaptive and flexible business and operating models;*

- ☐ *They tailor their skills and expertise to each experience rather than producing set-piece transactions;*

- ☐ *They are perceptive and insight driven;*

- ☐ *They are context aware, and;*

- ☐ *They are mobile.*

Spend the time needed to create a thought out and well-planned plan of action, focused filling one or more niches in the BIG-BIM ecosystem. Look for opportunities within the preconceived notions and design your offerings and structure, much as you would any other project.

Size Is Not the Critical Issue

We need to trust those with whom we work.

The size of an enterprise is less critical to a connected process in a BIG–BIM ecosystem. Technology blurs the line between individuals, small, and big businesses. Using mobile technology, an individual can bring a team of thousands to bear on an issue. Using cloud-based tools, a small business can use the same technology as her largest competitors. Traditional large businesses no longer have a technology edge, as anyone can bring the same tools and resources to bear.

In today's mobile, crowd sourced environment, it is imperative for large corporations to build and maintain trusting relationships. People have experienced too many problems as they interact with big business; highlighting the fact that many large corporations are not designed to maintain trust in a digital age. People are no longer sure that large enterprises can be trusted to help when things go wrong.

Because of the air of mistrust that exists, big businesses need to truly focus their energies toward their customers. Corporations that rely on words and not deeds are quickly exposed. Today even the biggest players must earn trust. Becoming a reliable advocate to help people understand and use BIG–BIM has advantages that come when large companies focus on building strong, trusting relationships that:

Bring a high level of people resources to bear on projects that require a lot of figure out time.

Bring specialized skills from many directions to bear on large, multiphase projects.

Bring a level of comfort to other large owners that prefer to work with corporations of similar size.

Small businesses are often taking the risk to do something that they have never done. They understand that their customers' trust is based on transparent, inclusive, and accountability-based business practices. Small businesses have real advantages in an environment where people seek certainty about things, and can:

Adapt quickly to today's way of doing work. They need to consult and convince fewer people to get things done.

Create a hierarchy that is easy to understand. Since they are small, they are already a flat organization, and everyone does a bit of everything.

Zero in on their individual skills and talents. They can concentrate on applying their resources where and when needed.

Take advantage of the Internet, as well as current and next-generation technology to level-up with the biggest corporations.

Size is only one area where the traditional approach is under siege. Facility owners are tired of the waste and errors. The news media make cost overruns and mismanagement of projects into feature articles. The industry struggles with tight fees and standards of care that don't fairly apportion risks and rewards. The attacks spring from construction processes that have not adapted to the changes in our society.

Whatever the size of your business, do what is needed to change for the better, and you will see benefit. Use the power of the today's tools and processes to increase certainty of outcomes. Build for the long-term, and focus on achieving the best for all concerned... no matter whether you are a sole-proprietor or a corporation with thousands of employees.

Decide How to Adapt

In preparing for battle I have always found that plans are useless, but planning is indispensable. — Dwight D. Eisenhower

We cannot avoid the pitfalls that come with industry wide change. As any soldier knows, *no plan survives the first contact with the enemy.* Can we learn to balance planning with action? To enable us to eliminate the train-wrecks before moving forward? Knowing that as soon as we decide something, the issue will change and need another decision? How can we keep up with the pace of change?

Too often, we act as though we can work out everything before we proceed. We make plans and create tools. We develop complex and arcane standards and attempt to define every contingency. All to minimize errors when we finally move forward. In today's world, is this truly the best way? Are mistakes, of all kinds, unforgivable even when we correct and move on to other things? Is perfection our only option? Does more planning result in zero errors? Not by a long shot.

It seems like many have missed the upheavals in other parts of our world. Other sectors have learned the hard way that the conservative, let's wait and plan and see what happens, approach is a formula for disaster. We cannot afford to continue this way. Things are changing too fast.

The ebb and flow of information happen so quickly that the ability to connect facts to support decision-making has become critical. At the pace of the Internet, we rarely have the luxury to focus and handle issues in isolation. When we do, as often as not, we are working with degraded data. We need to be able to interact with the latest information so that when we decide, we are working with the most recent facts.

Will we embrace the change and become more agile and capable, or something else? The construction industry must expedite the process. Or, the process will accelerate on its own and leave us behind. Things need to change if we are to bring the industry into the twenty-first century. We have three options:

1. Revolutionary change; discarding all that went before, much like happened in the travel industry. In this case, the industry will be under pressure to begin anew. New leaders will invent an entirely new process. Many will be left behind.

2. Evolutionary change; building on the best parts of the traditional process and replacing those that no longer work. The industry can connect the old with the new. Many will adapt, and some will be left behind.

3. Maintain the status-quo and fall back on tradition. Instead of responding to the situation the industry faces, worry about consensus and hope that the world will adapt to revert to what we know. Others will take our place and do what we now do cheaper and more efficiently.

In any of these cases, a different way of doing business is the result. In the past, systemic changes to the building industry required centralized control. The United Kingdom is currently attempting to achieve the promise of BIM using a 2nd Industrial Revolution, command-and-control response, and 3rd Industrial Revolution tools, to solve a 4th Industrial Revolution problem. No single entity can drive these changes using the old ways of working. The construction sector is too complex and splintered.

Together, we can do better. The building industry no longer needs to depend on command-and-control hierarchies. Individuals now have the authority to make the changes without permission from those above. Such is the App Economy that surrounds us. But, we need to accelerate the pace.

Five years once seemed like a long time. Now five years happens in a relative instant. The industry went from most people never having heard of BIM; to most people either using BIM, claiming to use BIM or to knowing that BIM will soon be a necessity. When the building industry transitioned from hand drafting to computer-aided design and drafting (CADD), the same process took more than fifteen years.

We already have the tools to use real-time data to our benefit. Building Information Modeling, coupled with Geographic Information Systems (GIS), facilities data, mobile devices, and the Internet all help us to capture connected knowledge. We use rules-based planning systems to capture and connect knowledge at all levels. If you can describe something, you can capture its essence in writing or as data. If you have captured something, you can define its relationship to other knowledge, and things.

The ability to interact with the vast stores of information that surround us is changing the world. Information has even changed how we react to the world. The usual way no longer produces the desired results. The only thing left is to decide how we will adapt to the changes.

Err on the Side of Daring

Plan for how you fit into this world of information. You don't have to have a grand and sweeping strategy. But, you do need a plan. Your plan should be a peek under the hood to look in detail at how you do business. Decide how you want to proceed.

Know that the environment that you work in is ever-changing. Change how you approach traditional processes. Find the means to add lifecycle methods. Embrace the new tools and new paradigms that create BIG-BIM ecosystems.

We have not done a good job of tailoring how we use our resources. In most cases, our processes remain linear. If you traditionally rely on linear processes and established norms, find ways that enable innovation and rapid development. The systematic approach makes it difficult to connect just-in-time decision-making with design and construction. It makes involvement in operations and management difficult at best.

You have a place in the BIG-BIM ecosystem and can add value to the mix. At today's pace of change, clutching to the old ways is no longer the best solution. Do not focus on strategies that require you to begin anew. That is the last resort. Begin by folding current and evolving technology into your traditional approach to creating new ways of doing business.

Technology gives you the ability to forecast with better data. It enables you to react quickly. It allows you to study a change in detail and provides the data to justify new ideas. By applying the rules that govern how bits of knowledge interact, you can assess options more quickly and more accurately than ever before. Where planning once relied on broad generalities and rules-of-thumb, one can now simulate real-life using BIG-BIM.

Today's world requires that one takes risks to move ahead. Increased speed and risk traditionally beget increased error and higher failure rates. BIM and connected processes give you the tools to go into an environment that uses informed decision-making to reduce your risk and to predict outcomes better, to minimize failure. Build just-in-time-decision-making into your plan. Critical decisions delayed create many of the problems that become visible to the larger public. Key decisions made too late in the process are an endemic problem. Poorly timed decisions are a root of all future problems.

Realize that it is best to err on the side of daring. As an industry, we are making too many cumulative mistakes and wasting resources using cautious approaches. We make too many errors by being conservative. Decision-making must be better. Forecasts must have greater accuracy. We must become more flexible and must plan with longer horizons. Otherwise, improvement isn't possible.

Plan of Action

The cautious side of your mind is at work. You are concerned with who will lead the change in your organization. You fear that your corporate culture will aggressively resist the change—since you are reshaping your culture and your routine ways of doing projects.

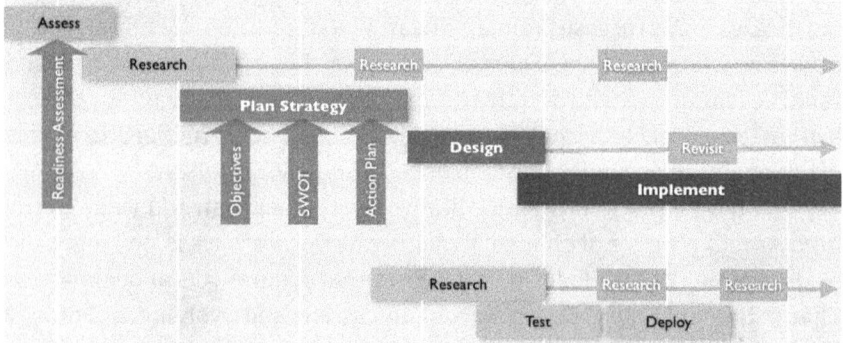

How will you bring the BIG-BIM ecosystem into your life and work? What steps will you take? You have a good idea of the concepts and scope of the change. You are creating a vision for remaking your business. You recognize areas where connected processes might give you a competitive advantage. You may have even started to build your business case for connected workflows and processes.

Many excellent tools and books are available to assist you in this exploration. My favorite books are *Business Model Generation* and *Value Proposition Design* by Alexander Osterwalder, et.al. These books (and the associated web-tools) offer unique perspectives on moving beyond outmoded business models to design the enterprises of tomorrow. Search and you will find many additional resources to guide your efforts. If you don't know exactly where to start, follow these steps:

Step 1. Assess what you have now;

Step 2. Plan your strategy;

Step 3. Plan and share it everywhere;

Step 4. Implement (just do it), and;

Step 5. Change how you work.

Step 1: Assess Readiness

Question everything about your world today. Understand the environment in which you now operate. Where do you provide value? Whom do you serve? Who supports you? How do you create value? What makes you unique? Your answers are colored by the type of work you do.

Are you ready for BIG-BIM and connected processes? If so, start with introspection. Look at how you do business. Look at how you interact with your supply chain: your advisors, consultants, and suppliers. Understand how your customers will react to a new way of doing things. Assess how you organize projects, produce documents and how your staff may respond to the change. This step is an internal appraisal of your present situation.

Your goal is to create a clear picture of who you to guide the next steps. Stay away from sweeping generalities and focus on the details of what you do and how you do it. Here are some things to consider:

- ☐ *Who are your key partners?*
- ☐ *What are the key things that you do?*
- ☐ *What are the essential resources you need to do what you do?*
- ☐ *How do you create value? What do your customers see as your value proposition?*
- ☐ *What products and services do you provide?*
- ☐ *Who do you work for and how are your relationships with them?*
- ☐ *Who do you plan to reach and serve?*
- ☐ *How do you communicate with your customers? How do you deliver value to them?*
- ☐ *What does it cost you to do business? How do you calculate your fees?*
- ☐ *What are your dependable revenue streams? How much money do you generate from each customer? What are your overhead costs?*
- ☐ *What is the composition of your team? What makes them come to work every day?*

These are but a few of the questions you should be asking. Involve as many of your friends, family, associates, and staff as possible. Other businesses have gotten valuable data by having staff members independently prepare their assessment. They have found value in measuring how well their teams understand what they do and what connected processes mean. It becomes a good starting point for further discussion. Budget several weeks for this process.

Many have found that mind mapping software is an ideal medium for documenting and communicating in any business change process. With mind mapping, you process snippets of data about yourself. You organize them to find patterns. You brainstorm and see where your thoughts take you while keeping track and building a map of how you work. Others can quickly understand and comment.

Step 2: Plan Strategically

SWOT Analysis guides you to assess your perception of the things that drive your business. The process helps you to identify positive and negative factors that promote or inhibit an organization's efforts. When you do SWOT, you assess both the internal and external factors that affect your business.

You started your strategic planning process by gathering information about what makes your business unique. At this stage, you understand your company in the context in which you work. Now you plan the path forward. Planning is critical. Without a strategy, you react to problems. You never get ahead of the curve. In simple terms, strategic planning helps you to:

☐ *Define your objectives for connecting your business;*

☐ *Document your financial conditions and history; and,*

☐ *Document your customer base and markets.*

Use a structured approach to assess the things that impact your future direction. Start by formally specifying your objectives. What are you going to do? What end state do you plan to reach—a phased-in approach to little-bim or a fully connected BIG-BIM focused business? Remember that you are seeking to identify the critical factors in achieving success. Your efforts should produce clear and well-prioritized strategies—not lists for list's sake.

One tool to consider is the SWOT Analysis. SWOT (Strengths, Weaknesses, Opportunities, and Threats) is a structured planning method that helps one identify actions required to achieve one's objectives. SWOT is a questioning and brainstorming process.

Strengths and Weaknesses are internal to your operation. These are the features that give you an advantage or disadvantage in your market. You identify your strengths and understand your weaknesses. Take into consideration; resources, knowledge, product(s), communications, technology, location, staff, money, capabilities, and capacity.

Opportunities and Threats are external. You identify things that can cause trouble and then plan how you will take advantage of the opportunities. Take into consideration macroeconomic issues, black swan events, politics, current events, trends, cultural changes, the marketplace, and the competition.

Keep the internal and external factors separate until the end. Be critical once your strengths, weaknesses, opportunities, and threats are documented and prioritized. Are your objectives attainable, given your assessment? If not, revise your goal and repeat the process. Match your strengths to the opportunities to find the competitive advantage.

- ☐ *Where are the gaps between your strengths and the opportunities?*

- ☐ *What do you need to do to convert your weaknesses into strengths?*

- ☐ *Can the threats be turned to opportunities?*

- ☐ *Can you see new markets?*

- ☐ *How can you minimize or avoid the risks?*

- ☐ *What are the factors that will be critical to your success?*

Take enough time to do your planning well. It will pay off in a big way as you move forward. Budget a couple of months for strategic planning. Next, use the knowledge from your SWOT to design your path forward.

SWOT is an organizing tool. Used in collaboration with your team, SWOT underpins the change process.

Step 3: Share Your Plan

You cannot put too much emphasis on your plan. It must become of primary importance to everyone in your business. When it is complete, publish your plan and talk about it with your business colleagues. If you don't involve your staff, the odds of failure increase dramatically.

Use the information you gleaned from your SWOT Analysis to guide your vision for the future. From the outcomes of your assessments, look at the best ways to optimize your strengths and to mitigate your weaknesses. Develop a plan for exploiting your opportunities and defending against threats.

Prepare how best to adopt meaningful plans of action within your wider business strategy. Begin by planning and designing your connected processes. You will need operational, resource, and project plans for strategy implementation. Break the plans down into bite-sized pieces and prioritize them.

Write an implementation plan. Create a plan that builds step-by-step and allows you to achieve small, visible successes. Answer the following questions:

- ☐ *What do you want to do in the future?*
- ☐ *What are the steps you will use to get to your goal?*
- ☐ *How will you meet your strategic goals?*
- ☐ *What tools and resources will be required?*
- ☐ *How much will it cost? How will the costs be financed?*
- ☐ *What will your business look like five years from now? Ten years?*

Designing your process may take several iterations. Use the structure outlined in this book and your skills and experiences as a starting point. Allow two weeks to one month for creating the plan.

Step 4: Implement

Don't connect everything at once. Do what you can, right now. Over time, you will be able to build more linkages into the larger world of BIM. Start with a plan and build your processes step-by-step until you are a connected practice. Use this book as your guide. Begin to develop your projects in a BIM environment. Find new ways to create small successes. Tell your consultants about your new process. Market your new abilities and work in a connected way. Become an evangelist for connected processes.

As you transition into a connected business model, you will need to embrace change to become a life-long learning organization.

Three or four months have passed. Some will have completed the assessment and planning process much faster, and others may take longer. However long you took, the initial process is complete. Now you are ready to start. You know where you are going. Your plan is in place. You have a vision for your future.

Now jump in and get started. It is better and more profitable to spend your time doing something than it is to obsess about having a perfect plan, even if something needs to change later. Whatever you have decided, the process will evolve as time passes. A connected business system isn't static—in fact, it can change every day.

Because of this, your plan should be fluid and adaptable. Connecting your business usually requires significant change. As with any change of this magnitude, things will not be perfect. You will make mistakes and encounter barriers. Stay the course and adjust as you move forward.

In the beginning, you will find yourself in a state of constant adjustment and correction. You should plan a regular cycle for revisiting your strategies and solutions. Change them as you grow and become more expert in the process. As you move forward, plan for a minimum of quarterly or biannual reviews of your status.

Step 5: Change

Becoming a connected practice takes time and commitment. As your BIG-BIM ecosystem rolls out and matures, you will be able to do things that were once only dreams. To get the maximum benefit, focus on changing your business to handle the future, keeping in mind that you may need to change behaviors, and the way you do business.

Be self-aware—know and understand how you work;

Embrace the philosophy of fail-fast. Move on rather than continuing flawed processes;

Engage others earlier in more collaborative ways;

Maximize knowledge and productivity in the front-end of projects;

Adjust fee structures as appropriate;

Consider your new ways of working, and;

Manage liabilities.

These attitudes and actions that you develop will define a philosophy that enables connected workflows. Next, we explore the changes that drive business in the BIG-BIM ecosystem.

Change: Self-Awareness

Knowing yourself and understanding how your business provides services is the first step to successful BIG-BIM. The effort begins with information and management.

Long held practices must change to enable building information modeling of any kind. By understanding and articulating how you work, you create a framework for connecting technology in ways that work best for you. By tailoring your processes, you deliver the benefits available from the best tools and high-performance processes most recently available.

☐ *First, understand how you do business. Look at how you set up projects and how you generate solutions. Know your skills and deficiencies—your strengths and weaknesses.*

☐ *Think ahead to avoid trouble and avoid the pitfalls.*

☐ *Realize how interconnected you are with others. Observe how to provide value in this new world. Expand your vision of the world and your vision of where you fit in the built environment.*

☐ *Question everything and dig into the processes used by others. Break everything down into its smallest components. From these elements, you will create processes that work for you.*

☐ *Find the best places to use your resources. Baby steps work quite well in this environment, and a smooth transition is possible with planning.*

☐ *Decide how fast you will make the change. People accept change at different rates. Some prepare better than others. Some have more money, more support, and can handle faster transitions. Some like to go fast. Some like a slow and steady approach. Be proactive. No matter the pace you set, tailor your speed to your ability to handle change.*

☐ *Capitalize on your strengths and find ways to overcome your weaknesses. Move to a process designed for today, and tomorrow.*

Read more about the new ways to do business included in the Case Studies throughout the book. Connecting technology into any business requires managing change. How you approach staffing, customers, and consultants will adjust based on the business processes you choose. In an information-centric world, your implementation strategy will require adjustments to business and design processes, a commitment to embracing new technologies and a high level of responsibility.

Constraints impact everything we do. Studying TOC and its applications, you will find that either you can manage constraints or they will control you in unpredictable and sometimes harmful ways. Conversely, if you try to manage everything, you are not managing anything. Management by constraints is a balancing act. To assess your current approach, consider using a process based on the Theory of Constraints (TOC). TOC and the Toyota Production System (TPS) are two of the proven management theories that can be coupled with the most successful parts of your current business processes to help you to plan and manage better.

In 1984, a physicist turned business consultant; Dr. Eliyahu Goldratt published a book entitled, *The Goal*. He theorized that any business could improve its results through applying scientific methods to resolving organizational problems. Goldratt suggested that each business has a single constraint that limits its performance relative to its goal.

By managing this constraint, the company can overcome obstacles to production and become more efficient and responsive. Finding and managing this constraint in your organization is critical. Theory of Constraints looks at an organization as a system rather than as a hierarchy. Goldratt's theory explains why Agency-Construction-Management works. It is also a primary driver behind Toyota's success. The Theory of Constraints underpins many of the management approaches that work best today.

There are many constraints on how you do business. By identifying these constraints and one-by-one managing them, you can control the performance of any process. Sciral and Northrop Grumman's Flying Logic is a Theory of Constraints based visual reasoning tool for understanding complex systems, and is one tool that you may want to consider as you begin to explore your skill sets and how to do what you do better.

In our explorations, we identified *Costs*—in all forms—as the primary constraint on most built environment processes today. We came to understand that management of cost constraints is the single most important change that you can make to improve how you support your customers. We found that managing cost constraints changes outcomes in positive and customer-centered ways. Best of all, there is proof. Managing cost-as-a-constraint has worked for over forty years! Ask any successful Agency Construction Manager.

With proper cost controls, much of the poor documentation, cost overruns, and other problems cited by customers in recent years is manageable. By not managing cost-as-a-constraint, the problems have increased in the past twenty years and have become endemic in many markets. You can dramatically improve the outcomes of design and construction processes by managing cost constraints.

Study how you can manage cost constraints throughout your process and apply the Theory of Constraints to your organization with these four steps: 1) Identify THE constraint on your process; 2) Decide how you will use the constraint to improve performance toward your goal; 3) Make the constraint important—give it power by connecting it into your process; and 4) Embed the constraint into your everyday work processes.

Change: Fail-Fast-and-Move-On

Until the advent of Apps, it was usually best if one assumed that any new technology would be tested in detail and proven in the market before you adopted it. The fully-develop-extensively-test- and-only-then-deploy approach is no longer always the best approach. Today this approach at best delays action, and often signals a failure... especially for customized software deployments.

The world is changing at an ever-increasing rate. New technologies and new ideas abound. Some are good. Some are bad. Most only add to the complexity. Today, we quickly explore options. We search for tools that offer what we deem to be the best approach to our problem. As lifelong learners, we adapt to changing tools, devices, and systems. We try new things, discarding those that don't work and adopting those that provide dramatic benefits.

Formalized processes such as agile development have been created to take advantage of these new ways of operating. We need programs that demonstrate new ways of working and thinking; new forms that are more collaborative, innovative, and connected. There is a need for new patterns of working that allow people *to fail-fast-and-move-on.*

Without risk, there is little improvement. Without innovation, there is little growth. At our best, we constantly experiment, fail early and often, and learn as much as possible in the process. Without some failure, there is little progress. Accepting, and even embracing, processes that recognize failure as the price of innovation is one step toward adopting connected processes in your enterprise. Without such an approach, many of our best-known inventions might never have happened.

However, failure is not always acceptable. You should weigh failure against the potential outcomes. We cannot accept failure in some highly developed and critical systems. Such systems need to be intolerant of failure, with zero errors. None of us wants to be on an aircraft, with the pilot in failure mode. That would be a disaster.

Where tasks are critical or human life is involved, consider checklists driven processes. We expect the pilot to use a checklist before takeoff. The list is created from years of study and experience by experts and includes every potential failure point. Should any errors be found as the pilot steps through the list, item-by-item; correction is immediate, or the flight is scrubbed. Such is the stuff of pilots and surgeons.

BIG-BIM enables us to simulate failures early, so that later in the lifecycle when the systems become critical, we minimize the chances of failures. Finding the potential problems in the early stages of planning is one reason for prototyping with computer models. One takes the risks and makes the mistakes, well before the plane is built or flown. We make models and use them to identify the failure points before we build.

Ask yourself: When are failures okay? When are failures unacceptable? Remember that this is a balance between innovation, and cost of repairs, cost in human suffering, cost of resources, cost to credibility, etc.

Innovation stops when a system can tolerate zero failure. In a zero-failure situation, fear rules. People become obsessed with trying to be perfect, and there is little forward movement. Few people take a chance and nothing changes. Innovation rarely happens and when it does, it is rarely significant.

At the other extreme is chaos. Many ideas emerge, but little gets done. Progress stops when no one takes responsibility for outcomes. When failure is always acceptable, at any time in any process, it can be catastrophic.

Balance risks that enhance innovation with reliable performance. Most of us draw the line when significant capital, time, or resources are required to correct a failure we minimize failure, and; we eliminate failure when lives are at stake. BIG-BIM makes thinking this way viable in the construction industry. We can now rapidly simulate and visualize to find the problems before we spend significant time or money.

The Level of Detail concept, as originally conceived, is a framework to front-load failure in information models. By connecting data to models to represent location, massing, and other decision-making information, we simulate failures... With a minimum of effort and fuss. Virtual failures are easy to fix. Failures become much more of a problem when we pour the concrete, or after the project is complete and in operation. This distinction is one of the critical issues in information modeling and connected decision-making.

In today's world of cloud computing, information modeling, and model servers, definitions such as Level of Detail allow a lot of flexibility—if we use the technology correctly. It all depends on collaboration and connected processes that move systematically from concept through documentation into realization. And an enlightened view and understanding of the value and hazards of failure.

BIMStorms are designed to embrace the concept of fail-fast-and-move-on, with little or no risk. They might be thought of as online brainstorms using BIG-BIM. Investigate BIMStorms and run a small-scale one for yourself, or join a BIMStorm that is in progress. BIMStorms allow you to establish a virtual project program and explore solutions that can be landed in 3D in a real-world manner using free programs such as Google Earth.

Change: Collaboration

Team members become more valuable by learning to work collaboratively. They use education and natural skills to complete tasks in ways that allow others to do better work. They develop their ability to create and manage complex processes.

Collaboration among members of a network benefits from processes that allow team members to develop their craft. Members gain expertise gradually as they see what worked and what did not. They fail-fast-and-move-on, rather than being corrected through punitive means. Failures resolve by doing tasks again and doing them right.

To do such things communications must flow freely. Clarity and rapid access to authoritative data are but two of the principles that keep the communications flowing. Time spent finding and pulling information from many sources is inefficient and impedes communication. Many of the tools change when you adapt to a BIG-BIM ecosystem. Foremost among them is e-mail. E-mail is not the primary form of communication within those working in the ecosystem.

E-mail is not secure. It isn't robust or dependable enough for BIG-BIM communications. It allows manipulation and confusion. With electronic mail, one can conceal mistakes and defer decisions, which undermines collaboration and efficient teamwork.

An e-mail can become an avoidance tool. How often have we heard: what e-mail? ... you sent me an e-mail? or; I never saw any e-mail like you describe? Such things happen often. It is easy to lose or misplace emails; intentionally, or not. E-mail does not work well in the world that depends on timestamps and transparency.

Something better is needed. BIM Mail is one solution. BIM Mail allows a message to be sent from a location or object in a model with a comment and a time stamp.

Embedded and connected communications reduce the chance for error and streamline data flow. BIM Mail supports collaboration by placing transparent communications in-context. A BIM Mail attached to a light fixture in a room carries the design and construction team's conversation about the fixture.

Why was the fixture selected? Why did the designer feel that this fixture was needed? How were cost problems overcome? How did the supplier accomplish the task? Were trade-offs made? Why is the wiring one way versus another? Does the fixture fit into some larger systems which aren't evident?

Much as the fixture's BIM object might include size, weight, lumens, supplier, cost and other data; we could add conversations to the object; however, the effort would be enormous.

BIM Mail gives the model context. Use it to make decisions and track decisions. Use BIM Mail to form the basis of better downstream understanding of how a project got to the current state; eliminating the need to rebuild logic as things change over time; adding the component of concurrent thought. With BIM Mail the project's lifecycle logic is transparent for all to see and understand. BIG-BIM enables this additional level of complexity, without adding significant effort. Here are real-world examples of the impact of BIM Mail:

At the component level

With email: A mechanic does a search for communications about Air-Handler-A and a list of e-mails appears. Is that everything? Are some e-mails tagged as HVAC-A rather than Air-Handler-A? Are critical e-mails missing? Has something gone astray? Is this an opportunity for error?

With BIM Mail: The mechanic views the model of Air-Handler-A in her tool of choice, on any web-enabled device. She then selects Air-Handler-A's BIM Mail. All related communications connected to this component appear. Date and time stamped. Easy, with little chance of missing information.

At the site level

With email: An Owner's Representative opens her e-mail client and sends an e-mail with the subject line: Problem with Grading *to the Architect's boss. The boss forwards the e-mail to the Architect, with the revised subject line:* Problem with Grading—FIX THIS TODAY. *The Architect returns from lunch and gets annoyed and accidentally deletes the e-mail. Not knowing what else to do (and not wanting to upset anyone), he does nothing more. The Owner's Representative wonders why no one took care of the problem. The boss gets busy and forgets to follow up. A little problem gets magnified. Feelings get hurt. Lawsuits follow.*

With BIM Mail: The Owner's Representative opens the BIG-BIM site model on her web-enabled phone and posts a BIM Mail with copies to the Architect's boss. Since the Architect is the design lead, he automatically receives notice of a new attachment to the site. Should the Architect defer the announcement for later, the system sends reminders. When he clicks the site on his tablet then clicks on the location's BIM Mail he sees the communication in-context. With all the facts needed to reach a solution. He adds a quick comment to the BIM Mail and forwards to the Civil Engineer, who upon receipt resolves the problem in five minutes. The Owner's Representative opens the site an hour later, reviews the issue and the correction. Problem solved.

Similar scenarios can happen at the building and room levels of detail. This kind of precisely tracked communication leads to improved collaboration that results in dramatic benefits—across the lifecycle of assets.

With the need to conduct business in a quick and efficient manner, this system provides the opportunity to view comprehensively and update data typically stored in numerous locations and media formats. An effort that consumes far too many person-hours. — Public Works Director.

Change: Maximize the Front-End

It is the building industry's simplicity on the microscopic level and complexity on the macro level that led us to focus on COST as the single unifying constraint in the industry. Businesses large and small, of all shapes and sizes, are driven by costs, in one form or another.

We work in a world of highly interconnected processes. Tapping into these connections gives us the ability to impact things far in the future. They also give us two choices. We can make a difference in ways that increase the chance of future success. Or we can continue to work in a partial vacuum, disconnected from the larger issues that affect the industry. It is as simple as that.

Many things must change if we are to move to a BIG–BIM ecosystem. Some of the changes involve technology. Most do not. Most are people related. They include changes in mindsets and ways of looking at the world. These human-focused changes are the most complex and challenging to manage. They are the drivers behind BIG–BIM.

The construction industry is exceedingly diverse. Most businesses in the industry are small, focusing on small subsets of the built world. The industry isn't a place of uniformity in workers, or much else.

Understanding the individual components isn't too difficult. Reading and changing the system is much more complex. The interconnections seem infinite. One must take this into account when you study how to adapt to the BIG-BIM ecosystem.

Obviously, there are many constraints in any process in the built environment. If you try to manage them all, you will end up not achieving much of anything. Using concepts that we learned from the Theory of Constraints, we found that by controlling costs, we could control the downstream process, in a positive and customer-centered way.

Many fall into the trap of reacting to events. They allow the constraints to take over, rather than being proactive. They jump from crisis to crisis. Poor documentation, cost overruns, and late delivery are often the result. As an industry, we must stop the cycle. Treating the industry as an interconnected system that can be managed by constraints is the first step.

Change: Adjust Structures

Frank Lloyd Wright said, *Man builds most nobly when limitations were at their greatest.*

In Mr. Wright's day, the construction industry was entirely different. There was more time to contemplate and evaluate. In today's context, the pace was glacial.

This is the reason that many of today's construction professionals resist adding new limitations to their workflows. They resist adding costs as an additional constraint to the design and construction process. They fear that managing costs from the beginning will harm their design process. This attitude is hurting the industry and is a cause of design and construction issues.

Often there is little connection to financial reality. Solutions marry others to aesthetics or functionality, supported by unfounded promises about cost and other details. Leading to projects that start unfavorably and create downstream problems. Costs are often little more than an acknowledgment: *We think the project will be under your budget.* Rather than a managed constraint: *Our system shows that you should plan this amount for THIS specific solution.* One pushes the cost to some future date, for others to handle. The other starts a discussion, today.

Until recently there was merit in professionals thinking that adding costs as a constraint was not viable. No tool existed for assessing early stage costs without imposing significant additional effort. Adding cost-as-a-constraint would have required that other critical aspects be dropped and replaced by cost estimating. Few firms had the fee or inclination to go this route. Today, this position is no longer viable.

Tools exist to allow continual cost predictions. At a level of detail that supports decision-making at the earliest stages of planning and design, with little or no intervention. The design changes and the costs vary proportionally. All involved can have a conversation and make decisions about values that correspond to the level of detail of the design. Decision-making information comes as a by-product of other tasks.

To allow us to eliminate airplane crashes in the virtual world. Before the issues become critical in the real-world. We can now tweak the issues found to advantage, and concentrate on costs from the moment a project is conceived. We can capture early decisions and use them to accelerate the process, using BIG-BIM tools to capture, visualize and analyze.

The tools and techniques are available. It takes willingness and new attitudes to make it happen.

Consider the traditional design and bidding document preparation process. In this process, there are numerous opportunities for early decision-making to increase efficiency. There are also many places where one can lose any time and money saved by a more efficient process in other areas. Maintain the early gains as the process moves forward.

Today's reality is that even with a connected process, one issues bidding and construction documents. The industry may be slated to hold profit-bid-auctions with everything else managed at cost via models connected to data and blockchain database technology.

Blockchain is the technology that underlies bitcoins and provides a trust based chain that enables one to be sure about transactions, without intermediary financial institutions. But this remains on the horizon.

Owners find themselves with a dilemma. They want their project to move forward, as rapidly as possible, and they want to be sure of the outcomes. However, at each stage of the traditional process, the owner is required to sign-off on the work before the team can proceed to the next step, mostly without facts to support the decisions. Most decision-making information only becomes known after the owner has spent most of the money.

With a connected process, one reverses this situation. The team arrives at the start of physical work with much of the work done—in the virtual world. Critical decisions are made early and included in the project prototype. The team has confirmed and the prototyped solutions are backed up by repeatable fact.

Production templates are set to generate any files or paper that may be required—plans—elevations—sections—details—schedules—et al, in a process that is automated. coordinated, labeled, and in the preferred formats.

If all team members work in a BIG-BIM framework, the project is self-organized, interference checked and tied to the ecosystem. BIG-BIM, Industry Foundation Class exchanges and connected data mesh efficiently. The effort to produce construction documents comes down to cleaning up and packaging. The production team does not have to reinterpret or wait for decisions. They assemble the materials. It is more controllable and predictable. With fewer conflicts and errors.

In today's connected processes, we remain welded to some form of bid and construction documents. Right now, the difference between a traditional approach and what is sold as the connected approach may be little more than a different focus and more efficient tools. When we look at today's design process, even with little-bim, much does not compute.

The process seems to guarantee that there will be problems somewhere along the line. Little effort goes toward heading off downstream problems or controlling costs from beginning to end. Today too many design and documentation processes go something like this:

The team starts with Schematic Design creating concepts for owner approval. Outcomes depend on the designer's abilities and knowledge. The Owner's support requires a lot of faith and trust. The team supplies little real information beyond sketches and lovely images.

During the next step, Design Development, the team develops the project's systems. Up to this point, the process has been solitary. There has been near zero input from engineers and no input from builders. Ideally, the team adds to the value and detail from the Schematic Design. At worst, the team revises and redoes the approved concept.

Next, the process moves to Construction Documentation. The design team hands off to the production team. If the design team got the required decisions, documented them correctly and finished the process under budget; the production team's work is simplified. If not, the production team takes the handoff with a significant disadvantage. Because of the handoff and the need to finalize details, critical project decisions continue. The production team finds themselves having to reinterpret and implement the work of the design team. Sometimes with the design team's involvement. Sometimes without input, while trying to make up for lost ground against the fee.

Is it any wonder that projects have cost overruns and errors? What could be done better in a more connected process? How many potential tweaks did you identify? Let's look at the process from the designer's perspective. The process goes something like this:

The designer reviews the owner's program and develops a concept. The owner is quoted a cost-per-square-foot that is no more accurate than the budget she formulated in the Space Needs Program. The Schematic Design phase uses between 10% and 15% of the fee.

The design team then develops the concept to define the systems. With a well-managed process, they build upon the first step. The team refines the idea, and the engineers create system concepts. The designer's cost estimator improves the cost-per-square-foot estimate. Design Development uses 15% to 20% of the fee.

The production team then produces construction documents. With a smooth process, they build upon the first two steps. Traditionally, this is where the design team and the owner make most of the detailed decisions for the project.

Sometimes the decisions require significant changes to the work completed in the first steps. Near the end of this process, the designer's cost estimator prepares the first estimate based on unit costs and assemblies. Construction Documents use 30-45% of the fee.

The procurement team then packages the solicitation and bids the work to constructors. Since there has been little (if any) interaction with contractors before this, the designers issue the work and then hold an office betting pool to see who guesses the closest. Procurement uses about 5% of the fee.

Finally, the owner receives bids, and the chips fall where they may. They could be high. They could be low. Common wisdom suggests that the bids are usually high. If the bids are high, the designer works with the contractor to cut things out to get to budget—she re-engineers but does not get much value in return. Any redesign is intended to cut things out. Usually without additional fees. The design team then has 15-25% of their fee remaining to administer the problems caused by these after-the-fact changes.

What is wrong with this scenario? From the perspective of connected processes and best use of the—everything is wrong!

When the project's bids are over the budget, the owner usually incurs the extra costs. Either by adding off-budget funds or, in the form of funds to pay for redesign and rebidding. The owner also bears the costs of the items the team may value-engineer out after bidding and other problems that develop—even when the overages result from poor cost management by the design team.

Designers must learn to match the work effort to the available money if they hope to be profitable. When the costs to develop a project, exceed the fee for the project, they are in big trouble. If you are a designer or design firm, how often have you forgotten this simple equation?

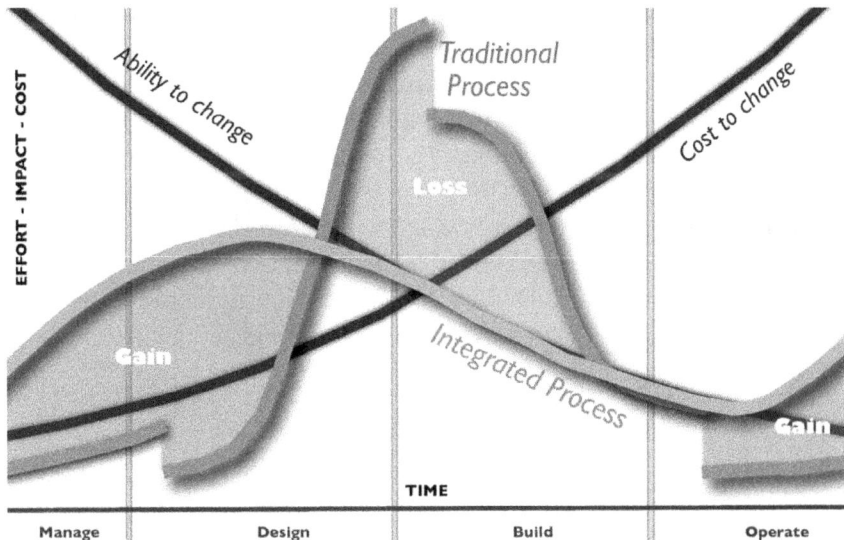

The Cost-of-Change curve focuses on the fact that the ability to change without consequences diminishes as projects move through the development process. BIM helps us to front-load the process, to take advantage of changes... before they take significant resources.

The fact is that designers have come to value their process much more highly than others do. In today's market, the way that many designers work is not effective—not for the owner, and certainly not for the designer. If this continues, it will always be hard to move the industry toward a fact-based approach to design and construction. There are many reasons that we are in this situation:

> People work their way into traps that get them (or their projects) into trouble. Too often with hidden problems that happen when they least expect them. They have not embraced or understood the tools that might overcome the problem.

> Excessive time is spent in refining for aesthetics' sake only, with little or no fact-based proof that the designer has the correct solution.

> The ability to develop efficient projects is undercut by not making the proper decisions at the appropriate time in the process.

> Mundane questions such as: how and how much, are not asked or forgotten.

> Often there is a mistaken belief that designers understand what drives owners, and what makes construction efficient. With little, or no, factual support.

Step back, look at the character traits of a good construction professional and compare them to the character traits that would get the most from the traditional process. There are significant misalignments. The traditional process is much like an assembly line—Getting high volume from a large contingent of semi-skilled laborers. The process does little to leverage anyone's ability to create sustainable and high-performance solutions.

The process is fraught with disconnected tasks, repetitive work, and things better done by computers. The process moves from gateway to gateway, building detail as you progress. It is inefficient and unwieldy. It's a linear process in what has become a non-linear world.

Connected processes and BIG-BIM focus on just-in-time decision-making to improve predictability and give more assurance of outcomes. They require a very different approach and a different set of questions:

- ☐ How can we more closely align with the characteristics that we associate with good design and construction delivery?

- ☐ What can we do to reduce or eliminate mundane and repetitive input and other tasks?

- ☐ How can we transparently capture our knowledge to inform the future in sustainable and resilient ways?

- ☐ What is the best way to synthesize the complex data that surrounds us?

☐ *How can we reduce the workflow problems that currently plague most businesses in the building industry?*

☐ *What changes need to happen to enable creative professionals to focus on what they do best?*

☐ *What can we do to improve the process and do a better job for our customers?*

Change: New Way of Working

We looked at fee allocations in the early stages of the traditional process. It became obvious that the costs need to be allocated differently in a connected process. In a connected process, the work effort is greater in the earliest steps than in the traditional approach. Fee percentages need to adjust to match, assigning a large proportion of the costs to the front-end efforts.

Connected processes and BIG-BIM help us to focus on just-in-time decision-making to improve predictability and give more assurance of outcomes. For designers, the greatest benefit of the BIG-BIM ecosystem may be the ability to foster a higher level of understanding for everyone concerned; moving toward design solutions which are both beautiful and backed up by fact. To illustrate the structure that one may encounter for connected design and documentation, consider the following process:

1. Develop a Validation Study. The team of experienced architects, engineers, and constructors work in close collaboration with the owner and the using organization. Within the study, the team analyzes needs and objectives and creates prototype models. They prepare a schedule and project strategy. The team creates Cost Models, cost assumptions and comparisons. The team runs solar, sustainability, and other analyses. They spend the time to review all of this with the owner; getting the appropriate decisions as the study progresses. They document the decisions made and embed them in the prototype. The Validation Study becomes the framework for capital budgeting, procurement, and all future development. The Validation Study becomes the virtual box containing all the parts required to design and build what the owner needs. Validation uses 20-25% of the fee.

2. Add detail to the validated prototype. There are two main options. The first is to move forward with the design concept built into the Validation Study if the owner feels that it is the best solution.

Is the validation-concept the best option? If so, you continue to add detail to your conceptual models until they are ready for the next step. Alternatively, the team starts a new prototype from scratch using a validation process as the control for projects that are too large, too complex, or require special handling.

For such projects, a large company or a signature designer may be a better option. In this case, the validation becomes the framework for managing the process, serving as one of the constraints to create the best solution. The validation prototype becomes the base from which to evaluate any new solution for compliance with owner needs. In either case, one can extract the necessary data in any form required. The team embeds detailed consultant data. They output model views to create procurement documents or prepare for more detailed modeling in the next step. The team refines costs and analyses. The prototyping of the design solution uses about 25% of the fee.

3. Create contracting documents. If procurement is through general contracting, the team adds more detail to the prototype to bring the model to a level where they can extract public bidding documents. The bulk of work on this prototype involves composing sheets, cleaning up sections and conducting quality assurance operations. The team refines costs and analyses. The construction prototype uses 18-22% of the fee.

4. Package the documents and bid the work to contractors, or negotiate pricing from the constructor team. Since they have shared the material and solutions with constructors and the owner from the beginning, all have a clear idea where the project is going. The team focuses on responding to all questions and concerns. They let nothing drop through the cracks. The goal is to eliminate uncertainty at the bid table. The Procurement process uses about 8% of the fee.

5. Finally, receive proposals. You are still at the mercy of market forces. However, you have now analyzed, tested, and verified to a level where you have eliminated confusion and the need for most contingencies. Experience has shown that the bids will be within 5% of the budget you validated in the first step. You now have about 20-25% of the fee to administer a precise and well-understood project.

It is interesting to note that early stage design fees increase in a connected process. To compensate for the initial efforts, and to take advantage of the perceived value, the process requires that you front-load costs, compared to the traditional process. Although the fees occur at different levels, in different steps, the combined cost has proven to be less than or equal to the standard costs.

The connected approach gives the owner a high degree of certainty while retaining at least as many fees to administer the construction process as in the traditional process. The opportunity is to focus your creative energies on getting quality decisions early and to minimize downstream problems. Become more focused on getting the best decisions made and less focused on production. Handle the first day issues. The chances of success at the end will increase. A process like outlined above creates the opportunity to refocus the direction your projects take.

The process moves decisions to the beginning, focuses the designer's energy on creating the correct solution, and allocates the funds to support the effort. By moving decision-making to the beginning, the owner is more engaged in the process. These methods make customers more confident and sure about where their project is heading.

Some questions to ask as you move toward becoming a connected part of a BIG-BIM ecosystem:

☐ *How can I best use BIM and my knowledge-base at the beginning of projects, to make every decision, as early in the process as possible?*

☐ *What do I need to do to conceive the design using building information models from the start of the process?*

☐ *What changes must be made to manage costs? Where can I add value in the new process?*

☐ *Can I use building information models to communicate with constructors and suppliers early in the process?*

☐ *How should I tailor procurement to customer requirements and the most efficient delivery process, for our location?*

Experience has shown that facility owners highly value processes that front-load decision-making—once they understand the issues and experience the benefits. The BIG-BIM ecosystem enables decisions with greater understanding. When things go wrong; everyone understands why.

Change: Manage Liabilities

As an industry, we are risk averse and fear the unknown. We hesitate to step on a new path, even when it might lead to correcting many of the problems we face. Yet, our world is changing, like it or not. We have two options: proactively change to embrace the future, or; find something else to do.

In the perfect world of the future, we will be able to design and solve problems without a care in the world. Arguments and finger-pointing will be things of the past. Lawsuits will be outdated, and transactional law practices will be long forgotten. Everyone will work in perfect harmony, sharing data with no concern for intellectual property rights. We waste nothing.

Yeah right! That isn't going to happen—not anytime soon. The reality is that we work in an environment where traditional delivery processes and our approach to risks and rewards all contribute to distrust and adversarial relationships. Construction professionals must watch what they do all the time. Each project phase is independent of those that precede and follow. We focus on avoiding risks in our individual niche. We cling to our traditional ways. Even when our customers complain and society forces other industries into new forms of working. Often against their will.

There are risks in any move or new endeavor. The move to a BIG-BIM ecosystem is no exception. BIG-BIM is a disruptive change, best approached with open eyes. You are already wrestling with this change. In fact, you have already made similar changes in many other areas of your life. You are trying to figure out how to protect your assets, your reputation, and your family. These are important considerations as we move forward. Consider these issues which affect professionals in the building industry:

When we embed incorrect data in a model, what happens? Who handles inaccurate information and how is risk assigned when it is unclear who created the data (or who created the problem)?

Answer: Tracking the quality of data is an evolving issue with few sure answers; the wild-wild-west of BIM. In current little-bim projects, tools such as COBie and BIM Execution Plans are the weapons of choice to manage these issues. However, recognize that they are stopgaps requiring significant manual effort to enforce.

Does your insurance cover the potential risks and exposures from this change? Do standardized agreements address the new problems that come with this change?

Answer: In most cases, insurance carriers are responding positively. Standardized contracts are in a continuous state of development to respond to the changes.

Will connected processes alter the standard of care that we are responsible for providing?

Answer: Standards of care are changing to acknowledge little-bim and Integrated Project Delivery systems and will change much more as BIG-BIM becomes widespread. Look for standards of care that embrace the quality of delivery and collaboration, responsibility for the environment and stewardship of lifecycle assets.

As BIG-BIM takes hold, the need for today's manual data entry will vanish as connections to reliable information and clear responsibility tracking become widespread. Until then, this is an area that needs special care, close monitoring, and active quality control.

Note: Time stamped tracking for who did what, when, where and to whom, is an inherent part of any BIG-BIM ecosystem, TODAY.

How can I share the risks equitably across the entire project team (including the owner)?

Answer: Explore Pain-Share/Gain-Share project structures. Standardized agreements focused on Integrated Project Delivery offer frameworks for ways to contractually share risks. Consult with one of the growing lists of attorneys that embrace more collaborative, less transactional legal practices for guidance and assistance.

What information do all team members share to deliver on their responsibilities?

Answer: Not to be flip, but what don't they share? BIM and collaborative teams require team members to play fairly. The goal is for everyone to work to achieve agreed upon outcomes. Everyone takes responsibility for project outcomes. Rather than each member focusing on their niche and personal benefit. Team members prosper when the team prospers.

What legal and financial exposure will I have when I front-load information and decision-making?

Answer: First day mistakes are the bane of the construction industry. How many times have we seen an ill-advised early decision, manifest and grow as the project moves forward? Front-loading decision-making requires that one pre-negotiate financing to match workflow changes.

Anecdotally, better information coupled with increased communication and understanding reduces the potential for downstream error and legal exposure. By eliminating the potential train-wrecks early, the team can focus on the directions that offer the greatest chance of successful outcomes. By involving the correct team members at the beginning of the decisions, we reduce the likelihood of unintended outcomes. We can't predict everything, but we can do a better job of assessing potential outcomes. Business, as usual, is no longer enough. The problems outweigh the benefit of remaining with the traditional approach.

The biggest benefit from traditional processes may be that there are precedents. We know-how to react since most problems have happened before. We also know that, when somebody makes a claim, our insurance carrier and attorney will know-how to respond. Since the system is in place, we can continue to work as usual and let someone else handle the problems.

Take your insurance agent or attorney to lunch and see what they say about BIM. Have they been trained in the latest thinking about managing risk with BIM and connected processes? Are they fluent with the issues, both positive and negative? If not, start the selection process to identify advisors that understand where you and your business are heading.

Workflow
little-bim Authoring Software

Put your preconceptions aside. None of the noise matters to your decision. If the software does not improve your process and provide you long-term connected data, don't buy it. The costs of little-bim software products pale in comparison to the direct and hidden costs of a 12-month trial that turns out to be a mistake.

Little-bim is the part of BIM that has passed the tipping point to become a commodity product. Yet, carefully selecting a little-bim platform is vitally important and deserves careful consideration. In this arena, brand name recognition means less than one might think.

Any of the vendors that sell Industry Foundation Class (IFC) certified products can sell you a little-bim solution that will get the job done. These vendors develop all types of strategies for getting people to purchase their products. They try everything from reduced feature limited versions to giving away updates for non-BIM legacy products, to subscription services. Ignore the vendor hype and forget the marketing that surrounds the little-bim authoring tool market.

Too many of those that have tried to implement BIM tools based on their legacy systems or vendor recommendations have seen suboptimal results. In fact, depending on how one defines the term, many of them have failed. Such an approach to BIM tools can be an excruciating experience.

Sometimes the vendors are more interested in making a sale than in imparting the truth. Battles for market share and dominance among software and hardware vendors leads to messages designed to put products in the best light. Sometimes reality gets lost in the hype. BIM Washing is rampant. Find products that are a comfortable fit and which enable you to be productive.

In a world of interoperability, the monolithic approach favored by most little-bim vendors is old-school. Based on their experiences with legacy products, many professionals continue to believe that a single product line is needed to do BIM—Not so. In fact, no single project line or individual tool can do all the tasks required.

The real winners from monolithic product lines in this area are the vendors, not the users. Today you should aim toward using the best tool for the job at hand, rather than using the same tool, or product line, for all things. Find the product that lets you do work, as smoothly and efficiently as possible. Your selection should consider such elements as:

☐ *How much training will be required to be productive? How intuitive is the interface?*

☐ *How much will it cost annually to stay up-to-date?*

☐ *How much storage capacity, of what type, will be required to archive your work safely? Can you keep your files on an encrypted drive for increased security?*

☐ *What workflows are standard? What workflows can be done using either workarounds or add-on products?*

☐ *What file exchanges are standard? What data interchanges are standard? Do they work in both directions?*

☐ *Are appropriately trained people available for surges, should you get busy and need short-term help?*

☐ *Are senior staff and non-techies able to use the tool, or is it only for the technical at heart?*

☐ *And, much more.*

Communication, Connection, Interoperability, Knowledge, and FACTS drive BIM. Focus on creating the most efficient and effective way to support your needs. Once you start to improve your processes and begin to see success, you can then widen your reach. If you are like others that have taken this path, you will, over time, add more capabilities. You will create greater value in the built environment.

The better one understands the underlying needs of any business, the easier it is to find one or more BIM solutions. Take it a step at a time. Make the changes in the way that works best for you and your customers.

Most users focus on the graphic modeling capabilities with some steps into clash detection and other analysis built into the system. Remember to also seek opportunities to exploit the *I of BIM* beyond schedules and other internal uses.

Desktop little-bim authoring systems are typically file-based, welded together software applications with the data tightly embedded. Data is usually internal rather than able to interface with external databases. This data is hard to access and subject to data rot. Both may limit your long-term benefits.

Data rot is almost a fact of life for many today. Whether one saves electronic files in the cloud, on a local server, or on digital media; stores paper in file cabinets or cardboard boxes; or archives rolls of prints, the information may not be current, and may not be valid. Authoritative data needs to live.

Some vendors are making strides toward greater access to the information in the models created using their systems. The ability to fully capitalize on the information side of little-bim systems isn't mature. Data interchange via IFC and COBie can be quite advanced, but be aware that no two tools have the same capabilities in this area. To fully use the information side of little-bim solutions requires expertise and training. Simplicity and clarity are often missing.

Each of the major little-bim authoring tools has a different approach to BIM. Each does some things exceedingly well and others not so well. Dig deeply and you will see that each has pros and cons that will impact how one works. Find the tool or tools that most closely aligns with your workflows, strategy, and philosophy. Your projects may require any number of processes unique to your organization. You can improve any of them with a BIM solution. Finding the right product may take some trial and error.

Testing little-bim products

The following approach to testing little-bim products has worked for others:

☐ *The first day you download a little-bim software trial version, go through the product tutorial, step-by-step.*

☐ *Alternately, sign up for the vendor's one day introductory course.*

☐ *The second day, begin a new project. It should be a project that is typical for your business, whether a new facility or a renovation. This should be something real, not something from the tutorial. Do not select the project for simplicity. You want to make this a real-life test.*

☐ *By the end of the third day, your model should include—floors, walls, roofs, doors, windows, stairs, toilet and kitchen fixtures, and a basic ground plane. As a minimum, you should have produced photo-rendered images, presentation-grade plans, and elevations. These images should be at a quality level that is good enough to present to customers, with no apologies.*

☐ *Extract the areas for all spaces with quantities and areas of doors, windows, and wall and roof surfaces. Some people going through this process have also produced a virtual reality model or tested their model on mobile oriented systems such as BIMx™ at this point.*

You have created your first prototype. You have had a productive three-day exercise much of which should be billable. If you are comfortable with the product, you may have found your modeling tool. If you cannot achieve at least this level of product by the end of the third day, try another modeling tool.

Case Study
Control Your Projects

No matter how critical an issue is, sometimes you cannot change a preconceived notion. Sometimes the local situation and pressures force people to make the wrong decisions. As a professional, you still must try.

If you're not the lead dog, the view never changes, quipped Ian Thompson, vice-president of Standing Stone Consulting Inc.

Mr. Thompson's comment came on the heels of a meeting with a school superintendent to discuss how to structure our team on a new project. The superintendent required a textbook approach, and she could not conceive of why a high school might need CPTED (Crime Prevention Through Environmental Design) support.

We left without convincing the superintendent of the value in connecting safety and security at the beginning of projects. The meeting was one week before 9/11.

Over the years, how many projects have you seen that started with a flawed plan? How many were under-funded? How many were over-scoped? How many missed a critical piece that led to failure in the end?

A primary goal of BIG-BIM is to avoid this type of failure. These failures usually happen because of small, easily correctable flaws at the beginning. Conceptually it is simple to correct them at the beginning. In practice, it is much harder.

The design and construction process is rooted in tradition. As a group, industry professionals give too much power to legacy systems when they should be making changes using good business sense. The days where one could work without connecting to the customer's business systems have passed.

Technology is commercially available to allow construction professionals to do a much better job at controlling outcomes, from the very start of every project. They no longer must rely on manual, linear processes to produce quality work. We now have databases, the Internet, and BIG-BIM. It is time to become leaders in making the change.

We saw a scenario play out repeatedly—the owner hires a team without keying them into the realities. The team creates a concept that responds to aesthetic requirements but misses an issue easily handled at an earlier stage of the process. They build a facility that is too large or too expensive, or in some way out of sync, and problems begin. The organization struggles to operate the facility and then (and only then) the realization occurs that they missed something important.

Much too late to fix the problem a lot of money, legal services, time, or other resources are expended to correct the problem.

It seems simple — start right. As we completed more projects, we saw a disconnected process. People forgot the basic equation. Moreover, downstream problems usually followed the early stage bad decisions.

Case Study
Scenario-Based Planning

Security consultants apply Crime Prevention Through Environmental Design (CPTED) principles and techniques to encourage appropriate behaviors, discourage inappropriate actions are, and improve emergency response capabilities, at the earliest stages of projects. By combining security principles, operations parameters, properties of destructive devices and facilities data, these professionals improve their ability to predict outcomes—before a tragedy occurs.

Gaming and disaster simulation are time-tested approaches to preparing emergency responders for new and unexpected conditions. Planning for emergency response and damage mitigation is one area that the BIG-BIM ecosystem supports. Traditionally security has been bolted-on projects either late in the design process or after construction. This after-the-fact approach limits options and is at best an afterthought that leads to safety and security failures.

Since 9/11, security forces have become more visible, vigilant, and efficient. Today, first responders are well trained, better equipped, and have learned how to respond to unexpected situations to protect critical assets. BIG-BIM gives them the ability to consider an almost unlimited range of issues that influence response.

First responders can now analyze their options well before the completion of detailed design and construction, using an appropriately structured Building Information Model. Much as we use models to identify *trains wrecks* to increase the certainty of outcomes in other areas of the built environment.

With a BIG-BIM ecosystem, knowledge from many sources connects to simulate potential scenarios. By combining operating data and safety and security best practices with explicit imagery, it is possible to generate fact-based simulations and view potential outcomes. Post 9/11, such simulations of safety and security issues have taken advantage of BIG-BIM's capacity to mash-up data, to speed solutions and improve understanding to create the safest environments possible. A couple of examples of this capacity to use BIG-BIM for early stage assessment and scenario planning include:

1. *During the deployment of US troops to Iraq, professionals could assess the security and force protection status of bases located on Charleston Harbor, while the facilities were on lockdown. By using a combination of little-bim, data-rich models that included facility assessments, and GIS the team created and visualized options. The team identified potential problems and created multiple scenarios designed to mitigate and manage the threats quickly, from five-hundred miles away.*

2. *As part of the safety and security planning of a major community college system, professionals used BIG-BIM to visualize and assess response to threats that might impact students and staff. Scenarios for potential threats to an on-campus daycare center required evaluating refuge areas, the creation of mitigation strategies and finding secure external assembly areas sized to the population. Synchronized to first responder capabilities and response times.*

Simulating the principles of crime prevention and emergency management helps security professionals balance security needs. Scenario planning for emergency response depends on the capacity to model both physical and operational excellence, quickly and accurately. A security response built without proper operational changes will fail.

A scenario planning system enables the user to understand what the owner does and how they do what they do. Gaining an accurate understanding of the owner's mission is a fundamental step in developing a comprehensive, connected strategy. Planning created in the scenario planning system must be based on real needs, not on a generic security approach.

Tactics must then be devised that provide long-term performance and value, appropriate to each owner's situation. For every scenario, there is more than one solution. There are many ways to reach the desired goal. It is up to the security consultant, the designer, and the owner to determine the best solution. The solutions will include the identification of the risks, and then determine how the environment contributes to making the facility vulnerable to the threat.

Finally, the team identifies ways to mitigate the risk. You then translate your findings into implementable goals to create plans to make them happen in support of the day-to-day operation of the facility. Scenario planning allows you to respond to the physical and operational issues so that solutions:

☐ *Identify and prioritize the assets that need to be protected;*

☐ *Define the level of threats the organization and facility may face;*

☐ *Determine the vulnerabilities from the identified risks, and;*

☐ *Evaluate the risks to the mission of the organization.*

BIG-BIM overlays operational data with asset data to give security professionals the tools they need to rapidly customize each facility, area, organization, campus, or distributed network of buildings. You evaluate the impact on the environment; visualize and estimate costs; set standards that inform a rules-based system, and; support the owners' needs for a safe and secure environment.

It is critical to define the scope of the problem, matching needs to available expertise, and engaging the right people to manage emergency response. The system must accommodate and connect new experts without requiring everyone to be in the same room. Collaborative, highly responsive, and open systems are needed to ensure success in this environment.

In the fast-paced and chaotic world of emergency response, data, and information rule. Using data from a central repository that archives everything, emergency response leaders link information in new ways. Doing this, they can understand better and leverage available resources. Use the same information that supports building, business operations, maritime conditions, and other things that influence the built environment, to reach high levels of situational awareness, fostering real-time, fact-based decisions.

Including security input early in the process has the effect of reducing redesign and minimizing costs while achieving high-performance safety and security systems. You ensure the selection of appropriate tactics that fit with the overall security goals and actual facility use. By developing and connecting security first, you work within the local environment instead of security becoming a bolted-on item after completing design and construction.

The adage one-size-fits-all does NOT apply to security and emergency response planning. What works well in one situation often fails in another. Each facility exists in a unique context and needs an equally unique plan.

Case Study
Children's Theater

The ability to quickly extract and use the data from the model, coupled with a connected process allowed the CTOD early, complete, and detailed information to support fundraising and the development of the theater program.

What are the interesting aspects of this project?

Use of BIG-BIM at earliest phases of organization development.

Use of BIM to chart the way forward in detail.

Process validated the use of BIM to study organizational structures, physical requirements, and operations issues in-context.

Location—Delmar, MD, USA.

We don't have much money. We don't have a site. We are still putting a board together. Nevertheless, we have a vision. We must plan for the next thirty years.

Budgeting, raising funds, property acquisition, and organizational development were the opportunities that the Children's Theater of Delmarva (CTOD) presented. The Theater created an opportunity to apply commercial off-the-shelf (COTS) technology and techniques developed to define a new organization.

Summary

The Children's Theater of Delmarva was truly a labor of love. Founders of such performance groups are often highly motivated and enthusiastic visionaries. Their energy and focus are critical to success. The founders created a unique and exciting program that became one of the community's tools for exposing youth to the performing arts. They offered the opportunity to plan not only a new building but also a new organization, using BIM.

The CTOD's founders considered a permanent home to be crucial for long-term growth and continued success. Supporting the need was the overwhelming success of the theater's signature educational show, *The Stand-Up*. This show began as six local children performing to become a mad dash for performers to become one of the first fifteen to respond at open auditions for each show. The goal was to allow *The Stand-Up* to grow from six to twenty-four performances each year while allowing more children to perform in each show.

The group modeled the program to serve as an outlet for youth to encourage them to satisfy their passion while building skills in the performing arts. The program was designed to strengthen the relationship of the entire family while creating a tradition in the performing arts. Participant growth and program needs drove the CTOD toward the creation of a permanent space.

The founders could access and evaluate projected costs based on accurate quantities extracted from the model. Even at this early stage in development, the group's producers and directors analyzed sight lines and visualized backstage traffic flows using the project's virtual building models.

Creating a plan and framework for a new organization with a vision started with a blank slate and few resources. Making the solution into a reality required them to engage all stakeholders. Collaboration among the design team, the founders and participants were critical. Seen from the perspective of participants or funding sources, the process was easy to pigeonhole as an academic exercise.

I had a vision, if you will, of a theater that would provide for children's productions and a venue for professional productions that would bring in money to support the children's theater program. My background is in events planning and fundraising— in getting people to provide things at little or no costs. However, I had no idea where to start.

I figured that seeing an expression of my idea would be a huge first step. I communicated my vision and asked what we could create for minimal dollars. What we got was huge. We got 3D renderings, a strategy, and a detailed estimate that gave a good idea of the direction we should go. They gave us legitimacy. — Carlos Mir, Founder, Children's Theater of Delmarva.

Funding raising for design, land acquisition, construction, operations, and endowments required easily understood plans that represented all parts of the organization's operations. From the beginning, the core team included the founder of the theater, an accounting business with a strong business planning background, the board of directors, parents, and the design team.

The process involved directors of some established community theaters across the country that provided input and reviews. Lenders, bankers, realtors, leaders of other non-profit organizations, and the youth that made up the Theater's lifeblood drove decision-making. Connecting all involved in the process was critical.

Building support systems and awareness was one of the groups' greatest accomplishments. Due to the lack of a permanent home, the group structured the CTOD's programs to make the best use of open-air venues and small community facilities. The city did not have a solid, Broadway-quality venue that could help youth grow and learn how to become better performers, in a caring, safe, and supportive atmosphere. Sets, equipment, and costumes were designed to function in found spaces, with an eye toward future connection into a permanent venue.

The community began to take the Children's Theater seriously. Producing successful shows without a home gave the group the influence to move forward, and the graphics captured people's imaginations.

The next step was to create an organizational development study that the group could be proud to take to patrons, banks, and the Rural Development Administration to start the process of funding the theater. The group had to be thoroughly prepared when asking people and corporations to give large sums of money.

The group's leadership had high confidence when presenting *A Theater for Tomorrow*, with its graphics, renderings, and detailed estimates and accounting. The process allowed them to produce a far more complete report for less money, much earlier in the development process than normal.

Outcomes

We are a small group of people, parents primarily, that is concerned with providing a performing arts program for our children and the children of the community. It is important to have a venue that our children's theater can call home. We have been quite successful as a theater without walls. This approach has been right for our children, but it isn't sustainable. We need a theater and a plan for generating the revenues to operate it, long-term. Our understanding of the building process ends there.

We got much more than images and estimates, but also a long-range development plan that we could get our hands around. It is amazingly clear how the proposed facility will meet our needs. We now understand what we must do to achieve our dream. Federal government funding sources have been very impressed with the work and the detailed plan. The study has already convinced a patron to commit the first $100,000 toward our project. — W. Frank Brady, Member, Board of Directors.

The Children's Theater of Delmarva (CTOD) was designed to be an integral part of the community and to provide youth with education-oriented experiences that enhance the area's overall cultural experience. The organization successfully worked with a broad range of young people and adults to support this mission. They operated without a permanent home and survived by the generosity of those with existing facilities and by renting needed space.

The group's goal was to define the steps that they should take to reach their long-range vision. The first task was to develop a concept model to generate public interest and attract funding for planning. With planning funds in hand, the process opened to the community. Next, a design vision developed to include projected costing data and a validated analysis of the group's program needs.

The validation process included extensive research on comparable facilities and involved the directors of some successful theaters. The design team, working together with the group's Producers and Directors created performance schedules and used them to predict income and expenses to support a plan for long-term funding. From this data, the theater could raise development funds and begin negotiations for their preferred site.

BIM worked well to support the development of new non-profit organizations, as the founders explore the many factors that go into starting right and becoming established in their communities. By building in BIM before expending detailed design and construction funds, the shortcomings, possibilities, and opportunities all become clear and available to decision makers—early in the process.

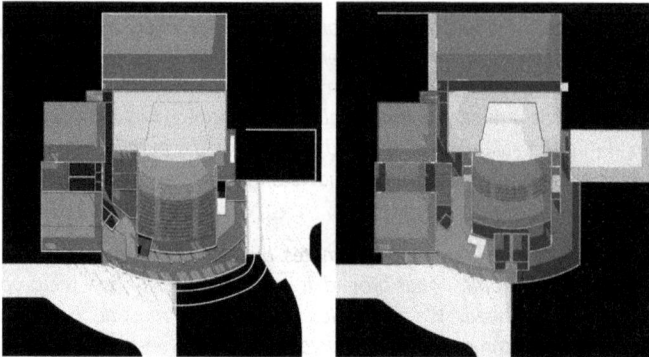

The facility's main venue was to be a formal Broadway-quality theater with stepped, fixed seating. A black box theater also allowed freeform performances within an open and creative neutral space. The facility was designed to support multiple simultaneous productions, allowing the main arena to host a larger production while the black box theater hosted a smaller house production. Supporting the theaters were dance studios, classrooms, administrative support, and all necessary behind the scenes spaces. Studios for professional quality audio/video production and audio/video/lighting control were also incorporated.

BIG-BIM is particularly useful for communicating and documenting group discussions and decision-making sessions. Helping the group understand and decide.

Early stage planning does not always tell people what they hope to hear. Not all projects move forward to implementation. BIG-BIM exposes the problems that are likely to occur in later stages of projects by bringing early decision-making information to the table. By studying the alternates, supported by data, groups can make the best and most informed decisions about their projects. Sometimes the decisions made are not what the optimists among us hope.

During the process, many things became clear to this group:

Without the proposed theater, their ability to provide for after-school programs, theater camps, workshops, at-risk youth programs, and traveling shows became severely limited.

The group needed a home to survive. As a theater without a fixed home, the organization could only function if the founder was willing and able to produce shows, fundraise, and promote his vision.

Lack of significant underwriters and community financial support could not be overcome by performance revenues or external grants, making the project financially unfeasible.

Continuing as a theater without a home was not sustainable. When all the facts were understood, the group elected to abandon the project and have since ceased operations.

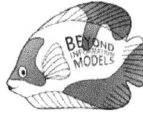

SEVEN
PROCESS OVER PRODUCT

Integrated Project Delivery isn't the end-product of information modeling. Integrated Project Delivery is a process that helps leverage information models for stakeholders.

The products of information modeling include better collaboration, enterprise integration, connected decision-making—and, a measurably better world. One creates clarity by studying organizational structures, physical requirements, and operations issues in-depth, early. You capture intelligence and rules to manage knowledge in all you do.

The chapters that follow contain a compilation of common misconceptions, essays on the state of the industry, suggested solutions, workshop exercises, and lessons learned that apply to your work as you move toward the BIG-BIM ecosystem. These essays address the background, triggers and logic that are the foundation of the issues covered elsewhere in the book.

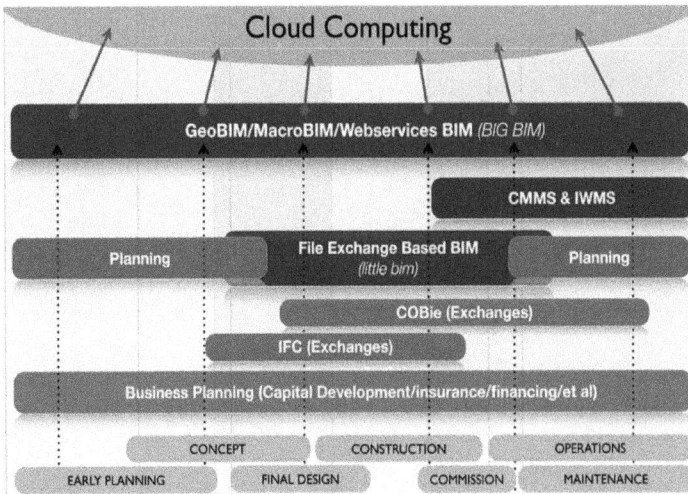

Curmudgeons

Over-building models with too much information and duplicating information that already exists results in lost productivity. Just as it did when the curmudgeons walked the earth.

The pioneers of BIM began their explorations in the 1970s. The '70s were an era of confusion, conflict, and change. McGovern lost to Nixon in 1972, and by 1974, Nixon had resigned. Intergraph was getting off the ground, and AutoCAD was not on the horizon. The floppy disk and the microprocessor had recently appeared. Most were still punching cards—if one used computers at all. Most considered Toyota to be a cheap import aimed at those with limited resources. Ford Motors was the gold standard. Futurism was in full swing. The possibilities were endless.

Every drafting room of that era seemed to have a curmudgeon. It was his (they were all male) job to keep everyone on task. His desk was usually at the back of the open studio (the studio had to be open because that was the latest innovation). From this lofty perch, he could spot the malingerer and that worst of all offenders—the Pouche'er. One found them by following the staccato tap-tap-tap of their technical pens as they rendered every drawing in sight. This villain was responsible for lost profits, delayed drawings, and the business' inability to make money.

Although exaggerated, this characterization has been common among generations that grew up with hand drafting and CADD. It is likely that overdrawing and excessive detailing has been a problem since the days of the medieval Master Builder.

Step forward to today. The drafting room has gone the way of the dinosaurs. There are no drafting tables. The standard tools of the 1970s are museum pieces. Now, if you have internet access, a fast computer, and a mobile device, you have the world at your fingertips. You can do it all, and do it anywhere.

The BIG-BIM ecosystem makes it possible to replicate the real-world, in the cyber-world. We simulate, model and connect. The line between this cyber world and the physical world is becoming hazy. Disruptions are careening through our entire system of production, management, and governance as we move from the Information Age to the Connected Age.

How efficiently you work in this new world will still affect your outcomes. The drafting rooms and curmudgeons many be gone, but one can still be unproductive and wasteful—faster than ever before in human history. Improved tools and processes alone don't make things better; how you use them is the key, as always.

Reduce Waste

Technology, knowledge, and the physical world are aligning as the 4th Industrial Revolution or Connected Age takes hold. In this environment, the building industry is positioned to step up and find solutions to the world's most pressing problems, if we can overcome some significant issues.

We spend most of our time in our buildings. It is not surprising that the built environment wastes five times more than other industries. We have tools that give us the ability to understand and manage information so we can avoid this waste. We have processes that enable us to work with wicked problems. Most importantly, we are coming to recognize that the downward spiral cannot be solved by just computerizing traditional processes.

The industry is highly fragmented, and the complexity makes solutions difficult. In an industry made up of thousands and thousands of small, independent enterprises, even the largest organizations tend to rely on a system of disconnected and independent production. Tools and processes that make other industries more productive have not translated well to the built environment sector.

Discordant competition, a high incidence of extremely self-actuated entrepreneurs, and the highly cyclical nature of the building industry color perceptions. Traditionally, those that become most successful tend to have a *what's in it for me?* approach. They fight for projects, fight to respond to errors, and fight to make a profit in a highly competitive world. Adversarial relationships are often a dominant theme.

New tools that benefit some are either ignored or not considered to be relevant to other groups. In other industries, a small number of technology creators can develop software tools that support well defined processes industry wide. In the building sector, each group and subgroup believe that their needs are unique. As other industries improved productivity, following the advent of personal computing, the construction sector has been in continuous decline. Could this parochial attitude be to blame?

Too often ego, fragmentation, and outside forces manipulating the industry to overcome larger economic issues drive the industry. Solutions that do not take these into account do little more than mask the waste and inefficiency.

Technology vendors and large corporations have worked to develop systems that respond to a task, or at best project–oriented needs. Most of the systems they have created have been extensions to processes that continue the fragmentation, poor communications practices, and lack of connection. Most of the tools do little more than computerize operations that will never be able to handle the complexity that characterizes the industry.

The complexity and breadth of the issues seem daunting. Overcoming them has led many to give up and focus on personal benefit, knowing that they are at the mercy of forces they have no ability to control. This is the place to start. We need to believe that we can fix the problems.

☐ *Use technology as a force multiplier, rather than as a replacement for doing things the old ways.*

☐ *Focus on developing open tools that improve our ability to respond to the people, business, and economic issues.*

☐ *Deliver tools that handle second-order problems, rather than just building upon the traditional approach.*

☐ *Embrace systems thinking, just-in-time delivery, and similar procedures that offer insight into new ways forward. Interconnecting the tightly focused silos of activity is the path to making the industry less susceptible to the whims of the economy.*

☐ *Embrace connections and become truly collaborative. Rather than doing little more than acknowledging the trends, while continuing the what's-in-it-for-me business practices.*

☐ *Become centers of open-data; no longer supporting each industry group as a rigid, disconnected fiefdom.*

☐ *Participate in the changes, to become active stewards of a world, less driven by ego than by pragmatic, common sense.*

☐ *Rethink our view of projects to take on an asset focus.*

When properly interconnected, computers can process massive amounts of information to inform and guide decisions. In ways, that are very fast and comprehensive. With the right type of knowledge, archived in easy to access data storehouses, computers can supplement the human brain's ability to analyze and find patterns to make good decisions in a complex and fast-changing world.

With wisdom, intelligence, and creativity, people can use technology to supplement the things that they have learned, to maximize the chances of making good decisions. BIG-BIM and BIG Data offer a path to correcting traditional processes that no longer deliver value. When we learn to move beyond tradition to embrace connected business practices, then we will be reducing waste on a large-scale.

An ASSET is an item, thing or entity that has potential or actual value for an organization. An asset can be anything from tangible and physical items such as precious metals, machinery, vehicles, equipment, buildings and land, and current assets, such as inventory; to more intangible items such as patents, trademarks, copyrights, goodwill, company reputation and recognition. — Mash-up of Wikipedia and ISO-55000.

Case Study
The Long View

The Town's Director of Public Works commented: *We got down to the details early. Decisions resulted in significant time and money savings. The documents reflected decisions. The response to our input was a quick evaluation with clear, understandable graphics. Adding this to a fluid design process that eliminated the course of stop-go, stop-go too often found in the design community led to successful, intimate relationships between the owner, designer, and contractor and allowed for painless change solutions when necessary.*

The interesting aspects of this case study include:

Facilities management and GIS connection within BIG-BIM to position facilities, over time, for better long-term management and operations.

Successful Design-Build collaboration optimized using little-bim within a BIG-BIM ecosystem.

Connection of new team members into a little-bim process to enrich outcomes in an early use of BIG-BIM.

Location—Ocean City, MD, USA.

Although home to only slightly more than 8,000 full-time residents, Ocean City, Maryland's average summer population exceeds 250,000 vacationers. This dynamic fluctuation in population requires an infrastructure and support system that can respond well to the needs of a small town and a small city. In this environment, early stage planning, accurate capital budgeting, and coordinated project delivery are critical.

Opportunity: Manage municipal facilities on a 10-mile-long barrier island.

Correctly positioning and designing municipal installations in a resort community is a challenge unto itself. Facilities serve the population surges experienced in every beach season, yet function economically year-round. Facilities must withstand storms and a corrosive environment, in a tight fiscal environment, that's hard to administer.

Opportunity: Manage a diverse group of stakeholders in a small town with big assets.

City Engineer—Public Works Director—Director of Emergency Services—Volunteer Fire Chief, Volunteer Fire Company—City Manager—Mayor—Town Council. These groups (and more) all had a stake in and strong opinions about town facility design, building, and funding.

Needs and agendas vary and are often in conflict. Communications and *knowing that we are right, going in* are essential to a smooth and orderly capital development program. A connected approach with the right experts delivering an economical and efficient process was the solution.

A Superintendent employed by the Town commented on the first project: *We got a hell of a deal. The design was perfect. We developed healthy relationships early, leading to smooth communications and coordination throughout the project. This relationship has continued after move in where the contractor has returned to fix or repair minor concerns.*

Opportunity: Plan, design, and construct facilities in a seller's market.

Regularily newspapers run stories of bids that exceed the budget. Often by more than twice the published estimate. The Town was no different. Costs were usually over budget and rarely did projects finish on time. A different way to do business was required, and Town leaders were willing to try a new approach, even if it seemed risky.

The Town of Ocean City initially contracted to consolidate facilities to house their Public Works Department administrative and repair functions. The projects were designed and constructed with a minimum of problems, under tight time constraints, and under budget.

Project assignments have grown to encompass public works and emergency services facilities throughout the ten-mile long coastal island community. The key to this process is the owner having a representative who knows construction and how the parts go together.

The Ocean City Public Facilities Development Program uses high-performance management systems and off-the-shelf technologies to support municipal requirements—efficiently and cost effectively. Overlaying everything is a focus on cost constraints. Connected forward-thinking, collaborative planning and design processes identify values and success strategies early. Projects use connected, information-supported workflows.

Connected processes enhance the municipality's ability to communicate issues and decisions to all team members, quickly and efficiently. Projects develop within a GIS construct, using readily available and mature design tools. Every project is georeferenced. Where practical and beneficial, projects have been tested and prototyped using a broad range of analysis systems and interoperable software tools, allowing teams to envision better, build, manage, and maintain Town facilities.

The combination of optimized traditional processes with building information models that interface with GIS and CAFM enable teams to create powerful environments that support the Town's ongoing capital development projects.

Safety, security, funding availability, stakeholders' needs, and long-range planning connect into the process. A range of professionals in Crime Prevention Through Environmental Design (CPTED); First Response/Emergency Services, software development, accounting, real estate appraisal, hotel/motel/restaurant development and operations, and; metal building manufacturing took part.

The Town can visualize buildings accurately with three-dimensional modeling capabilities, using the wealth of model data included to extract information from the very first concept. The building information models help teams to identify costs and a success strategy very early in the design process. The models then became a vital part of the design practices and efforts to deliver the best quality customer services.

Opportunity: Optimize the Town's ability to respond quickly.

Emergency and public works personnel must respond immediately, even when visitors overload the solely available access route. Unique to this team were connected emergency services experts. The team created a Call Volume Study to help the Town determine optimal station locations and to best manage the growing call volume. The team also coordinated the Volunteer Fire Company's first strategic planning process and prepared concepts and program estimates for completing the Town's entire fire facility program.

The Town's Director of Public Works commented: *The projects have our fingerprints all over them. The process used for the design and construction of our offices and shops gave us the opportunity for detailed input to meet our needs now and gave us flexibility for expansion within the original footprint for future needs. The benefits of the process are amazing. We conduct business in a quick and efficient manner. This approach allows us to view and update data typically stored in numerous locations and media formats, an effort that consumes far too much time. The models streamline access to building data and allow the transfer of information from design and construction to facility management. The process eliminates tedious, repetitious tasks.*

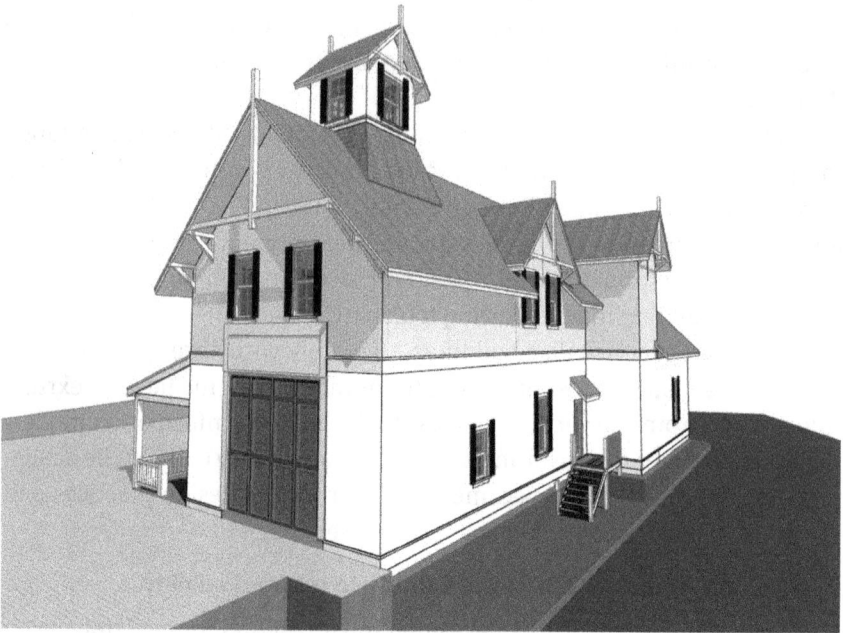

The location study concluded that the Town's most remote station was the priority and should be expanded, noting: This expansion is vital since this station is your first responder to control any situation in the North until additional support can arrive. Due to the strong potential for traffic gridlock that prevents support from other stations, this station should be designed and equipped to be self-sufficient for a significant period.

Often one's greatest benefits come from embracing projects while maintaining a big-picture outlook that creates long-term value for one's customers. The often-unspoken need for increased lifecycle benefit is one of the reasons that the lines between little-bim and BIG-BIM are rarely clear or clean cut. Often something as simple as—*design a new office and workshop* will over time, expand to encompass georeferenced master models, web-based facilities management, strategic planning, emergency services, and more.

By maintaining a long view, the small engagements can lead to bigger things that take new and unforeseen directions that create value for one's customers. Municipal capital programs offer a diverse mix of built environment assets. Traditionally design and construction of built environment assets happen piecemeal and have not been georeferenced. As-builts are inconsistent and projects are often late and over budget. BIG-BIM processes give municipalities the ability to correct these issues without sacrificing efficiency, even in one-off situations.

Traditionally, owners reward professionals for completing projects. The reward system has not changed, but now customers are also focusing on the long-term sustainability of their assets. This change of interest is the case whether they communicate this fact to you, or not. There is a growing realization that one's capital assets are more than individual items in isolation.

Manage Better

In the building industry, many push back against the idea of managing information. How often have we heard comments like, I didn't get into architecture, or construction, or... to manage data.

Computerization has not worked to the built industry's advantage. Where other sectors of the economy have moved toward an App-focused approach that connects software to the physical world, the building industry has retained a general bias toward file exchanges and welded together software systems. This bias has resulted in the industry lagging other areas in achieving the productivity benefits that come from connection.

2D CADD solutions and spreadsheets were the first attempts at automating industry processes. Rather than improving things, studies suggest that these file-based tools have contributed to a long-term decline in productivity, industry wide.

CADD files have little computable-intelligence, are not interoperable and require complicated management controls. They increase the potential for error. The refined and finished document look that comes from these systems gives a false sense of quality, rather than providing improved coordination and clarity. Even little-bim authoring tools offer only marginal improvements when used for task automation. In this mode, BIM is little more than high-priced computer-aided-drafting on steroids.

Design and construction have always required that one work with data, and lots of it. The planning, design, construction, and operation of any facility requires management of massive amounts of information. The industry has always revolved around data management.

We may call it something else, but it is still information management. One has long needed to marshal all the potentially relevant data and then sort, filter and massage it into useful project information, using notes, books, Rolodexes, and stacks of index cards. We have a long history of managing massive amounts of data to get things done.

Now the goal is to use the information to streamline and eliminate waste to get more for our efforts. To do this most effectively, it helps to approach BIG-BIM with an open mind. Often when presented with new technology tools, construction industry professionals become mired in the details.

How will the software draw this type of line? If I put a door in this wall, what happens? We seem to forget the underlying necessities as we delve ever deeper into the details of the features. At times, we are our worst enemies. We push vendors toward continually add features as their primary way to keep customers coming back, rather than forcing software developers to focus on the important things, like data exchanges. This emphasis on tools to do the same day-to-day tasks in new ways perpetuates a cycle that is not productive.

We are ending up with little-bim systems that are incrementally becoming more complicated, without truly solving the problems that need resolution. We can no longer allow vendors to push features just to sell more software.

Add to that the fact that connected processes and building information modeling are not about buying the right software. Both are about adopting new management methods that make information easily available, in a shared environment that connects to and mirrors the real-world.

Rather than looking at connections from a systems perspective, many building industry professionals have spent money and time to automate tasks in their offices. They added word processors, spreadsheets, analysis programs, scheduling, estimating tools and Computer-aided-drafting and Design (CADD) programs to improve specific tasks. In many offices, little-bim has taken the same direction.

Over time, as they automated more things and added more tools, offices found that task automation comes with some problems. The problems became severe as fully computerized companies use a dozen or more applications, from electronic time sheets to digital image libraries, each with a separate database.

Today the norm is a mixture of individual seats of software on personal computers and hosted applications on local servers and the Cloud. Each computer runs software applications that rely on file exchanges and have little or no ability to share data via web services.

It is no longer enough to automate manual tasks with the computer. Using the computer as a glorified typewriter is a waste of time and money. With this approach, it is impossible to overcome the challenges the industry faces. The industry needs to embrace technology as a force multiplier to develop new ways of doing business.

BIM isn't an automation of tasks. When viewed from the perspective of task automation BIM becomes another drafting tool—little more than another software purchase. It is a much more sophisticated tool, but a drafting tool nevertheless. Often the task automation approach can be tracked as a major factor in failed or sub-optimal BIM deployments, whether people understand this fact, or not. BIG-BIM and connected practices require something much different. The approach is well outside the building industry's usual practices.

With the file exchange approach, people end up inputting the same information for each tool or manually moving data from one database to another. Both options are time-consuming and error-prone practices requiring revision with every software update.

Files or Information?

One does not have to do things in precisely the same way that others do things, if the work fits into the ecosystem. Sustainability and resilience are byproducts.

With BIG-BIM, one connects information in standardized ways, using regulated and shareable archives. As new technology emerges, it can read and manipulate the data—even for technology that we today cannot remotely envision.

Rather than starting over, with every new tool, one moves to a cycle of reading data filed in a standardized and reusable format. One gives up some control, but in exchange, the system enables organic growth of tools for understanding decisions before we expend significant resources.

The data comes from many sources and represents the state of an asset and its connections to the built environment. Each bit of data accounts for a discrete part of the whole; it minimizes repetition. We are no longer required to sort out multiple versions of the same information which removes much of the confusion and potential for error. The authoritative source supports each type of data; you use it with confidence. Making such things possible is why standards are so important.

The focus of many built environment professionals has been on a different vision. Much of the energy and attention have gone toward defining exchanges and codifying standards. The tools that have resulted have focused on file exchanges, rather than on web services transactions, to create systems that require a lot of training or expert intervention to function properly.

Too often the efforts have been overlaid with self-interest and need to control all interactions, all in the interest of interoperability. The focus has been on rigidly constraining the interchange of information between welded together software products rather than on flexible and open-standards that establish an industry norm, and then getting out of the way and letting things happen.

Interoperable data exchanges do not solve the problem by themselves. If tomorrow we woke up and every welded together software product on the market could magically talk to and understand every other product, the problem would not go away.

- How often have you tried to open a file from *version X* of your current software, only to find that you cannot open it with the latest *version Y*?

- Have you exported a COBie file from your desktop software and sent it to the owner? Only to get a call telling you that the file contains duplicate room names or numbers and will not open?

- Have you ever found the disk with the specification for a job completed ten years ago, to find that none of your machines have floppy drives?

- How many times have you tried to access a CD burned six years ago and concluded that it was unreadable?

- Have you exported an IFC file from your software and sent it to a coworker for import into her software program? Only to receive and email describing all the things that didn't translate and complaining about the need to redraw?

These are some of the day-to-day issues that can overshadow concerns of interoperability. Such machine and file issues matter less as the Cloud dominates today's computing world—if we use the Cloud for web services based data exchange, rather than as a file server housed off-premises.

Apps that push and pull data from multiple sources are rapidly making files-based interchanges outdated—in most other parts of our daily life. Not in the minds of many in the construction industry.

When it comes to BIM, many construction industry professionals have a death grip on their 3D-graphics-bound, welded together software tools. Not understanding that INFORMATION is, and always will be, the most important part of the work they do. For these folks, little-bim is a commodity, replacing CAD with something that makes nicer images.

Cloud-based BIG-BIM servers are changing the equation, and there are hopeful signs from some of the file-oriented systems. The file and graphics-bound servers that relate to BIM in the building industry are starting to respond to the need for information management connected to graphics. Tools such as Trimble's *SketchUp* are starting to find ways to connect graphic oriented models with Cloud-based objects and data in more open and shared ways.

Information is at the center of the next generation of change in the building industry. Soon more will come to understand the urgency and move from file-based information to secure shared information on the web to allow information to flow when, where and how people need data to improve our world.

It is a dichotomy. The same people that insist on the focus on graphics and files cannot live without their mobile devices. Rare is any meeting where they aren't glued to their smartphones and tablets. Cloud-based apps support their personal and business activities. They rely on information—without knowing what they are doing?

Case Study
Owners Changed Before

Each time technology changed, owners had to bear the costs to resurvey, re-input and replace their entire system.

A primary goal of BIG-BIM is to enable owners to move away from the cycle of starting anew each time a new technology appears. For owners, the information-driven approach represented by BIG-BIM may be the ultimate step in moving away from the throw it away and start over approach that has long characterized their relationship with technology in the industry. BIG-BIM is a practical way for owners to reuse their information over the life of their facilities.

Owners of facilities spent a lot of time and money to implement new technologies over the past fifty years. Typically, they threw away old systems and started over every time a new regime (or approach) came into vogue. Owners, and the enterprises they represent, lost inertia, resources, and information. Often ending up with halfway implementations and ongoing usability problems that took years to correct. The changes that occurred in the production and archiving of construction documentation is but one example:

1. Owners historically archived ink on vellum and pencil on paper. When they needed data, someone searched through the file cabinets and field verified their paper records—the time-tested approach;

2. They then began to use plastic lead on Mylar media. This change had minimal costs since nothing much changed for the owners. In fact, this medium improved owner's archival abilities;

3. Then pin-bar compositing systems were developed, ushering in what would later become complicated CADD layer conventions and would create significant archival difficulties;

4. Then large owners invested in CAD (Computer-Aided-Drafting) on mainframes. Each station cost a lot of money and the technology that fostered this change was so new that few gave thought to the realities of archival data. Data became inaccessible due to format incompatibility and tape drives that quickly became obsolete;

5. Then the standard moved to CADD (Computer-Aided-Drafting and Design) on minicomputers. Archived data did not carry forward due to software revisions and format incompatibility, floppy disks and Winchester drives;

6. More recently, the standard became personal-computer-based 2D CADD. Archived data is subject to data rot due to lack of interoperability, complexity of standards and lack of long-term storage media. File systems became so involved and hardware dependent that it became difficult to access archives quickly;

7. Then a few owners moved to 3D CADD on desktop computers. But the data was not database driven, not intelligent, usually not interoperable and did not comply with a single standard;

8. Forward-looking owners became advocates for BIM with the expectation that such tools and processes would overcome industry problems. Little-bim quickly moved toward becoming the industry's standard of care. Most systems relied on complex, prescriptive requirements. Due to the file-based data exchange based deliverables, much of the output is currently subject to Data Rot. Work product from these systems will NOT carry forward into future, information centered systems.

9. And now owners are moving to BIG-BIM ecosystems that mirror the BIG Data and web services oriented tools for connected decision-making and e-commerce on the Internet. BIG-BIM ecosystems are software agnostic and designed to connect data to give users just the information they need to make decisions—across the life cycle of built environment assets.

Step Back and Assess

Barreling ahead without a plan can work against everything you are trying to achieve. Too often, those new to BIM have gotten far in the process, only to find out that much of their work was for naught.

Making your customers' lives better, saving them money, and staying profitable is what connected business processes accomplish. When you create a process, that helps you to do better work, more efficiently—you provide your customers with greater long-term value.

Building a connected business does not happen overnight. It isn't a matter of switching off the lights after a day of working the traditional way and coming in the next morning to a new, better approach. It is a change management effort of consequence.

Think ahead about your information models. One must sometimes add things that are not needed today, knowing that they will be required tomorrow. The issues may seem small or large, but they will happen, costing you time and money.

Each of us must decide how to proceed with our models. There are many decisions to make. If you plan to analyze your building for sustainability, address what additions you need, at the beginning. Forget this step and something will need to be reworked as you move forward—usually at the time that causes the maximum amount of aggravation. The same goes for any analysis tool. Build in the assemblies and details needed to achieve the end goal of your effort.

A model for Design-Build will be different than one for a connected project workflow. A model for O&M will be different than either of the others. Create prototype models that contain the right information for each use type, while looking forward to future needs. Viewed from the perspective of the overall process, modeling in BIM happens fast; sometimes too fast. Design models constructed in haste, without thought to the future, can undermine projects.

There is little excuse for the designer that models only for the task at hand with little or no thought to construction or operations. Nor is the constructor blameless when only a bit more than clash detection is possible with her models. Not surprisingly, it is usually the most productive and aggressive of us that fall prey to such shortsighted approaches to modeling.

Because BIG-BIM is so oriented toward the long view, your actions need should always focus on planning your path forward—before you act. Models must be well conceived and built to a repeatable standard that supports lifecycle value. Models must support what comes next.

Do not minimize the risks and let your ego drive you to barrel ahead without a plan. Large and small, your success depends on thinking through the consequences of your actions. To be successful in the transition to connected processes, one must understand where one is headed and plan for the changes, in all things. The changes you create can be evolutionary, but often they will cause a revolution.

BIM in all forms is about making early decisions. Each step of the way, one needs a plan that always focuses on future needs. Without such an approach, one invariably ends up in a cycle of rework that wastes resources. Always think about where you are heading.

Case Study
Rapid Assessment

The entire process took place in a morning.

A BIG-BIM oriented approach requires good business sense and most of all; it requires good common sense. Some time ago, we were retained to convert a basement area for a group of attorneys that we had known a long time. In fact, we had done the interiors for their first offices—before BIM.

At this project scale, most experienced designers would give the customer a quick top-of-the-head assessment of the project, write up an agreement and start detailed design. Now we work differently. We start even small projects with a subtle difference.

We first got authorization for a minimal validation process. We did a quick site survey and assembled a basic model designed to act as a data container. The model was nothing more than a zone object capable of defining areas, furniture, finishes and other project data.

The project was too small to warrant a complete prototype model. But from the limited information available, we created a Cost Model using parametric, rules-based data maintained in our system. The Cost Model responded to the project scope, quantities, timelines, and other customer requirements.

We then sat down with the attorneys and went over the project logic. They understood the issues and cost risks. They could now decide how to proceed, with useful facts. They could move forward with certainty. They had the data to look at their options and were active participants in the decision-making; before they had to invest schematic and design development dollars. We could have given them our informed opinion. Instead, we gave them facts to help them make decisions.

This validation exercise is a small example of the types of activities that can occur in the first phases of every project. Quickly making clear and organized information available to customers early is one way we use a connected process. We validate the facts of each task before the conventional process even begins. Such methodologies are what drives the BIG-BIM process. It is a collaborative process that recognizes the value of team members. The process works to achieve high-performance and economic value for customers. It meets strategic goals and creates a safer, better-managed world for those who follow.

We are in the middle of a cycle where the industry is experiencing revolutionary change. While little is entirely new, this is a time where changing how you look at projects gives you many advantages. As apparent as it may seem, providing your customers with better early information makes it easier for them to see what lies ahead. Making you more valuable; you become the one that can make new things possible.

Change the Focus

Not long ago, one might buy software without needing to worry about whether it could share information with other tools, or work across the Internet with your bookkeeper in Bangalore. Today this is no longer true. BIG-BIM workflows revolve around teams working toward common goals.

The *I* in BIM is where the solutions to the building industry's problems lie. Information that is easily accessible when and where needed is the key.

Sit in on a presentation from any BIG-BIM expert and you will hear of the world where the ability to exchange information between systems, processes, and people is critical. When team members know the value they deliver, their performance is enhanced.

Project planning, design, and construction take most of the time and space when people focus on BIM. Most find it surprising when they learn that these three areas make up only 18% of the total construction industry. They get the lion's share of the attention. Why is that?

Go to a seminar, attend a lecture, or pick up a BIM book and you will find ways to use BIM for planning. Much advice and detailed steps for creating concepts and document production using BIM workflows fill books and blogs. You will find information about construction use of BIM, everywhere you look. Sit in on a presentation from any BIG-BIM expert and you will hear of the world where the ability to exchange information between systems, processes, and people is critical.

Factoring the rest of the lifecycle back into the building industry equation is what is under discussion. BIG-BIM enables value across the full spectrum of the industry. Some people just may not realize it yet.

Does it make sense to focus on planning, design, and construction? What about the remaining 82%? Shouldn't acquisition, maintenance, operations, recapitalization, and disposal also be considered? In these seeming outliers is where the major opportunities lie. To embrace the full range of the building industry needs, we need to change the overall focus from merely developing projects to getting the customer certainty about the lifecycle needs of his or her assets. When everyone embraces this shift in focus, beautiful things begin to happen.

With a project focus, tasks are more about the needs of the service provider than the needs of the customer.

What is the architect's fee? Can she make money at that rate? How much will the contractor charge? Will the project be finished on-time? On-budget? The customer pays the bill, but the focus is on those delivering the project, especially when it comes to BIM.

With an asset focus, building data is connected and accessible throughout the facility's lifecycle. From that information, you can accurately simulate the building in its present or proposed future state, in-context. Managing assets is the best way to become customer focused.

What needs to happen for all involved to successful? How much money should the owner set aside to achieve here goals? Have we found the potential problems before we pour the concrete? How will we design the building so that the owner can sustain the operation for the next thirty years? What should the team do to make the building resilient in a hurricane?

The customer still pays the bills, but now the focus is on a long-term asset. This subtle change in focus is critical to successful BIG-BIM. Help your teams shift toward managing assets:

☐ *Recognize that change is a team sport. Increase the numbers of alliances with others focused on similar goals. Consult and involve your supply chain in decision-making. New alliances are but one side of the BIG-BIM coin. Build your personal ecosystem.*

☐ *Keep an open mind and don't be afraid to try new things. Explore new and evolving technology. Design, test, and apply tools to manage information. The App Economy is rapidly changing the game. Tools that worked well yesterday may not work so well today.*

☐ *Use innovation as a management tool. Develop new insights, explore new roles, and understand new viewpoints. Design thinking and a systems approach to management are an essential in BIG-BIM.*

☐ *Change how your business works. Build an environment fully engaged in positive change. Record information to confirm decisions or to create future value, not to track blame. Create value rather than profiting from waste. Move firmly toward processes that add value.*

☐ *Become a lifelong learning environment. Increase understanding so that everyone can grow to meet the need. Significant knowledge and sapience are required to find the problems as early as possible. Do everything you can to build a solid team grounded in the needs of BIG-BIM.*

Life-Long Learning

Many are locked into a process, and no amount of truth will move them. They fear the loss of creativity. They look at the computer as a production-only tool, even with the body of proof that shows otherwise.

The misconceptions about BIM are legion. Many of the worst mistakes come from those in charge. Many professionals that are in the middle of their careers or later, need to consider if their resistance to change is holding back their enterprises. Too many still believe that it is not possible to do the things that learned to do by hand as well on the computer. They could not be more wrong.

These are the same people that don't commit to the effort to learn how to use an ever-evolving set of digital tools. They cling to the belief that they will always be able to sketch by hand and have someone draft it for them on the computer. They are forcing the usual approaches; instead of solving the problem. It is time for them to change, or they should get out of the way—no matter how lofty their view of themselves.

Each of us has done new things before, and we can change again. It is a time where each of us must be a life-long learner.

Today's best tools allow unprecedented levels of freedom while eliminating unnecessary work. Used correctly they allow freedom while overlaying constraints. They offer the ability to break the rules, knowing what the rules are, and knowing the impacts of decisions. They eliminate a lot of the mundane and repetitive work, both for ourselves and for the others that must carry on after we finish.

To correct industry problems, we must make a leap of trust. Life-long learners are prepared to take the risk to do things they have never done. They have a confident relationship with the unknown, and use it to keep moving forward.

A BIG-BIM ecosystem is always evolving. We must too. Being dedicated to learning and change may be the greatest asset for those who work in the built environment of tomorrow. Be a life-long learner. Embrace change. Enjoy the life-long journey.

Case Study
BIM Metaphor

With BIG-BIM, you push and pull data from many data repositories that archive everything. Networks of authoritative data are linked to incorporate the many information sources. You mash-up the data from many places to understand and make decisions with the facts.

There are many ways to use building information models. Some use the tools in isolation, much like the early adopters in the late 1980's. Some are further into the change and embrace collaborative processes.

Both approaches fall under the heading of little-bim. A few are moving to BIG-BIM, embracing the ecosystems that will make up the world of BIM tomorrow. Similar cycles of adoption abound outside the building industry. One that resonates with many took place in the accounting industry.

... little-bim is like computing (circa 1987) before the internet and early in the Information Age. Local Area Networks (LANs) were not in widespread use.

Using tax preparation as an example: One moves away from pencil and paper to improve how you prepare your return and simplify the computations. You depend on software that you have loaded on your desktop computer. You don't know whether the databases included are up-to-date. In fact, you don't know that there are databases behind what you see. You load new versions of the software as they become available. You share files with your accountant via sneaker-net or paper. You print out and mail your tax return.

In the building industry context: You replace AutoCad with Revit, Archicad, Bentley or one of the other little-bim authoring tools, on a personal computer. Improvements are internal to your office and your projects. Your BIM is little more than computer-aided-drafting on steroids. You model your project. You begin to explore simulation software on data from your model. You get all the benefits of real 3D CADD and then some. You start to become virtual building proficient.

This is what most of the construction industry understands as BIM today. In this mode, people worry more about what software they should use, than about work practices and business processes.

... little-bim is like computing (circa 1996) using files and other single use outputs that connect to a local network and are transitioning to internet connectivity.

Taking the tax preparation example one step further: You now have centralized files from last year. You share the tax schedules with your accountant so that more eyes are available to pick up mistakes. Your accountant takes your data and checks it for you. You either print out and mail your return or try e-filing.

In the building industry context: You are beginning to be more collaborative. You are learning ways to share information on a project-by-project basis. You are still limited to desktop software and the data embedded in these tools. Although now your local network is supplemented by the Cloud. Information is beginning to be decentralized and shared among your connected associates. You begin to do conflict checking, cost modeling, and process simulation, in the context of your projects.

This is the mode that most people are working toward, and what the big firms are doing. People continue to worry about what software they should use and are just beginning to figure out that they need to change how they do business.

... BIG-BIM is like the networked enterprise, becoming a part of the Internet of Things in the Connected Age.

To finish the tax preparation example: You access your tax information in external databases that someone else maintains. When the government passes a new law, it connects immediately. You access to the latest versions of everything, knowing that the background data is up-to-date. When you try to input illegal or illogical information, you know it immediately. You add your information and standardized processes verify it and connect it with the central repository. The system reacts in standardized ways, depending on the need.

In the building industry context: You are working on a global scale with live data. Your projects are no longer in isolation from anything or anyone. You connect data from everywhere. You understand what you are doing in a big world context. No longer is your building's context limited to the surrounding buildings or the neighborhood. You set constraints to control your work. Your customer's business requirements affect the solution. You know the impacts you make on the environment and other resources.

When you analyze your options, your results are repeatable and as accurate as possible. You are working with real-world information—not assumptions, guesses or opinions. You avoid unworkable options before you spend time on unproductive tasks. Data and information are kings.

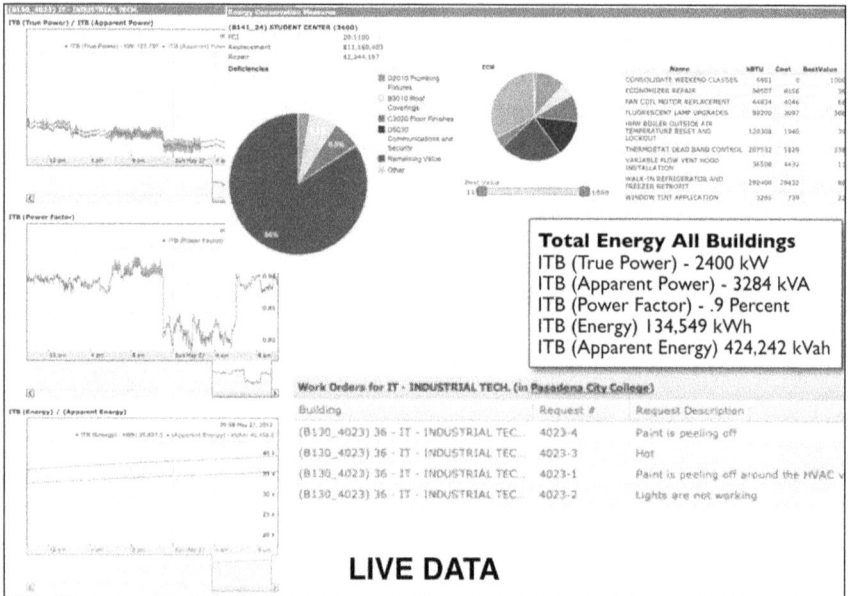

Total Energy All Buildings
ITB (True Power) - 2400 kW
ITB (Apparent Power) - 3284 kVA
ITB (Power Factor) - .9 Percent
ITB (Energy) 134,549 kWh
ITB (Apparent Energy) 424,242 kVah

LIVE DATA

You create or manipulate the data using an almost unlimited set of tools. Motes and sensors link live data to give you a real-time understanding of what is happening.

You manage at the appropriate level of detail using the best available data. You have the detail that you need to make informed decisions, without seeing (or needing to see) the underlying complexity of the system. No longer must one be an expert to interact with the information.

The data is sharable, interoperable and grows over time, becoming an invaluable resource. The system is universal and sustainable to make our world a better, more efficient place to live, work and play. BIG-BIM is the democracy for the built world, cutting through the fragmentation that has been the hallmark of the industry.

EIGHT
FIRST DAY MISTAKES

Facts supported by imagery and presented using tools that maximize understanding are the currency of the Connected Age that is before us. Delays to *study the issue* and *go/no go decisions* that take months are not appropriate responses in this fast-paced environment.

Framework

The problems we experienced were affecting everyone who interacts with the built environment at any level. We found that people and organizations everywhere were suffering.

We realized that we had our own first day problems. For some time, we felt that we were fighting everyone. No matter what we did, it seemed like our projects were always over budget and late. Contractors seemed to be fighting us at every step. Our designers and engineers appeared to have stopped coordinating their work, and every project was a battle. We needed to do something else, but we didn't know what that something else was.

Adding more people to monitor the process seemed to make things worse. We learned the hard way that you cannot add inspectors, especially when they don't know the contract, in the middle of projects. It became apparent that throwing people at the problems wasn't the solution. We needed to make bigger changes. Most people didn't seem to care or understand what was causing the problem; they were just fed up with the outcomes.

We asked owners to make decisions based on graphics, anecdote, and experiential knowledge. Without thinking it through, we asked our customers to trust our brilliant, rational logic, without real data. We asked them to use their judgment to decide, even when they had a minimal amount of actual knowledge or reliable decision-making information from which to form their opinions. We inadvertently led owners to make decisions that in retrospect, had unintended consequences.

Our customers found themselves exposed to public scrutiny every time they approved a plan. Being politicians, seeking a safe direction, or a scapegoat, often seemed more important than finding a fix to the problems. It was easier to cover one's backside or shoot the messenger than to find a fix.

The public our customers represented was tired of projects with problems, budget overruns, and disasters. They expected every project to be an undeniable success, with clear indications of wise spending and high-value results for the money spent. How we got there rarely rose to the level of public scrutiny.

In 1996, we decided to tackle the problem head-on.

Talking about the issues and an open dialog started the process. We did our research, looking for new ways of doing things and new tools that might offer a solution. We concluded that a lack of systems to support early decision-making was keeping us from resolving the issues.

Finding tools and procedures to understand issues better, early in the process, become the critical task. If we could enable better decisions at the beginning of projects, we could reduce the problems. We could increase our customer's confidence in the outcomes, and get better buy-in from the community.

In this process, we found that talking about technology caused people to tune us out. They either didn't care, or the details were always too complicated. The details were not relevant to most people; they wanted little more than to make sure that things happen correctly.

People preferred to open a browser, click on an icon, and participate in the decision-making process with straightforward, easy to use tools. Either, *just take care of it* or, *make it easy for me* were the primary responses. Facebook or Expedia for the building industry, seemed to be the best approach.

Why waste energy trying to get people to do things they don't want to do? People wanted simple and easy to understand solutions. Complicated strategies would do little more than create confusion and boredom.

Now that we had a direction, our first job was to analyze the problems and find solutions. We had people talking, a lot of public input about what people wanted, and we knew some of the things that were creating problems in our projects. We had a hunch that we were not alone in our quest, but didn't understand how widespread the problem truly was.

Sometimes when people focus on their little slice of our world, they forget to concentrate on global problems. I guess that's what happened to us. Since we didn't know better, we just jumped in and started to develop solutions that made sense to us. We tested hundreds of software and hardware tools, both individually and as part of systems.

We created an environment for trying anything and everything that popped up on the Internet. Our testing had a goal of finding the best and most beneficial solutions. Some we kept, and we use them today. Some we discarded for a variety of reasons. Some never worked; some used to work, and some are beautiful.

These were real-world explorations. Ours were not ivory-tower tests. Rather, we used the tools on real projects. If they worked, great, if not, we moved on and looked for the next possibility. This exploration was a ten-year journey. In those years, we learned volumes about how systems for managing technology and systems for managing people differed.

We learned that we needed to change how we educate people to create adaptable, lifelong learners capable of connecting the technology.

We learned about interoperability and model servers.

We learned about ways to manage by constraints.

We came to understand that little-bim tools might help us perform better, but BIG-BIM processes tied to the larger world were what it would take to solve our problems.

We came to the realization that we needed to drive the process, even at the education and technology levels.

In the beginning, the design and construction process seemed to be broken. With no fix in sight. People complained about the problems. Electing new politicians, every time there was an election was not solving the problem. Nor was finding a replacement design and construction team after each hiccup. No one seemed to be stepping up to create an environment that would provide the solution. That's why we just had to start and try to do the right thing. You can too.

People want things to be under control. They want to know where things are going. They want to understand how things relate to each other in ways that improve decisions. Correctly applied technology and systems thinking gives us the tools to make this happen.

Case Study
Repeating Struggle

A friend quipped, *All the big problems happen on the first day,* after she heard the story of a facility manager that oversees facilities for a 400-bed medical center. Never was this truer.

Design is the honeymoon period, and we are always under construction. We hire a design team, and the architects create beautiful ideas—everybody loves the vision.

If we have hired a construction manager to control the design process, we get reliable information. If not, we look to the designers for details to assure ourselves that the sketches meet all our needs. We get 'pretty pictures,' but we rarely get reliable decision-making information at this stage. The images get people excited. The designer asks us to take it on faith that everything is worked out. The decision to move forward becomes strongly weighted by emotion rather than by facts.

By the time, we can understand the details, the designer has invested much time developing the concept. If everything is as required, life is good. If not, someone spends more money to make corrections. Unfortunately, the costs often fall on us since we approved the 'pretty pictures.' The tendency is to move forward after tweaking the sketches since no one wants to spend the money or take the time to start over.

When we receive bids in this environment, they are often drastically over budget. Then everyone panics and the designer gets defensive. The project gets "bought out" or "value engineered" and things get lost in the process...

Construction starts and many changes cost extra money. We juggle the changes within the contingency, so not everything can get done. Finally, we move in, but the problems are still not resolved, so...

We struggle to operate in the facility—and issues continue to crop up. Then the more self-aware people realize that we missed something important at the beginning, but no one admits it because to do so would make them look bad.

By the time, we do the next project, most of the players are new, and those involved in the past conveniently forget what happened the last time.

Any building owner might tell such stories. Create a BIG-BIM ecosystem that enables early, fact-based decisions to avoid similar problems. Handle the *first day* issues and assure life cycle benefits. Listen to understand the places where BIG-BIM can help.

Identify a building owner. Sit down with him or her and ask questions such as:

- [ ] What steps do you take when you begin a new project?

- [ ] How do you establish your budgets? What happens when things change?

- [ ] How do you make early decisions? Do you have solid facts or must you rely on the knowledge in people's heads?

- [ ] How much time is spent to find the facts needed for decision-making?

- [ ] What happens if you lose an old-timer and must rely on a new hire to make the same decisions?

A Connected World

Today, things are much less linear and much more connected to the world around us than ever before.

Since the first publication of *BIG-BIM little-bim,* there has been a groundswell of professionals and stakeholders experiencing their first work with information modeling systems. These modeling systems offer significant improvements in visualizing and documenting projects. There are some obvious benefits to users, and that is where most focus their attention.

That is where they see the fast return on investment, and that is where most stay, often missing the larger opportunities. Too few have continued to aggressively develop more connected tools and processes.

This approach to BIM continues Industrial Age, assembly line thinking, where work went step-by-step, relying on semi-skilled workers. Find a problem in need of a solution. Identify a tool or process to deliver the solution. Implement and repeat.

Part of being a professional is the ability to share information in ways that make it possible to gain benefit from connections and accessible data. There are many ways to share and profit from the lifecycle information you create and access. Conceiving the tools and processes you need and using them to exchange information is a core part of how you interact with BIG-BIM ecosystems.

The mobile world and the App Economy has created thousands of excellent tools that can actively maintain links to live information. Adding to this is a new class of purpose-built middleware systems that create bridges to live information and simplify the use of data.

These systems' ability to support data as a living resource is today delivering on the promise of BIM servers described in earlier editions. Such systems are among the first, and most critical, components of any BIG-BIM ecosystem.

Beliefs

BIM is about human interaction and collaboration enhanced by technology. It is about how people think about and use technology, and new ways of doing business. Without the connections between people, technology, and the physical world we may never learn to overcome the issues that our first day mistakes create.

You can buy every piece of software in existence. But without making the changes to how you think about the building industry and how you work, you will not dramatically improve conditions. You must adapt to the people side of the change, or you will never reach the full potential of BIM.

As you read this book, you have learned about the context and the tools you need. In the end, you decide what you do with them. You get to choose how, when and where to move. By understanding the underlying principles and consistently using what you know, you can create your personal vision and move your business toward connected practices.

Some of the changes will seem counter-intuitive, and may conflict with the things that you have been taught. The change to BIG-BIM will require you to examine your beliefs and understand them at the most basic level. Willful ignorance will get you in trouble in this environment and a bit of soul searching to understand the root of your professional beliefs will take you far, for this change touches upon the entire scope and breadth of your business.

The changes may require you to reassess much that you know. You will need to reconsider things that may have worked for many years, and there are new skill sets that may require training to master. You may find it difficult to adapt to them all.

Keep a positive attitude, be introspective, do your research and become involved with those further along in the path to change, and all will be well. Because BIG-BIM ecosystems are so revolutionary, it can be difficult to get one's mind around some of the changes. While it may seem hard, paradoxically, BIG-BIM is easier to master than little-bim. Don't let anyone tell you that you cannot make this transition, because YOU CAN!

Lead the Change

Step up and help owners sort through the hype and sales pitches. Show them how a BIG-BIM ecosystem can capture what they have today and future proof what happens from this day forward.

Building owners have long understood that operations and maintenance costs make up the lion's share of the costs over the lifecycle of their properties. Many others are beginning to realize that this is an area prime for connection into a holistic approach to information sharing.

But owners are having a hard time driving the changes that will be required to serve their best interests. Vendors are inundating them, and other professionals are pushing business-as-usual using new permutations of file-based welded together software products. Some of the vendors understand the market and are clamping old-tech to keep the business. Others don't understand the market and hype the tools that make them money. None is truly providing what the building owner needs.

Think of the opportunities BIG-BIM presents. When you focus on the assets, you begin to change the building industry in a big way. Saving money and resources for the life of built environment assets.

The change begins to level the cyclical nature of the industry. As the focus moves away from being solely on aesthetics and short-term project execution, you begin to influence the areas with the greatest potential for savings and efficiencies. Owners end up with a more productive process and facilities that are more efficient.

You lead owners away from storing data in files to making information available in real-time on mobile devices. By helping to connect the owner's business needs with assets and infrastructure, you enable them to make more sustainable and resilient decisions. To be effective with BIG-BIM, you must become more than just a designer, or contractor, or manufacturer, or supplier. Think about assets like a building owner.

When you take the long view, you resolve mechanical clearance issues early. Critical devices connect seamlessly to ensure maintainability. Connected data informs and enhances the owner's ability to make decisions. You and your customers no longer toss information over the wall to other professional disciplines in other phases. The right information flows to support the work of all involved.

Gain knowledge about the owner's mission and other business needs. Look for the value that lies beyond your legacy self-interests and take a long view of the built environment. Become an advocate for connecting, capturing, and reusing all the things that happen over time. Lead others toward a more resilient and sustainable future. Make three lists:

- ☐ *List ten people that you know, or have supported long-term. Focus on those with influence in areas related to what you do.*

- ☐ *List ten companies that you have worked with more than once. Focus on those that can cooperate with you to form a strong supply chain.*

- ☐ *List ten friends, acquaintances or colleagues that might be a resource as you move forward. Focus on those outside your usual circle.*

Assess each person or company on your list:

- ☐ *How well do they understand connected business processes?*

- ☐ *Do they understand and use BIM?*

- ☐ *Are they oriented toward new things? Or, traditional and unchanging?*

Prioritize your lists to identify *who is most likely to listen and respond positively. Give them a call and start to build your personal BIG-BIM ecosystem by working with them on Workflows in this book.*

Get the Benefits, Today

Manage project constraints from the beginning. Do this and you will begin to control your first day mistakes.

Have you ever dreamed about a time when you could call up the site details for a new project in real-time? Without hiring a surveyor? Without visiting the site? Have you ever dreamed about a time when you could open a file and have all the as-built and as operated details for the remodeling project that you just won? Have you ever wished that you could understand how your new customer's company works, without doing weeks of diagnostics and fact-finding? Well, now you can.

With BIG-BIM, you can design your process to take advantage of the information that surrounds us. You can make it possible for everyone to be more involved, more knowledgeable, and better able to make informed decisions. You can see significant improvements in your business.

Building Information Modeling is, as an idea, so universal and so wide-reaching that it can include anything that you can imagine. If it touches on the built environment, BIG-BIM can make our lives better and the built world more sustainable and resilient.

You (and your customers) cannot wait for someone else to figure out the complex systems and standards for you. You have, within your current resources and available tools, the ability to deliver the benefits of BIG-BIM, today. Moreover, using these resources and tools in new ways, you can produce better outcomes and happier customers. Why not get started?

Sometimes, one must overcome issues before one can change. There is often much inertia to overcome. However, if one looks at BIG-BIM as a business decision to deliver better outcomes and better customer support, the decision becomes easy. Focus on how you deliver projects and appropriately apply technology.

You can have the benefits today. The tools are available and have been for more than twenty years. BIM is about getting results—right now. BIM lets you use the tools and processes that work well—today. BIG-BIM allows you to position yourself to take advantage of other technologies as they become commercially available.

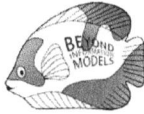

MORE CASE STUDIES

The design fiction and the case studies that follow are designed to highlight the possibilities and opportunities that BIG-BIM provides in situations that require early stage analysis and planning for resilience. The materials have four goals:

1. At the community level, the they involve everyone.

2. At the organization level, they connect business needs with state-of-the-art mission delivery and sustainability to better support the community.

3. At the system level, they promote resilience and comprehensive strategies for the future of the system and the community.

4. At the facility level, they help stakeholders make design decisions in a way that connects people with business needs.

At all levels, they supplement and enhance other material earlier in this book.

Design Fiction
BIMStorm Cork Point

One creates a system that allows people to ask for help, to take risks, and to develop new things without fear. Everything builds around this concept

BIMStorm Cork Point illustrates the process for using BIMStorms to plan and design new flexible and adaptable healthcare systems in small communities that respond to people, the environment, and constantly changing conditions. It is a long-term, ongoing BIMStorm designed to parallel the development of the Cork Point Health Complex. The process goes something like this:

Part 1—Preparation and Fact-Finding

Transparency and openness are needed for people to fully buy into the process. When participants recognize that a process is driven from a command-and-control perspective, interest wanes and fewer people participate. Over time, a truly collaborative process that allows people to innovate without fear will accomplish much more than any linear command-driven approach.

The core group meets to understand the key resources that will be involved in the process. As the discussion evolves, marketing and promotional concepts are solidified. Without letting people know what is happening and making them feel welcome, none of the rest will be possible. The core team's planning is designed to identify and manage the overall process so that as many people as possible can participate, in any way that they feel comfortable.

Communication systems are put in place at the beginning. Team members shift all communications to systems embedded within the BIG-BIM System. The goal is to connect all communications to the models so that nothing is lost. Behind the scenes communications using e-mail can easily undermine the collaborative process.

The team identifies and documents the source data, existing resources, and scheduling issues that must be addressed. While the core group is planning, others are cataloging and accessing existing knowledge about the project location, the community, the county, and the region. As much as possible, this information comes from existing geographic information systems connected to the BIG-BIM System.

By subscribing to government and private geographic information resources, the system makes property information, topography, water and other natural resources, cultural background, existing facilities, transportation, utility, demographics, and other public information available to the BIMStorm.

When they are available, the group connects building information models that local architects have built in the past. These models provide valuable information about the location of existing structures and historic buildings that may be rebuilt as the process moves forward.

As gaps in the data are identified, the group decides on experts to input the required data. In some cases, scanning and digitizing of hand sketches is required. Some information, particularly related to existing facilities and historic building resources, must be either laser-scanned and normalized, or scanned and imported from standard blueprints and other documents.

Part 2—Engagement

As these planning and data collection processes take place, the second part of the process begins. Marketing and promotion of the big-picture ideas are rolled out in the community and the region. Participation is solicited. Facebook, Google Docs, and other social networking tools are deployed and actively used to create interest and to accept input. The goal is to get people involved, using every tool in one's toolbox.

A series of public meetings begins the process. The meetings take many forms. Some are traditional open meetings with core team members inform those who attend about what is happening and take questions. These meetings depart from tradition in that the goal is to create a dialogue with participants, rather than convincing them of the Cork Point's position.

The goal is to listen, not tell. Each of the meetings has a set of core members. One or more members act as the event manager and moderates the discussion. At the same time, another group operates the BIG-BIM tools to reflect the discussion that takes place during the meeting. When practical, team members work at the meeting site. At other times, this activity is provided from remote sites.

As the group explores possibilities, participants see their ideas pop up instantaneously. A discussion of a new housing development results in an information model of a housing development on the site in question, with costs and other information immediately available.

The discussions quickly focus on people's concerns. Participants become engaged in the process, because they can see that their views are being considered and incorporated into the record. This is not talk to fill the void. This is a discussion to achieve results. And everyone knows it. Participants are encouraged to provide input to the system using their mobile devices. The information created is also projected for all to see and follow along with the discussion.

Meetings also occur in community groups such as the Rotary, the Chamber of Commerce, and churches. The goal is to reach as many people as possible. Other meetings are focused on prominent people who will then recruit other participants. Strategic planning, systematic data collection, and collaborative participation get BIMStorms off on the right track. Everything that follows became easier when the team focuses on these early tasks. One starts the process by creating an environment that gives the BIMStorm the greatest chance of a successful outcome. It is essential to begin the process right.

Part 3—Organization

If you live within reach of the project, you know about the process. You have had more than one chance to have your voice heard. If you attend a meeting or post to a social networking site, your input has been recorded, and you know it. The scope and possibilities have attracted a lot of interest.

Most of these professionals came from the design, engineering, and construction industries. For the first time a significant number of environmental scientists, specialists in social systems, and health-care planners are also participating. Everyone feels as though they are part of the process.

People start by learning to use web-based software focused on Service-Oriented-Architecture, so that they can actively participate. Some people will jump right in but most take a bit longer to get acquainted with the web processes. No matter how people learn to work with web-based systems, there are resources available to make it happen.

A series of webinars are held to illustrate the workflows that participants will need during the process. A workflow used by some people for BIMStorm Cork Point might look like this:

☐ *First, a spreadsheet is created using a template. The spaces, floor levels, and room sizes for the building under consideration are added to the spreadsheet.*

☐ With this spreadsheet in hand, it takes sixty seconds to enter the system, select the studio, add and name the project, add and name a scheme, and set the site location, either through Google Earth import, latitude-longitude, or by adding a bounding-box.

☐ Thirty-seconds more and one has imported the spreadsheet to create spaces and floors. One names the building and verifies that the spaces in the spreadsheet are imported. One has an information massing model after a total time expenditure of ninety-seconds.

☐ Next, one starts to lay out spaces. You begin the design process. Space numbering, space areas, and sizes and costs are generated automatically. In five minutes to two hours... depending on the complexity and scope of information you include... you have a completed design concept information model.

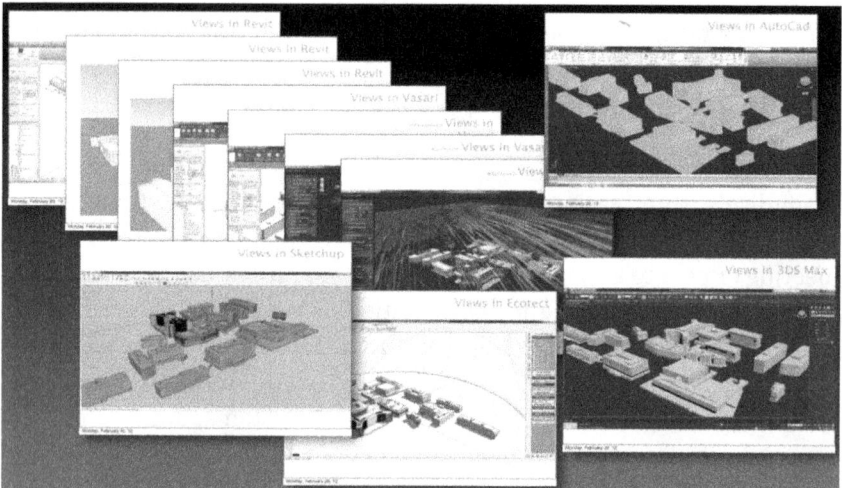

Seed files to Revit, Vasari, AutoCad, SketchUp, 3DS Max + many more

The model can be exported to other tools for more detailed analysis and further development. The model carries with it not only the data you have added, but also the data the system automatically generates.

Even after exporting your model for action by others in other tools, you continue to add information. When the work by others is done, they will re-import their work and it will automatically update and add to your model, making your model richer and richer each time.

You include details about the site, building, and rooms. At the room level, you add furniture, fixtures, and equipment in both 2-D and 3-D from component lists. You input other building systems data and define space attributes, types, security zones, privacy, and finishes. You add heating, ventilation, and air conditioning systems to rooms. All while continuing other design tasks.

At any point in the process, you output reports detailing information in the model. These reports are dynamic. As you change the size of a room, everything else changes to reflect the additional square footage. Enlarging the area increases the cost. As you generate multiple schemes, you can compare your schemes side by side. The comparisons enable you to assess energy, cost, security, sustainability, operations and maintenance costs, and other project data.

In ten to forty-five seconds, your data can be directly exported from BIG-BIM in the Construction Operations Building Information Exchange (COBie) format for use in operating and maintaining equipment in the building you are planning and designing. Since the COBie data is maintained in a multi-tabbed spreadsheet format, an additional ten to forty-five seconds lets you re-inject the data back into the system after you make changes.

Twenty-seconds is all it takes to export your information for other information modeling systems that comply with international standards. When your export is opened in other information modeling systems, they automatically generate models with spaces, equipment, and furniture. These models contain information that you created in the system. By retaining system information, these models can export new data generated as it is further developed. Other participants explore options remarkably quickly using similar work flows.

Most of the people that are participating in BIMStorm Cork Point do not see the complexity that underpins the process. They take advantage of the information and graphics to understand the problem. Once people understand the background facts, it becomes easier for them to provide solutions to problems that they face. Once the solutions are analyzed, viewed, and validated, the community can reach a consensus for how to proceed.

There were basic rules for how people work with the system. Just as one would not send a fax to Expedia to book an airline reservation, a BIMStorm requires dynamic collaboration not dependent on static data sources. The rules for participating in BIMStorm Cork Point revolve around collaboration.

☐ *When communications and information are not accessible to all, collaboration becomes difficult. Sharing, transparency, and information in standard formats that all can see and use underpins everything. This provides a way to understand the reasons behind decisions and thought processes that people are using as the decisions are made. The leadership team must make sure that as many people as possible understand these rules when BIMStorm Cork Point starts. These basic concepts make this possible:*

☐ *This is a digital process. Everything is documented in digital format using information models. Traditional ways of working, hand sketches, and notes can be used, but they must quickly be scanned and input for all to use.*

☐ *Participants need to work within the system as much as possible. Real-time collaboration with others is essential. Minimize situations where things happen in isolation, disconnected from the system.*

☐ *Do not manually enter data sets. When working in other systems or software, this manually entered information is transferred as you export data from the system. When working in other applications, import your results to the BIG-BIM server regularly. You should avoid going for long periods of time without importing to and exporting from the system. This ongoing workflow between applications results in one spending less time manually coordinating data.*

☐ *The goal is continuity of data in the ecosystem. Save your work in the BIG-BIM ecosystem. Do not save to file servers or other media. The goal is to create a lifecycle resource where data remains alive and active. A file on a hard drive, a DVD, or other media is subject to data rot, from the moment it is saved.*

☐ *There is no single way to interact with the system. Some will view information and obtain reports. Others will complete planning and other design tasks. Yet others will enter detailed data manually and through imports from spreadsheets and other databases. Some will require extensive use of the system and others will only reference information. The goal is to let people to work in ways that they are most comfortable, using the tools that they know best. If everyone works with the same data in a collaborative process, the BIMStorm will be successful.*

BIMStorms use a pretty standard process. By the end of preparation, much of what has been talked about in concept will be thought out and organized. The process is a network of complementary but independent interactions and not linear. Things do not progress from A, to B, to C...

The BIMStorm creates the ability to plan for the long-term, by doing the right things up front. Even is uncertain times. The process is inherently robust and allows the organization to find the most cost effective ways to work with the community. Rather than defaulting to the lowest cost solution, the BIMStorm gives us the ability to find the right solution at the lowest reasonable cost, without sacrifice. The process works to eliminate uncertainty and reduce misunderstandings.

Design Fiction
Four Days of BIMStorm

Most of the participants are working remotely. One of the big advantages to this process is that you didn't need a large area where everyone can come together face-to-face. Everyone comes together, but it is all virtual. Only a few people physically working at the headquarters site.

The activities during BIMStorm Cork Point, might look something like this:

Day One: People are excited. They are ready to start.

Participants know that they are part of a life, and community-changing event. The core team expects that a lot of design decisions will quickly emerge. The excitement is building as the site opens for BIMStorm Cork Point Day One. Today the planning and hard work will begin to come together. Everybody is ready. Everyone has started to work by the time that the Hospital officially opens BIMStorm Cork Point.

The planning team seeded the BIMStorm with as much existing information as possible. Participants open Day One by reviewing the Google Map sketches, Google Earth boundaries, and information from old-fashioned land surveys and US Geodetic Service mapping. Where possible, community goals and criteria have been converted to visual representations that overlay Google Maps. Background information for healthcare and facility staffing needs have been refined so that it is easy for all to follow. For those more fluent with numbers, the spreadsheets and databases are also embedded. One of the beauties of the BIMStorm process is that professionals all over the world are also online, ready to support the effort.

There are engineers in Sweden, Tokyo, Germany, and Ireland ready to begin analyzing concepts that the community develops. The core team expects that these engineers will provide much of the most sophisticated energy and environmental analysis, in conjunction with local environmental scientists.

Designers in Korea, Norway, and Finland are ready to begin the process of validating models. They are also developing time scheduling scenarios.

In Buenos Aires, London, Paris, Boston, and New London, Connecticut, graphic design experts are prepared to deliver visualization models as solutions develop.

Architects in Milwaukee, Denver, and Chicago are adding their health-care expertise, coordinated by the core team.

There are teams of emergency response professionals, transportation engineers, cost managers, constructors, social scientists, change management experts, business planners, urban designers, and many other professionals participating.

Each group of professionals is supported by a BIMStorm certified expert whose mission is to use their knowledge where it is needed to smooth the information flow. The fact that experts across the world were involved does not diminish the local effort. The local Chambers of Commerce have their own group, led by a local architect. Architects and engineers across Delaware, Maryland, and Tidewater Virginia were all dialed into the process.

The Hospital's staff has four groups:

1. One group is made up of physicians and specialty health-care providers,

2. Another group is made up of board members and administration staff,

3. One group comes from the elder care center,

4. The last group is made up of facilities and maintenance personnel.

The four groups representing the hospital are the only groups in the BIMStorm that were directly supported by paid professionals. In most cases, the professionals that were donating their time to this effort look at it as a combination of benefits. At one level, the professionals benefit by experiencing the latest technology first-hand. Few of these professional's peers will be so lucky. At another level, the professionals benefit by the recognition and credibility that participation brings. In the past, BIMStorms had won unprecedented recognition both in mainstream media and professional awards. Most importantly, the professionals learn much more than they teach in this environment.

In California and various other locations, teams are assembled to support the effort. Over the next four days, the team will monitor and support the BIMStorm—24 hours a day. In Pasadena, California it is four o'clock in the morning. In Europe, it is two o'clock in the afternoon. In Tokyo, it is nine o'clock in the evening. Participants quickly learn how to juggle the time zones. The system's ability to foster collaboration across time zones is one of the factors that allows the BIMStorm to produce so much decision-making information so quickly.

As participants in one time zone end the working day, those in other time zones are just beginning. After one group spends the day inputting and resolving an idea, the outputs are passed to others for further development while they sleep. In this way, an architect can lay out a building, go home for dinner and a decent night's sleep, and return the next morning to see the energy analysis completed by an environmental engineer in San Diego; the mechanical systems completed by a mechanical engineer in Sweden; and the structural system completed by a structural engineer in Tokyo.

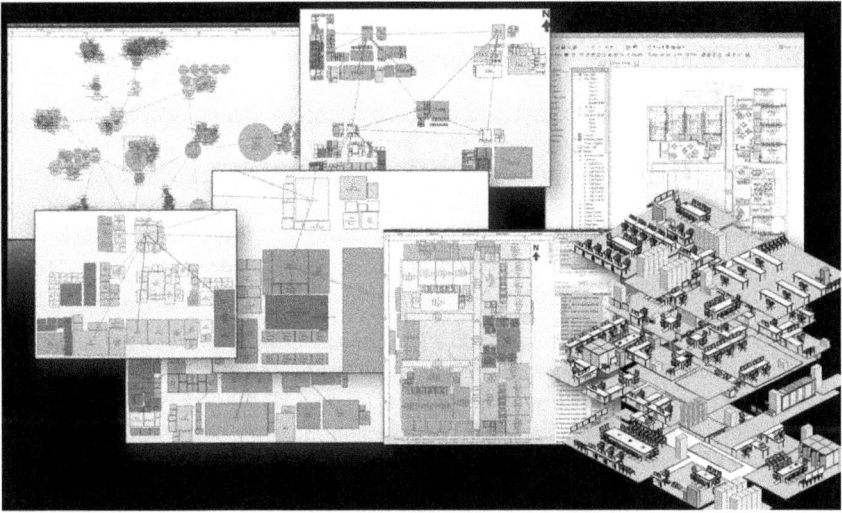

Concepts emerge at many stages of development, simultaneously; all share and build upon the same data. This cycle continues throughout the BIMStorm and is repeated by many different teams. There is no way to get a faster education on the future of information modeling and collaborative practice than by working in a BIMStorm.

Day Two: The day starts slowly.

Yesterday, participants explored many options and made a lot of progress. Late last night, as people became tired and went home, it was unclear what might happen with their studies. This morning, everyone is excited to see what those in other time zones might have created while others slept. Much of the work today will revolve around the evaluation of options.

Groups see the metrics of schemes in-context. More schematic buildings are developed for analysis. Overnight, while some slept, they have been assigned specific tasks, as the starting point for study at the highest levels of detail. By the end of Day Two, the selected strategy will be shared to all for further development.

Several of the schemes were studied by energy analysts in Europe. Attached to the models is a lot of energy data. Even better, there were a series of energy visualizations showing how the schemes would respond at different times of the year. The work by the energy analysts in Sweden is of interest. Their initial recommendations suggest that, with proper planning, Cork Point has the potential to become a zero-energy organization. In fact, it might well be possible that the facility will produce more energy than it used.

An urban planner in California and an urban designer in Seattle have added detail to the most promising concepts. The ideas from Seattle were especially intriguing. They focus on many of the environmental issues that will set Cork Point apart, if managed properly. This afternoon, when these planners on the West Coast are back in their offices, local leaders plan a working discussion with them to focus on the layout. In the interim, the team will examine some other alternatives.

While the engineers are working on detailed analysis, some architects are refining the blocking and stacking models to develop early thoughts about style, enclosure concepts, and costs. Using this information plus the site conditions that were being developed, they have exported to Trimble SketchUp to begin the process of visualizing how the project would look.

By tomorrow morning, they should have vignettes and sketches that will help people know what is being proposed. Since the goal is to develop people-centered places, their sketches will focus on how the facilities relate to the water, how pedestrian and vehicular transportation works, and the spirit of space. From an urban and architectural design perspective, the goal is to determine the essence of Cork Point.

Planning committee members are now on site, supported remotely by health-care consultants in Chicago, Oslo, San Francisco, and Washington, DC. The healthcare consultants started the process of defining what the new Cork Point organization would look like several months ago. They spent much of Day One in meetings to reach agreement on both the overall business concept and the exact space needs to achieve their goals.

Today, the healthcare consultants are in the process of converting yesterday's whole discussion into spreadsheets using templates. Much of what they want to create involves an entirely new direction. Yet, the new direction is grounded by many years of healthcare precedent. The requirements for many of the services they are defining are well known. The needs for procedure spaces, exam rooms and clinics, surgery and diagnostics, and other spaces are straightforward; the uncertainties arise from volumes and relationships.

Projecting numbers of visits and the spaces and personnel required to support them has been difficult, especially as the hospital is moving toward decentralized services supported by technology. The concern is that creating a system based solely on managing wellness may skew the numbers. The traditional focus on curing sick people will result in quite different metrics than will a wellness focus.

Coupling the changes in delivery paradigms with increased use of sensors, analytics designed to identify problems early, and increasing reliance on services delivered directly to people in their homes, historical information may no longer be accurate. The team realizes the potential problems and are making reasonable estimates of needs.

The system gives them the ability to compare several concepts side by side. As the options develop, the system allows the team to make direct side by side comparisons that feature the schemes' net and gross areas, construction costs, and line-by-line operations and maintenance costs. Using this information, the team eliminates some schemes, adds other schemes, and finally focuses on a preferred solution.

First, the group adds room names and room sizes to a spreadsheet template, assuming all spaces are on one level. Next, they import this spreadsheet into the system, giving it a name and adding an executive summary that described the theory behind the scheme.

The system then creates an information model of the spaces and lands the spaces on the site. Space relationships and room design are not completed now.

There is nothing that one could call a floor plan. There are only groups of boxes laid out across the site. Even without formally laying out the boxes to get a floor plan, the team has significant decision-making data.

The system creates placeholder cost data, as well as standards for support spaces such as corridors, elevators, and stairs. Immediately the team gets feedback on gross areas, costs and other factors needed to guide their thinking. The process repeats until the group had modeled most of their options. Each option explores different possibilities. Each option allows the team to evaluate different what-if scenarios.

As the team focuses in on a preferred solution, the hospital designers began to create basic footprints of buildings. The first schemes lay out the room boxes with the entire organization on one level. The team soon finds that a one level solution would never fit on the site and quickly reallocate rooms by floor to make multistory buildings.

The hospital designers then began the process of laying out the floors. Since they were working over live geographic information system mapping, they received immediate visual feedback. The designers create schematic diagrams that directly respond to the program needs assessments.

By the end of this exercise, the planners, and the designers all agree on the two most responsive solutions. These solutions will be shared for further development. After an energetic and productive day, the team heads for home and a full night's sleep, knowing that others will continue to improve the two schemes overnight.

Engineers are already in the process of analyzing foundations and structural systems.

Based on the preliminary massing of the two schemes, energy experts are developing zero-energy analysis.

Architects have exported the schematic layouts to desktop building information modeling systems and refining the buildings.

Overnight, experts worldwide analyze, develop, and examine how the schemes will go together. By the next morning, the core team has much more information to work with and will further refine their decisions.

Day Three: Today's focus is on timely decision-making.

Project overview presentations begin to outline the way forward. Short working sessions fill in gaps. Final decisions would get made tomorrow. Today, the team must make sure that everything is ready to go. The output that has come in from remote teams seems to confirm both concepts that were shared the previous night. Either scheme could work. Since both have merit and neither has obvious flaws, the team decides to proceed with both. Tomorrow they will become the basis of a community decision for the future.

Building on the work developed overnight by the architectural teams, the designers are developing the schematic models. They continue to organize plan layouts and are refining the buildings' massing.

Last night the engineers made progress on the design of the structural systems. As the design and massing of buildings progresses, the structural engineers quickly reflect the changes.

Several architects have worked on building exterior options overnight using desktop BIM applications. The architects' solutions have been reimported into the system and are under evaluation.

Construction managers have exported area and volume data to enable them to develop detailed estimates of cost. Structural concrete and steel estimates are also in progress, using quantity data extracted from the models. As detailed cost information is developed, it is added to the system to refine comparisons between schemes.

Throughout the day, the schemes are becoming increasingly real. Structural systems evolve to the point where one could see bolted connections. Building skins include specific materials and fenestration. Urban design concepts connect transportation systems, landscaping, streetscaping, and lighting. The models include LEED checklists, energy data, and layouts of spaces with furniture.

The last two hours of the day, the whole team meets physically and to consider early concepts. The construction managers conduct a presentation on projected costs and quickly connect the team's feedback. Overnight the work will continue. The focus has now transitioned toward the next day's public decision-making process.

Day Four: the day starts bright, hot, and humid; typical weather for a summer day on the Eastern Shore of Maryland.

Much detailed design and documentation remains, yet much of the planning and development concept is finished.

Building program development has progressed to a level that traditionally could be called design development. Size projections, schematic layouts, and other conceptual design aspects are well established.

Structural estimates are finalized. The building enclosure estimate is finalized. A complete building exterior estimate will be completed before the public presentation begins.

The construction managers are refining with their program estimate, backed up by design assumptions, preliminary schedules, and a lot of data.

Models for the site, roads, adjacent structures, the environment, foundations, and residents have been combined for quick review and analysis.

The team is ready for the final presentation. BIMStorm Cork Point has reached the point where decisions must be made. The core team leads off by reviewing what has happened over the last four days—describing the effort for those attending in person and via the Internet.

Each person that participated has contributed a minimal amount of time. Because of the intensity of the effort, the process seems to some to be overwhelming, but the fact is that most individuals who participated still had time for other normal business tasks even while participating in the BIMStorm. The process leveraged the skills and knowledge of many people.

Over the four-day process, several thousand people worldwide worked to define the new Cork Point. People got a broad perspective and feedback about their ideas. With many involved, the group produced more. With many involved, no individual became a bottleneck for others.

Government Leadership Case Studies

The case studies that follow represent several of the prototypes that the US government has undertaken as they work to implement BIG–BIM ecosystems. Each of the prototypes included faced a series of issues that impact on all government agencies seeking to make changes of this scope and scale.

The following six case study prototypes are a sampling of the phased-in development, oriented toward BIG–BIM, which began soon after the turn of the century, and is continuing to take place in the leading government agencies.

Case Study
Integrated-Decision-Making

*The data about our facilities, is more valuable than the physical facility themselves —
Admiral Thad Allen, US Coast Guard.*

What are the interesting aspects of this case study?

The first documented concept of Levels of Detail.

*Stand-alone Building Information Models began to converge with Geographic
Information Systems and facilities management in the Road Map.*

*Many of the tools and processes of little-bim emerged in the context of the needs
of an enterprise scale owner.*

*Established how business systems to connect in near real-time with business
information systems, building information, geographic information, mobile and
fixed asset information, and many more systems.*

*Proved that it was possible to connect decision-making data to business
objectives to improve understanding and outcomes using a BIG-BIM ecosystem.*

*Software programs evolved to support the search for Integrated-Decision-Making (IDM) and a
simple, easy to use Industry Foundation Class (IFC) model server to support Road Map
prototypes.*

Location—Worldwide.

The US Coast Guard's Shore Facilities Capital Asset Management (SFCAM) Road Map included 25,000 real property assets including buildings, structures, and utilities. The 30-million square feet of spaces on 420 improved sites, have an average age of 37 years and are valued at over $7 billion. Also, the Coast Guard leases of more than 3-million square feet of building space.

The entire inventory is managed by the USCG Civil Engineering Program by about 1,400 military and civilian employees. The impact of the USCG's Road Map was worldwide and was the beginning of BIG-BIM thinking in the building industry.

Seeds of the Future

The Coast Guard's SFCAM Road Map project and follow up prototypes made possible commercially available BIG-BIM ecosystems and seeded many of the little-bim processes that we now take for granted.

To succeed, the USCG needed to create a Building Information Model for the organization's entire facility inventory. After modeling sample USCG facilities in Washington State, South Carolina, and New Jersey in little-bim, the team realized the costs and constraints associated with such models was great.

Questions about the viability of large-scale little-bim programs led to the creation and documentation of a Levels of Detail approach that allowed all facilities to be first modeled using very simple models that could hold a significant amount of information. How would the building information models be maintained? How would decision-making information be extracted without a little-bim expert always in the middle of the process? One of the major roadblocks to the success of the pilot projects revolved around this little-bim approach. How was the team to model 23,000 facilities in a short period, within currently available funds?

The team established a hierarchy of BIM detail, making it possible to model and georeference every existing USCG building at a level of detail appropriate to the available data. Data, a middleware mash-up engine and overlaid tools supported connected decision-making needs. The tool set and system was designed to reduce redundancy and connect open-source and proprietary data in easy to use and standards-compliant ways that enable future growth.

By focusing on the information required for decision support, rather than on graphics, the models came together quickly and at minimal cost. Development began with models of low-level graphic detail and rich data-detail, and came with cost and time constraints. Instead of taking the time to create highly detailed visually oriented models, this approach allowed quickly generated, simple models that grow richer over time.

Founded in 1790, the United States Coast Guard is informed by tradition. Their missions, facilities, departments, and individuals create a decision-making environment with wide-ranging economic, social, political, and environmental impacts.

The Shore Facilities Capital Asset Management (SFCAM) program represented the USCG's commitment to evolving and maturing their organization in a rapidly changing world. The resulting business process engineering roadmap changed and improved how the USCG managed facilities over the asset lifecycle. The analyzes, systems, and resulting prototypes became the seeds for many of today's standards of practice for BIM and connected business processes.

USCG leaders found themselves forced to confront significant, life-impacting decisions with too few facts, tight budgets and little tolerance for error or failure. Adding to the complexity, late in the twentieth century: the organization lost significant numbers of knowledgeable staff; their missions continued to expand, often in the harshest environments imaginable; and, they faced a tightly constrained funding environment stretching into the far future. Such constraints led to their search for ways manage better with fewer assets.

The team of Coast Guard personnel and consultants assessed existing technologies, conducted intensive logic analysis, and evaluated the flow of data to identify key relationships between critical activities and assets.

Existing USCG data was normalized and validated as accessible at an enterprise level. The information was then available in BIM and other distributed systems within the USCG.

Bringing this standardized data into a BIG-BIM ecosystem resulted in a typical USCG facility having two million data points connected into BIM. Manually linking the same data points into stand-alone little-bim would have been a impossible task. A service-oriented-architecture approach to web-based data sharing was crucial to this success.

The ecosystem of tools had to support the ability to assess the impact of decisions on future conditions. The tools were to provide a flexible connected decision-making process designed to help users understand and explore options.

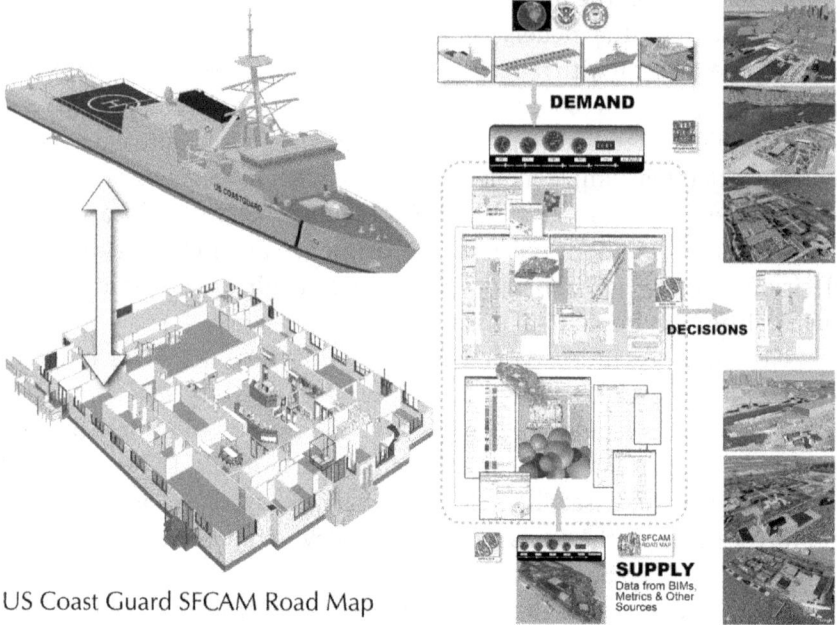

US Coast Guard SFCAM Road Map

The team documented workflows and coordinated missions across the spectrum of planning, design, construction, and operations of the organization. The goal was to understand and connect needs, constraints, and tasks to support Integrated-Decision-Making.

The focus was to understand the impacts of decisions by establishing a broad range of metrics, standards, and visual information available to those tasked with making organizational decisions.

The Road Map recognized the potential for industry change using BIM and other processes. Rather than wait for software development to respond to identified needs, the team elected to use a mix of commercial off-the-shelf software and web-enabled data tools to answer to the Coast Guard's requirements.

Enterprise Metrics

The SFCAM Roadmap Team developed many assessments along with the resulting indices and standard metrics. A partial list and description of these metrics and evaluations includes:

Condition: Condition Indices (CI) indicate the status of assets at various levels of detail. The indices can be weighted based on the replacement value of their sub-elements and rolled up into a higher-level index.

Component Condition Index (CCI) is calculated to produce a score of 1 to 100; it is used to determine the rate of deterioration and to make a repair, replace, or maintain decision on that component. CCI is weighted and rolled up to produce the System Condition Index.

System Condition Index (SCI) indicates the condition of the systems of a facility. SCI is created by weighting and rolling up the Component Conditions Indices.

Facility Condition Index (FCI) indicates the condition of a facility. The USCG divides their facility assets into 14 systems, and each system further subdivides into components. FCI is created by weighting and rolling up the System Conditions Index.

Readiness: The Mission Readiness Index (MRI) derives from Condition Index calculations and a system's relative position on its Deterioration Curve. Deterioration curves are unique for each system. Each has an elbow where decay begins to accelerate. The angle is used to determine MRI.

Dependency: A Mission Dependency Index (MDI) identifies the relative importance of a facility to a command's missions. Procedural guidance for MDI assessments is available on an internal, secure website. In addition to its other significant uses, MDI is used to optimize assessment costs by determining assessment priority. Higher MDI facilities receive more detailed assessments than those with lower MDI.

Utilization: Space Utilization Index (SUI) compares actual space use with either USCG or other space standards to determine if space is over or underutilized.

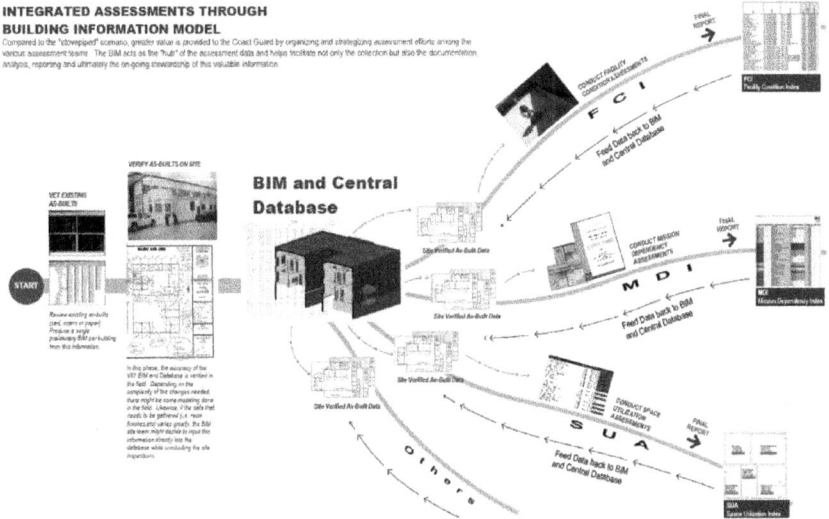

Facility Assessment metrics were developed or upgraded to collect Readiness Data. The data is used to support Facility Metrics that depict the condition and performance of facilities.

Deterioration Rates
20 year design life

Condition Index (CI)

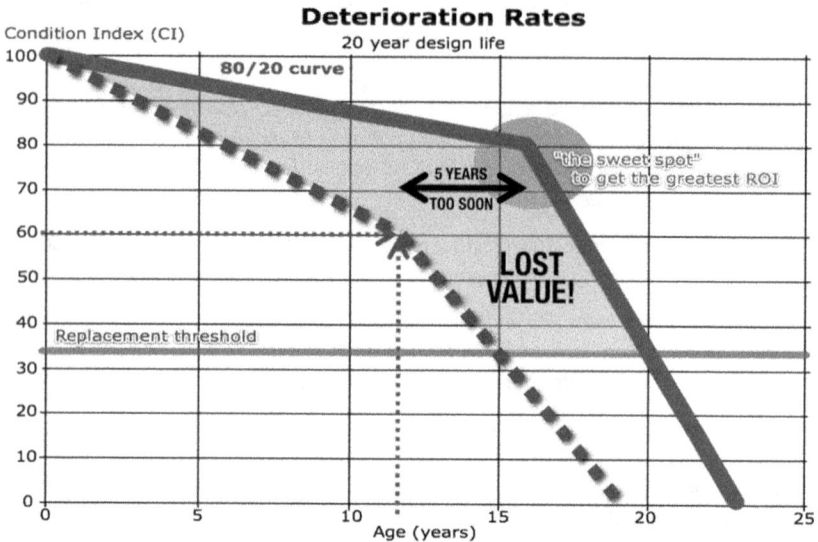

A system is ready if it is above a specified CI. The arbitrary selection of a CI (of say, 85) is not an appropriate way to evaluate all systems. An exterior motor may have a 90/10 curve and at 85 is well below a high MRI rating while a roof with an 80/20 curve would be well above at that same 85 condition index. This index can be rolled up similarly to the CI's. MRI gives the USCG the ability to build business cases around repeatable, capable of being audited, and valid Return-on-Mission data. The effect on CIs and MRI is predictable for any funding scenario. With the penalty costs expressed in dollars or the degradation of a mission, asset managers can make optimized decisions and communicate results to their customers.

Criticality: The System Criticality Index or (SKI) is a measure of the importance of each system to the mission of the building or infrastructure asset. It is either calculated based on homogeneous groupings of category codes or is user defined. Like MDI, SKI can be used to focus assessment dollars on those systems with a high impact on Mission Readiness.

Suitability: The Suitability Index (SI) indicates the ability of the asset to perform its operational function by comparing the occupant needs based on intended use of capabilities based on existing attributes. SI is a prioritization factor for repair or replacement decisions.

Force Protection: The Force Protection Index (FPI) measures the ability to protect the mission capacity of a facility through a comprehensive threat, vulnerability, and loss analysis. The assessment provides supportive reasoning and photographs and expresses the return on investment for alternative scenarios as the basis for planning and decision-making.

Property: The Real Property Assessment (RPA) provides the meta-data review for property lines, meets and bounds, site data, and lease information.

Codes: The Building Code Compliance Measure (BCC) assesses compliance with building and life safety codes and specific deficiencies regarding penalty costs.

Environment: Environmental Compliance Assessment (ECA) evaluates both building environmental health (lead based paint, asbestos or mold), and environmental issues, such as National Environmental Policy Act and historical issues, and express deficiencies regarding penalty costs.

Overlays of metrics, coupled with low level of detail graphics and existing data combined to allow the USCG to generate decision-making support materials in near-real-time. The goal was to seed an institutional change management process across the organization.

As part of the effort, the project team used design thinking and planning skills, expert logic analysis and team member concepts of a connected practice strategy to identify pilot projects that supported this level of business process change. The first uses of the system connected assessment data and made efficient use of information possible throughout the life of a facility.

Many of the USCG pilot projects that came from the SFCAM Road Map were precursors to other connected asset management approaches using a BIG-BIM ecosystem. Some of the other projects include:

Connecting Google Earth and Open Geospatial Consortium standards to link BIM and GIS in many projects, including the National Capital Planning Commission's Southeast Ecodistrict.

Supporting the General Services Administration's Public Building Service in early stage planning for relocations, and space use efficiency improvements.

The framework for much of the California Community College's BIG-BIM ecosystem.

The underpinnings and seed for the US Department of Defense, Defense Health Agency, and US Department of Veterans Affairs FED ifM and SEPS2BIM initiatives.

The SFCAM Road Map and the resulting projects are the seeds of many BIG-BIM issues included elsewhere in this book. Some of the benefits that have come from SFCAM include:

☐ *Adaptable systems that assist lifecycle data management, one of the highest forms of information connection.*

☐ *Improved ability to access and use data to make better decisions as early as possible.*

☐ *Ability to retain, capture and manage near real-time corporate knowledge. Providing new staff with reliable, simple to access contextual data not subject to data rot or otherwise easily lost as experienced staff retire or move to other opportunities.*

☐ Ability to predict when and where to expend resources to best support mission requirements using facility condition information and task dependency measures.

☐ Support for open-standards and links to distributed systems through web services that allow multiple solutions for intelligent and automated construction sites.

☐ Ability to create and manage furniture, equipment, and materials in object databases linked to almost any inventory, procurement, or manufacturer data program. Suppliers can use this centralized data for automatic shop-drawing generation and other functions. Manufacturers such as Fypon LLC use such systems.

☐ Ability to create living archives of actual conditions of multi-facility enterprises to assess better how facilities affect missions and business processes. Over time, such libraries of data form the basis for fully connected enterprise BIG-BIM. Currently this is one of the few approaches that manage the data rot that effects most little-bim implementations.

☐ Ability to generate BIG-BIM at the building, space, and component levels with connections to business needs and mission requirements.

☐ Capability to automate design to expedite an organization's mission support systems. Users interact with connected data to make decisions in real-time.

☐ Ability to combine automated design with dashboard views of data without resorting to software technical support.

☐ Ability to link institutional knowledge to support automated design and catalog the experiences that make one special.

☐ Ability to create customized systems for automating processes that link parameters in a database to visual images to enable rapid assessment of multiple solutions for complex problems.

The Coast Guard tools connect data to allow users to review issues such as space planning, facilities management, and assets management within a geospatial construct. Tools are easy to use and designed to support users at all skill levels. The goal Is to enable ease of use by non-experts, with minimal outside expert support—a foundation of BIG-BIM ecosystems.

Case Study
Rapid Planning System

Although the tools are familiar and require little or no expert intervention; underneath, the algorithms are complicated and designed to process the complex tasks of planning, constructing, and managing a project such as a Sector Command Center. The processes involve many specialists, with many factors to consider and resolve.

What are the interesting aspects of this case study?

BIG-BIM Planning Systems to Support the USCG Integrated-Decision-Making Process.

System using historical data to connect it into a BIG-BIM ecosystem that quickly produces preliminary solutions.

Connection of early stage security and Force Protection planning.

Tools that flexibly respond to codes, staffing standards and operational requirements that are both known and implied in existing and new building situations.

Location—Worldwide.

The US Coast Guard Sector Command Planning System is but one part of what the SFCAM Road Map defined as Integrated-Decision-Making (IDM). The Road Map laid out the processes necessary to fulfill IDM needs, and the Sector Command Planning System helps implement many of the processes. The rapid planning tool the project team created works as an integral part of the overall strategic planning process for the implementation of all future Sector Command Centers.

Traditionally, Coast Guard planners first establish preliminary estimates and determine the feasibility of projects based on published design criteria. The initial estimates then follow a linear design process that, on average takes ten months to complete per Sector Command Center. The new Rapid Planning tools changed this dramatically. The team finished all thirty-five SCCs in only 60% of the time traditionally required to create ONE SCC.

Development began with the team working with USCG staff to custom fit tools for the unique needs of a Sector Command Center facility type. Once customization was complete, USCG architects and engineers were trained to use the tools with little or no emphasis on BIM. Users saw and responded to a system that worked much like familiar multiuser web-based systems.

These projects occur worldwide, at a fast pace. Requirements range from maintaining Coast Guard missions, to the day-to-day support of the operators of the SCCs. The processes and tools answer questions such as:

What does a plan look like for an SCC in Honolulu? How is it different from an SCC in Miami?

What is the estimated construction cost for such a project in New Jersey versus Nome, Alaska?

How much square footage is typically needed? Is the required area different in San Francisco than in New York City?

What type of furniture and equipment is required? Can the specified furniture be procured efficiently in Anchorage?

The tools respond to this type of question and much more.

Some problems facing the SCC planners are glaring. Because they get much attention, they tend to be straightforward to solve for this type of project. Other problems that may be equally important are easy to overlook and can fall-through-the-cracks. In the traditional process, Force Protection is such an overlooked problem.

Poorly designed or after-the-fact Force Protection undermines the mission of the Coast Guard and increases vulnerability to threats. Early planning for Force Protection is a fundamental element of any Coast Guard project, and anti-terrorism force protection (AT/FP) is but one of the easily overlooked factors associated with the design of any Sector Command Center.

The tools take AT/FP design parameters far beyond fences and security guards to address Continuity of Operations Planning (COOP), as well as protection for environmental, plumbing, electrical, communications systems. Also included are sourcing potable water, food, and other items that might impact missions.

The planning tools include the capacity to model scenarios and present alternative ways of accomplishing national anti-terrorism and force protection mandates. Situations go well beyond criminal acts and terrorism to include real-life incidents such as hurricanes, floods, tornadoes and, other events not considered to be terrorism. Force Protection is but one of the many issues built into the system. The tools allow the design and planning team lots of analysis and development flexibility. A connected graphical interface enables the team to produce quick diagrams in plan views. Moving blocks of space or positioning furniture pieces, as needed.

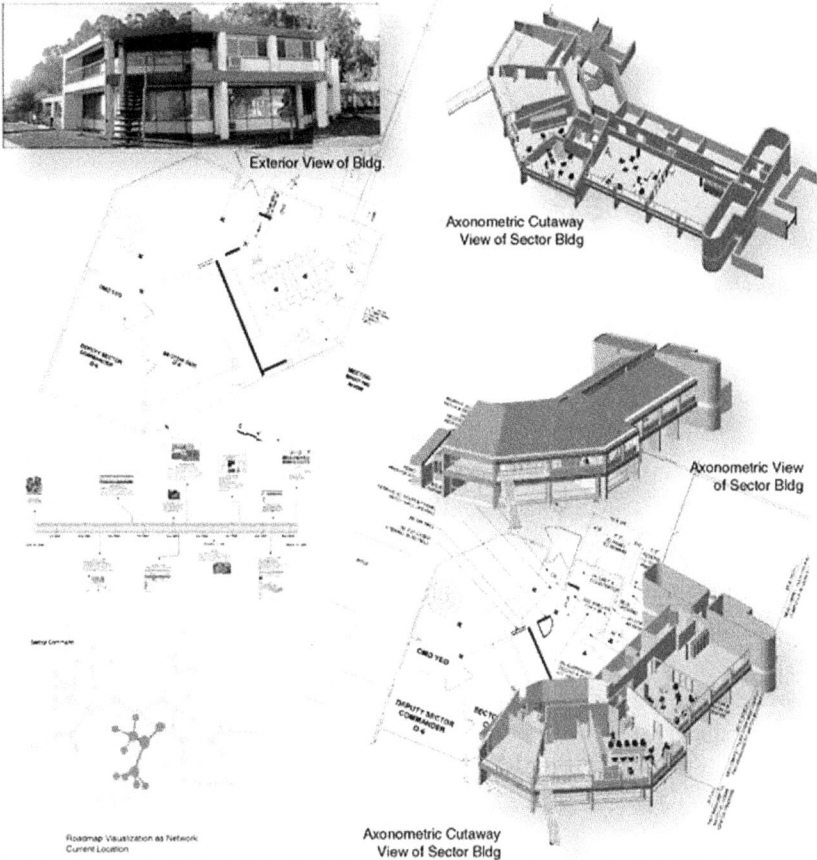

Exterior View of Bldg.

Axonometric Cutaway View of Sector Bldg

Axonometric View of Sector Bldg

Roadmap Visualization as Network
Current Location

Axonometric Cutaway View of Sector Bldg

The Sector Command Planning Tools go far beyond traditional architecture and engineering planning and design processes to embrace a range of social and environmental impacts. Vulnerabilities are identified and mitigated or eliminated.

The system also enables:

☐ *Embedded Coast Guard rules in a modeling format that allows Coast Guard planners to visualize the facility as a 3D model.*

☐ *Automatically generated models as data is entered, without user intervention, so that data entered is not influenced by any solution developing in the system.*

☐ *Web-based functionality that allows easy access by users with many different skill sets. However, the tools remain fully functional on standalone computer workstations and laptops.*

☐ *Decisions within the system link to databases, producing detailed reports related to cost and square footage, as required.*

☐ *Exploration of scenarios and presentation of assumptions, associated costs, and impacts on the lifecycle of the facility as planners focus in on their preferred solution.*

☐ *Creation of interior architectures using Sector Command Center modules that embed adjacencies, ergonomics, equipment locations, staffing, and finishes. Modules available within the system include: Search and Rescue Operations Center; Vessel Traffic Center; Communications Center; Port Operations Center; Field Intelligence Support Team; US Navy Joint Harbor Operations Center; Port Partners; Surge Staffing Components; Briefing/Conference Room; Office Space; Restrooms; and Break Rooms.*

☐ *Visualization of the options available using a comprehensive set of data representations to analyze scenarios for potential* train-wrecks, *to eliminate the options with the highest likelihood of failure.*

Gradually the processes focus on the situations that offer the strongest set of benefits to the Coast Guard. In the end, the selected options became the one deemed most appropriate to each site.

To validate the effectiveness of the system, the Sector Command Planning Tools were test-run in a 'real-world' project. The test-run involved using the tools to support design charrettes and development of rapid Request-For-Proposal documentation for the USCG Station San Francisco on Yerba Buena Island. Based on the resounding success of this test-run, the tools were used in implementing the full Sector Command Center program of thirty-five Centers.

The Sector Command Planning System, using a BIG-BIM ecosystem and developing new functionalities to support rapid planning received both AIA Technology in Architectural Practice and FIATECH Celebration of Engineering & Technology Innovation awards.

Case Study
Housing Product Line

Surprisingly, front-end work can exceed the actual BIG-BIM implementation efforts. Cleaning up old stovepipes and non-normalized data is usually the first task. Months of preparation, followed by hours of BIG-BIM ecosystem application is the way it typically works. Clean and organized data becomes the foundation for the long-term benefits of establishing a BIG-BIM ecosystem.

What are the interesting aspects of this case study?

Housing System Development to enable integrated decisions.

Initiative to capture the business processes and information needs and standards implemented by subject-matter communities.

Comprehensive strategy report and recommendations to leverage industry standards.

Making all assets visible to all levels of decision makers, to best optimize resources while achieving mission objectives.

Location—Nationwide.

At the enterprise level, the application of a BIG–BIM ecosystem can require significant effort outside the scope of traditional design and construction processes.

For organizations with large asset inventories, large staffs, and much information, the front–end efforts to make this shift are often enormous. Normalizing data, planning for accessible and resilient data structures and other preparation and cleaning tasks are often the first tasks. Without such front–end efforts, a BIG–BIM ecosystem may not achieve the value and benefit that is possible. With them, enterprises see significant improvements to their operation and ability to improve decision–making processes. Long into the future.

Total Asset Visibility

A significant management effort to transition from a regional command–and–control approach to a unified national framework took place in the US Coast Guard. The actions aligned with the principles laid out in the Coast Guard's Information Management Strategy (IMS) for their Civil Engineering Program. The IMS was a first step in establishing the necessary procedures, protocols and standards for re–engineering and modernizing the Coast Guard's current processes to take advantage of the concepts included in the SFCAM Road Map.

The initiative was a comprehensive effort to analyze the Coast Guard's business processes and data systems, including GIS and BIM capabilities. A key objective was to enable the USCG to achieve *Total Asset Visibility*. Total Asset Visibility refers to the presence, configuration, and capability of all assets to become visible and accessible. To achieve this challenging goal entailed interview of all the key subject–matter communities within the Coast Guard to establish critical data relationships and workflows.

In 2011, the Coast Guard's Housing System became one of the first product lines to undergo the shift to Total Asset Visibility. The Coast Guard's Housing Product Line initiated in–house and contracted efforts focused on updating and maintaining available housing information.

The goal was to establish standards, develop uniform processes and comprehensively assemble all elements of information and data affecting strategic decision–making for housing acquisition, retention, divestiture, operation, and maintenance. The USCG first established validated database information, including the condition of the housing inventory, energy/water consumption, availability by locality and status of environmental remediation for the entire stock of family and single housing.

Using a BIG–BIM ecosystem, the project teams then captured the current as–is condition information, collecting standard information from legacy systems. The system can assimilate the legacy data from the Coast Guard's Oracle Fixed Assets and their internal housing database, the Housing Management Information System.

Bringing the Coast Guard's Housing System into a state of Total Asset Visibility resulted from the concepts developed for the SFCAM Road Map. Subsequent prototypes and proofs-of-concepts, refined by the IMS, led to the condition where the USCG could re-engineer their product lines to be Integrated-Decision-Making tools to support its missions far into the future.

Case Study
Live Masterplanning

Higher education masterplans are more than the process of planning for the future. They require an understanding of the past and the current conditions and projection into the future, to envision optimized outcomes. When enhanced with a BIG-BIM ecosystem, masterplanning enables enterprises to understand better the impacts of decisions, now and into the future.

What are the interesting aspects of this case study?

Road mapping for Live Masterplanning in Higher Education.

A broad range of facility metrics, standards and visual information tied to the institution's business and academic processes results in better organizational decisions.

Linking the entire lifecycle of facilities, business needs and the needs of academic programs to maintain a common operating vision in near real-time.

Development and application of high-speed planning tools and other information modeling based resources for higher education masterplanning.

Location—New London, Connecticut, USA.

Live masterplanning requires constant adjustments based on capturing changes as they occur and is not an isolated activity to be measured once every five years.

The United States Coast Guard has long been a leader in the use of advanced technologies to manage facilities and operations. The US Coast Guard Academy undertook several BIG-BIM projects following completion of the organization's SFCAM Road Map and other enterprise BIM foundation projects. Chief among the projects was the creation of systems to replace the traditional five-year masterplanning cycle with live decision-making tools.

Decisions made every day affect stakeholders on many levels. When a masterplan is prepared, and updated sporadically, we may lose much of the nuance and undermine our ability to respond correctly. Rather than tailored responses based on up-to-date information, decisions increasingly rely on anecdote or parrot what may be old standards and directives.

Traditionally masterplanning revolves around the collection of data to document changes that occurred since the last masterplan. Based on the data collected and stakeholder wishes, desires and projections for future conditions, decisions were then made to define the future state of the enterprise over the next five years. These efforts resulted in static, printed documents, usually consigned to the shelves of those in authority. Never, or at best rarely, were such documents accessed.

Field surveys, interviews, and enterprise-wide data collection are people-intensive tasks that take place with every masterplan. The process of gathering, sifting and validating information is costly and time intensive. It is bad enough the first time but done every five years this becomes a significant drain on resources.

Rarely is the data collected in reusable ways and seldom is the logic behind decisions documented. Nor are the resulting recommendations, captured in accessible digital formats. At best, masterplanning work products become the equivalent of accessing the Internet, printing today's flight schedule and returning two months (or two years) later to make travel arrangements using the information one printed. Much of the data collected and most of the goals set by such masterplans became obsolete the minute they are printed and saved.

Every five years the process starts over and follows the same trajectory with new people, new constraints, and new issues. The process is typical throughout higher education. One creates static solutions to define future directions on a schedule demanded by funding sources, accreditation groups, and higher education standards. In the past, this approach may have been unavoidable because of the limits of technology. No longer is this true.

The Academy's Masterplanning Road Map is a vision, with instructions. A living document with a set of data that can be used today and tomorrow to expand the value of the Coast Guard Academy facility data connected to business processes and academic needs. The Road Map connects education, mission, and services to allow Academy masterplans to become a living record of the past and for the future.

The Coast Guard Academy realized that technological constraints are disappearing and took the opportunity to change how they create masterplans, design, construct and operate. Much as defined in the SFCAM Road Map, the Academy started by creating an environment that enables live plans, informed by BIG-BIM.

Understanding the process requires one to link the entire lifecycle of facilities, business needs and the needs of academic programs. To reach this level of information connectivity, the US Coast Guard Academy began by accelerating their use of advanced tools using Building Information Models, Geographic Information Systems, and related data to document and manage the institution.

Next, the Academy embarked on a program of capturing their facilities in a BIG-BIM ecosystem. By consolidating legacy information and current conditions, the resulting ecosystem minimizes data rot and enables users to access lifecycle data in many formats.

With information about the Academy's premises and other seeding data in place, the Coast Guard created a Masterplanning Road Map document to guide consultants. This electronic deliverable is searchable and focused on identifying opportunities to change how Academy personnel, academics, and experts create and use facility data to support live masterplanning activities.

The Masterplanning Road Map acknowledges that there are opportunities that come from the data already collected and stored in the BIG-BIM ecosystem. Identifying these foundation opportunities gives the Academy the ability to build for the future. With a solid starting place for implementing wins that result from the data and tools now in place. The Road Map also:

Identified and created facility operations and decision-making processes that guide users in applying the masterplan system;

Prototyped and validated the tools needed to connect data to allow users to review issues such as space planning, facilities management, and assets management within a higher education geospatial construct, and;

Provided a connected decision-making process with the flexibility to understand and explore options while considering the impact of decisions on future operations.

The ability to achieve live masterplans that connect the many parts of higher education enterprises is groundbreaking. The concepts and ability to deliver living systems are rapidly becoming the standard for university campus facility and masterplanning.

Unlike the traditional approach, establishing a higher education ecosystem enables a living system that changes in near real-time as things change on campus. BIG-BIM is enabling a movement toward live masterplanning to replace the traditional five-year cycle of static, file-based updates at schools across the country.

Case Study
Real-World Chess Games

Within BIMStorms, people learn ways to visualize and convert legacy data rapidly. They test hundreds of tools to find the right tools for each job; and have concluded that the use of brute force to make technology tools do things at the fringes of their capabilities is not beneficial to asset lifecycle management.

What are the interesting aspects of this case study?

Using BIG-BIM to plan for renovation of occupied historic university housing.

How do decisions that involve complex relationships between many random processes and programs get reconciled to arrive at the optimum solution?

What solution is most likely to succeed?

Which solution is least likely to become a train-wreck?

Location—Charleston, WV and West Point, NY, USA.

BIMStorms have been used to test BIG–BIM concepts under stress. When hundreds of professionals, distributed around the world focus on the needs of one area, the problems come to the front. Things break or don't work the way one expects. Conversely, new things happen, and breakthroughs in understanding and capabilities pop up to fix problems using new tools and processes. Highlights from an early BIMStorm in West Virginia provides one example:

The BIMStorm started with a three-week moderated public comment process. Concerns about gentrifying neighborhoods, housing opportunity, recreation, water taxis and more came to the forefront. The process included a live, face-to-face group and others connected via the internet.

The remote team documented discussions. Contemporaneous text notes were projected for all to see. Everyone could see their input as it appeared on monitors in the meeting room. People heard the comments, and everyone saw the proof.

In the second week, the comments focused on projects. What will happen to my neighborhood if more old houses are torn down and replaced with MacMansions? If we build new housing at the confluence of the Kanawha and Elk Rivers what will it look like and how much would it cost? Discussions about the possibilities went part of the way to helping people find answers, but much was missing.

The team deployed a BIG-BIM ecosystem for live viewing, operated by the remote note taker. Rather than talking about solutions, the team could then show visualizations of potential solutions and data for the items under discussion—directly reflecting comments. Everyone walked down the route of a new bike path—in the computer. The team modeled start and stop points for a new water taxi system. Solutions for housing developed. As participants raised their concerns, they now saw potential solutions pop up in-context. In BIM, in geo-space, with costs, areas and much more.

The dynamic of the meetings and entire BIMStorm changed. Now, rather than merely documenting words, the group actively participated in the conception of futures for Charleston. Making decisions based on facts and solutions. Reaching consensus as a group, they eliminated the potential train-wrecks.

The BIMStorm in Charleston, West Virginia refined new ways to engage groups with diverse training and experiences. The BIMStorm built on legacy data to improve understanding. enabling integrated decisions that reflect facts about design, context, time, and costs tied to user needs, resources and much more.

BIMStorms are vehicles to test and refine how to best apply BIG-BIM ecosystems in the real-world. They seek the best ways to improve legacy processes and bring experts and the public together to promote understanding. Many things have been learned in BIMStorms and then moved out into the world to support real projects. One example took place in New York.

US Military Academy at West Point

Project management in places like West Point is inherently complex. There is an almost sacred quality to the buildings. Tradition and honor overlay everything. Stakeholders have varying backgrounds and technical expertise. Business needs drive the owner's requirements. The Cadet Housing areas at West Point are listed on the National Historic Register places, clustering tightly around Cadet assembly areas that get heavy use many times every day.

There is little or no leftover space. Any work on, or around, the buildings must not impede operations of the Corps of Cadets, except in well-rehearsed, pre-planned ways.

The Army's approach to planning for design and construction activities in these areas has traditionally been a drawn-out process. Ideally, everyone who's work may touch on the facility over the lifecycle has input: the architects and engineers that will design the project; the builders and suppliers that will put the project together and; the facility managers that will manage the building for the full lifecycle are all engaged. It falls to the appointed project representative to moderate the disputes and sift through the confusion to respond to the widely varying needs of the institution.

Planning for the reconstruction of the Barracks at the US Military Academy at West Point is one place where the lessons learned in BIMStorms made new and exciting things happen.

Data is traditionally captured on paper and in files. The process requires the preparation and review of many reports, before anything proceeds. The process occurs so often that much support data exists, in many forms:

- *Mapping of Cadet Housing in standalone GIS, floor-by-floor, room-by-room; taking GIS into the realm of facility management tools;*

- *Documents with detailed guidance for formations, personnel, logistics, operating orders, codes, standard procedure, utility plans, delivery routes, history and, oral and written traditions that support day-to-day functions;*

- *Individual criteria and requirements for each of the support areas: medical, food service, security, scheduling, academics, and all other programs associated with higher education and the military, in a variety of forms;*

- *Standards for design and construction: seismic upgrades, historic restoration and upgrade, accessibility, life safety, construction procedures, force protection and security are a but a few of the codes documented, and;*

- *Budgets, financing needs, allocation methods and, legislative procedures the interact with all other factors.*

The team deployed systems that interconnected with these existing data sources to rapidly create planning tools that allowed Army planners to develop rapid what-if scenarios. The systems enabled the modeling of construction activities, overlaid with cadet formations and movement areas, all while outputting costs and other decision-making parameters in near real-time. The process went like this:

Connect to standalone GIS data and directly generate BIG-BIM blocking and stacking models at the space level. Taking less than one week, 1.1 million square feet of space went from GIS plans to IFC compliant, computable BIM.

Meet with stakeholders and decision makers to document requirements for construction, short and long-term needs, funding, access and, overcrowding issues. BIG-BIM, mind maps, and web collaboration tools captured the input.

Create project phasing concepts, in response to available funds. The BIG-BIM include 3D frameworks at the space level, costs (construction, operating and energy), sequencing (project timing, construction lay down, cadet formations), overcrowding (the chess game of coordinated movement of occupants during renovation).

Army planners were then able to extract data from the BIG–BIM ecosystem in many formats to suit internal and external requirements as the project moved to acceptance, approval, funding, procurement, and implementation.

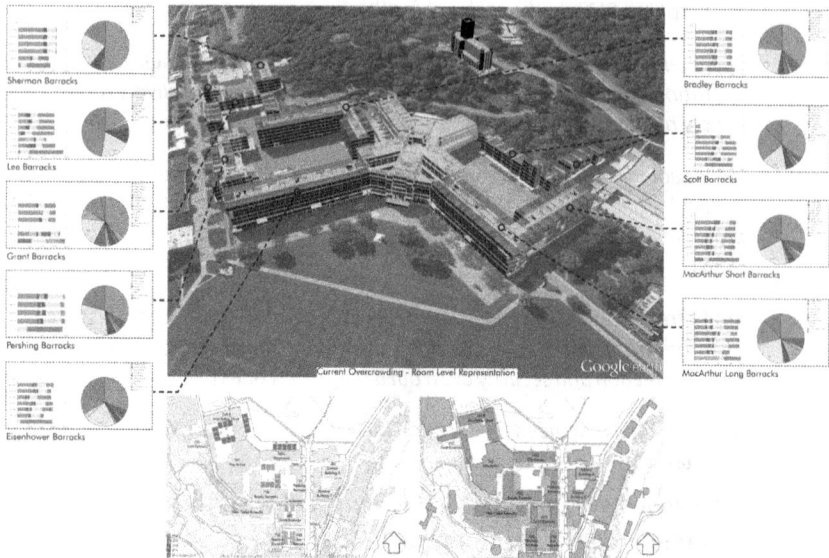

BIG-BIM, as prototyped in BIMStorms, enabled West Point leadership to look at the issues, in-context and connected, to plan proactively for the renovation of their Cadet Housing Areas, in a fraction of the time required for the old process.

The models the team created enable rapid what–if scenario planning to allow West Point to assess the impact of decisions. If we have one–hundred additional cadets in Year 4 of the renovations, where will they be housed to minimize overcrowding? If fewer funds are available for Year 2 of the renovations, what will be the impact to the program downstream? If we accelerate the renovation of two buildings, what will be the adjusted cost?

This process of consolidating information and assessing how best to proceed has long faced Academy decision makers. Before BIG-BIM, completing the process took so long that many decisions had to be made based on incomplete and out of context information. Traditional methods for making such decisions were linear, disconnected and broken into separate silos; creating inefficiencies and risk of unplanned outcomes.

Case Study
Seeding the EcoDistrict

A BIG-BIM ecosystem was used to create a user-friendly geospatial tool focused on capturing existing information to support downstream urban design and planning scenarios with lifecycle controls. The ecosystem connects planning and program requirements to validate design solutions, in the context of implemented projects.

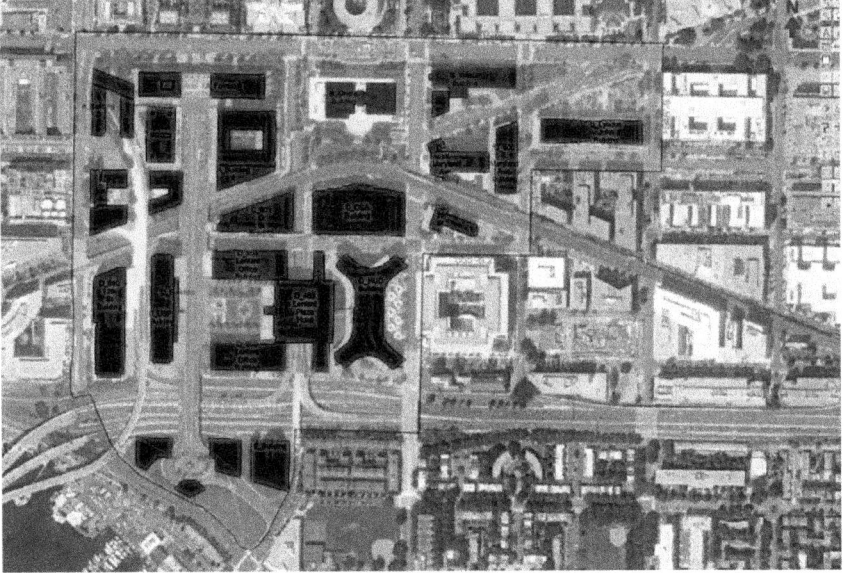

What are the interesting aspects of this case study?

Creation of a framework for EcoDistrict Development.

Seed data to start revitalization aimed at creating a mixed-use neighborhood and cultural destination.

Planning structure to guide development of a community that is well-connected to the balance of DC. Restoring connections to the adjacent National Mall, the Capital, the Potomac Riverfront and more.

Prototype of tools to enable a high-performance environmental showcase for lifecycle sustainability and resilience.

Tools for supporting the development of an economically successful public/private partnership that thrives because of the Ecodistrict.

Location—Washington, DC, USA.

Executive Order 13514 mandates the phased-in compliance of federal government buildings with Energy Efficiency Guiding Principles. Longer term, the executive orders mandates new federal government buildings to all be Zero-Energy buildings.

The executive order states: The Federal Government must lead by example ... To increase energy efficiency; measure, report, and reduce their greenhouse gas emissions from direct and indirect activities... To design, construct, maintain, and operate high-performance, sustainable buildings in sustainable locations; strengthen the vitality and livability of the communities in which Federal facilities locate, and inform Federal employees about and involve them in the achievement of these goals.

The Southwest EcoDistrict is an urban design and planning project conceived by National Capital Planning Commission (NCPC) to comply with Executive Order 13514 by transforming the corridor and its environs into a model sustainable community. Ecodistrict planning has been shown to yield greater environmental and economic benefits than traditional large-scale urban planning and building strategies.

The Southwest Ecodistrict is a comprehensive approach to transforming one area in the nation's capital into an incredibly sustainable workplace and livable neighborhood. The fifteen-block area Southwest of the Smithsonian *Castle* and the National Mall is bounded by Independence Avenue and Maine Avenue between 7th and 12th Streets. The Ecodistrict encompasses 110 acres of public and private land.

The SW Ecodistrict Plan lays out a roadmap to direct development and positively contribute to Washington's economic vitality and environmental health. The plan aligns community and agency goals, using district-scale sustainable practices to connect land use, transportation, and environmental planning with high-performance buildings, landscapes, and infrastructure.

The ecosystem enables fact-based decision support for those that will create and manage the area over the lifecycle of the Ecodistrict. The goal is to improve access to information, connect urban design and land use to publicly validated needs and to capture, manage, and reuse most of the energy, water, and waste generated on site.

BIG-BIM embeds the methodology used to identify the benefits, opportunities, and lifecycle costs of implemented improvements to the Ecodistrict. The decision to use a BIG-BIM ecosystem to capture and organize project information came early as a reaction to traditional processes that were disconnected and had stalled the progress of the many entities involved in the project.

Each of the participating organizations had their ways of doing things. Stakeholder groups had hoards of data firmly locking into siloed tools and processes. Mediating between conflicting approaches and consolidating the available background data took more time than did producing results. The rigid reliance on legacy information was impeding progress and undermining the ability to achieve the Ecodistrict's stated goals.

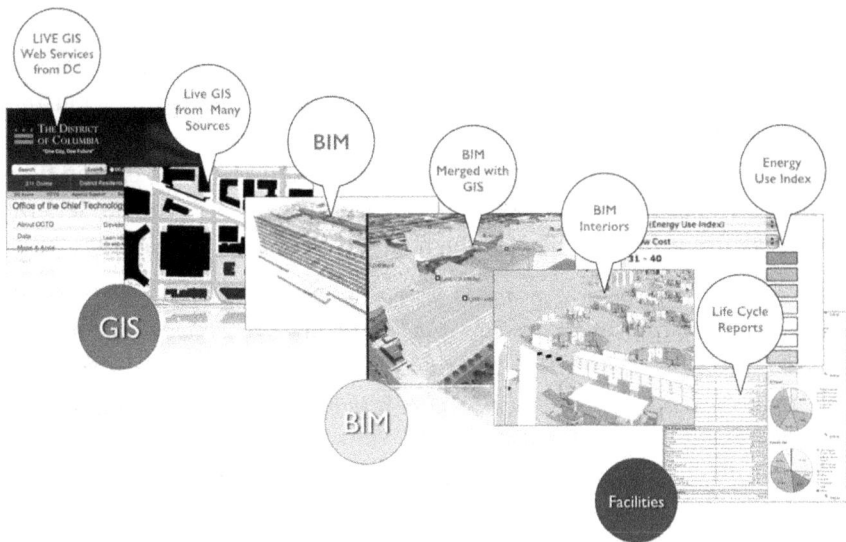

The team created a real-time BIG-BIM ecosystem that is interoperable over the lifecycle of the project and does not rely on a BIM or GIS-centric approach. Other ecodistrict projects depend on the file-based import of BIM to their GIS system and then use GIS to simulate real-time interaction. Reliance on such a file-based approach is not the long-term solution.

The SW Ecodistrict embraces real-time interconnections supported by live data, to achieve live views of information that support Integrated-Decision-Making. GIS, BIM, and facility management data are connected. When the footprint of a building or site changes in BIM, the system reflects the changes in GIS. When streets or sidewalks change in GIS, they reflect in BIM.

The tools and data that support the Ecodistrict are a mash-up of real-time connections, or Geo-BIM. Information from buildings, geographic systems and operations interconnect to support decision-making. The system 'seeds' future planning and development, enabling the BIG-BIM ecosystem to become the long-term repository and clearinghouse for all Ecodistrict data. Servers talk to other servers to reduce redundant information. Authoritative data pushes and pulls from and to sources throughout the EcoDistrict, exponentially increasing the development and management possibilities and opportunities.

Design teams get the facts they need before builders pour concrete. Planners see the impact of their decisions before codifying their plans. Managers see the ground-truth tied to real-time data to decide better. Public stakeholders view live information to understand better their neighborhood in-context.

There are many needs and many ways to respond. In the Ecodistrict, people react based on real-time information, rather than supposition and innuendo. The BIG-BIM ecosystem contains live models of all existing buildings within the Ecodistrict. These models were created based on files in many flat-CAD formats and scanned forms provided by the US General Services Administration. Few of the models originated in little-bim.

After converting and consolidating the legacy documents into the BIG-BIM ecosystem, models were populated with information or connected to external databases to include spatial, energy, and other environmental and systems.

The system also includes exterior walls, roofs, slabs, doors, windows, stairs, and other facility information to allow urban design visualization and analysis.

A group of little-bim analysis tools prototyped and computed energy baselines for all buildings. Actual energy usage from historical records and local energy sensors was then connected to the baseline data to enable the visualization and real-time control of power and systems.

Data from a wide variety of other facility related sources make the models in the Ecodistrict's BIM-BIM ecosystem into real existing conditions models designed to support downstream development needs.

With the many datasets, models enable studies of capacity, current usage, and other analyses. Users can access the BIG-BIM, add layers of information, and interact with the existing information, within a geospatial framework tied to the real-world.

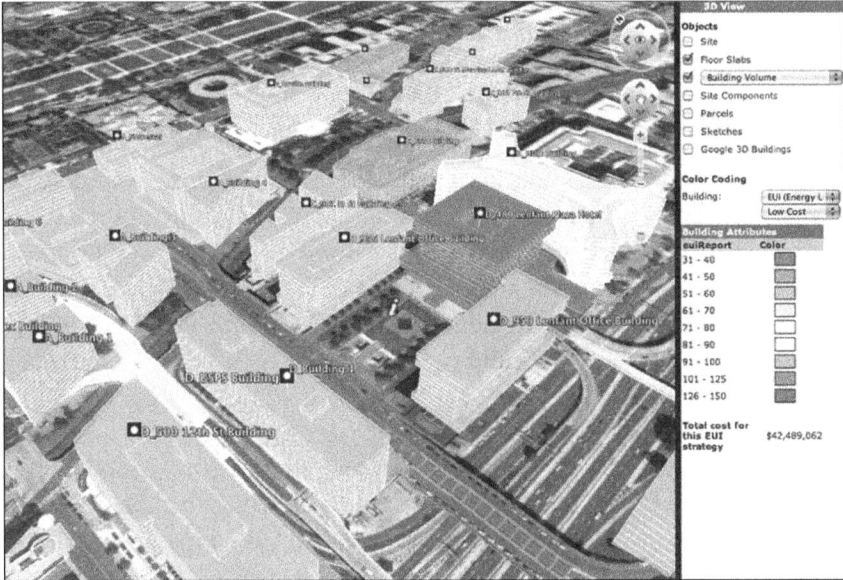

The BIG-BIM ecosystem supports SW Ecodistrict planning and is a national example for fact-based urban design decision-making support to achieve solutions that handle the needs of all stakeholders.

Influences

The Southwest Federal Center, between the National Mall and the Southeast Freeway in Washington, DC, is the antithesis of a walkable community. The brutalist architecture and massive Federal government office buildings that dominate the area have long overshadowed the need for a coordinated long-term vision.

Where other parts of the Capital are pedestrian friendly, this is a land for cars, office cubicles, concrete, and above ground trains. The area needs a long-term solution to correct the constant changes that created the current conditions while accommodating existing infrastructure and government agency space requirements.

Two efforts drive the need for the SW Ecodistrict:

1. **Monumental Core Framework Plan.** This plan recommended the most efficient use of federal property, and proposed that new cultural sites and museums be in the area south of the National Mall to catalyze economic development.

2. **Executive Order 13514 (Federal Leadership in Environmental, Energy, and Economic Performance).** Signed by President Obama in 2009, this rule sets aggressive targets for energy, water, and greenhouse gas reductions for federal buildings.

A Task Force of Federal and local agencies direct Southwest Ecodistrict planning. Members include: The National Capital Planning Commission who leads the effort; the District of Columbia—Office of Planning, Deputy Mayor for Planning and Economic Development, Department of the Environment, and Department of Transportation, and; all US Federal government agencies with building footprints within the boundaries of the ecodistrict.

Development of BIG-BIM data to support the planning effort began in 2009. Hearings to create public support and comment took place from 2010 through 2011, and the Task Force issued a draft plan in 2012. Approval of the Southwest Ecodistrict Plan occurred in 2013 with amendments added in 2014.

> *People use the tools that work best in their individual and corporate workflows. Tools used ranged from spreadsheets to BIM, to GIS, to LIDAR, to SketchUp, and much more. Stakeholders have access to the information they need, in the software format, they require, when they need it.*

Case Study
BIMStorm Chronology

BIMStorms began to show people what is possible with BIG-BIM. As BIMStorms have matured, they have evolved to include such things as community service and disaster recovery. Connecting the built environment into community programs and individual action accelerates recovery efforts and helps people to understand their world, in-context.

BIMStorms have also became drivers in the movement toward what some call Geodesign. With Geodesign the ideas detailed by visionaries such as Ian McHarg and Buckminster Fuller began to happen, as building information modeling in the cloud and geographic information started to unite. As the complexity of the built environment increased, this alignment has resulted in better, more informed solutions.

Decisions are made earlier in the process, with more accurate and reliable data. No longer does each area of technology need to operate in isolation. Multiple technologies and knowledge domains connect, to the benefit of all. The ability to interact with all systems and all areas of the built environment is one of the highest and best uses of the vast stores of data available.

The US Army and others used BIMStorm processes to plan the relocation and reorganization of military bases. Cities have used the procedures to prepare for the urban and community impacts of significant changes in employment and tax revenues. The California Community Colleges System, the Department of Veterans Affairs, the Department of Defense Health System, and other enterprises continue to use elements of BIMStorms to improve their processes.

BIMStorm Timeline

Wim Scheele, Director of Project Development, City of Rotterdam, Netherlands commented: *We were not aware these types of solutions even existed. Best of all, we are now able to keep the relationship between our financial estimates and the design, since both drive us in our decision-making. The BIMStorm involves us, as a client, within the BIM process, where we didn't have this relationship before.*

2007—BIMStorm Rotterdam, was the first BIMStorm.

This BIMStorm was part of BIM Caseweek Rotterdam LIVE initiated by the Rijksgebouwendienst Department of Ministry and VROM, (ie. the Netherlands' version of the US General Services Administration). Virtual participants from California and Hawaii worked in collaboration with the CADVisual team in the Netherlands.

2008—BIMStorm LAX demonstrated the power of cloud-based BIM.

The event took place over a 24-Hour period, and included participants in eleven Countries. 133 Players created 420 virtual buildings totaling 54,755,153 SF. Participants travelled zero miles. The process encouraged architects to embrace new ways of project delivery that expand their impact upon the environment and help improve their business and management skills.

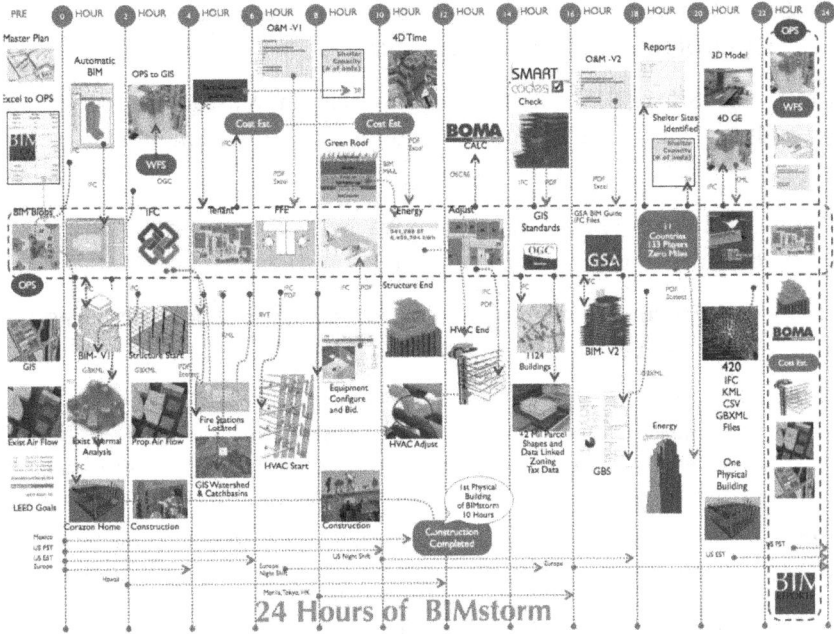

24 Hours of BIMstorm

The work produced during BIMStorm LAX was the equivalent of 2,800,000 pages of print documents.

2008—BIMStorm West Virginia, was a lead up to the West Virginia Expo in Charleston, WV. This BIMStorm was first to focus on extending the concept to the public.

Organized as a series of public meetings, on site and remote teams captured community issues and used the tools to engage the public. In a typical session, a downtown resident expressed the need for housing at the confluence of the Elk and Kanawha Rivers. The remote group would then, in near- real-time, create and display housing solutions in the location under consideration.

Enabling the public to see their ideas immediately reflected in Google Earth, with building massing, areas, costs, and other materials are incredibly powerful. People left the process knowing that their ideas are understood and reflected in the ultimate solution.

2008—BIMStorm The Big Easy Way, took place soon after Hurricane Katrina, in New Orleans.

This BIMStorm looked at emergency services, connecting geographical information system data to support urban planning and new downtown structures. BIMStorms' ability to engage people locally with experts anywhere in the world offered significant benefits in the disaster recovery process.

2008—BIMStorm Pasadena, California included the signing of the Declaration of Information Independence.

2008—BIMStorm BIM for the People in Boston, Massachusetts enabled an audience of 400 to create 130 building information models in 90 Minutes.

2008—BIMStorm Build London Live was an international juried competition centered on the Greenwich Peninsula in London.

2008—BIMStorm Associated General Contractors of America, was the focus of the AGC BIMForum in Lake Tahoe, Nevada.

Teams started with a high-rise design and ran through a series of construction reviews including detailed analysis of structural, MEP and curtain wall systems. In a few days, a process that normally took weeks or months, revealed options that might never have become known in a traditional linear approach.

2008—BIMStorm Connecting Buildings to the Earth, took place in Vancouver, Canada.

2008—BIMStorm Alexandria BRAC, focused on US Federal Governments Base Realignment and Closing program's impacts.

2008—BIMStorm Tshwane/Capital Alliance, took place under the auspices of the National Capital Planning Commission (NCPC), the central planning agency for America's capital, as they hosted the Capitals Alliance 2008: Greening the World's Capital Cities, in Washington, DC September 15-18, 2008.

The conference assembled planners, designers, architects, and policy-makers from national capitals around the world to explore the role of capital cities in creating a greener planet. This year, the Capitals Alliance focused on a planning charrette of Tshwane, the capital of South Africa. BIMStorm Capitals Alliance allows participants from around the world to observe and design.

2008—BIMStorm Washington DC1 was the focus of the 2008 EcoBuild Conference in Washington, DC.

2009—BIMStorm buildingSMART alliance/COBIE 2, focused on the value and power of COBie as part of Ecobuild in Washington, DC.

2009—BIMStorm Metro Los Angeles, was a Web2.0 collaboration to study innovative transit solutions for Los Angeles, CA.

2009—BIMStorm Build Hospital Live, studied high-performance hospital planning with buildingSMART in Oslo, Norway.

2009—BIMStorm Plan Haiti, was a real-time BIM collaboration in support of Haiti earthquake recovery. The earthquake in Haiti and the tsunami in Japan are both the subject of BIMStorms focused on the recovery process.

2009—BIMStorm Connectivity Week in Santa Clara, California focused on connectivity and the use of BIG-BIM within the realm of the Internet of Things.

2010—Low Carbon Collaboration BIMStorm, was launched to promote the concept of using less carbon to collaborate on projects.

> *Participating schools included: the University of Southern California, School of Architecture/as part of a five week Low Carbon Collaboration BIMStorm course during Spring 2009; the University of Southern California - The Sonny Astani Department of Civil and Environmental Engineering; Virginia Tech WAAC; Pennsylvania State University, Computer Integrated Construction Research Program; Catholic University, School of Architecture; and the Royal Danish Academy of Fine Arts, School of Architecture.*

> *The program highlighted the ways that BIMStorms enable collaboration processes that happen at a stunning pace. They minimize the need for traditional carbon heavy communications like face-to-face meetings and travel. The building industry is poised to promote a "green practice" with sustainable project management processes.*

2010—BIMStorm 13514, Washington, DC, was the focus of the 2010 Ecobuild Conference with emphasis on implementation of Executive Order 13514, Federal Leadership in Environmental, Energy, and Economic Performance, signed by President Obama on 5 October 2009.

2011—BIMStorm® Connects the World, was a live BIMStorm event at Qualcomm in San Diego, California.

2011—BIMStorm Getting Real with BIM, planned for projects in Chicago, Illinois with a total value of $14 Billion in 90 Minutes to kick off Getting Real with BIM, GIS, and Facility Management program.

2011—BIMStorm Hong Kong, was a 60 Minute planning process for 79 buildings that were completed using crowdsourced Information Models submitted live from an audience of 200 during Kimon Onuma's keynote presentation at the GeoDesign Summit at ESRI. Redlands, California.

The BIMStorm was based on input from the audience using iPhones, Androids, and PCs to submit BIMs in real-time for a mash-up during the beginning of the presentation. Within 30 minutes 68 new buildings were submitted from audience totaling $13.67 Billion US of construction and landed on a site in Hong Kong. At the same time, Balfour Beatty of Fairfax, Virginia submitted 11 buildings totaling $2.54US Billion of construction to the same site.

The aggregated total area of all the buildings submitted was over 36 million square feet. During the live BIMStorm three ONUMA team members in Pasadena, CA coordinated and arranged all 79 buildings on a site in Hong Kong.

A typical design and construction process would not occur at this pace or with this many people. The intent of this BIMStorm was to demonstrate that the technology exists to make this happen and that even those that with minimal knowledge about the underlying technology can use simple tools to interact in real-time.

2011—BIMStorm BIG-BIM BANG, focused on Washington DC's first EcoDistrict to capture existing site and facility documentation, site analyzes, energy and environmental data, and much more to inform future development.

As an offshoot of this project, examples of ways to use real-time sensor data and live device control emerged. With the framework put in place, the district is becoming a national showplace for fact-based decision-making in the environmental and sustainability realm.

2011—BIMStorm Japan, was planned in response to the devastation from the 11 March 2011 earthquake and tsunami. The event was coordinated by Ryota Ieiri, journalist and blogger in Tokyo, Japan.

2012—BIMStorm OKC, was a joint effort of the University of Oklahoma was the sponsor and the Oklahoma City Planning Office to look for ways to better manage the future of the city.

The program brought together students from disciplines such as architecture, construction science, planning, and engineering to join in a partnership with the City of Oklahoma City and industry participants for the virtual BIM event. Students developed design alternatives that could be tested and analyzed in BIM to verify feasibility and construction.

Industry partners provided insight to students about real-world solutions. The dynamics of students, city officials, and industry partners all working toward one goal has implications for each group with information sharing, problem-solving, and solution testing. The virtual team context offered OU students a differentiator and experience uncommon to most students of the built environment.

BIMStorm OKC used existing GiS to illustrate BIMs that enable high level management of urban systems by public agencies.

2012—BIMStorm COAA, was completed in conjunction with the Construction Owners Association of America, in Miami, Florida. The focus was on one of the 112 campuses of the California Community Colleges.

Owners saw how their project requirements can evolve from program requirements through design and into construction using BIM and open-standards such as COBie, IFC, and web standards. Participants gained knowledge on what is possible today and could view results live on smartphones, tablets, and computers.

2012—BIMStorm Show & Tell, was 3-day track of 90-minute sessions covering applications for: Healthcare; Facilities Management; Education; Geospatial Planning; Open-standards, Web services and, Model Servers; COBie; and more.

On the expo floor in the BIMStorm Theater, an additional 16 short courses free to all attendees showcased the latest technology advancements, new products and services that make it all happen. The Theater highlighted software developers, technology evangelists and AEC firms to show their solutions to help attendees better understand the process and actively engage in owner driven scenarios for managing new projects and existing portfolios of facilities and infrastructure.

2013—BIMStorm Mars City, Washington, took place in conjunction with NASA and other US Federal government agencies, Washington, DC.

Highlighted the importance of BIM and Facilities Management in the life or death environment that will impact any settlement on Mars. The goal was to use BIG-BIM to learn, explore and find the problems, before making the big step of traveling to Mars.

2013+—BIMStorm LIFE, in Washington, DC. focused on the essence of the issues now coming to the forefront of the industry. Decisions start from stakeholders, the community, the owner, a city, and more. It is not about the *project.*

The things happening today touch on all parts of the life cycle and ecosystem. Why do we build what we build? How do we reduce risk? How do we predict the future? Or, at least respond resiliently to future events? How do non-BIM users interact with decision-making? How can we fit into this ecosystem?

2015—BIMStorm Healthcare Hack in Pasadena, CA. Combined program with the BIM AEC Hackathon. The AEC (Architecture, Engineering, Construction) Hackathon was created to give those designing, building, and maintaining our built environment the opportunity to collaborate with innovative technologies and its developers and designers.

This hackathon was a forum for improving the industries that affect all that live or work in the built world and is quickly becoming a global community of innovators that include all elements of the built environment.

2016/2017—BIMStorm Data Independence, focused on letting people experience the next-generation of Building Information Models to use web services to manage and process building data in advanced workflows that are incredibly simple for the end user!

Participants observed or directly participated and experienced how these new tools are used. No experience was required, first timers and novice BIM users, as well as Owners and members of the AEC industry saw the power and possibilities.

This BIMStorm sought to take the Building and Design industry a step closer to the modern Google, Amazon, Facebook, Twitter age. Behind the scenes, driving much of the advanced functionalities we see in these modern technologies is something called web services. It is NOT important for people to have a technical understanding of Web services to participate in this (any other) BIMStorm, although if you are a developer, the program can provide more technical information.

Case Study
GeoBIM Proposal

There is a delicate balance between understanding the technology, business case, culture, standards, building industry and trends and defining a successful change process that is strategic and implementable. A balance must exist. If one focuses too much on technology or legacy data, you have a recipe for failure. The goal is to avoid the pitfalls that occur in facility transformation projects while guiding the organization on a logical path.

What follows is a sample of the steps one takes to position an organization in the BIG-BIM ecosystem. The goal is to make it easy for the owner to commit to the full implementation of a BIG-BIM ecosystem, creating an informed environment within the enterprise. This process provides the organization's leadership with real, asset-focused benefits that come from working with informed environments, and; demonstrates the power and possibilities from becoming a leader in the BIG-BIM ecosystem. The initial work efforts include three major steps:

1. Initial Consultation

Customize the process to the enterprise, through an initial consultation program, designed to validate the owner's needs and wishes. A doctor wouldn't perform surgery without a proper diagnosis; this initial consultation works in the same way. The initial consultation starts with a strategy built around understanding the organization's existing systems and requirements:

- ☐ *Identify current data availability and ease of access.*

- ☐ *Expose data systems that are held captive by outside vendors and software constraints.*

- ☐ *Explore external linkages into organizational data.*

- ☐ *Assess human limitations and roadblocks.*

These reviews quickly establish a trajectory for the project. Use this knowledge to create scenarios for the future:

- ☐ *Develop an overall view of the current condition and short and long-term goals.*

- ☐ *Create a conceptual prototype.*

☐ *Generate recommendations for further steps needed to support the transition to an asset management ecosystem.*

☐ *Inform future actions with the organization's strategic goals and the various drivers for those initiatives.*

Deliverables

Look for team members with the expertise to model future outcomes and create proper project trajectories. As the team guides the project, they establish a foundation for success that considers organizational needs connected to knowledge of the areas that can become problems. Prepare a brief that details the opportunities and possibilities and includes:

☐ *Documentation of potential solutions in outline form.*

☐ *Assessment of current data sources, documentation, system types and accessibility.*

☐ *Analysis of existing conditions to define a trajectory for further development and implementation.*

NB. If, at this point, it becomes apparent that the selected team is not an ideal fit for the enterprise's needs, then the owner is free to take the report to another team to continue the process. In complex (or even simple projects) there is always the need to allow for adjustments, as the project proceeds.

2. Begin Implementation

The next step is to discover, start-up and expose high level functionality. At this stage, strategic information is accessed and normalized with the goal of rapidly making legacy data computable and useful in the ecosystem. Review of an enterprise's data always leads to a starting point for future development. As the team examines the current state of facility data:

☐ *The team evaluates the extent of non-standard or non-normalized data sources.*

☐ *They create systems that maximize usability and access to the data, in the form needed by all classes of users.*

☐ *And, they seek ways to maximize use of current data, without delaying implementation of BIG-BIM tools.*

☐ *Clean up and organization of legacy data are secondary to the efficient use of structured data. At times, a decision must be made to move ahead with new information structures, rather than forcing the use of legacy data.*

Scores of datasets, in many formats, exist within most established enterprises. These datasets are in the form of spreadsheets, MSAccess databases, SQL databases, document management systems, accounting systems, and GiS systems. Or, held within, welded together software systems, such as Revit, ArchiBus, Maximo, et.al. Since much of this data is file-based, it is subject to data rot and often of little long-term value.

The welded together little-bim systems that most are familiar with continue to have a purpose, though primarily in the design and construction realms.

Often access the many systems in any enterprise is very limited, due to training, access, and many other impediments. A small number of individuals can access and use some of the data for their purposes. Rarely do you find enterprises where the data and sophisticated tools are in full use. The goal is to change this paradigm.

Deliverables

☐ *Create a working prototype of the system. The prototype includes deployment of middleware populated to show significant uses of the system.*

☐ *Create a BIG-BIM studio, branded for the organization, designed to become the hub of current and future development and an information repository.*

☐ *Outline phasing and costing for budget usage.*

☐ *Outline regulatory issues and global impacts.*

NB. Where available, use existing organizational data and documentation, adjusted to weave in changes. Where information is not currently available, deploy placeholder images, data, and documents to show what is possible. Projects that implement the best of today's BIG-BIM technology must be prescriptive but not so rigid as to be brittle. A delicate balance between flexibility and rigidity must be established to create favorable outcomes.

3. Embed Across the Enterprise

Now is the time to connect to new projects and processes to build a series of small wins and AHA! experiences in the members of the enterprise. The goal is to work with all systems now in place, or that will be in place in the future. The cultural shift that is needed is often more of a challenge than the technology itself. The goal is to identify the catalysts to initiate and guide change within the organization.

☐ *Create a systematic approach for interconnecting business processes, to facilities, to operations;*

- *Work with in-house and external teams to interface detailed design and construction processes with the organization's BIG-BIM ecosystem;*

- *And, develop a process support system to overcome roadblocks and issues that may occur.*

- *The system is used to seed the little-bim and other systems with all the pertinent information currently in the owner's systems. As the design progresses, the information that is critical to owner needs can be pushed back to the ecosystem, enabling the owner to evaluate design performance, assess the impact on future financial needs, etc.*

- *When the project moves to construction, the system does much the same for the contractor, now documenting the information coming from other systems and data structures during the building process.*

- *As the project moves toward completion, the system seeds commissioning, captures adjustments and at any time can push the data to facility management for operations and maintenance use. After construction, the system continues to enable the aggregation of a owner's information, with or without a Integrated Workplace Management System.*

Deliverables

The system acts as a clearinghouse or 'neutral' repository for the data and graphics designed to provide context for users—not to directly contain the detailed graphics. Because of this, the traditional design/construction personnel can continue to do what they have always done if that is all they choose to do. The system imposes very few additional requirements on them. However, should they wish to expand their horizons into property management, early stage validation, O&M, et al. the system ties things together to enable the opportunities.

For design and construction, one might think of the BIG-BIM ecosystem as program requirements on steroids, at the beginning of design; coupled with a repository that captures the data created as design and construction progress.

The ecosystem is localized and tied to the enterprise's needs to the greatest extent possible. It adapts and adjusts as needs change and progress occurs. When deployed, the ecosystem should:

- *Demonstrate the look and feel of the organization and the context in which it works.*

- *Create a strategy for planning viability, organizational ideas, and long-term outlooks.*

- *Identify and implement new systems and projects.*

☐ *Convert low-hanging-fruit into implementable results in the near-term, progressing to increasingly long-term goals and solutions.*

One must know where the building industry is going to avoid the gotchas in the implementation process. The team must guide the organization through the process, allowing the enterprise to build upon the team's knowledge to educate and keep everyone informed and on the path to lifelong implementation.

Where initiatives such as those in the United Kingdom focus on graphics via Levels of Detail/Levels of Development, the BIG–BIM ecosystem can function at any LOD at any stage in development. Within the ecosystem, one sees 3D boxes representing projects, buildings, and spaces. Any of these boxes can (and does) carry detailed data at a very high level of accuracy and completion; dependent on the data sources connected.

Immediately after importing a spreadsheet that lists Room Name, Room Size, Floor Level, one has an entirely functional Work-Order-Management capability, accessible from any web-enabled device. If you add Room Number, you also have the ability for users to link directly to their space and the ability to immediately seed facility management.

Case Study
California Community Colleges

This material supplements and continues the CASE STUDY: BIM–GIS–FM FUSION earlier in the book.

The California Community College (CCC) System enrolls 2.6 million students each year, in 72 districts, encompassing 112 campuses, 72 approved off–campus centers, and 23 separately reported district offices. The System's assets include 24,398 acres of land, 5,192 buildings, and 72.4 million gross square feet of space.

Using the *ONUMA System* as both a planning and mash–up engine the FUSION+GIS+ONUMA platform allows data from many sources to be combined to tell new and compelling stories about the environment. Before this system, information was often in disconnected data structures that required manual manipulation to understand and use.

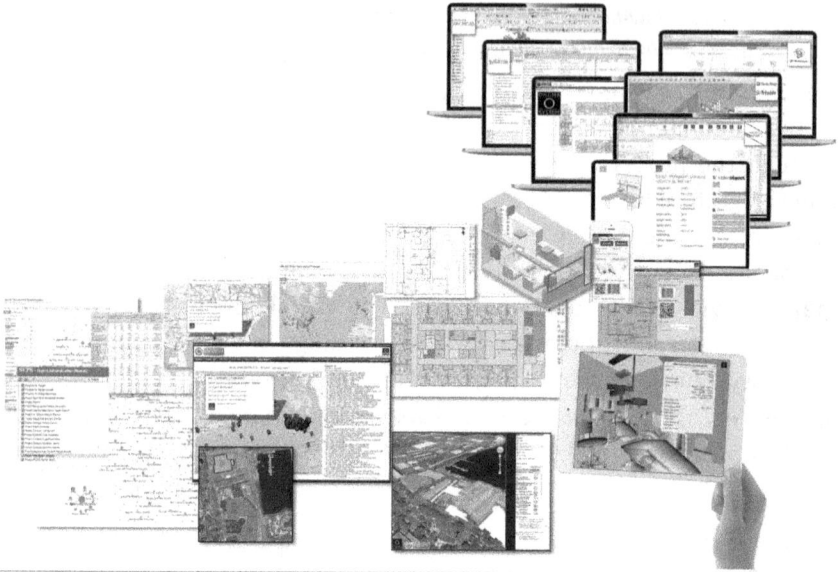

Within the CCC system, one can now see such things as detailed building information models, overlaid streaming live in an adjacent window.

California Community Colleges empowers community colleges through leadership, advocacy, and support. CCC's Finance and Facilities Planning Division oversees distribution of local assistance, capital outlay funds and construction and remodeling of new facilities. The Division uses web-based tools to assess, coordinate, plan, evaluate and manage projects efficiently.

The Foundation for California Community Colleges develops programs and services to save millions of dollars, promote excellence in education, and provide learning opportunities for students throughout the state. The Foundation also supports the system through individual initiatives, statewide awards, and direct donation. Within the first nine months, many benefits were realized from the FUSION+GIS+ONUMA platform.

User Interface Benefits

☐ *The system is simple for both managers and users to learn and use.*

☐ *Enter data once and control changes to that data. Users view data in many ways for greater insight and effectiveness.*

☐ *Orient new employees to facilities management more efficiently.*

☐ *Lightweight real-time data is accessible on multiple devices, including iPhones & iPads. Provides a light weight version of BIM for the planning stage that can easily be ported to more feature-rich little-bim systems when doing design and construction of a building.*

☐ *The entire California inventory is accessible in seconds.*

Management Benefits

☐ *It is inexpensive compared to the purchase of a full-featured enterprise scale BIM System. GIS layers from the Foundation's GIS server are visible now for all districts and linked to BIM. Fifty-six GIS layers connect to BIM for planning purposes on the Mira Costa College campus.*

☐ *Define criteria and address more objectively any equity issues between the district, school campus, or individual buildings.*

☐ *Develop procurement strategies and bulk purchase plans.*

☐ *Streamline project management, tracking and reporting functions for submission of bond funding and loan requests, grants, change requests, and development and phase documentation.*

☐ *Package projects to support facility renovation and renewal to protect mission-critical teaching, research, and support functions.*

☐ *New solutions are emerging from vendors who now see an easy way to connect with web services to the system.*

Decision-Making Benefits

☐ *Conduct scenario planning, thereby making planning more efficient and robust.*

☐ *Sensors and building automation systems at Glendale College, are connected to the platform. Giving the college the ability to monitor real-time data and control devices directly from the BIM.*

☐ *Traditionally, classroom scheduling is managed in tabular formats. Now one can visualize classroom schedule in a variety of ways in the model. Several solution providers of classroom programming are evaluating how to link to the system.*

☐ *Many districts are requesting increased access and functionality. The initial roll-out of the system in March of 2011 was intentionally kept simple to minimize the risk for overwhelming users with new functionality. Individual districts such as Chabot / Las Positas, have found features that support their current needs.*

Capital Planning Benefits

☐ *Prepare Project Plans and five-year Capital Improvement Plans online. Project program requirements now generate BIMs automatically. These models can be used to check program requirements against designs.*

☐ *Update, certify, and track space inventory status, project status, and forecasts (work status, full-time equivalents per college, etc.) online while permitting enterprise view-only access.*

☐ *Monitor, view, interpret and understand the overall performance of projects with a variety of funding streams that span multiple fiscal years to manage risks proactively. Generate mandated reports from data that exists within the system.*

☐ *Access the latest procedures, such as enterprise Facilities Business Processes and Best Practices from the AEC industry that have the potential to add value to the portfolio of facility management tools.*

☐ *Consultants use the system as a tool for dynamic masterplanning. Districts have recognized the value of having planning data that is dynamic. Where assumptions can be edited to create new results rather than locking them into static document-centric deliverables. Ability to maintain living Masterplans that update as a change occurs in the enterprise.*

☐ *The California Investor Owned Utilities are evaluating how to use the system to manage and reduce energy consumption to create scenarios based on their goals.*

Data Benefits

☐ *Reduces data rot by minimizing the use of documents and files.*

☐ *Uses the best of current Internet and Cloud computing technology.*

☐ *Errors in the FUSION database become obvious and editable.*

☐ *Efficiencies enable the management of complex data in simple formats, allowing teams to focus on value-added tasks. BIG-BIM expands the value of information in the management and GIS systems already in place.*

☐ *A by-product of this activity is that all project data passes through the system in BIM IFC format. Data is COBie-compliant, included in GIS, and accessible by other tools as file exchanges or as real-time data, through web services.*

First districts to implement

San Joaquin Delta Community College District
Long Beach Community College District
Citrus Community College District
Los Rios Community College District

Rancho-Santiago Community College District
Foothill-De Anza Community College District
Sequoias Community College District
South Orange County Community College District

Districts added between March and December 2011:
Chabot / Las Positas
Los Angeles Community College Mission East
Glendale College
Peralta Community College District
College of Marin
Riverside City College
Mira Costa College

Participating Design & Construction Organizations
Architecture / vbn—Laney College, Marin College
Balfour Beatty Construction—Riverside City College
HMC Architects—Mira Costa Masterplan
Pankow Construction—COBie for LACCD
Broaddus & Associates—COBie for LACCD
Nolte Associates, Inc.—GIS Layers for MiraCosta

Technology Applied
FUSION System—https://goo.gl/HRsjun
CCCGIS—https://goo.gl/cJqneB
Onuma System—https://goo.gl/uKslBh

Participating Support Organizations
Greenbuild Energy IRIS— https://iris.thegiin.org/
Byucksan Power Energle
Lavelle FasBridge
Powersmiths WOW—https://goo.gl/QY8biH

Standards Applied to the system
BIM—Building Information Modeling
IFC—Industry Foundation Classes (ISO/PAS 16739)
GIS—Geographic Information Systems
OGC—Open Geospatial Consortium
COBie—Construction Information Building
Information Exchanges Used or Enabled
W3C—Worldwide Web Consortium
XML, GBXML, BIMXML
SOA—Service-Oriented-Architecture
Web services—REST, SOAP
SQL -Structured Query Language
SVG—Scalable Vector Graphics
oBIX—Open Building Information Exchange
BACNET—Building Automation and Control Networks
OSCRE—Open-standards Consortium for Real Estate

Open-standards, and web services allow a scalable platform that encourages other web-enabled solutions to link. Within the open-standard FUSION and CCC GIS database, users can access and use a variety of planning, management and administration resources moving from a worldview, through the site, building and space views. The data visible is a mash-up of data from a variety of sources, filtered to the needs of each view.

BIG-BIM has Arrived

Following the unfolding change is interesting. What I came to call little-bim started as a grassroots effort, led by small, nimble practitioners. Building Information Modeling began as software for improved visualization and document production.

Early users found new and unexpected benefits that had little to do with graphics and production. It became apparent that BIM could be a force multiplier, impacting every aspect of the building industry. As the early adopters got deep into this new tool, they changed how they worked.

Shortly after the turn of the century, a rough outline started to develop. Some evangelists remained mired in the logic of last generation software development. They focused on little-bim using welded together products relying on import and export of files, within the design and construction context.

Others saw the revolutionary advancements taking place with the internet and embraced what I came to call BIG-BIM. They focused on loose connections between apps and a services-oriented approach to the building industry.

Along the way, it became evident the changes would always be little, without a BIG push. The push had to come from the top-down and involve people industry wide. Small groups could no longer work in isolation if BIM were to move to the mainstream. That is when the US Coast Guard, the US General Services Administration, the state of Wisconsin, and others came to the forefront. These national leaders helped to create clear and convincing evidence of the power and benefits that come from BIG-BIM.

Years later, many continue to worry about software, not understanding using BIM that way rarely works. They approach BIM like a software upgrade, not believing stories telling of a new way of working changing everything. They make critical mistakes, undermining the benefits. They get frustrated and spend their time arguing about the sophisticated technology they don't understand.

Some cannot get their minds around the fact that with BIM, the thing that matters is people. Figure out the people issues and the technology gets a lot simpler. Most people do not care how BIM works. They want to get things done, with a minimum of effort. If we make that happen, we will be a success.

Much has occurred in the world since the release of the original *BIG-BIM little-bim* in late 1996. The changes are impacting everything and everyone in the building industry. No longer is the use of BIM an option for most designers and builders. Many are yet to make the leap, but most know at some point, they must change. All disciplines are discussing and trying to determine how they fit into the BIM ecosystem.

It is my sincere hope that *BIG-BIM 4.0* will help you to chart a sustainable and resilient future.

My earlier books focused on new ways of working in architects' offices. Other disciplines had to read-between-the-lines to figure out how they fit the picture. I completely rewrote this version for a general audience, because BIG-BIM affects us all. If you live, work, and play in the built environment, BIG-BIM is and will continue to impact your life. It may be called any one of several hundred names, but it is still BIG-BIM.

When I wrote *BIG-BIM little-bim,* BIG-BIM was a concept. Collaborative systems, sustainable ecosystems, and model servers were just beginning to emerge. This book builds on *BIG-BIM little-bim* to focus on establishing the ecosystem that matches your plans with the little steps needed to achieve competency in BIG-BIM.

We need systematic and dynamic approaches that allow us to fold together technology and today's business processes to improve the way we work. Such decision-making processes are already happening in many industries. The travel industry, healthcare, financial markets, music distribution, lodging, personal transportation, and other industries are transforming their core business processes. Information over web-based mobile devices is enabling people to make faster and more informed decisions to improve their productivity.

Much has changed. The Internet continues to transform our relationship with data, systems and welded together software. Functional model servers exist in the Cloud, and one can access and use them today. Web services underpin many of the tools we use every day. This complex system affects us all, every day in everything we do. We can no longer afford the distorted thinking that pervades the building industry.

Now is the time to make the effort to see this world as it is. Beliefs grounded in evidence, rather than emotion or desire, are the foundations to becoming a BIG-BIM expert. Use your critical thinking skills to evaluate and use new tools and processes to better the built world. Even though the evidence may at times contradict your initial beliefs.

In the recent past, we relied on experts to stand between us and the things we lacked the training or ability to control. These experts were our interface to the complexity. Only by moving beyond our reliance on experts-as-interface, will BIM move into the mainstream.

Simple, easy to use tools that don't need one to be an expert, are no longer a dream. These tools enable any savvy Internet user to benefit, and people are using them today.

Organizations such as the California Community Colleges, the US Veterans Administration and the Department of Defense Healthcare System use BIG-BIM. They embrace a more systemic approach to the lifecycle of their assets. Their approach mirrors the way that data operates across the Internet. They are finding the change efficient and beneficial, TODAY. You can too.

Fondest regards, Finith E. Jernigan, FAIA

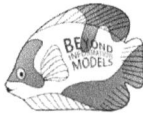

APPENDIX

When people continue to demand proof that BIM and connected processes work, they waste time and energy. The processes have been proven to work for assets of all types and sizes. Do whatever research you need to convince yourself, but don't let that stop you from jumping in and starting the change. Otherwise, you will be left behind.

One day house build by familia Corazon as part of BIMStorm Los Angeles in 2008. 133 Players created 420 virtual buildings totaling 54,755,153 SF, and managed this volunteer-focused house build in Mexico, from Maryland.

Glossary and Definitions

It is recommended that one stay away from peppering discussions with the Ds below (esp. those above 3D). They are included as you will encounter them in your BIM travels.

2D—Analogous to painting or hand drafting. The architect's equivalent to word-processing. 2D computer graphics deal primarily with geometric entities (points, lines, planes, etc.). Blueprints, construction documents and anything output (or drawn on) paper are 2D.

3D—Analogous to sculpture. Prior to computers, architects manually constructed perspectives and physical (cardboard, Foamcore, balsa) models to represent a project's concept. Today computers have automated concept visualization. These 3D graphics can be exported to rapid prototyping systems to create physical models. 3D computer graphics rely on much of the same programming as 2D computer graphics.

3.5D—3D with the addition of limited object technology (minimal object intelligence and not connecting NCS or IFCS) or, 3D with implied movement (Ken Burns effects, trees blown by wind, moving people, etc.). This is not BIM, no matter what you are told.

4D—Building Information Model with the addition of time (virtual building model with scheduling).

5D—Building Information Model with time and construction information additions (virtual building model with cost and project management).

nD—The 'n' represents additional overlays of data, or visualization to the Building Information Model, beyond the dimensions represented by 2D and 3D. Often an indication of BIM Wash.

AECOO—Architecture, Engineering, Construction, Ownership, Operation

aecXML—Architecture/Engineering/Construction-oriented Extensible Markup Language. Internet-oriented data structure for representing information used in BIM.

Agency-Construction-Management—Delivery process where a construction professional organization is retained to exclusively support the owner, acting in the owner's interests at every stage of the project. The owner, with the assistance of the construction manager retains separate entities for design and construction.

Agile Development Environment—Agile development focuses on adaptive planning, evolutionary development, early delivery, technical excellence, and continuous improvement, as a rapid and flexible response to change, as opposed to the highly regulated and micro-managed development methods favored by others. Agile development teams subscribe to the twelve principles outlined in the Agile Manifesto http://agilemanifesto.org/principles.html. Continuous development of valuable tools, embracing change, frequent delivery of working products and simplicity by maximizing the amount of work not done, are characteristics of the process.

AJAX—Short for asynchronous JavaScript and XML, Ajax is not a technology, but a group of technologies. It is a set of web development techniques to create asynchronous (in the background) Web applications that can send and retrieve data from a server. Ajax decouples the data interchange layer from the presentation layer. It is common to substitute JSON for XML as JASON is native to JavaScript. Per Wikipedia, et.al.

Asset—An item, thing or entity that has potential or actual value for an organization. An asset can be anything from tangible and physical items such as precious metals, machinery, vehicles, equipment, buildings and land, and current assets, such as inventory; to more intangible items such as patents, trademarks, copyrights, goodwill, company reputation and recognition. Mash-up of Wikipedia and ISO-55000.

Asset Life—the period from asset creation to asset end-of-life.

Asset Management—the coordinated activity of an organization to realize value from assets. Asset management includes four fundamental principles: Value: assets provide value; Alignment: uses the organization's mission and strategic objectives to guide resource decision-making to optimize performance; Leadership: organizational values, goals and objectives determine how value is realized; Assurance: assure that assets will fulfill their required purpose.

Authoritative Source—A managed repository of valid or trusted data that is recognized by an appropriate set of governance entities and supports the governance entity's business environment. From National Institute of Science and Technology (NIST)

Beyond Information Models—Uses currently available technologies and couples them with proven business management techniques to achieve connected practice results—today, efficiently, and economically. Beyond Information Models firms have changed their working practices, methods, and behaviors to better support their clients. They practice small is the new big and achieve significant practice improvements.

BIG-BIM—is the business process changes and the steps needed to connect data from everywhere to understand what you are doing in a big world context. Business requirements, building industry data, geographical information and real-time operations intersect to support connected decision-making using interfaces tailored to individual users and needs. Data and information are king. BIG-BIM pushes and pulls data from distributed, shareable, and interoperable repositories that interconnect to encompass everything about assets. You create or manipulate data using an almost unlimited set of tools in a sustainable process that is no longer in isolation from anything or anyone.

BIMStorm—BIMStorms demonstrate the power of faster and better communication, fuller stakeholder participation and, up-to-date...real-time information. Information models and Connected process data grows over time...allowing the management of facilities from beginning to end... without recreating the data at every step. The programs better align project needs, scope and budgets using BIM and connected processes.

BIM Wash—BIM Wash is a term describing the inflated – and sometimes deceptive – claim of using or delivering Building Information Modeling products or services. An organization which commits BIM Wash is typically engaged in promoting its unwarranted claims. From *BIM ThinkSpace: Episode 16: Understanding BIM Wash.*

BIMXML—Describes building data (sites, buildings, floors, spaces, and equipment and their attributes) in a simplified spatial building model (extruded shapes and spaces) for BIM collaboration. This XML Schema was developed as an alternative to full scale IFC models to simplify data exchanges between various AEC applications and to connect Building Information Models through Web Services.

BLOCKCHAIN—Per Wikipedia, blockchain is a distributed database with a dynamic list of records (or blocks) that are timestamped, linked to a previous block, and secured from tampering and revision. The blockchain underlies bitcoin and serves as the public ledger for all transactions. Any compatible client can connect, send transactions, verify, and compete to create new blocks.

Building Information Model—1. To manage project information including data creation and the iterative process of exchanging data through the built environment value network: BIM includes processes by which the right information is made available to the right person at the right time. BIM adds intelligence to project data to allow data to be interpreted correctly removing attribution errors and assumptions. Or—2. To create or work with a single archive where every item is described once: Graphical representations—drawings and non-graphical documents—specifications, schedules, and other data are included. Changes are made to any item in one place and changes flow through the system. Or—3. To represent physical and functional characteristics of an asset digitally in a reliable archive of asset information, from conception onward: without open-standards and a focus on shared data, it is proprietary, not interoperable, and not BIM.

CAD Object—These objects are symbols and 3D representations that are static (line work with little or no intelligence). These objects are instance-based, i.e., each use requires a new instance of the object, tailored to the specific situation. This approach requires a significant library of objects (i.e., one object for each size of window, another for each type of window and another for window detail). This approach results in significant storage and file size requirements to store repetitive and unconnected information.

Complicated—Difficult to understand, but have an understood set of rules. If you follow the rules, step-by-step, you can solve complicated problems. Quadratic equations and building Boeing-747s are complicated tasks, but if you know the rules they can be completed successfully.

Complex—Do not follow the same pattern as complicated tasks. One does not know where things are heading until other things happen. Things are likely to happen, about which you have no knowledge or control over. The unknowns and uncertainties that characterize complex tasks make them difficult to solve with traditional tools. With real-world experience, you can prepare for the known, unknowns that happen in complex situations. Other things are outside your control. It is the things you don't know, that you don't know that make complex tasks so difficult to resolve. Farming is an example of a complex task. Many things can be planned; the farmer can choose the right time to plant, can use the land properly, but weather, pests, and the other things that cannot be controlled make the difference between success and failure.

Composable Enterprise—A highly connected organization with business processes supported by on-demand services that are acquired and leveraged from the cloud and APIs, furnished by outside providers or through internal data centers. The services, which tend to be small and lightweight, are themselves complete systems, and are connected to the composable enterprise through APIs, in the manner of building blocks. Definition copyright Forbes Insights and Mulesoft.

Construction-Management-At-Risk—Delivery process that delivers projects within a Guaranteed Maximum Price (GMP) in most cases. The construction manager acts as consultant to the owner in early project phases and becomes the equivalent of a general contractor during the construction phase.

Construction Operations Building Information Exchange (COBie)— COBie is a open-standard data schema, designed around a spreadsheet format. It contains a subset of of building related information focused on handover of data between construction and facility management. COBie is a subset of Industry Foundation Classes. COBie enables interchange of information using tools long been available within Computer Assisted Facility Management applications. This enables an interim level of interoperability between design and construction BIM authoring tools and legacy CAFM, without either set of tools becoming fully IFC compliant. COBie may be replaced at some future date as data interchange becomes more resolved and robust, or as Service-Oriented-Architecture approaches supersede the current welded together software approach to interoperability.

Data Rot—Refers to the degradation of stored data, especially when the data is unchanged over time, ie. degraded bits of data on a disc render it inoperable when access is attempted. Data rot occurs in any situation involving file exchanges or storage, even when the appropriate hardware and software systems are still available. Data rot occurs when information requires hardware and software that is no longer available and/or staff that does not have the training and equipment to effectively access and use the information. The very act of saving live information into files (whether paper or electronic) creates data rot. Paper files have traditionally been stored in the 'Boiler Room' in file cabinets and Bankers Boxes which are rarely (and only with great effort) accessed. Current file systems rely on storage on media, internally or in the Cloud, often with complex indexing systems, that are analogous to storing paper in the 'Boiler Room.' These systems have the same issues as their paper counterparts. Maintaining live data on model servers with simple human interfaces is one way to reduce data rot.

Design-Bid-Build—Delivery process where an owner hold separate contracts with separate entities for design and construction. In today's environment, this is the traditional method for procuring design and construction services, especially in the United States.

Design-Build—Delivery process with a single source of accountability for both design and construction.

Design Fiction—Design fiction is an emerging technique for prototyping complex scenarios and opportunities in times of rapid social change and increasing complexity to help people understand how they can comfortably coexist in evolving ecosystems and other organizational and mental models. Design fictions raise questions about a product or idea's place in the world, rather than describing the most idealized or optimal future. What will this approach mean in my life? Who will the product help and who could it hurt?

Data Normalization—The process of organizing and restructuring data tables to enable sharing and web services between databases. One either creates tables with agreed upon names and structures, or creates translation tables between data tables so that one can read or write to a table in the proper place and relationships.

Ecosystem—Paraphrasing Wikipedia: An ecosystem is a community of living data and rules in conjunction with the nonliving components of the environment (things like applications, files, computers, etc.), interacting as a system. These live data, relationships and physical artifacts are regarded as linked together through data exchanges and development cycles and informed information flows. As ecosystems are defined by the network of interactions among authoritative datasets, and between living data and their environment, they can be of any size but usually encompass specific, limited portfolios (although some scientists say that the entire planet is an ecosystem). BIG-BIM ecosystems form when applications and related processes allow information sharing via live data exchanges for use by both experts and non-expert stakeholders over the entire lifecycle of a building or anything that we can build. Ecosystems are larger than the original owner's platform and solve technical problems by making it easy to connect or build upon a range of tools and processes to allow new and unpredictable uses that solve industry problems. Products connecting to the ecosystem are of substantially greater value than the core products used alone.

Emotional Intelligence—Emotional intelligence is what builds influence, drives proactive behaviors, fosters concern for others, and builds enduring relationships. People using their emotions effectively leverages the power of the teams needed to solve problems in our built environment and education ecosystems.

Enterprise Client or Customer—In the context of BIM, an enterprise client is an organization, business, company, or agency that operates in an environment that includes multiple assets, repeat projects, large multi-functional facilities, or other assets that require coordination of people, places, budgets, and other resources to function. Enterprise clients might include such groups as: US Coast Guard, US General Services Administration, California Community Colleges system, local school districts, medical centers, planning groups, city/state/local governments, fire/police/first responder organizations, property developers, lending institutions.

Facility Management—Per the International Facility Management Association (IFMA), facility management, *encompasses multiple disciplines to ensure the functionality of the built environment by connecting people, place, process, and technology.*

Federated Model—Federated models combine models from multiple disciplines to allow collaborative and connected workflows. A master model acts as the framed of reference and models from team members are then connected into the master. Once connected, tools such as Autodesk's Navisworks enable the master model to be queried for clashes between elements in the model and other uses. By breaking the modeling effort into smaller parts, this approach allows for large, complex projects. The process is usually dependent on high level hardware and software resources. File storage, versioning and other issues require significant resources and expertise that becomes difficult to maintain outside the development environment as projects move into operations and maintenance.

First Order tools and techniques—Simply follow the rules and focus on doing things the right way. They are the foundation for expertise and process compliance. Scheduling software is a first order tool.

First-Principles—Basic principles include the assumptions and basic knowledge that are the foundation for any other undertaking or activity. Math first-principles are called axioms or postulates. First-principles ground the texts, arguments, ideas, and themes that underpin society and are fundamental to the design and implementation of tools, processes, and solutions in the built environment. Without understanding the principles behind things, responsible and reflective action is difficult or impossible. http://en.wikipedia.org/wiki/First_principle

GDL—Geometric Description Language. A scriptable language for programming intelligent objects using a fraction of memory of other modeled objects. A GDL object can store 3D information (geometry, appearance, surface, material, quantity, construction, etc.), 2D information (plan representation, minimal space requirements, labels, etc.), and property information (serial numbers, price, dealer information, URL, and any other kind of database information). Multiple instances of the same object but with different appearance, material, size, etc. are kept together in one object. GDL is one of the important formats as the Internet emerges as the best communication platform for the building industry.

Geodesign—Geodesign is an emerging subset of both GiS and BIM professionals, focused on environmental scale design decisions. Geodesign is one subset of the ecosystem that is forming around BIM to enable global scale connections. Per Wikipedia: Geodesign is a set of techniques and enabling technologies for planning built and natural environments in a connected process, including project conceptualization, analysis, design specification, stakeholder participation and collaboration, design creation, simulation, and evaluation (among other stages). Geodesign is a design and planning method which tightly couples the creation of design proposals with impact simulations informed by geographic contexts.

Georeference—Refers to exactly locating something in the virtual world, via coordinate systems. Georeferenced buildings are tied to established coordinate systems such that they can be rapidly located in their proper place and time. Latitude, longitude, and elevation are three of the coordinate systems for referencing a location. Georeferencing allows for high level studies of relationships, causes, and effects in a real-world context.

GiS—BIM can be seen as a Geographical Information System focused on building scale information. Per Wikipedia: GiS is a computer system designed to capture, store, manipulate, analyze, manage, and present all types of spatial or geographical data. The term describes any information system that connects, stores, edits, analyzes, shares, and displays geographic information. GiS applications are tools that allow users to create interactive queries (user-created searches), analyze spatial information, edit data in maps, and present the results of all these operations. GiS is a broad term that can refer to several different technologies, processes, and methods. It is attached to many operations and has many applications related to engineering, planning, management, transport/logistics, insurance, telecommunications, and business. For that reason, GiS and location intelligence applications can be the foundation for many location-enabled services that rely on analysis and visualization. GiS, BIM and Facilities Management connected in service-oriented-architecture design patterns are the three disciplines that taken together offer the greatest promise for correcting building industry problems.

Granular/Granularity—Refers to the extent to which something can be broken down into smaller parts. Coarse-grained items are said to have fewer parts or options than Fine grained items. For data, coarse-grained data might look like: Address = 1402 S Dogwood Drive, Suite 200, Tempe, AZ, 54321, USA. Fine grained data for the same information might look like: Street = S Dogwood Drive; Addressnumber = 1402; Suite = 200; City = Tempe; State = AZ; Postalcode = 54321; Country = USA. Finer grained data may increase input and storage; while being more flexible.

Hyperbolic discounting—Preference for a reward that comes first. The value of later rewards are discounted, often rapidly discounting value due to delay, no matter the time involved. A reflection of a *I want it now* bias and a strong tendency toward inconsistent choices when considering future situations.

IAI—International Alliance for Interoperability was the forerunner of what is now called buildingSMART International. IAI's name was changed with the recognition that the name did not resonate with most industry practitioners. IAI was a subset of the International Standards Organization (ISO), charged with developing standards for standardizing how software represents data.

IDM—Information Delivery Manual is a document-mapping building processes, identifying results and describing actions required within process. Information needs to be available when it is needed and maintained at an agreed upon level of quality. The Information Delivery Manual identifies a set of construction processes and defines the information required at each stage. ISO 29481-1 specifies methodologies for the format of the IDM. IDM, the Data Dictionary to map alternative terms for common elements) and IFC form the BuildingSMART interoperability model.

IFCs—Industry Foundation Classes define how things such as structure, doors, walls, and fans (as well as abstract concepts such as space, organization, information exchange, and process) should be described so that different software packages can use the same information. Although IFC structures data in a neutral way, the standard is still focused on monolithic files and processes. IFC is an official ISO document (ISO 16739:2013-Industry Foundation Classes (IFC) for data sharing in the construction and facility management industries.) The current version is known as IFC 4, replacing (ISO/PAS 16739:2005 Industry Foundation Classes, Release 2x, Platform Specification) which is also known as IFC 2x3. IFC2x3 is the version in most common use today, and IFC 4 is just starting to gain traction. IFC 4 does not yet have a certification process in place, but will have one very soon.

IfcXML—One of the hundreds of XML based textual data formats. Defined by ISO 10303-28 *STEP-XML*. Derived from the neutral and open Industry Foundation Class object-based file format. This format is suitable for interoperability with XML tools and exchanging partial building models

Information Model—General term for shareable, organized models of things that represent the relationships, concepts, rules, operations and other parts of things. Can represent an individual component or highly complex systems. Can be focused on buildings (Building Information Models), business processes, software engineering, data, semantics, and many other things. http://en.wikipedia.org/wiki/Information_model

Integrated Practice—Uses early contribution of knowledge through utilization of new technologies, allowing teams to realize their highest potentials while expanding the value they provide throughout the project lifecycle

Integration—The introduction of working practices, methods and behaviors that create a culture in which individuals and organizations can work together efficiently and effectively.

Intelligent Object—These Building Components can behave smart, i.e., they can adapt to changing conditions. The user can easily customize them through an interface. These objects are rules-based, i.e., they incorporate rules that define how the object adapts to other objects, database calls, and user input parameters. Because of the rules base, each object can represent an entire subset of an entity, i.e., one window object can represent an manufacturer's entire window line and can generate all 2D, 3D, details, finishes, shapes, and profiles. This results in significant decreases in the space required to store the equivalent information and results in very small files.

JSON— JSON is simple, way to store and transmit structured data. It is a lightweight, open-standard data interchange format that is easy for humans to read and write, and easy for machines to parse (break into components) and generate. JSON is compact, easy to use, maps easily to data structures used by most programmers, and works well with all programming languages. It is the most common data format used for asynchronous (in the background) browser/server communication, replacing XML which is used by AJAX, per Wikipedia, et.al.

Lifecycle—the stages involved in the management of an asset, including: acquisition, use and disposal phases.

LOD—The Level of Detail or Level of Development concept defines a long-range plan for information models that can be implemented much like one might implement a contacts database: over time. As buildings progress from planning, through design and construction, into operations and maintenance, and then renovations, the model accumulates increasing amounts of information. LOD represents the amount and type of data that is accumulated in a model at each of the stages. By sequentially adding data in planned ways, the modeling process can be streamlined to maximize efficiency and minimize costs. Managed properly one builds upon the data from each previous LOD to create a virtual representation of the building, with minimal waste. Within BIM Execution Plans LOD has become a means of defining levels and types of elements to be modeled at each project stage, effectively becoming a means of defining the quantity and type of work product.

LCA—lifecycle Assessment is also known as lifecycle analysis, LCA is a cradle-to-cradle environmental impact assessment for built assets. The energy and materials used, along with waste and pollutants produced from a product or activity, are quantified over the whole lifecycle to determine a more balanced, total cost of a product, system, or asset.

little-bim—is the application of advanced software and processes using files-based data exchanges via monolithic product lines, translators, and import/export. Replaces 'flat-CAD' with BIM authoring and/or analysis tool(s) on networked computers. little-bim leverages work product and efficiency, but improvements are internal to projects. little-bim is computer-aided-drafting on steroids. Data is secondary to graphics. Advanced graphics, conflict checking, cost modeling and process simulation occur, but are project-by-project oriented exercises. Focus is on software products and current profitability, often ignoring or misunderstanding lifecycle benefits.

Mash-up—A mash-up is a web application using information from more than one source to create a new service in a single graphical interface to enable easy, fast integration, often using APIs and data sources to create enriched results that were not part or the original reason for producing the raw source data. For instance: facility condition data, space use, construction status, cost basis, and a floor plan might all be *mashed-up* with a Google Earth view to show facility information in geospatial context. Wikipedia, et.al.

Model Server—Model servers allow centralized storage of live information models allowing them to be accessed and modified via the Internet. Model servers are a critical element in the long-term management of building information that will be hosted, added to, and manipulated by a large audience over a building's lifecycle.

Multi-file approach—Multi-file systems use loosely coupled collections of documents, each representing a portion of the complete model. These documents are connected through various mechanisms to generate additional views of the building, reports, and schedules. Issues include the complexity of managing this loosely coupled collection of documents and the opportunity for errors if the user manipulates the individual files outside the drawing management capabilities.

NBIMS-US—National BIM Standard. Standard for how information is presented via BIM, currently under development with the cooperation of the AIA, CSI, and NIBS. The National CAD Standard is a subset of NBIMS. The 2201 page, National BIM Standard—United States® (NBIMS-US™) is a consensus document, where many ideas are brought together, presented to a variety of people representing different parts of the industry, discussed, debated, and subjected to the democratic process to determine which ideas rise to the stature of inclusion.

NCS—National CAD Standard. Graphic standard for how information is presented via CAD systems, developed with the cooperation of the AIA, CSI, and NIBS.

NIBS—National Institute of Building Sciences is a non-governmental organization, authorized by the U.S. Congress in the Housing and Community Development Act of 1974, Public Law 93-383. NIBS supports the NCS and the buildingSMART alliance in the United States. In December 2014 NBIS/buildingSMART alliance ceased to be the United States representative to IAI/buildingSMART International.

Normalization—Per Wikipedia, normalization is the process of organizing the columns (attributes) and tables (relations) of a relational database to minimize data redundancy.

Object-Oriented—A computer program may be a collection of programs (objects) that act on each other. Each object can receive messages, process data, and send messages to other objects. Objects can be viewed as independent little machines or actors with a distinct role or responsibility.

Open BIM—An open-source approach to collaborative design, construction and operation of buildings, based on open-standards and workflows. Open BIM is an initiative of software vendors using the buildingSMART Data Model. This model incorporates data (ISO 16739) via the IFC file format, terms (ISO 12006-3) using the International Framework for Dictionaries to map technical terms that have the same meaning, and process (ISO 29481-1) per the Information Delivery Manual.

Parametric—Objects that reflect real-world behaviors and attributes. A parametric model is aware of the characteristics of components and the interactions between them. It maintains consistent relationships between elements as the model is manipulated. For example, in a parametric building model, if the pitch of the roof is changed, the walls automatically follow the revised roofline.

Platform as a Service (PaaS)—per Wikipedia, PaaS is a category of cloud computing services that provides a platform to allow customers to develop, run, and manage applications without the complexity of building and maintaining the infrastructure typically associated with developing and launching an app.

Prototype—A working model used to test concepts, impacts, and ideas quickly prior, to physical implementation. Integral part of a system design process created to reduce risks and costs. Can be developed incrementally so that each prototype is influenced by previous prototypes to resolve deficiencies, refine solutions, or increase understanding. When a prototype is developed to a level that meets project goals, it is ready for construction.

Sandbox—In computing, a Sandbox is an online isolation environment or virtual space where untrusted programs can be run and code changes can be tested without risk to the host computer or operating system. Depending on the implementation, a Sandbox can take on many forms ranging from a tightly restricted space that tightly constrains what can occur to emulation of a complete host computer or computing system that only limits direct access to host resources.

Sapience—per Wikipedia, sapience is often defined as wisdom, or the ability to act with appropriate judgement... in a complex, dynamic environment.

Second-Order techniques—Use first order tools and higher level skills to adapt, modify and improvise to focus on doing-the-right-thing. They are targeted on achieving the end goal. Google tools and the Onuma System are second-order tools.

SOA—Service-Oriented-Architecture can be described as a part of the larger vision that Bill Gates has called the digital nervous system. The OASIS Group defines SOA as: A paradigm for organizing and utilizing distributed capabilities that may be under the control of different ownership domains. It provides a uniform means to offer, discover, interact with, and use capabilities to produce desired effects consistent with measurable preconditions and expectations. SOA enables vendor, product, and technology independent loose coupling of tools to allow repeatable business processes. SOA allows the connection of widely disparate applications in a web environment across multiple platforms. Services within SOA are defined protocols that describe how data is combined to create ad hoc applications built mostly from existing software services and legacy data. Within the SOA framework the user is presented with a simple interface focused on their need. Users access and interact without knowledge of the service platform or the underlying complexity.

Single model approach—Revolves around a single, logical, consistent database for all information associated with the building. The building solution is represented in a single virtual building that captures everything known about the asset. From this database, all project visualizations, analysis, and management information can be extracted. The Single Building Model approach has been found to become unwieldy and hard to maintain at scale and has therefore fallen out of favor for all but the smallest little-bim projects.

Super-wicked problems—Wicked problems that include the added attributes of: 1) Time is running out, 2) No central authority has control or responsibility for the problem, 3) Those seeking to solve the problem are causing the problem and, 4) A strong tendency toward hyperbolic discounting of future costs and impacts.

Tame problems—Well defined with a straightforward problem statement. They can be complicated. You know when you have reached a solution. The solution is either right or wrong. You solve most tame problems using similar methods and the results can be tested, and measured. Most of the project management tools that we use today will only work as designed on tame problems. The ability to solve tame problems is a part of professional development and is a step toward proficiency. Tools for managing tame problems can be called first order tools.

Value network—The Value Network adds an extra dimension to the concept of Value Chains. Value networks represent the complexity, collaboration, and interrelationships of today's organizations and environment. Value Chains are linear and Value Networks are three-dimensional.

Wicked problems—Solutions to wicked problems usually involve significant numbers of people changing their behavior and mindsets. A wicked problem is a moving target. When you think that you have solved a wicked problem, usually all that you have done is to identify a new problem. Even defining a wicked problem is itself a wicked problem. Wicked problems don't have a stopping point. There is no test of solutions to wicked problems. Rather than right or wrong, a wicked problem can usually only be described by better or worse. Every wicked problem is unique and can be considered a manifestation of another problem. http://www.nautilus.org/gps/solving/ten-criteria

Writeboard—Collaborative Web-based text development system that allows for editing, version control and change comparisons.

Definitions are compiled from a variety of sources including: Wikipedia, technology vendors, NIST, OASIS, NBIMS, and others.

Bibliography

Recommended reading for those who want more information on the subject:

Alexander, Christopher et al. A Patten Language. NY: Oxford University Press, 1977, ISBN 0-19-501919-9.

American Institute of Architects and Dennis J. Hall, FAIA, FCSI. Editors. Architectural Graphic Standards, 12th Editon. Wiley. ISBN-13: 978-1118909508, 2016.

Branko Kolarevic (Ed.), Architecture in the Digital Age – Design and Manufacturing, Spon Press 2003.

Caudill, William Wayne. Architecture by Team. NY: Van Nost Reinhold, 1971.

Cheng, Renee, Questioning the Role of BIM in Architectural Education, AEC Bytes Viewpoint #26, July 6, 2006.

Cohen, Michael; March, James; Olsen, Johan, A Garbage Can Model of Organizational Choice, Administrative Science Quarterly 17, JSTOR 2392088, 1972.

Cotts, David and Lee, Michael. The Facility Management Handbook. American Management Association, NY, 1992, ISBN 0-8144-0117-1.

Dettmer, H. William. Goldratt's Theory of Constraints: A Systems Approach to Continuous Improvement. NY: Asq Quality Press, 1997.

Deutsch, Randy. BIM and Integrated Design: Strategies for Architectural Practice. Wiley. ISBN 978-0470572511.

Deutsch, Randy. Data-Driven Design and Construction: 25 Strategies for Capturing, Analyzing and Applying Building Data. Wiley. ISBN 978-1118898703.

Duran, Rick. Understanding and Utilizing Building Information Modeling (BIM). NY: Lorman Education Services, 2006.

Eastman, Chuck and Teicholz, Paul. BIM Handbook: A Guide to Building Information Modeling for Owners, Managers, Designers, Engineers, and Contractors. Wiley. Apr 19, 2011. ISBN 978-0470541371.

Elvin, George. Integrated Practice in Architecture: Mastering Design-Build, Fast-Track, and Building Information Modeling. Hoboken, NJ: Wiley, 2007.

Feldmann, Clarence G. The Practical Guide to Business Process Reengineering Using IDEF0. NY: Dorset House, 1998, ISBN 0-932633-37-4.

Forbes Insights, Mulesoft, Opportunity on Demand-The Rise of the Composable Enterprise, 2016, Jersey City, NJ, http://www.forbes.com/forbesinsights/mulesoft/index.html.

Forsberg, Kevin; Mooz, Hal, and Cotterman, Howard. Visualizing Project Management: Models and Frameworks for Mastering Complex Systems. Hoboken, NJ: John Wiley & Son, 2005.

Friedman, Thomas L. The World is Flat: A brief history of the twenty-first century. NY: Farrar, Straus, and Giroux, 2005, ISBN 978-0-374-29279-9.

Fuller, R. Buckminster. Operating Manual for Spaceship Earth. Carbondale, IL: Southern Illinois University Press, 1969, ISBN 671-78902-3, Lib of Congress 69-15323.

Fuller, R. Buckminster. Intuition: Metaphysical Mosaic. Garden City, NY: Anchor Press/Doubleday, 1973, ISBN 0-385-01244-6, Lib of Congress 72-182837.

Fuller, R. Buckminster. Buckminster Fuller: Anthology for the New Millennium. NY: St. Martin's Press, 2001.

Fuller, R. Buckminster. Critical Path, NY: St. Martin's Griffin, 1982.

Gallaher, Michael P.; O'Connor, Alan C.; Dettbarn, John L. Jr.; and Gilday, Linda T. Cost Analysis of Inadequate Interoperability in the US Capital Facilities Industry. US Department of Commerce Technology Administration, National Institute of Standards and Technology, Advanced Technology Program Information Technology and Electronics Office, Gaithersburg, MD 20899, August 2004, NIST GCR 04-867, Under Contract SB1341-02-C-0066.

Gladwell, Malcolm. The Tipping Point: How Little Things Can Make a Difference. NY: Back Bay Books, 2000, ISBN 978-0-316-31696-5.

Goldratt, Eliyahu M. What is this thing called Theory of Constraints and how should it be implemented, Toronto, North River Press, 1990, ISBN 0-88427-166-8.

Hamilton, Kirt, et. al. National Institute of BUILDING SCIENCES. The Academy for Healthcare Infrastructure, Collaborative Research Program, 2015, ow.ly/8OmW3o3rot8, AHI_WhitepaperTeam1.pdf. USA. The American healthcare industry is facing overwhelming uncertainty in every segment. This collaborative research program focuses on issues that are vital to improving the performance of the healthcare facilities industry. Includes traditional Capital Project Management Process plus two enhanced Processes and (12) Principles and Observations for the future of healthcare Capital Projects.

Hatch, Alden, Buckminster Fuller, At Home in the Universe. NY: Crown Publishers Inc, 1974, Lib of Congress 73-91509.

Heery, George T. Time, Cost and Architecture. NY: Mcgraw-Hill, 1975, ISBN 0-07-027815-6.

Hino, Satoshi, and Jeffrey K. (Fwd) Liker. Inside the Mind of Toyota: Management Principles for Enduring Growth. Portland: Productivity Press, 2005.

IFMA and Teicholz, Paul (editor). BIM for Facility Managers. Wiley. ISBN 978-1118382813.

Koch, Richard. The 80/20 Principle: The Art of Achieving More with Less. NY: Bantam, 1998.

Kunz, John and Gilligan, Brian. 2007 Value from VDC / BIM Use survey, Center for Integrated Facility Engineering (CIFE) at Stanford University, 2007.

IfcWiki-open portal for information about Industry Foundation Classes (IFC), List of certified software, http://www.ifcwiki.org/ifcwiki/index.php/IFC_Certified_Software and Free tools that support IFC, http://www.ifcwiki.org/ifcwiki/index.php/Free_Software.

Jantsch, John. Duct Tape Marketing, Thomas Nelson Inc. Nashville, TN: 2006, ISBN 978-0-7852-2100-5.

Jossey-Bass. Business Leadership: a Jossey-Bass reader, Jossey-Bass, San Francisco, CA, 2003, ISBN 0-7879-6441-7.

Kieran, Stephen, and James Timberlake. Refabricating Architecture: How Manufacturing Methodologies are Poised to Transform Building Construction. New York: McGraw-Hill Professional, 2003.

Kotter. John P. Leading Change, Boston: Harvard Business School Press, 1996, ISBN 0-87584-747-1.

Kymmell, Willem. Building Information Modeling (BIM). New York: McGraw-Hill Professional, 2007.

Liker, Jeffrey K., and James M. Morgan. The Toyota Product Development System: Integrating People, Process, and Technology. Portland: Productivity Press, 2006.

Liker, Jeffrey. The Toyota Way, McGraw-Hill, NY, 2004, ISBN 0-07-139231-9.

McKenzie, Ronald and Schoumacher, Bruce. Successful Business Plans for Architects, McGraw-=Hill, NY, 1992, ISBN 0-07-045654-2.

Nisbett, Richard E. and Ross, Lee. The Person and the Situation. Philadelphia: Temple University Press, 1991.

Osterwalder, Alexander, et.al., Business Model Generation. Hoboken, NJ: John Wiley & Sons, 2010. ISBN 978-0470-87641-1.

Osterwalder, Alexander, et.al., Value Proposition Design. Hoboken, NJ: John Wiley & Sons, 2010. ISBN 978-1-118-96805-5. (www.strategyzer.com).

Redmond, A., Alshawi, M., West, R. and Zarli, A., A Critical Review of BIM Assessment Practice for Construction Management Students, CIB W078 2013, International Conference on Information Technology for Construction, Tsinghua University, Beijing, China, 2013.

Redmond, Alan, Smith, Bob and West, Roger, Evaluating A Cloud BIM Model 'Situation Analysis' Based on a Usability Review, Anglia Ruskin University, Tall Tree Labs, Trinity College Dublin, published in BIM Academy Proceedings, 2016.

Ritchey, Tom; Wicked Problems: Structuring Social Messes with Morphological Analysis, Swedish Morphological Society, 2007.

Rittel, Horst, and Melvin Webber; Dilemmas in a General Theory of Planning, Policy Sciences, Vol. 4, Elsevier Scientific Publishing Company, Inc., Amsterdam, 1973.

Rogers, Everett. Diffusion of Innovations. NY: New York Free Press, 1995.

Roundtable. The Construction Users, WP 1202 Collaboration, Integrated Information and the Project lifecycle in Building Design, Construction and Operation, pub Aug 2004 and WP 1003 Construction Strategy: Optimizing the Construction Process, pub 2005, 4100 Executive Park Drive Cincinnati, OH.

Dana K. Smith, Michael Tardif. Building Information Modeling: A Strategic Implementation Guide for Architects, Engineers, Constructors, and Real Estate Asset Managers. Wiley. ISBN 978-0470250037.

Smith, Ryan, Integrated Process and Products, Assembling Architecture, Building Technology Educators' Society Proceedings, 2009, p.67.

Toffler, Alvin. The Futurists, NY: Random House, 1972, ISBN 0-394-31713-0, Lib of Congress 70-39770.

Toffler, Alvin. The Eco-Spasm Report. NY: Bantam Books, Feb 1975.

Toffler, Alvin. Future Shock. NY: Bantam Books, 1970.

Toffler, Alvin. The Third Wave. NY: Bantam, 1984.

Watson, Donald and Crosbie, Michael J. . Time Saver Standards for Architectural Design: Technical Data for Professional Practice, 8th Ed. McGraw-Hill Education, ISBN-13: 978-0071432054, 2004.

Wilfrid, Thomas Nelson, The Garbage Can Model reopened: Toward improved modeling of decision-making in higher education, dissertations available from ProQuest, paper AAI9026670, 1990 *http://repository.upenn.edu/dissertations/AAI9026670.*

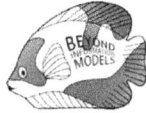

SPECIAL SUPPLEMENT

Onuma Inc. graciously provided readers with a free trial EDITOR license, to get started. The free license gives you the tools needed to explore the system and experience BIG-BIM for oneself... at no cost. Review the capabilities and features of this license at http://onuma-bim.com/license

The exercises that follow use the Onuma System to act as both an expert system creating and visualizing building industry data, and via web services to connect live data to decision-making.

Recipe for Real-World BIG-BIM

Follow these steps to begin your exploration:

1. Send an email to BIG-BIM@onuma.com.

    Upon receipt, you will receive an email containing a code and instructions for how to sign in for a free time-limited license to get you started. After completing the sign-up processes, you will be an official member of the BIG-BIM Studio. You are ready to rock!

    *Once you log in, you will be taken to the Studios page. At this point, you should see only one studio—**BIG-BIM**. Explore the Support Files drop-downs on the right side. Here you will find Templates for uploading data, Advanced Options with instructions for connecting via web services, as well as Plugins for Revit, Archicad, Navisworks, and SketchUp.*

2. Click the BIG-BIM icon to go to the Project List page.

    As you move into the system, you will notice that the organization of pages at every level is similar:

    The Black Top Bar contains general information such as Help and New Features. The buttons in this area provide detailed advice and videos on using the system.

    The second horizontal black bar contains controls for moving around in the system. The left side includes links to the system hierarchy. In the system, Schemes are organized by levels:

    Site Plan—This level accesses the whole site and allows you to see all the buildings at once.

    Floor Plan—This level accesses one building, one floor at a time and allows you to see the spaces in the building, on that floor.

    Space Plan—This level accesses one area at a time and allows you to see all the components and furniture in that space. You will find that each level uses similar controls and buttons, adjusted to the data needed at each level of detail. i.e. you see different information at the Site Plan level, Floor Plan level and Space Plans level.

To the right are links to Settings, Reports, Comparisons and a button for Bugs and Comments.

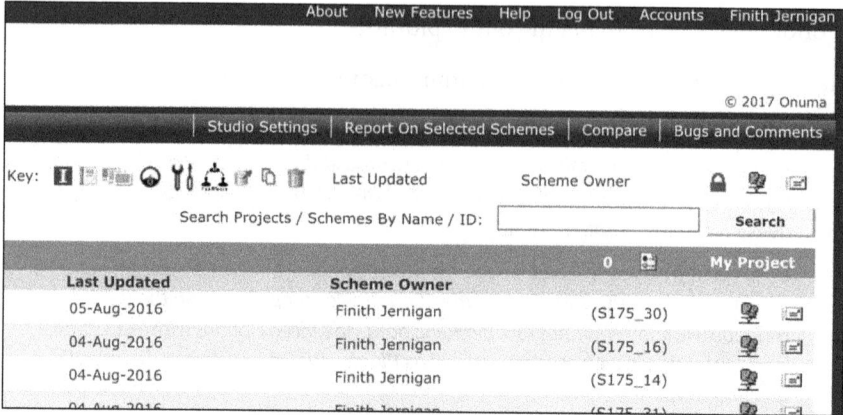

Below the horizontal black bars is the work area. Here you will see additional control buttons, My Projects and other information geared to the level in which you are working in the hierarchy.

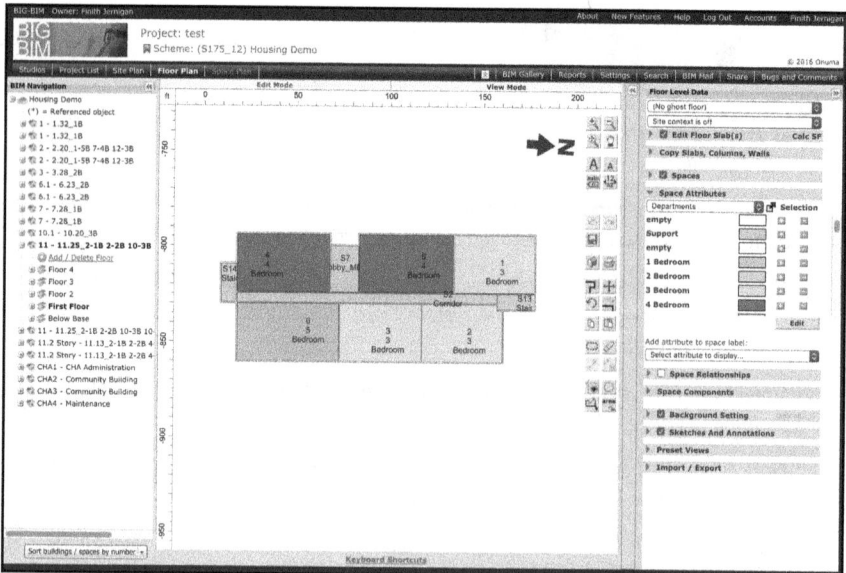

3. Create your first project.

Click the Add New Project button on the left side of the second horizontal black bar. The Create Project window will open. Give your project a Title. Project Number, Budget, and Description are optional. Click Proceed.

Projects can identify a program such as New High School. *Schemes within that project could be used as studies to evaluate that project in various locations. Projects can also be used to manage a series of existing buildings, like* University of Southern California Existing Campus *and the schemes within that project could be each of the existing buildings on the campus.*

4. Next, click on the blue Add Scheme button.

   Next, there is a list of options for seeding your new Scheme. Depending on the information that you have available each of these options will create a BIG-BIM model. For now, start your exploration with a blank slate. You can come back to the other options later.

5. Click the blue Add Empty Scheme button, to open the Add Empty Site window.

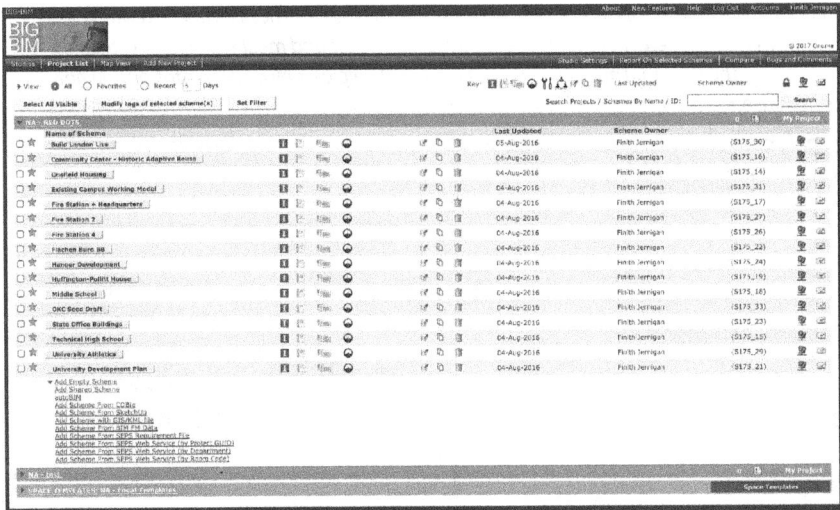

Give your Site a name and select your preferred measurement units and currency. Component Category and Value Lists are optional. Next, find your site location on the map by typing in an address. Use the tools at the top center of the map to quickly set the corners of your site. Use the Hand Tool to move around the map, the Polygon Tool to add the corners of your site, and the Rectangle Tool to create a site with parallel sides.

6. Once you have created a closed polygon around your site, click Proceed.

   The system creates your georeferenced site and takes you to the Site Plan page, ready to start adding Buildings, Spaces, and Components. Share Projects and Schemes, should you wish others to see them. For more information on sending and sharing schemes, see Sending and Sharing Schemes within any Help button.

7. The system responds rapidly to change, rather than relying on a fixed pattern of updates.

The system is continually updated. To work to best advantage, one should embrace the multi-tier Help tools linked to the site. Help is available in various formats. Helps, Bugs and Comments, Videos, and BIMStorms allow one to self-teach and bring the system's tools and processes together for live field tests.

Online help, user manuals, and how to documents are available at onuma.com/manuals. The features in the system update often, and the online helps highlight the most up-to-date information.

The Bugs and Comments button within the system connects directly to technical support. Questions or problems should be posted to Bugs and Comments from within the project, at the location one is working. Submitting issues from the place in which the problem occurs provide context, and improves response and corrective actions when needed. Descriptive comments and pertinent screenshots also aid in better responses.

Videos document many of the tools, capabilities, and processes that create value within the system. For many, the videos are the best and most efficient way to learn about the system. The videos include technical help as well as presentations on how to use the system.

Did you encounter a bug? Or did you simply want to make a suggestion for an improvement?

Please Bug Us!

Name
Finith Jernigan

Please describe the issues you encountered as clearly as possible:

Please attach screenshots or files that might help to find the problem or fix the issue:

Choose File | No file chosen
Choose File | No file chosen
Choose File | No file chosen

Submit

Close Window

:: copyright by Onuma.com 2017 ::

New Features
Using Onuma
Onuma Connectivity
Onuma Tools and Views
Onuma Animations
Onuma Hotkeys

ONUMA Help

Search

CONTACT

Using Onuma System

- **Bugs and Comments**
- **Getting Started**
- **Onuma Main Menu**
- **Georeference and Elevation**
- **Creating Projects**
- **Creating Schemes**
- **autoBIM**
- **Local Templates**
- **Sharing Onuma Schemes**
- **Background Settings**
- **About Spaces and Buildings**
- **Adding Furniture**
- **Sketching In Onuma**
- **Site Components**

Onuma System Connectivity

- **BIM Gallery**

BIM Tube page *https://www.onuma.com/products/BimTube.php includes links to many of the concepts and real-world examples of the system in use.*

Vimeo Channel *http://vimeo.com/album/1512903 includes projects and step-by-step How-Tos.*

YouTube Channel *https://www.youtube.com/user/KimonOnuma/ includes additional how-tos and presentations for some of the more elaborate and specific uses of the system.*

Recipe for BIG-BIM From Thin Air

In the first workflow, you joined the BIG-BIM Studio and created your first project, scheme, and site. You are ready to experience some BIG-BIM magic—you will create a Building Information Model out of thin air.

Most projects begin with Owner needs listed in various ways. Some jot their lists on paper. Others maintain their lists in their heads. Other lists exist in spreadsheet form. For building projects, the lists are often in a spreadsheet and include room names, room numbers, types of occupants, areas required, ceiling heights and many more data points. For a house, the list may be straightforward. For other project types, the lists can become long and involved.

When properly formatted, the data in these spreadsheets can be converted to data-rich 3D massing models and landed on Google Earth.

A properly established BIG-BIM ecosystem captures this seed data from the formatted spreadsheet to create simple massing models that help people get a basic understanding of the project. The massing models act to orient you in space and contain both embedded seed data and whatever data you choose to include in the formatted spreadsheet.

You can create a simple starting point for what may be a very complex endeavor. Over time, this seed data can grow and change, but now there are electronic records of the original lists for comparison through the entire lifecycle. Let's add a Building and Spaces to your project.

1. Begin by downloading the MS-Excel Import Template from the Onuma System Studio page, under Support Files/Templates at the upper right.

X = imperial (feet/sqft) - Please remove X for metric dimensions									
Instructions in second worksheet									
ID	Floor Number	Space Name	Space Number	Space Area	X	Y	Space Height	Department	type your column header here	Value List: type your value list name here
	1	Office	101	300				Offices		
	1	Lobby	102	400				Support Rooms		
	1	Coffee Shop	103	500				Support Rooms		
	1	Kitchen	104	250				Support Rooms		
	2	Office Manager	201	200				Offices		
	2	Meeting	202	600				Meeting Rooms		

File from https://www.onuma.com/plan/helpfiles/Onuma_XLS_Import_V13.zip

2. Extract the .zip folder.

You will use the Onuma_XLS_Import_Simple.xls spreadsheet for this Workflow. Use this file to add and edit the information that you want in your BIG-BIM spaces. This spreadsheet enables you to upload spaces or create new buildings containing spaces.

You will also find the end user licence and the Onuma_XLS_Import_Advanced.xls which can be used for projects with many data points. You will need it at some time in the future. The Onuma-Excel-Import_readme.pdf includes additional help on importing MS-Excel files. Tabs in the two spreadsheets contain simple instructions for their use. Your can also go to https://www.onuma.com/manuals/OpsExcel.php for the manual for importing using MS-Excel.

3. Spreadsheets in the system require data to be organized in defined ways to import correctly into the system. The rules for this spreadsheet are:

    The X in cell A:1 indicates that the spreadsheet data uses Imperial (feet/sq ft) units. Delete the X if you are entering your information in metric units. Do not change any other item in Rows 1 through 3.

    Leave no blank or incomplete rows in your data.

    Cells in Yellow are mandatory. *Every Row must include data for Floor Number (Column B) and a Space Name (Column C).*

    Cells in Light Blue require either a Space Area (in Column E) or X/Y dimensions (Columns F/G).

    All remaining Columns are optional (Column A, and Columns H through N).

    Starting at Column J, you can replace the text type your column header here *with custom Text Attributes. Each scheme can have up to fifteen Text Attributes, i.e. you can add a total of fifteen columns for Text Attributes.*

    You can also add Value Lists. Format example—Value List: Floor Covering. This will add a value list with the name Floor Covering. *Attributes in value lists can be used to color code Plans in the system, and you can add a total of thirty columns for Value Lists.*

4. Add information about your spaces starting at Row 4.

    Include Floor Number (decimal), Space Name (text) and either Space Area or Space length and width (all decimal). Use an existing building, work from another spreadsheet that tracks your current spaces, copy the values from the spreadsheet example, or make something up to test. Include as many Rows of Spaces as you wish. Many of the Schemes in the system include thousands of spaces that flow bidirectionally, importing and exporting via spreadsheets.

5. Save your spreadsheet as a .xls file.

The system requires Edit Mode for most actions you will take. In View Mode, many of the systems functions are locked to prevent those with View-Only rights from accidentally making changes.

6. Import the .xls file containing your data into your Scheme, to create a new Building and Spaces.

   Start at the Site Plan level. Near the top of your browser window look for: Scheme: (system assigned number) your project name. *Site Plan is highlighted in the Black bar below.*

   If you see the Red VIEW MODE words overlaying the Map pane, click Edit Mode in the White bar above the Map.

   Click the Import button located on the right side of the Map and Add Objects panes. An Importer window will then open. Select Import New Building and Spaces with Spreadsheet. Use the pop-up to choose your .xls file and Click Import.

   The Importer will then open a confirmation window that lists each of your spaces. Input your new Building Name, near the bottom, and click Proceed and Close to finish the import.

7. Once the system completes the import, you will see your new building as a Blue box on the map pane and the BIM Navigation pane on the left side.

   Click the plus icon and you will see Floor 1. Click the plus icon on Floor 1 and you will see links to your new Spaces. Double click the Floor 1 icon, and you will see your Spaces as blocks, ready for you to configure and rearrange. Double clicking the Blue box on the Map pane will lead you to Site Plan level data. Explore the many links and tools in the system. You now have an official BIG-BIM model of your Building, with Spaces and Data, ready for further development.

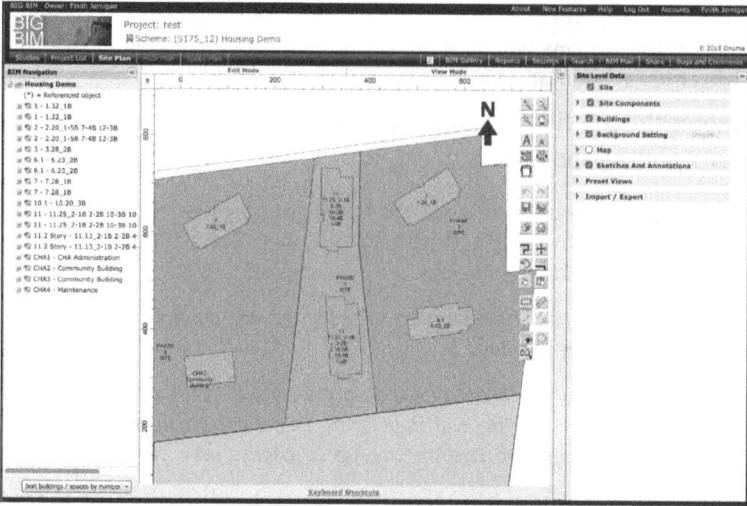

Click the Keyboard Shortcuts link at the bottom of the central window to get a cheat sheet on the drawing window tools.

Exploration with a Global Perspective

Let's go through a simple exploration. First, visit—*http://goo.gl/odbBDH*—and you will find yourself at the center of what can be called a Red Dot Model.

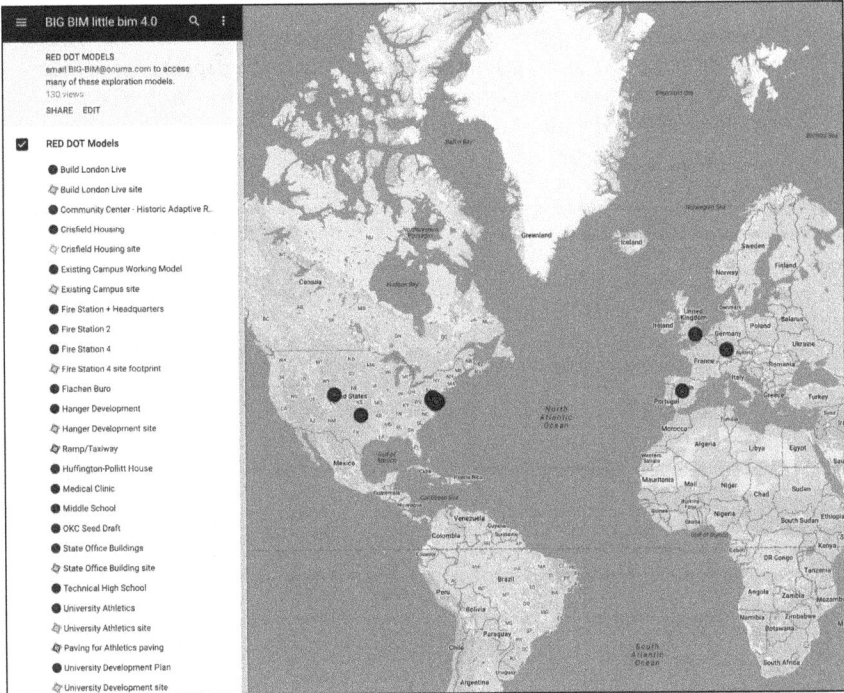

Click any of the Red Dots and you are taken to the project's location and presented with data—area, energy use projections and more. Click any of the other links in the sidebar see a site plan with additional project information. At the bottom of the sidebar data with each Red Dot is a link to the project's BIM Gallery for live plans, detailed reports, and downloads. Click around. Look at the links on the BIM Gallery.

> *The username and password that you received in the Recipe for Real-World BIG-BIM Workflow will be needed as you explore the BIM Galleries. If you missed this step earlier, go to Real-World BIG-BIM Recipe in the Appendix for the detailed recipe to get started.*

Get a feel for what you might do with such a portfolio of project information at your fingertips. Consider the implications and benefits that come from data shared over the web to visually assist consensus decision-making. Pay attention to the Reports tab in the BIM Gallery.

Files like these can be used in projects to initiate project planning and requirements definition, in the format you need to work on the project. What benefits come from auto-generated, live reports, even at this level of detail? Can you do this with your current software tools, with as little effort?

Think of the red dots as the view of your assets from space. Zoom in gradually, as needed to support what you need to get done. View the site to understand in the context of the surrounding area. View the building to understand spaces, to find your way, and to understand relationships. View individual rooms and the components that they contain. Always knowing that the data is consistent for all steps.

GLOBAL DATA

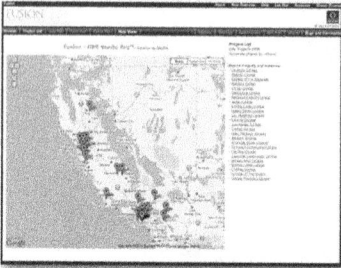

SITE DATA

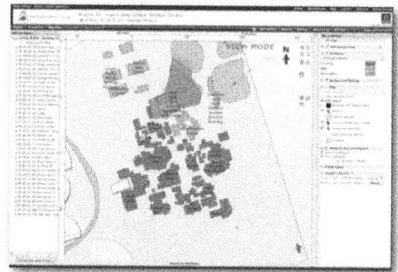

BUILDING DATA

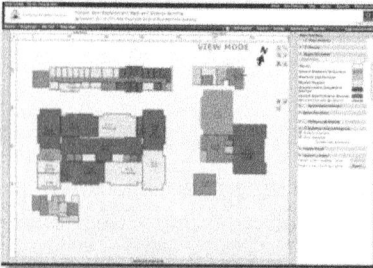

ROOM DATA

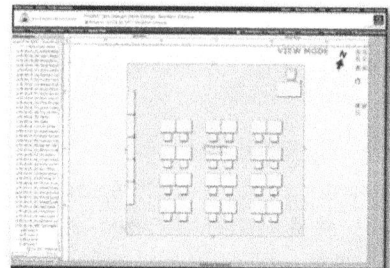

The Onuma System includes a range of plugins to enable you to work with your data using a variety of little-bim tools. Consider maintaining your live data in the system. Your little-bim tools can then be used to enrich the assets you maintain in the system for the life cycle of your facilities.

Support Files

Flash Player in Safari > version 10.0

System Requirements

End User License Agreement (EULA/SLA)

Templates

Advanced Options

Plugins

Export your BIM from your CAD files to Onuma or import BIMXML files into your CAD program:

Download the ONUMA - SketchUp Extension:
ONUMA-SketchUpV16-Plugin.zip (March 21, 2016)
(Manual)

Download the Onuma - Navisworks Plugin for Navisworks Manage 2012 (V2 - October 20, 2012):
Onuma-Navisworks-Plugin-2012-V2.zip
(Please note: Extract archive to desktop before copying plugin into correct folder)

Download the Onuma - Navisworks Plugin for Navisworks Manage 2013 (V2 - October 20, 2012):
Onuma-Navisworks-Plugin-2013-V2.zip
(Please note: Extract archive to desktop before copying plugin into correct folder)

Download the Onuma - Navisworks Plugin for Navisworks Manage 2014 (September 23, 2013):
Onuma-Navisworks-Plugin-2014.zip
(Please note: Extract archive to desktop before copying plugin into correct folder / use the plugin folder in the 'Program Data' path!)

Download the Onuma - Revit Plugin for Revit 2015, 2016, AND 2017(V5.40 - August 26, 2016):
Onuma-Revit-Plugin-2015-17-V540.zip

Download the Onuma - Revit Plugin for Revit 2014 (V5.30 - May 17, 2014):
Onuma-Revit-Plugin-2014-V530.zip

Download the Onuma - Revit Plugin for Revit 2013 (V5.23 - May 29, 2014):
Onuma-Revit-Plugin-2013-V523.zip

Acknowledgements

I have not attempted to cite all the authorities and sources consulted in preparation of this book. To do so would require more space than is available. The list would include federal government agencies, AIA chapters, customers, libraries, institutions, and many individuals.

My most special thanks and all my love to Beth. Without her support, none of this would be possible.

My thanks to my friend and colleague Kimon Onuma, FAIA, president of Onuma Inc. of Pasadena, CA for his insight and support with examples and concepts throughout this book. Mr. Onuma has long been a thought leader in the BIM world. His conception of the Object Genome, organizing the objects that underpin BIM technology, helped many understand the complexity and power of the process. Mr. Onuma won the 2007 American Institute of Architects BIM award for the US Coast Guard Web-Enabled BIM Projects and the 2007 FIATECH CETI Award for the Sector Command Planning System for the US Coast Guard. Design Atlantic Ltd worked on both projects with Onuma. Mr. Onuma's groundbreaking contributions to the future of information in the built world will affect us all for many years to come.

My thanks and sincere appreciation to the group of national and international experts that took their time to review and comment on this book—In Ireland: Professor Alan Hore, Alan Redmond, Paul Sexton, Ralph Montague, and Shawn O'Keeffe; In Germany: Professor Alexander Malkwitz, Oliver Lindner, and Volker Krieger; In the USA: Chip Veise, Deke Smith, Devin Jernigan, Josh Plager, Kevin Connolly, Michael Chipley, Michael Scarmack, Paul Adams, Peter Cholakis, Thomas Dalbert, Yong Ku Kim, Forrest Huff, Hugh Livingston, Jared Banks, and John Roach; In the UK: David Churcher; In Spain: Professor Farid Mokhtar Noriega, and; In the Netherlands: Joost Wijnen. Be assured that they contributed to this being a great book and that I am fully to blame for any errors.

About the Writer

Finith Jernigan uses proven systems and technology in new ways to help people everywhere move toward a more sustainable and connected world.

Finith is a visionary architect whose unique style bridges the gap between novice and expert. He is an expert whose creative writing style makes technical information transparent to users at all levels of expertise.

Anyone who has read literature on change in the building industry knows that the focus is often on expert users. Every discussion focuses on technology. There is little attention dedicated to those just getting started. Finith is an exception, introducing new tools and processes into the mainstream, making complex ideas about the future of the built environment clear to everyone. He has made information modeling real for people.

Finith's award-winning books are clear guides to achieving the benefits that information models enable. In *BIG-BIM 4.0* he continues his no-nonsense descriptions of complicated concepts that made his first book, *BIG-BIM little-bim* directly applicable to building industry business processes that increase the effectiveness of building design, construction, and operation. With more than 40 percent of the world's resources focused on building construction and operation, many industry leaders predict that effective use of information models will help fight global climate change.

Commentary on Finith's Books

The buildingSMART alliance in North America is working the BIG-BIM issue and I believe that it is a very rich environment for significant transformation in the way we do business. Finith has done our industry a great service in pointing out this very concept. I heartily recommend this book be part of your mandatory reading. — Dana K. "Deke" Smith, FAIA, is known as the father of the U.S. National CAD Standard and, is the retired executive director of the buildingSMART alliance who worked to establish a BIM Standard to help improve adoption of the powerful BIM tool set.

As someone who co-founded and built a 20-person architectural general practice, and then moved to the client side of the table, this is a book I would urge any client to read. Although at first impression the author is talking to design consultants, it would also be particularly useful for facility managers and other client executives. — Gerald Davis, IFMA Fellow, ASTM Fellow, AIA, CFM President, International Centre for Facilities, Inc.

Kell Pollard, Associate AIA, LEED AP, at Bender Associates Architects commented: *A wonderful book that balances the dream of BIM in the future with the cold real-world facts of the profession. It addresses many of the frustrations and peeves I've developed over the last 4 years and formalizes many of the solutions I've stumbled upon. Very inspiring and very practical at the same time.*

James Salmon, President of Collaborative Construction and Founder at Collaborative BIM Advocates commented: *Finith is a true pioneer in this arena, having practiced what he preaches in BIG-BIM little-bim for years. This book will help you connect the dots in your minds eye between planning, design, construction, operations, and maintenance and will show you the difference between thinking of electronic design - i.e. little-bim - and thinking of smart buildings and smart infrastructure. If you don't own it buy it.*

BIG-BIM little-bim, by Finith A. Jernigan is, simply put, the most accurate description of how to BIM that we have today. The book breaks down the concept of Building Information Modeling into "bim" (lowercase) as software modeling tools and "BIM" (uppercase) as the connected design and exchange of project data - Building Information Management. You cannot achieve BIM with BIM alone. You can be using BIM and be as far away from BIM as you were with CAD. - Nigel Davies, AECO Expert

Other Books by Finith Jernigan

BIG-BIM little-bim: The Practical Approach to Building Information Modeling - Integrated Practice Done the Right Way! Second Edition - softcover ISBN 978-0-9795699-2-0.

Path to Certainty: A BIM Chronology - softcover ISBN 978-0-9795699-3-7.

Makers of the Environment: Building Resilience into Our World One Model at a Time. BIM of the Book about Information! - softcover ISBN 978-0-9795699-6-8.

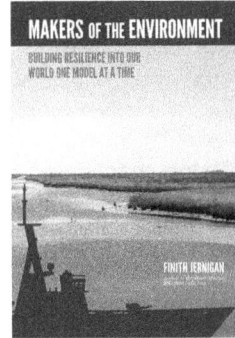

ORDER YOUR COPIES TODAY: *We recommend the purchase of physical books from either Createspace at www.createspace.com or Amazon at www.amazon.com. Purchase electronic copies at Amazon, Smashwords, the Apple Store, Barnes & Noble, Sony, Kobo, and numerous other online outlets. Contact 4Site Press for quantities greater than five copies. Postal orders: 4Site Press, PO Box 222, Salisbury, MD 21803, USA Email orders: fulfillment@4sitesystems.com.*

ABOUT BIG-BIM little-bim: *The award-winning BIG-BIM little-bim was among the first books to tell of the big changes happening every day in the world of BIM. The second edition of BIG-BIM little-bim expanded coverage of the practical applications of BIM for the entire construction industry. The book highlights the phenomenon of the worldwide BIMStorm, and gives user-friendly approaches that architects, engineers, owners, builders, facility managers, educators and students can understand and apply today. Finith Jernigan, an internationally recognized leader in BIM, shows you how to leverage resources, compete in a worldwide market, and become more efficient and productive in the planning, design, construction, and operation of facilities.*

ABOUT PATH TO CERTAINTY: *Path to Certainty, describes an architect's path from tradition to a more efficient and sustainable future. This book was designed to help students to understand the milestones and critical issues that led to the award-winning book, BIG-BIM little-bim to help them begin an exploration of how to leverage our scarce resources, compete in a time of uncertainty, and become more efficient and productive in the world of tomorrow*

ABOUT MAKERS OF THE ENVIRONMENT: Makers of the Environment *is a book written around scenarios that highlight what BIG-BIM can do today. The scenarios are fictional projections, not case studies. The scenes show readers some of the opportunities that come into focus as they embrace BIG-BIM.*

Using real-world, albeit fictional scenarios, Makers makes the case that BIG-BIM is here and in use today. Farming uses BIG-BIM to manage no-till farms to be more sustainable and efficient. Healthcare has become a connected system to respond to tight budgets and societal needs. Disaster preparedness and recovery are dependent on BIG-BIM from start to finish. The internet thrives on BIG-BIM apps and systems. As productivity and inefficiency decline, how can the building industry not do the same?

Makers is both a print book and a dedicated website. It offers readers links to the wisdom of others to improve understanding. The site is free to all and links to external information via Web-enabled devices, using tags. The tags let one embed information links into a printed book. Using the tags, readers can to jump to more detailed and technical discussions about topics included in the book. The tags use the Microsoft Tag format. They establish direct links to more information. Think of them as a glossary on steroids.